U-Turn

U-Turn

What If You Woke Up One Morning
and Realized You Were Living
the Wrong Life?

BRUCE GRIERSON

BLOOMSBURY

Published by Bloomsbury USA, New York
Distributed to the trade by Holtzbrinck Publishers

All papers used by Bloomsbury USA are natural, recyclable products made from
wood grown in well-managed forests. The manufacturing processes conform to the
environmental regulations of the country of origin.

LIBRARY OF CONGRESS CATALOGING-IN-PUBLICATION DATA

Grierson, Bruce.
U-turn : What if you woke up one morning and realized you were living
the wrong life? / Bruce Grierson.—1st U.S. ed.
p. cm.
ISBN-13: 978-1-58234-584-0
ISBN-10: 1-58234-584-8
1. Change (Psychology). 2. Epiphanies. 3. Insight. 4. Life change events.
5. Catastrophical, The. 6. Change. I. Title.

BF637.C4G75 2006
155.2'5—dc22
2006018634

First U.S. Edition 2007

1 3 5 7 9 10 8 6 4 2

Typeset by Westchester Book Group
Printed in the United States of America by Quebecor World Fairfield

For Jennifer

Contents

No matter how far you have gone on the wrong road, turn back.

—Turkish proverb

Introduction

One afternoon in Halifax, Canada, a guy named Bob—college undergrad, cut-up, and general underachiever—slipped into a campus auditorium with two pals to listen to a guest speaker up from Massachusetts. Actually, Bob's plan wasn't so much to listen as to mock. The speaker had come from the Student Missionary Movement, and Bob, a confirmed atheist, figured on plenty of grist for one of his cynical monologues. Bob and his pals stood in the back and prattled more or less continually, until the speaker, in a thundering voice, warned the three of them that they'd be on the next shuttle to hell if they didn't cut it out. Bob's buddies figured their job as agitators was done, and they beat a retreat. But something compelled Bob to stay. The man from Massachusetts wound up his spiel and launched into his pitch. The church needed candidates to volunteer for missionary work overseas. He scanned the hall. There were no takers.

Then a strange thing happened. There in the back row, Bob felt something under his elbow, a force, like a hand, the hand of a parent, perhaps, gentle but irresistible, pushing. Bob was raising his arm. *A volunteer? Excellent. Please, sir. Come forward.* Bob could have stopped things right then and there, claimed he was merely swatting a fly, or scratching his head, and vanished out the back door to resume his campaign of discreditation. But he didn't. For reasons that remain unclear to this day—no doubt some complicated subconscious calculus involving guilt, ambition, and filial duty—he walked, alone, toward the speaker's outstretched hand. His life had just changed irrevocably. A few years later he would find himself on a steamship bound for a remote village in North Korea. He would become a pioneering medical missionary for the Presbyterian Church, a man of such commitment that his name is now known to mission scholars worldwide: Robert Grierson, M.D., the Korean "Bethune." My paternal grandfather.

Obsession is too strong a word, but I confess that my mind returns often to my grandfather's conversion. Just what happened to him that day—and what it meant—has been a matter of heated family discussion, never satisfactorily settled. The old man couldn't explain it himself, except to say that he was "awakened." The instant it happened he knew that the man he used to be was gone, and the man he was somehow meant to be was born.

Flash forward a full century.

It was mid-November of 1997, and just outside of Eureka, California, a small group of environmental activists had marched down from their camp in the woods, toward the town courthouse. They were protesting the ongoing logging of the old-growth Headwaters rain forest, home to some of the planet's biggest trees. And specifically, on this day, they were demonstrating against the recent tactics of local police, who had sprayed some protesters with mace, adding insult to a campaign that seemed to be losing steam. A tall, young woman with a bright-blue backpack was among them. She had just wandered into town, and received crude instructions as to where to go, found this little group, and joined it, hanging to the back. She knew no one.

It was a highly unlikely place for Julia Hill, an ambitious young businesswoman and part-time model from Jonesboro, Arkansas, to find herself. Fifteen months earlier Hill, already the owner of her own bustling restaurant, was making a lot of money as a consultant to the bar industry. Julia Hill's thoughts were pretty much concerned with how things were going for Julia Hill—and the sky appeared to be the limit. Then one day, her Honda hatchback was rear-ended by a Ford Bronco. The crash totaled her car and sent her to the hospital with nearly fatal injures that would take the better part of a year to mend.

The flat-on-her-back convalescence enforced an unaccustomed level of introspection for Hill, who, as a rule, barely stayed still long enough to cast a shadow. But in that quiet space an insight opened up. Her life no longer seemed so perfect. Something was wrong; something was missing. In order to discover what that something was, she would embark on a kind of quest. She would have to discover again—if, indeed, she ever knew—who she was.

Some neighbors were planning a road trip to the West Coast, and Hill decided to tag along. A traveler they met en route steered them to northern California, and soon they were in Headwaters, amid the rum breath of the redwoods. The friends were itching to move on, but Hill knew she wasn't quite ready to leave. Alone now, she heard about the battle for the forest between the environmental activist group Earth First! and the company, Pacific Lumber/Maxaam, that owned the timber rights and had already felled a few million board-feet of trees that had been alive during the time of the Crusades. There was going to be a rally, and, curious, she found her way to Eureka.

She followed the crowd to the courthouse steps. A guy with a bullhorn said a few words to the protesters. It wasn't exactly like Henry V inspiring the troops. The mood was pretty light. In fact, it seemed less a serious undertaking than a party. Then he invited anyone from the public who felt moved to speak to come on up. What came over Julia Hill in that moment, she would later describe like this: "I almost felt like an invisible person was grabbing my arm, my heart, and pulling me toward the front."

She walked up to the microphone and set down her backpack. She said something that seemed utterly fitting for a young person in the middle of a California forest. "It's great that there's so much joy here. But while people are having fun at this rally, there are trees out there dying, falling to the ground, and it's killing me."

Julia Hill was extraordinarily naïve, both to the politics of the activist movement and, at that point, about the issues themselves. But she had a certain passionate *something*, and it caught the attention of an activist called Shakespeare, who invited her to come back to the local base camp.

For days that became weeks, Hill called this muddy, tent-filled, patchouli-smelling squat home. She did a little cooking and just generally hung around, waiting for an opportunity to make herself useful, for her vague sense of mission to resolve itself into something concrete. The moment eventually arrived. A warm body was needed to occupy a tree—a thousand-year-old forked redwood named Luna that had been marked for the lumber company's saws.

She had never "tree-sat" before. She had never tree-*climbed* before. (She had never even backwoods-*camped* before.) She had no training in nonviolent protest. But in the dispirited tail of a long protest campaign, a little enthusiasm goes a long way—and after a quick primer on climbing harnesses and prussock knots, she soon found herself, along with Shakespeare and another activist, on a platform eighteen stories off the ground.

Hill was told she would have to stay up there for five days: Could she handle it? She said she could. The endeavor felt right at some pretty basic level, "like the answer to a question I didn't even know I was asking."

The other activists soon rotated out of the tree-sit. But Julia Hill stayed. And stayed.

Hill stayed in the canopy of Luna for 738 days. She stayed through two seasons of lashing winter storms, provisioned sporadically by activists on the ground—when they could penetrate the security perimeter. When she came down, she was a radical environmentalist and an unwitting celebrity. (In the end, her efforts were something of a Pyrrhic victory: The forest all around was decimated but Luna still stands, and the company signed an agreement promising that she always will.) Hill now works for an environmental consultancy called the Circle of Life Foundation.

When I first heard the full story of Julia "Butterfly" Hill, I immediately thought of my missionary grandfather. It wasn't just the eerie similarity of the description of being "called"—the felt nudge of an invisible hand, the irresistible pull toward the front of a crowd, and a public commitment for which nothing in her life had prepared her and whose intensity she could scarcely imagine. Up in that tree, Hill experienced a half-dozen moments that tested her convictions, laid bare her ego, and cemented a kind of inner peace. During one particularly terrible storm on the eightieth day, Hill, sleep-deprived and borderline delusional, heard Luna "speak." The tree dispensed a pithy bit of wisdom of exactly the sort my grandfather, in his own journals, told of receiving just when he needed it, when his faith was wavering. What Hill heard was this: Let go. Trees that bend to the wind, live. Then and there she lost her fear of death. On a jerry-built platform not much bigger than a crib, she was, by her own description, reborn.

It occurred to me that the young man in Halifax and the young woman in California were very much alike. What had happened to them, at roughly the same point in their life, somehow seemed like the same thing. One had a religious conversion, the other what you might call a secular conversion, and the only reason for the difference, just maybe, was the culture they each grew up in. In my grandfather's time, here in the West, there was really only one "spiritual" narrative. If you felt the twinkling of conscience, a signal not readily identifiable as having come from within, it must be God on the line. But in Julia's time—which is to say, our time—there are other labels for such a feeling, and other outlets through which to do something about it.

I began to wonder: Could this second kind of "wake-up call"—a call not necessarily to be godly but simply true to oneself—be our version of religious epiphany, updated for a pluralistic, increasingly secular age?

The religious epiphany has certainly been the subject of much scrutiny, with generations of writers trying to capture that particular lightning in a bottle. William James, in his classic book *The Varieties of Religious Experience*, describes a typical "conversion" thus: The subject, emotionally exhausted, suddenly "feels a wave overpoweringly break over" him, leading to "a sense of perceiving truths not known before." Alcoholics Anonymous founder Bill W. described his moment of calling as a blinding light, followed by a "great, clear strength" that "blew right through me." Indeed, the breakneck religious conversion remains an enduring, and ever-more-dominant, American theme—part of the reinvention narrative of losts-now-founds, from slave-trader-turned-vicar John Newton to George W. Bush.

You hear much less about the "secular epiphany"—though I suspect only because no one has thought to frame it that way. In fact, though, these sorts of experiences may resonate perfectly with our time. Religious thinking stopped reflexively ruling human consciousness a couple of centuries ago; but the capacity to be "born again" is something no amount of postenlightenment science has quite been able to purge from our genetic code. By some definitions, having a moment of clarity and pulling a complete 180 in response *is* a spiritual event. If so, it may be among the last kinds of spirituality that participants in a culture increasingly reluctant to formalize a faith can freely admit to.

The grand U-turn is not all that common, but it's common enough. Every day, in almost every field, individuals perceive themselves to be on the wrong side of a divide. The "second brain" in their gut—that ten-billion-nerve knot—tells them their life must change. And, on moral, or at least deeply personal, grounds, they jump the gap. The apprehension can seem so sudden that it straightens them in their chair— and then seems inevitable. When a novelist or short story writer pulls off this effect, a small revelation lands hard on the reader, occasioning an understanding of the world in a new way.

When these kinds of epiphanies happen to real people, their lives change very quickly. It can be a compelling thing to observe. A full repudiation of the original position ensues. The Italian novelist Ignazio Silone, who was among the many intellectuals seduced by Communism, until Stalin's body count rose sufficiently high and the scales fell from his eyes, described his deconversion like this: One doesn't leave Communism; one is *cured* of it.

And so, computer hackers, having served their time and mulled their crimes, can be found working for the FBI to *hunt* hackers. Archconservatives carve out new professional identities as vocal liberals. Soldiers desert and organize peace marches. If a politician switches parties, we say she has "crossed the aisle." Others in humbler quarters routinely do the same thing: the ad executive who becomes a media critic; the butcher who becomes a vegan; the financier who, after a life of building equity, suddenly starts giving everything away. Every U-turn is in some sense a defection: You leave because you have to leave, blowing up bridges behind you, marching into the arms of grateful new colleagues while the shouts of the furious ex-colleagues ring in your ears. Max Weber, the first sociologist, coined the term *metanoia* to describe an experience that slices a life into a "before" and an "after" in this way. It is, as he put it, "the complete reversal of an individual's central attitude toward the value and meaning of life and the world."

An image springs to mind about people whose lives change on a dime, and it isn't very flattering. They are folks, perhaps, like the former chess grand master Paul Morphy, who at the peak of his career, when he was widely considered the world's best player, suddenly withdrew from the game, and from public life, to spend his days in his bedroom arranging women's shoes in a half-circle. Or the fisherman, immortalized in a Dave Smith poem, who narrowly escaped death in a storm at sea, and abruptly stopped fishing and took up farming—except that he pulled his plow around an unplanted field. The phrase *psychotic break* comes to mind. At the very least, to be seen stumping today for what you stood against yesterday looks, to the world, like instability at a minimum. U-turners become typecast. So clichéd, indeed, is the personal-journey narrative, and so facile are the supposed catalysts that anyone whose life actually seems to resemble the template comes off as either a charlatan or a dork.

But I can tell you, having considered the stories of more than three hundred U-turners, and interviewed dozens of candidates for inclusion, that the clichés do not hold up. U-turns brought on by mental illness can be spectacular and poignant, but they're relatively rare. The U-turners you'll read about here are, you could say, the opposite of mentally ill, and plainly unconniving. They are, indeed, extravagantly alive, and often wise and deeply attuned to the ground shifting beneath the feet of all of us.

Why do U-turners turn?

That question immediately fractures into a dozen others. Is there a type of person it's most likely to happen to? Is there a direction in which people tend naturally to turn? Are apparently damascene turns really as sudden as they appear? How do they differ, if they do, from the much slower changes of mind that ultimately point the turner just as perfectly in the opposite direction? (And what, in the end, is the difference between performing a U-turn and just, well, "growing up"?) Does the moment of truth always come, as W. H. Auden claimed love does, unbidden?

Watching the process unfold in even one life calls into question our notions about our very identity, which we might come to suspect is less fixed, more *contingent*, than we ever imagined. Why do people live the particular lives that they do? Does our story unfold because we "discovered" it—a core identity, a "true self," perhaps after a lot of missteps and dead-end roads? Or do we, rather, "create" our true selves, because identity is provisional, dependent on what we've experienced, and what has influenced us, and what we have decided to become?

"Conversion is an inner change of heart, not an outward change of allegiances," wrote Emilie Griffin, a born-again advertising executive, in her book *Turning*, to distinguish the event she experienced from the familiar swap-and-shop of denominations or congregations one often sees among the faithful as they fine-tune the dial. The parallel holds for secular turns, up to a point. Sometimes people whose lives change drastically have themselves, as individuals, not changed all that much. Shirley Rock, a former prostitute from the Midwest who—drug-addled and dependent on organized crime to keep her brothel running—made a 180-degree *exterior* turn when she went clean and became a pastor. But, in fact, her interior life remained stable: She was *always* sensitive and empathic and spiritual. In this case her public life simply caught up, finally, with the woman she always knew herself to be. The proof, then, is more than skin deep.

To be a moral U-turner is not simply to have made, say, a big job change; but rare is the true U-turn that doesn't leave some pretty obvious external changes for all to see.

It's not simply to be a "class traitor," since while you cannot choose your lineage you *can* choose your politics and your philosophy (and overturning a stance you've chosen seems a more radical move). But it could be.

It's not just to have jumped the spiritual divide in your particular

Introduction

discipline—like Gloria Steinem deciding that apparently a fish *does* need a bicycle, and marrying; or Albert Einstein admitting that, by golly, the universe *is* expanding. But it might be.

The test is not whether the way you view the world has changed, but whether something central to the way you view yourself has been recalibrated.

Americans, in particular, have a complicated relationship to people who utterly remake themselves. On one hand, reinvention is the great American myth. On the other hand, in the classic cases, people are reinvented in ways that call the "American dream" into question. More generally, U-turners make people uncomfortable, I think, because by sacrificing everything they seem to have broken an unstated rule. When a country drafts a constitution, it doesn't allow for a radical change in thinking. Sure, there will be lots of things that look like a bad idea a hundred years down the road, and you deal with these through amendments. But the founding principles are assumed to be eternal. U-turners haven't made amendments to the constitution—they've *thrown out* the constitution. Can anarchy be far behind?

For both the U-turners themselves and for the people in their lives, it's hard to overstate what is at stake. Colleagues and friends and spouses have a certain, understandable psychological dependence on the idea that the person they're working for, bowling with, or making love to is the person they think he or she is. Suddenly that person is gone. And now there is chaos. Marriages collapse. Children become estranged. A certain amount of scorn and ridicule is almost guaranteed to pound down like purgatorial rain upon the reverser. You watch through your fingers the U-turner on a course of self-reinvention—which can, in the moment, look an awful lot like a course of self-destruction. The culture doesn't understand this phenomenon, and because it doesn't, the consequences for many U-turners are grave.

But reversers themselves don't want our sympathy. For this is, at least subjectively, a generally positive phenomenon. The price paid is worth it, because the U-turner is now, at least, living an authentic life—perhaps even fulfilling, to some extent, Mahatma Gandhi's notion that "We must be the change we wish to see in the world."

One reason extreme behavior is so fascinating to observe is that it makes us wonder: How did it come to this point for this person? And then the question comes boomeranging back. The adage "There's nothing in any one of us that isn't, to some degree, in all of us" has a certain morbid ring of truth. While it is surely true that, as the emeritus Harvard psychologist Jerome Kagan puts it, "Not everyone could be a Gandhi or a Martin Luther," each of us is, I believe, more like these U-turners than we think. We may be reluctant to admit to sudden changes of mind because it makes us look flaky, but if we carefully examine our lives we can find inflection points—turning points—instants at which the fog cleared, leaving us changed in significant ways.

And so the question arises: What would it take to make us turn, not merely 15 degrees or 30 degrees, as a course correction, but 180 degrees: all the way around? If we were put under enough pressure, what are the odds that some fundamental fraudulence would be exposed? Are we really acting in a way consistent with our value system? Have we thought deeply enough about it—ever? And if we realized we needed to change, could we?

ONE

The Burning Spear

The Turning-Point Moment

"I had a sense that a knowledge more than human possessed me,
so that everything that had been confused was clear and everything
that had perplexed me was explained."

—W. Somerset Maugham, *The Razor's Edge*

Trr rue radicals, it's sometimes said, hide their essential fire within the most conservative of exteriors. Walk into the Atlanta office of Ray Anderson, chief executive officer of Interface, the world's largest commercial flooring manufacturer, and you will be greeted by a man in a navy-blue suit, with network-newsman hair, and an almost hypnotically slow Dixie drawl—the entire impression suggesting a man of soporific practicality, who leaves waiters exactly 10 percent, irons his underpants, and just generally toes the line. Listen to him hold forth for even five minutes on the nature of his business, however, and you will come to realize that all your assumptions are dead wrong. Ray Anderson is one of the most revolutionary corporate executives in America. But it was not always so. Something happened to him one July day in 1994 that would change him forever.

It was during that summer that the types of questions that get asked of companies when they reach a certain size—what are the spillover effects of all this growth?—began trickling in from Interface's customers. How ecologically sensitive were Interface's manufacturing processes? What was the company's environmental plan? Anderson, frankly, had no good answers. Like most corporate executives at the time, he hadn't given such issues a moment's thought. This was unhandy, because Anderson was now scheduled to give a keynote speech explaining Interface's nonexistent environmental stance to a task force of the company's managers. It was a deeply unsettling moment. "I had no clue what to say," he recalls, "except, 'We obey the law.'"

By chance, Paul Hawken's book *The Ecology of Commerce* had recently landed on his desk. Maybe there were some sound bites here he could crib. He dipped in.

"It was as if a burning spear had been plunged through my chest," he remembers. In Hawken's story of the doomed reindeer of St. Matthew Island—a metaphor for what happens when a species exceeds its "carrying capacity"—Anderson saw the future. He glimpsed his own company in a new light. He saw not the public face of Interface—the creamy broadloom blanketing American institutions from the National Capitol to the offices of MTV—but the hidden, private side. Whole lagoons of petroleum drawn daily to feed the manufacturing plants. Five billion pounds of Interface carpet moldering in landfills, slow-leaching chemicals into the soil for the next twenty thousand years.

He read on. "And as I did the spear went deeper. It dawned on me that the way I've been running Interface is the way of the plunderer."

Ray Anderson wept. And when he stood before the task force, he opened with the truth. "In twenty-one years of business, we've done more harm to the environment than I care to think about," he said. The more he had learned about the numbers, about how much the Earth has to produce to create a dollar of profit for Ray Anderson's companies, the more horrified he had become. Eventually a day would arrive, he realized, when what Interface did would be illegal. It would be deemed a kind of calculated intergenerational abuse: a tax on our descendants, in which they had no say. "Someday," he understood, "people like me will end up in jail."

Anderson pledged profound change. The firm's new aim, and motto, became "Zero Waste." The whole manufacturing process would be rethought. Instead of making new carpet from scratch, Interface would agree to take back old Interface carpet that had reached the end of its useful life, rip it apart, and reconstitute it—since the nylon particles never degrade. It was as if Anderson had suddenly shifted his gaze from the bottom half of a pair of bifocals to the top: from short view (profit this quarter) to long view (a viable world three generations down the line). And in that instant what sprang into view was a whole new business paradigm. "Linear must go. Cyclical must replace it. That's nature's way. In nature there's no waste, because one organism's waste is another's food."

"We look forward to the day when our factories have no smokestacks and no effluents," he would soon tell a shareholders' group. By 2020—the stated target date—"there will be zero scrap going into the landfills and zero emissions into the ecosystem. Literally, this is a company that will grow by cleaning up the world."

Ray Anderson should by all sound reasoning have become an industry pariah, and certainly the bane of his shareholders, on account of his naïve optimism. (It's efficiency and profitability, after all—not good intentions—that keep companies healthy.) But four years after his pledge of a total rethink, Interface's revenues had doubled and its profits had tripled. (Recycling done efficiently can save a company money, it turns out—in Interface's case, more than $300 million to date.) Within a year of the new production scheme, the company had cut its environmental impact by a third. Greenhouse-gas production from the company's plants worldwide is now down by more than 50 percent. (When I last spoke to Anderson, in May of 2006, crude oil had just nosed over $75 dollars a barrel. So even if its goals are overambitious—and they probably are—a company that has pledged, by 2020, not to take a drop of oil from the Earth, has everybody's attention.)

"Anderson's thinking is so advanced, and the efforts at Interface are so far along, that Interface ranks as the most highly evolved big company in the country," reported the no-pushover tech magazine *Fast Company* not long ago. "In terms of combining social responsibility and economic growth, no one comes close."

Psychologists often explain paradigm shifts by literally evoking them, with cunningly designed images that can be seen two ways, as figure or ground: a goblet or two human faces in profile; an old woman or a young woman. You see the image one way; there appear to be no alternatives. It's an old woman. Keep looking, the psychologist says. And then—"Aha!"—you see the other image, the young woman with upswept hair under a scarf. Once you've seen the young woman it's impossible to "unsee" her.

That's the way it works, too, for certain people in a certain set of circumstances. Their whole life becomes a paradigm shift. And just as with the faces and the vase, it's impossible, having experienced the shift, to go back to that other, older world.

Michael Allen Fox, a philosophy professor at Queen's University in Kingston, Ontario, used to be the guy journalists called on to rebut the arguments of radical animal-rights advocates. By his lights, it was okay to eat meat and wear leather. Within reasonable bounds, experimenting on animals was ethically defensible. On this subject, indeed, Fox wrote the book *The Case for Animal Experimentation: An Evolutionary and Ethical Perspective*. In it, Fox challenged Jeremy Bentham's famous position that because animals can suffer, they should be spared. In the grand accounting, Fox insisted, that premise doesn't hold up. Only if you believe that animals are our intellectual and moral equals should they be accorded "equal rights." Fox's own view was that any suffering a rat endures in a cancer experiment is outweighed by the benefits accorded human beings. That's still the majority position, and he argued it cogently. The book helped make his career.

But nine months after it was released came an event that must be every publisher's nightmare: The author decided that he disagreed with himself. Fox recanted after confronting a philosophical conundrum: What if extraterrestrials landed on Earth tomorrow? And what if they showed all the signs of "personhood": high intelligence, self-awareness, the capacity for complex speech? They had everything going for them that we did, and more—yet they were not human. Would we still have the right to enslave and kill and eat them? Fox decided that we would not.

The conclusion wasn't something he could simply note and acknowledge, before taking a bite of his roast-beef sandwich and getting on with his work. It set in motion a chain of other conclusions. The ethical presumptions—about the inherent entitlement of human beings—on which the experiments depended now struck him as dubious. And if the presumptions were wrong, the cost-benefit calculus of the experiments was meaningless.

Fox stopped eating meat, and encouraged others to do the same—as "the single most important thing anyone can do to relieve animal suffering." He no longer condoned animal experimentation. He wrote another book, *Deep Vegetarianism*. All of which made him an instant hero within the animal-rights movement and the scourge of many in the medical profession who once considered him a level-headed ally. "Scientists thought I was mentally ill," he recalls. "They couldn't conceive of how I could change my views like that."

The person who eats meat is very, very different from someone who rejects it on moral grounds, Fox now believed. Not different in the way that, say, someone who takes care of his health is different from someone who doesn't, or someone who volunteers is different from someone who doesn't. More like the way someone who considers a time continuum before and beyond his life span—a kind of afterlife—is different from someone who is perpetually focused on the present. The "vegetarian conscience" inclines people to see humans as part of nature, rather than apart from it. That, in these times, is a mental shift of Copernican proportions. The person Michael Fox was (and most people are) and the kind of person he became justified the label he has sometimes been given: the man with two lives.

Fox's recant pushed him, in a stroke, to the academic margins. Some colleagues still snicker privately about his "Planet of the Apes" thesis, and his previous work has been reassessed with the benefit of hindsight. ("Keep in mind," one review of *The Case for Animal Experimentation* warned, "that the arguments in this book couldn't even convince the guy who wrote it.") Fox seems unfazed by the criticism. He continues to teach moral philosophy, and to host workshops, tap-tap-tapping the beat of deep vegetarianism in his hemp shoes.

A story from closer to home (well, closer to my home): When she was twelve years old, the Canadian novelist and journalist Denise Ryan watched her mother, Angeline Kyba, perform a U-turn so abrupt, rejecting the roles of housewife and traditional mom, that it seemed ripped from the pages of Barbara Gowdy's novel *The Romantic*. Her mom had been the perfect fifties matriarch, a blond Grace Kelly knock-off who had worked as a nurse to put her husband through law school, without missing a beat at home. She made her own clothes and kept up the roses and was always there to welcome the kids when they returned from school, the house fragrant with the smell of fresh baking, a prelude to the dinner that would hit the table at six sharp. On Valentine's Day she sewed little velvet hearts on the children's clothes. One detail that betrayed the perfect, sunny exterior: At night, through the wall, Denise would sometimes hear her mom crying.

The day everything changed was the day Angeline's father died. "I dreamed I was alone in the universe," Angeline recalls. "And I realized: 'I have nothing. But I have to paint.'" Before the family could quite process what was going on, she was already tumbling away from them. She rented a studio space in an abandoned factory in downtown Toronto, leaving the kids, still nominally in her care, to rattle around the house that went to seed around them. Jeans and Jesus sandals—the de facto art-student garb—replaced the prim dresses of old. She painted through the night in the unheated studio and studied art theory by day. And then she completed the boho follow-through by moving to a coastal island in Mexico accessible only by sea, to a rented building without a phone or electricity—the ultimate "room of one's own." A few weeks after Denise's mother had gone for good, a postcard arrived in the mail. On the front was a photo of Richard Nixon shaking hands with Elvis. On the back, a simple message: "Insurance papers in the trunk at the bottom of the stairs. Will call when I've found a place. Love, Mom." So radical was the transformation that when Denise's brother saw Angeline later, in her new skin, her new life, he announced: "That's not my mother."

If you make a conscious decision to be on the lookout for these types of tales, they rise to meet you reasonably often, from the morning newspaper or over the back fence.

Not long ago a friend of mine noticed that the wasp's nest on the porch had grown to a flourishing colony the size of a lampshade, and she called an exterminator to come get rid of it. The guy came, and was getting the ladder out when she went to pick up some groceries. When she returned, the nest was gone—the queen dead, the rest of the hive's now rudderless population dispersed—but the exterminator wasn't. She found him sitting on the back steps, quietly sobbing. "It's this job," he said. "Every day—*every day*—I step into the chain of nature and take something out by killing it. What gives me the right?" Now, this wasn't some china-delicate young budding Jain, reluctantly helping out in the family business for a few weeks. This was a professional exterminator. It was *his* business. Now here he was, at midlife, staring into the gulf between who he was, at the core, and what he did for a living—a career path he'd chosen more or less by accident, without quite doing the emotional due diligence, but one that domestic commitments—kids, mortgage—prevented him from just abandoning. There was no easy way out.

For forty-five minutes he sat there. And then finally he got in his truck and left. In her mental rolodex, my friend crossed out his name: One way or another, she knew, next time she needed him he wasn't going to be in the game.

To the question, "What comes over these folks?" there are as many answers as there are variants of the U-turn experience. But Aldous Huxley described it this way: One day, one moment—and without the help of psychotropics—they see a door where there once was a wall. The door is irresistibly inviting, and through it they slip, into a subtler, more complicated, more morally freighted, place. "The man who comes back through the Door in the Wall will never be quite the same as the man who went out," Huxley believed. "He will be wise but less cocksure, happier but less self-satisfied."

The kinds of catalytic events that can make that door appear in the wall, urging people to pass through into new lives, can be roughly sorted into two types. There are the big things that periodically erupt—literally or figuratively—upon a whole population and are so seismic they change *all* lives somewhat (though some more profoundly than others). And then there are the things so small that they escape the notice of almost everyone, but that happen to resonate on the precise frequency of a select few.

Public events disastrous enough to make people frame the moment, almost immediately, in historic terms—to create at least the potential for shared moments of clarity across whole cultures—are rare. But we have just been through one.

For many North Americans, the response to 9/11 was the sense of having been relocated to a higher-stakes table, and stories abounded in the aftermath of fairly radical personal reappraisals as people asked hard questions of their immediate circumstances: Is this the kind of life I want to lead? Am I willing to accept these terms? Am I with the person I want to be with? For most people the furious burn of introspection was fairly short-lived; the collective charged moment that caused the whole world to look and feel quite different passed; the event that "changed everything" turned out not to have changed all that much. Lives resumed. "The bland surface of things closed back upon itself," as John Updike said, and everyone fell back into the old agreeable somnolence.

Well, not everyone.

On September 11, Pat Tillman—before he picked up the phone in his home in Phoenix and heard his brother say, "Turn on your TV right now"—had a routine day planned. He was going to eat breakfast and then ride his mountain bike to a training facility in Tempe for football practice. The prow-jawed, twenty-six-year-old starting strong safety for the Arizona Cardinals—comfortable in the midst of a three-year, $3.6 million contract playing for his hometown pro team—spent the day, instead, watching CNN.

The next day, the NFL sent out camera crews to canvass the reactions of the players. When a reporter caught up with Tillman, his reaction was different from the rest. "I play football, and it just seems so goddam—it *is*—unimportant compared to everything that's taken place," he said. "I feel guilty even having the damn interview. My grandfather was at Pearl Harbor and a lot of my family has gone and fought in wars, and I really haven't done a damn thing."

What followed for Tillman had the air of someone quietly putting his affairs in order. He fulfilled his contractual obligations and finished the season, and then he married his high-school sweetheart. On his return from his honeymoon, he promptly called his brother Kevin, who was also a professional ballplayer, in the Cleveland Indians' farm system. The two men rented a car, drove to Denver, and enlisted in the army. The first NFL regular since World War II to volunteer for military service, Tillman accepted a pay cut from $1.2 million to the $17,316 annual base salary for a new recruit.

It all happened so abruptly, Tillman never got a chance to—or was obliged to—explain himself. (He simply told his dumbstruck coach and managers that he "wanted to do something else.") All people knew was what they got from sporadic media reports: that both Tillman brothers had joined the Army Rangers and were headed for Afghanistan.

On April 22, 2004, Tillman's unit was ambushed by anti-Coalition rebels on a high mountain road in eastern Afghanistan. A firefight ensued, and Tillman, the ASU grad and hometown hero whom newspaper reporters were prone to describe as "living the American dream" was shot dead (by "friendly fire," as it turned out). That was that. No footage, no fanfare, no expectation on Tillman's part of any spiritual payoff. At the memorial service, held at San José's municipal rose garden, after someone said, "Pat is now with God," Tillman's youngest brother, Rich, furiously seized the microphone. "He is not with God, he is dead. He is fucking dead!" Senator John McCain stood up at the same ceremony and spoke of Tillman's "unexpected choice of duty to his country over the riches and comforts of celebrity." A lot of people didn't understand it. Some thought they did: The left-leaning Web site indymedia ran the story under the headline: "Dumb Jock Dies for Pipeline in Afghanistan."

The 9/11 attacks were the most dramatic event in the life of a generation, but they were, of course, just one point in an endless historic continuum of public events that serve as potentially pivotal moments in individual lives.

Jean Henri Dunant was a Swiss businessman based in Algeria in the mid-1800s. He needed to get the imprimatur of Napoleon III for the water rights to land he aimed to develop, so he traveled to meet the emperor near the northern Italian town of Solferino—and ended up blundering into one of bloodiest battles of the nineteenth century. In poor weather, under dubious generalship, the enormous French and Austrian armies stumbled into each other, and when the smoke cleared twenty thousand unattended wounded lay on the battlefield. And lay, and lay, until they were eventually put out of their pain by bayonets. Dunant, who had observed the carnage, was a changed man. The urgency of his business interests suddenly diminished by the scope of what he had seen, he wrote a now-famous book, *Un Souvenir de Solferino*, both describing the battle and proposing a plan for an internationally co-coordinated organization to care for people in such a future eventuality: the Red Cross.

The burst stock-market bubbles of 1929 and 1999 produced economic and philosophical refugees, their world destroyed, looking to be reborn from the ashes. (Po Bronson, a technology writer with a close eye on Silicon Valley, documented some of the '99 disasters, and his own observations about that now-earthbound subculture were the impetus for his book for and about lost souls, *What Should I Do with My Life?*)

Cataclysmic events, from genocides to earthquakes, tend to land with the force of spiritual omens—even for those who claim not to have a religious bone in their body. People pump for existential meaning. Whatever latent spiritual switch human beings have deep in the cerebral cortex—and as we will see, such a faculty does seem to exist—tragedies can turn on. Or off. "Is there a tipping point, in terms of the number of dead, when a catastrophe becomes suddenly capable of catalyzing doubt about the existence of God?" the writer Ron Rosenbaum mused in a recent *New York Observer* column, shortly after the scope of the South-Asian tsunami became clear. Whatever that hypothetical number is, the tsunami apparently surpassed it—for the week it happened, some noted, the archbishop of Canterbury himself was quoted airing his spiritual doubts.

The Truth about Bolts from the Blue

We are moved to ask a different kind of question after hearing stories of the Pat Tillmans and the Jean Henri Dunants—whose lives were upended by cataclysmic events—than after hearing the stories of folks like Ray Anderson or Angeline Kyba or the conscience-stricken bug man.

In these latter cases, where the catalysts are so subtle as to be all but imperceptible, we wonder, What is it about these individuals that they changed their lives so unexpectedly? In the former, the question seems to be, What is it about the rest of us that we *don't?*

In both cases, bewildered by the U-turn of a colleague or a friend or a spouse, we tend to go hunting for the source, the thing that set her off—figuring, quite naturally, that something that dropped down like a bolt from the blue and produced a conversion the U-turner never saw coming, ought to be easy to find. But we're really looking in the wrong place. The catalyst is not immaterial, but it's not really the heart of the matter. The answer has to do with receptivity.

Here's the secret about bolts that come from the blue:

They don't.

If we think someone has changed for no reason—or at least no good reason—it's only because we don't have enough information about his interior life, the ground that has been preparing for weeks, or months, or years, or decades.

U-turns happen because the turners are ready for them to happen. For a somewhat complicated matrix of reasons (which we will explore in coming chapters), these people are primed to respond. They are 99 percent of the way there, but don't realize it. All it takes is something to force them to see themselves from the outside in.

For James Kennedy, that moment came one day in a hotel meeting room in Garmisch, Germany, in 1987. Kennedy was an army lawyer charged with prosecuting homosexual soldiers, and he had been sent to take a refresher course on recent changes in the army discharge regulations for homosexuality and bisexuality. (These were changes in degree, not kind: Homosexuality was still grounds for discharge.) This was JAG grad school, a rat pack of macho men, and the other officers, some of whom Kennedy had gone through basic training with back in Kentucky, weren't exactly sympathetic souls; in fact, they cracked "homo" jokes throughout.

Kennedy had seen this before, at every stage of his career, and mostly tried to ignore it—even as he'd come to accept that he himself was gay. The army was what it was, and he was who he was. But now, sitting there amid the pastries and coffee urns, his mind skating over the whole breadth of his upbringing (for the view out the window was of sparkling Lake Eibsee, where he had vacationed with his family as a boy), something was different. A feeling was coalescing into fact. He had held it back as another officer, who had been quietly struggling with his sexuality, came out to him, and Kennedy did not open up in return. He had tamped it down as he daily enforced the Uniform Code of Military Justice, which in its failure to allow for circumstance was seeming more and more draconian by the day. The army didn't want people like him: fine. No, not fine.

It occurred to Kennedy, more or less in that moment, that the army policy on gays and bisexuals was not much different from the Nazis'. "*Fuck them*," he thought. "They are wrong, not me."

Up until then, it was he himself, James Kennedy, who had the choice to stay or leave. But now he saw things differently. It was the army leaders who had a choice. They could prosecute and discharge him if they wanted to, but this was something they now had on their head. One man's silent grievances had just become a big problem for the army: Kennedy would devote the rest of his life to defending homosexuals against prosecution.

Dramatic U-turns of this nature—"You're not the man you were yesterday," rather than the more familiar slow estrangement of "You're not the man I married"—are fairly rare. Rare enough, in fact, that they tend to get relegated to the human-interest pages and the category, among our conscious thoughts, of Things That Happen to Other People.

But it's worth taking a moment to ask why this should be so. Clearly it's not because all of us are satisfied with the lives we're leading and don't want to change. To choose to throw in all your cards and start again *seems* radical, but how many of us in some low moment haven't thought about doing just that, haven't fantasized about it—even to the point of imagining what kind of a butterfly effect such a decision would set in motion? What, then, stops us from doing it?

U-turns can be stillborn at two points in the process. Either we don't really recognize that impulse, don't value it as anything more than a passing whim—certainly nothing we should act on. Or else, for a variety of reasons—and there are very good reasons—we don't feel we *can* act on it. The first hurdle is an affair of the head: perception. The second is an affair of the heart: courage.

It may be significant that the very literary epiphany Sherwood Anderson experienced happened before he was technically a writer at all, in the sense that he hadn't published a word. A father of three, Anderson was managing a paint factory near Cleveland when he asked his secretary one day to take a letter (this was 1912). In the middle of the dictation ("The goods about which you have inquired are the best of their kind made in the . . ."), he simply stopped. She sat there with pen poised, then looked up. They stared at each other for a long while. Then Anderson said, "I have been wading in a long river and my feet are wet," and he walked out. He left the building and kept walking, down the railroad tracks, toward Cleveland. Four days later, still walking, disoriented and disheveled by this time, he was recognized, and taken to a hospital, suffering from exhaustion. Upon his release, pronouncing the job he had been doing "simply absurd," he quit—abandoning his family in the bargain—and moved to Chicago to devote himself to a life of writing.

Years later, holding forth to students, Anderson often referred to the episode as a kind of crossed threshold—the instant in which he left behind his bourgeois materialism for the life of an artist. And yet if a student had collared him, perhaps over beers at the end of the term, and said, "Mr. Anderson, what really happened to you?" he would have been stuck. The life itself must stand as explanation, he might have said. Or he might just have ordered another round.

Because, really, the moment itself defies a telling that makes sense. The metaphors the newly transformed reach for sometimes seem melodramatic, imprecise, slippery, even corny—but metaphors are all they have, because the experience is impossible to capture. It is the great white whale that cannot be drawn or described. Carey Hart, the first man to successfully perform a backflip on a motorcycle, a maneuver since dubbed the "Hart Attack," has tried to explain how it's done, the fine points. He has described the little adjustments with almost comic precision. But nobody really understands. You're just going up the ramp and then, at a certain point, you're on the other side. It's impossible to make the semantic trip with him if you haven't landed the same stunt and lived.

U-Turn

James Joyce had a hack at explaining the ineffability of the literary epiphany that detonates in a reader's mind. He called it an "aesthetic arrest," a kind of spiritual heart attack. It knocks out our capacity to comprehend it rationally.

At such times, like W. S. Merwin's narrator in the poem "For the Anniversary of My Death," who finds himself feeling suddenly, overwhelmingly full of gratitude, and "bowing, not knowing to what," there is a sense, even among the secular, of having been touched by grace. And for U-turners, somehow that feeling of renewed purpose makes bearable the job now at hand: to break camp and leave the site it took the whole first half of your life to find.

TWO

The Time of Reckoning

*When the Call Comes—And What's at Stake
If You Answer It*

> Everybody, I believe, has at least once looked in the mirror
> and said, "That is not who I am."
> **—David Ebershoff**

The Switching Yard

His business card at Apple read simply, "The Kid"—which got it just about right. For what Silicon Valley had on its hands, with Tom Williams, was a gunslinger in short pants. He was one of the youngest hires in the history of Fortune 500 companies when, at fourteen, he helped pioneer the computer giant's online music strategy—which became the online music industry. (This was, if not technically pre-Internet, before the Internet was a household word.) Not all who work at Apple live in Cupertino itself, but Tom Williams did. He was too young to drive to the office.

By age eighteen he had moved on from Apple to become an independent consultant, advising companies like Intel and Rupert Murdoch's Newscorp on their new-media business strategies. He was like Beowulf, plying his services to foreign kings—if Beowulf wore groovy shirts and lived in the Mercer Hotel.

But, this being the dot-com era, the really big bucks lay in venture capitalism. And Williams, being an opportunist, followed them—first to New York and then, eventually, to L.A., where a Svengali-like figure by

25

the name of Michael Milken took him under his wing. (Milken is, of course, the junk-bond financier who served time in the early 1990s for racketeering and fraud.) Williams developed formidable radar for knowing whether a business plan would or would not fly, and a Torquemada decisiveness. At Knowledge Universe, the venture-capital firm founded by Milken and Larry Ellison, The Kid was known to shut down multibillion-dollar pitches in under three minutes. He made his name saying No at a time when everyone was, by reflex, saying Yes. He chain-smoked, spent $18,000 a month on silk suits and late-night sirloins, and cultivated a surly rock-star persona.

And then, following a series of epiphanies of escalating strength, he left. Not just left Los Angeles—left *all of that*. He gathered every cent of his savings and pumped it into the creation of a nonprofit company that, he hopes, will redefine the way charitable giving is organized. At age twenty-eight, he stands against everything his whole career has thus far been about. "If you juxtapose Tom at thirteen" (in Victoria, British Columbia, running a software company out of his bedroom) "with Tom a decade later in Santa Monica, California, those two lives are diametrically opposed," he said, scarfing down a piece of apple pie.

Back in Vancouver, as we spoke, he had just become engaged to the pop singer Jessie Farrell. Which also seems about right. He himself looked as if he was about to open for the White Stripes: rock 'n' roll hair, couple of days of stubble, piercing hazel eyes, hipster shirt under a kangaroo jacket, and, judging from the lunch he was packing away, a blast-furnace metabolism. He resembles a little brother of Steve Nash, the Phoenix Suns guard who grew up just a couple of miles away from Williams in Victoria. Under the table, his leg was going like was tamping out a tiny fire.

He was, by his own admission, "under mind-numbing stress." More than working for Milken and Ellison? Oh, yes.

"Because never have I cared as much—it comes down to that. This is the only idea that I know needs to happen, should happen, and if it does happen in a big way, it'll be huge."

Plenteus Technologies, the nonprofit he founded and installed himself in as CEO, is an Internet company that aims to make matches between donors looking for causes and worthy nonprofit charities looking for donors. He was, when we met, overseeing a staff of seven.

To get to the bottom of what happened here—from corporate jets to save-the-world—it's worth looking way back, briefly.

The childhood? Not abnormal—like the ones that tend to kick unusually driven kids into the world. He was bright and curious and relentlessly analytical. On top of that, he had no notion of impossible. The son of a Joyce scholar, he was raised to believe there were no real limits to what he could achieve. In one feverish stretch, he read the entire Encyclopaedia Britannica. The intellect made him able to smoke out truth; the confidence made him able to speak that truth—to power, to whomever. That, ultimately, is why Michael Milken hired him. ("Nobody tells rich people the truth," Williams says.) In young Tom Williams, Milken saw, well . . . he saw himself at that age. "And that's both a good thing and a really scary thing," Milken later confided to a colleague.

The second trait that emerged early was this: To a rare degree in a young man, he knew himself. Which is to say, he knew his strengths and limitations. "I was never technically very smart; I was never a very capable programmer," he says. "But I understood selling. That's what I knew. I understood the communication of ideas; I could analyze ideas and then create my own ideas."

You could say that the very qualities that made Tom Williams a success in the world of high finance—truth and self-knowledge—were the ones that made him understand that he didn't belong there.

It happened in a series of steps—some of them so innocuous they didn't even seem like steps at the time. During his rise, there were, occasionally, faint transmissions from the core Tom trying to make themselves heard through the noise of the new life.

"A few times in that spell as a consultant—living in the Mercer—I thought, Geez, I'd really like to be *doing* something, instead of just coming into these business meetings—this sea of white shirts and blue shirts—shooting down the smartest person's idea in a couple of sentences, and leaving."

On one occasion a couple of years later, working with Milken to apply the screws to a Toronto-based company that had approached them for venture capital, he got a bad feeling. The deal on the table was,

Williams knew, more than fair. "*We* had more than enough," he recalls, "but Milken wanted to press for more. And I was like . . . why? Is this going to create a better company? Well, no. It's going to create a worse company because they're going to feel like they've been turned into employees, and it's their fucking idea! This was about allowing your greed to overtake your sense of what's going to be the best business decision."

Not right, no. He kept showing up for work, though, putting in those eighteen-hour days, at least for a few more months.

The beginning of the end came in an unlikely place: the ninth hole of a golf course in Palm Springs. It was the year 2000. Williams had flown there on the spur of the moment—Milken was out of town that day, and Williams wasn't needed in the office—to get in a round with his close friend Ross from back home.

"We were sitting there, lapping up the sun," Williams recalls, when his Socratic friend hit him with a simple question: "What are you passionate about?"

"Oh, you know," Williams said. "Bird-watching. Playing the cello." Holdover interests from his youth. His friend nodded without visible emotion.

"What?"

"Nothing."

The two sat there in silence. Williams turned the big driver, with its outsized head, in his hands. Over the next few holes, he kept coming back to the question, until Ross finally called a halt. "Okay, fine, I was just asking," he said. "But if you already know, why are you spending so much time thinking about it?"

Tom's friend Ross had known him since they were teenagers. He had witnessed the transformation: from the kid with passions to The Kid with the platinum cards.

Williams returned to Santa Monica. Within a month he had left Knowledge Universe, vacated his apartment, and moved to Canada "to decompress." Nothing overt had happened to force the move. What had happened, and was happening, was deeply subterranean.

Williams moved in with his pal Ross. He moped around. He slept in. "But we would have these middle-of-the-night conversations. We'd talk about politics, about Africa." Around 1 a.m. one morning, he found himself sitting in an all-night coffee shop, reading the paper. A boy named Randall Dooley had been murdered by his stepfather and mother. Ongoing, brutal abuse over months finally did him in. There'd been a breakdown in child services; no follow-up in time, and the boy died. Tom Williams didn't even get to the end of the story before he was crying.

Back in the apartment, tears turned to sobs.

"I understood that I'd finally answered the question Ross had asked on the golf course months back—my body had just answered it. Kids. I care about kids."

His friend said, "Well, what do you do about that?"

When Williams began researching charities—What was out there? How did they differ from one another? How did they work, at the level of human psychology?—one of the first things he discovered is that, in the landscape of human emotions, the cooling-off curve is steep.

"There's a moment of inspiration, and if you don't leverage it, you will lose that person," he says. "Because a potential donor is caught up in that moment of Randy Dooley; he wants to do something, but then it takes too much effort, and he says, 'I'll do that later,' and he never does. If you can't align the moment that somebody cares with a specific mechanism to enact that passion, you're lost. In everybody's life, that moment is unique. Mine came in that coffee shop. Yours may be completely different."

The big idea Williams hatched—the idea that would become the heart of his company, Plenteus—is what he calls the Five-Dollar Philanthropist.

"If you can show people that for five bucks and in less than five minutes they can get connected to something meaningful—and no other commitment is required—you have something very powerful. "But it can't be abstract. To get a real sense of affirmation, they need to see a picture of, say, the well being built."

To call the plan an obsession would be to understate things. One long-time friend diagnosed what had happened to his old pal Tom: "Man," he said, "you're *infected* by this."

Michael Milken had three cardinal rules of business.

Rule number 1: Never invest your own money.

Williams cashed in all his savings and sank every dime into Plenteus. (Not that he actually had that much to sink; he had spent most of it on *stuff*.)

Rule number 2: Be beholden to no one.

After cashing in his savings, the kid who'd prided himself on being financially independent since age thirteen asked his parents for a loan to help fund the company.

Rule number 3: Build back doors.

There was no fallback plan.

"Every self-preservation instinct said, Don't do it," Williams recalls. "But . . . I have to."

He began to reach out to his old contacts in the business world. He told them, "This is it. I've found what I want to do with my life."

It would not be accurate to say that the Capra-esque story of The Kid's turn melted their cynicism. People who knew Williams from his greedy, self-interested Milken days were immediately suspicious: What's the angle? What's in it for Tom?

Others figured he was just going through a phase. This nonprofit thing would interest him for roughly twelve minutes—just like all the other hot ideas this congenitally ADHD guy had hatched, mulled, solved, and moved on from in the past.

But still, everyone he asked for money gave something.

During lunch Williams took calls more or less constantly. One was from his broker. Williams had waited too long to exercise some put options and his hesitation cost him about $20,000. In California he'd have dropped that much in an hour on Rodeo Drive. But now that money had a different value. Now he had salaries to pay.

The money from those options, "I'm going to pump it all into the company. And that," he said, "is all I have left."

How are we to get our heads around what happened to Tom Williams? One approach is to think of him as a bomb that went off—that had to go off because, well, it was just time.

When people hear stories of other people's U-turns, with their ver- tiginous whirl of life changes—jobs suddenly abandoned, travel tickets booked, partners left blinking in shock—they often think of a time called *midlife*. And for those who are going to pull a hairpin reversal of values, midlife is indeed when they're most likely to do it. (Elliott Jacques, the psychoanalyst who coined the phrase *midlife crisis*, pinned the average reckoning point at age thirty-seven.) But there are a few outliers—like the tree-sitter Julia Hill and the wunderkind Tom Williams—whose stories seem to prove that the midcourse turn is more a developmental than a chronological milestone. You could say that Williams's crisis of spirit came just about the time he outgrew "precocious." When he was no longer the identity on his Apple business card, no longer had the comic jujitsu advantage of the kid in the world of men. When he had to defend himself as a man on his own terms.

"My mom calls what I did an elaborate form of running away from home—which is quite true," he says. "It's distinctly articulated in my case, but I think it's true of everybody. If you run away enough times, you'll eventually encounter yourself coming the other way."

Williams is not yet thirty. But considering that he was in a high-pressure job by age thirteen—a decade and a half earlier than most of us—and was deep into his career when he had his epiphany, his story makes sense as an expression of the moral restiveness of early midlife, the great switching yard, a transitional stage as dramatic as any since adolescence.

At this stage, Carl Jung observed, many people whose dynamism is on the wane—who present to the world merely the salt-and-pepper ash of consumed experience and wasted potential—ignite again. (In ways both constructive and problematic.) Extramarital affairs spike. Hardened violent criminals sometimes mysteriously reform, having passed into a phase of life in which guilt is felt particularly acutely. Increased spiritual chatter emerges on the broadcast channels of the secular.

What exactly is it about midlife that calls down these seismic shifts? Well, its status as the halfway mark is itself significant. Amid the intersections of multiple invisible graphlines lies the point where the young become the old: This apprehension has its own implications, some obvious, some not so much.

For men, the fortieth birthday, like the appearance of a little veteran's gray at the temples, has a certain talismanic ominousness, for many of the same reasons: You just crossed midfield, and you just turned the same age as your father—at least as you imagined him as a kid. (To kids, all Dads are forty.) If it's true that the young are underpaid for what they do and the old are overpaid (and, of course, it is), then somewhere around here we pass the point where, for the first time, we are worth less than our market value—a bracing insight.

A quirk of human neurochemistry makes dissatisfactions more readily accessible than satisfactions until around age fifty, when emotional stability sets in (it's dissatisfaction that sends us truffling in new places). But it's only now, creeping into midlife, that we *know enough* to put those dissatisfactions to constructive work. The declining line of our "vital innocence" has met the rising line of our "knowing experience"—and at the precise point of intersection, as myth would have it, comes enlightenment. Part of enlightenment, presumably, is the full appreciation of the (rather scary) obligations that come with the territory. For it's at this stage of life that the real heavy lifting is done: what the Hindu faith calls "the maintenance of the world."

Plus which, people around us are starting to die.

Interview subjects who are asked to look back and diagram the contours of their life cite, perhaps more often than anything else, the loss of a loved one as a turning point. Such an event forces a reevaluation of life goals and values.

A young Ted Turner, who had talked about becoming a missionary, abandoned God after watching his twelve-year-old sister die agonizingly of an immune-system disease, apparently helped not at all by his prayers. ("I was taught that God was love and God was powerful, and I didn't understand how someone so innocent should be made or allowed to suffer.") So, too, Mark Twain is said to have tipped to atheism when his meek and blameless brother Henry was killed in a steamboat explosion.

A sibling dies and we feel powerless and vulnerable. A parent dies and we understand in a terrible new way that our protector has stepped away, leaving a clear view of the grave. Suddenly, life becomes Hitchcockian. We can conceive of our end; the tension in our lives is, rather than expectation, a kind of suspense, which is a darker energy. (As the dramatists say, expectation is fulfilled, whereas suspense is *relieved*.) The shift, when you sense that your life is in peril, is from detached to engaged. "All men are mortal" ceases to be some abstract line in a famous syllogism, and is suddenly, chillingly, concrete. "*I will die.*"

But death may simply remind us, so that we can get on with things, that *the self we are now* needs to die—or perhaps already has.

Much has been made of how women are compelled by a shrinking reproductive window to make the single most prevalent U-turn human beings make—woman to mother, achiever to caregiver. Men, unencumbered by that constraint, presumably are exempt from that particular stimulus to change their life. But there's another clock, roughly synchronized with the biological clock, and this one men hear loudly ticking, too. It is what University of Chicago social scientist Bernice Neugarten called the "social clock" that reveals where you are in your life relative to what others have accomplished. It is a period of intense stock taking. Are you "on time"? If not, a kind of March hare angst can arise, the kind that drove Sigmund Freud to recurring nightmares that he had missed the train.

The sense we get, by midlife, that time is slipping ever more quickly through our fingers, is not just a cliché; it's a kind of relativity effect. Because our biological clock slows as we age, the events of the world seem, by contrast, to be accelerating; in fact, the "subjective midpoint" in most lives is around age twenty. (Those two decades, in other words, seem to have taken the same amount of time to pass as the five or six or seven that follow.) Mortality looms as a deadline, but this angst is not so much a direct fear of dying as a fear of squandering. "Work hard—you don't have as much time as you think you do," the magazine editor and writer Michael Kelly told a young acolyte, a piece of advice U-turners understand acutely. (Kelly's words proved prophetic; in 2003, Kelly was killed in Iraq while embedded with the army's third infantry division.)

Of course it's also true that, when we hear a ticking clock, it's probably because, for the first time, we're in a position to listen. "Look at people in midlife," says the psychologist Jerome Kagan. "What have they been doing? They've been raising kids, they've been too tied up in the responsibilities of life. From twenty to forty in America, my God: You have too many responsibilities. When you're forty, now, finally, you've got time to think." A fearless and searching moral inventory, or simply a hard look at the facts: however ambitious the excavation, the news is likely to come as a bit of a shock.

"I have become everything I hate," the business consultant and mythologist David Whyte recalls an executive telling him one day in the cafeteria of a large company. "Yet I am doing exactly what I always wanted to do." That's a common enough sentiment within a certain stratum of American enterprise that Whyte polished up a fitting response, wise yet simple as pie: *What you wanted in the past isn't necessarily what's good for you now.*

Every man should be forced to take his fortieth year off and look hard in the mirror, the Australian writer Steve Biddulph argues in his *Iron John*–inspired book *Manhood*. The point of the exercise? To reacquaint himself with himself, and put things right with the people who love him while they still do (if they do) before he goes even further off the rails. Because make no mistake, many guys in midlife, unless they actively do something to stop their ambitions from narrowing to a point, *will* go off the rails. Blind focus on work ensures that "our marriages fail, our kids hate us, we die of stress and on the way, we destroy the world."

(Losing) a Sense of Where You Are

If we can assign a verb to our passage through life, possibly the best fit is *drift*. We mark time and distance, and we may try roughly to hold a bearing, but we go where we're pushed. In other words, we become someone we aren't—or at least something we didn't start out being. Which is a curse at least as often as it's a blessing. That insight is as hard to act on as it is easy to grasp. In the present moment, there are always ways to explain and justify what we're doing, from the minor peccadilloes in an otherwise honorable life to pretty severe treason against decency. Until, finally, there aren't. That is, until something—some emotional event, or the accumulated weight of a thousand counterfactuals—forces a shift in perspective, and we actually *perceive* that what we're doing *is* wrong.

The Time of Reckoning

For the better part of five years Virgil Butler worked for the chicken-processing giant Tyson, at its slaughter plant in Grannis, Arkansas, close to his then-home just over the border in Watson, Oklahoma. It's not the kind of work you'd choose if it weren't pretty much the only game in town and, because your mom lives nearby, you don't want to leave.

The job consists of going to the plant each day and reporting either to the "hanging cage" out on the back dock, or the kill room.

If you're a "hanger," you take your place on an assembly line along-side seven other men. Down the belt come the live birds, at the rate of three per second. You grab one, spin it upside down, shove its legs into shackles and then reach for the next bird. "A lot of them die of a heart attack right there on the belt in front of you," says Butler. "They get to twitching, and they roll over on their back and their tongue comes out and their eyes roll back and that's it."

If you're on the kill floor, you first apply Vaseline to your face (the better to wash the blood off later), and enter a room that smells like spoiled liver left to burn in a pan. The Tyson chickens are supposed to be killed by a machine that slits their throat, but in an operation of this scale some are inevitably missed, so it's your job, armed with a very sharp six-inch knife, to grab these birds and dispatch them before they go into the scalder alive. It requires two cuts at the neck—one to the jugular and one to the carotid artery.

Soon you are standing in blood so deep you can feel it trickling in over the top of your nine-inch-high boots. "The blood's supposed to go down the drain, but you get a killer in there—even a good killer like me—and you end up cutting the heads off quite a few of 'em, cause you're working so fast trying to get them all killed," Butler says. The heads'll get clogged up around that drain and the blood can't go down, and pretty soon you've got a blood clot that's nine inches deep and eight feet long and six feet wide, and it takes three men to move it." At the end of each night shift, a diesel tanker truck pulls out of the Tyson lot filled with the blood of eighty thousand chickens.

"When you first go to work there, people get sick and throw up. I did. I'd come home and couldn't even stand to eat. It'd come right back up."

But soon Butler became inured to it. You had to. Otherwise, it would be hard to take watching bored and frustrated employees stomping birds to death, bouncing them off walls, pulling off their legs and running over them with forklifts, as Butler claims happened routinely in there.

"I *worked* at becoming desensitized for a long time. I tried really hard to—it made it a lot easier to do my job. It's like when you were a kid—the first time you said a dirty word. You looked over your shoulder, right? Well, you say the word enough times and pretty soon you don't look over your shoulder anymore." After a while, the chickens aren't animals. "They're like slabs coming out of the sawmill."

Butler got very proficient at this. Four times he was named employee of the month. In a job with predictably high turnover, Butler stayed on and on (taking time off periodically to recover from injuries—including arthritis in his hands, hips, knees, and back.) He was learning to do this, staying ahead of his misgivings.

But he had merely buried those feelings, not conquered them. "I just suppressed how I felt because I knew it would have been an unpopular opinion among the other plant workers," he told me. Others *felt* the same way, he maintains, but a culture of machismo prevented anyone from even bringing the subject up. "You get a bunch of guys around, and they don't wanna admit their feelings. In the back of your head, you're thinking, Man, this poor thing has forty-five days from the day it's born and here I am picking it up and slamming it into the shackles."

But to do this continuously—often for a double shift of eighteen hours—and then to return home to the trailer behind your mom's place where you live and, forgoing dinner, flop down, and the chickens follow you into your dreams, at the rate of 186 per minute—well, that took its toll. "The feeling just kept adding up and it kept getting worse," Butler says.

What finally forced the turn for Butler was the appearance in his life of a woman, an animal lover by the name of Laura Alexander. As they grew closer, Virgil realized that he could no longer get away with simply brushing off his work as pulling "the night shift at Tyson." One day the pair of them dropped by the plant to pick up a paycheck for some sick time Virgil had logged. She asked if she could see where he actually worked. It was a shift-change and the machines were idle—so, reluctantly, he agreed, and took her out to the hanging floor.

She was, predictably, appalled—and all the way home in the truck that night, near tears, she told him how much. In the dark of the cab, Virgil merely hung his head, silent. "I realized for the first time in my life, that I was actually ashamed at the way I made my living.

"When I had to admit it to her, it was almost like admitting it to myself. For a long time I just denied it went on. But once it had come out of my mouth, it was different."

In 2000, Butler quit. He started researching vegetarianism, and soon stopped eating meat. (Eventually, he quit eating all animal by-products and wearing leather.) He now runs a Web site that bird-dogs the chicken industry and supports animal rights. "It's been a good way for me to work through the guilt that I accumulated for so many years," he says, "especially since I always knew that the work I was doing was wrong and just kept justifying my actions and kept on doing it."

"The conscience is a brake, not a guide," wrote Rabbi Abraham Joshua Heschel. "It raises its voice after a wrong deed has been committed, but often fails to give us direction in advance of our actions." And by then, as Virgil Butler discovered, quite often we're pretty deeply damaged.

No one is entirely free of cognitive dissonance—the uneasiness that comes from holding beliefs that conflict with how we actually behave. But would-be U-turners may have kept it at bay all those months or years by offloading responsibility. Think of it as the Jay Leno Syndrome, an ethical problem for these passive-aggressive times. Leno's agent for many years was the ruthless Helen Kushnik, whose clients prized her for the money she managed to get them, and took something of a don't-ask-don't-tell attitude about the particulars of the negotiations. But Kushnik left a trail of scorched earth and furious business associates, and when complaints about her filtered through to Leno, and he eventually left her, she got the last word: "I served you steak every night, and you didn't have to see how I slaughtered the cow." Lots of people are unethical in the way of nice-guy Jay, which is to say, by default. They allow their ethical battles to be fought by others—thus delegating responsibility, you might say, for their own moral development. It's easy under these circumstances to lose track of who you are becoming.

There is a story the playwright David Mamet likes to tell—an insight he credits to the psychoanalyst and folklorist Bruno Bettelheim—about the Nazi salute, which the Third Reich cleverly enforced until it became habit. "Five hundred times a day, a thousand times a day, German citizens had to raise their arms and give this stupid salute. And if they didn't feel like doing it, after a while, every time they gave the salute they had to say to themselves, 'I'm giving the salute, but I don't mean it,'" Mamet explained to Charlie Rose. "And so they subsequently said to themselves, 'Therefore I am either a coward because I don't stop giving the salute, or I am a hypocrite.' So eventually the struggle was too great and they simply forgot about it and started giving the salute, and as soon as they started giving the salute"—voluntarily, without misgivings—"their soul was gone."

"If you start giving the salute to something you aren't, eventually it becomes something you are," Mamet said. "To deny what you are, to deny who you are, to deny what you want, to live a life of hypocrisy, has got to have an ongoing effect on self-loathing."

Smedley Butler, a decorated U.S. Marine general who led the invasion of Haiti in 1915, is better remembered for his Second Act as a fiercely outspoken opponent of war. (Butler's philosophical journeys actually took him full circle: from Quaker to soldier to antiwar crusader.) In a speech in 1933, Butler tried to sum up what took him so long to wake up. "I suspected I was just part of a racket at the time. Now I am sure of it. Like all the members of the military profession, I never had a thought of my own until I left the service. My mental faculties remained in suspended animation while I obeyed the orders of higher-ups. This is typical with everyone in the military service.

"Looking back on it, I feel that I could have given Al Capone a few hints. The best he could do was to operate his racket in three districts. I operated on three continents.

"For a great many years, as a soldier, I had a suspicion that war was a racket; not until I retired to civil life did I fully realize it," he wrote in

his book called, fittingly, *War is a Racket.* "Now that I see the inter
tional war clouds gathering, as they are today, I must face it and sp
out."

Clearly, behavior in the community we're part of can be so strongly
codified that even conscious *thoughts* of dissent tend to be squelched.
And that, for some people, is the blissful end of that. But for the Smedley Butlers of the world there remains, on some level, in precognitive
chambers of the heart, a tension, which only grows as it's suppressed.
It's the kind of tension you often see in people who are becoming aware
of their own values and, painfully aware in the deal, of a disconnect:
Those values don't match the script these people have grown up with,
and are expected to follow.

Dave Dellinger was raised in a well-to-do family in a Boston suburb,
the son of conservative Republicans (his father was a prominent Republican lawyer and friend of former U.S. president Calvin Coolidge,
his grandmother was a member of the Daughters of the American
Revolution). His was, in short, the kind of blue-blood pedigree whose
guarantee of American-style success can only fail if the kid actively,
royally screws things up.

Which young Dave was soon well on his way to doing. True, he had
graduated from Yale with an honors in economics. But by the late
1930s he had also spent months riding the freight trains with the
hobos—getting his meals on breadlines when he could—and had
dropped out of Oxford to drive an ambulance in the Spanish civil war.
Increasingly politicized, he had also, unexpectedly, found God.

In 1940, the draft bill was passed. Because he was a seminary student in New York at the time, "I was exempt if I just signed my name,"
Dellinger told NPR's Terry Gross in 1993. "But I thought that was a
bribe—some people are religious and can't kill people—but ordinary
people will do the real work of society." He refused to be exempted.
But he refused, too, to be conscripted. Which put him at risk of going
to jail.

He called up his father to tell him about this turn of events. It was,
apparently, the last straw. A jail term for his son would bring down
more shame on the family—but more than that, it would cement his

father's fears that his son had thrown away his life. More than *that*, it meant an end to his father's own ambitions, which he had by then transferred to his son. His father told him that if he, the son, didn't register for the draft, he, the father, would commit suicide.

Dellinger took it as his duty, in that moment, not to back off his stance, but to convince his father to change his mind. He did, using the persuasive skill that would later serve him well organizing antiwar protests, and earning him a place in history as one of the most prominent peace and social-justice activists of the twentieth century,

(In later life Dellinger and his father had a rapprochement. As Dellinger told the story, shortly before his death in 2004, what happened between the two men was not a mere truce but, all the rarer, reconciliation. "At the end of his life, he said to me that I had chosen the way of life that he valued and he thought was right.")

The early abolitionists, in Britain and America, often had to make the same choice, decide that the way forward was to reject what the family stood for. They had to reach the point where "I keep slaves because my father did" wasn't a good enough reason.

But some of the most powerful examples of this can be found among white South Africans who first opposed apartheid. It's hard to overstate just how strong was the family script, and the pressure to follow it, for Beyers Naudé (pronounced BUY-ers NOW-day), the South African cleric. Naudé's father was a potent force in the maintenance of apartheid: A minister in the Dutch Reformed Church, whose biblical translations into Afrikaans helped that language become the official tongue of South Africa, he was also the first chairman of the Broderbund, a kind of shadow government of Afrikaner leaders. Young Beyers was raised an Afrikaner nationalist in the church, and into early adulthood he seemed to be a chip off the old block, eventually assuming his place in the Broderbund. When, as an assistant minister in the church, he eloquently praised racial segregation, many Afrikaners proudly heard the father in the son.

Then came what Naudé would later describe as "the day my conscience came out of hiding." The massacre by government troops of citizens of the black township of Sharpville was the first of a series of events that shattered his faith in the ruling regime. He severed his allegiance to nationalism and, symbolically, to his family and his community. He began to support the liberation movement. He founded an ecumenical organization called the Christian Institute. He was sympathetic to both the ANC and Steve Biko's Black Consciousness movement.

He had an intuitive sense of the magnitude of the repercussions of his turnaround—and so it came as no surprise when he was defrocked and kicked out of the Broderbund. One day he turned to his wife and said, "We must prepare for ten years in the wilderness."

His prediction was accurate. The Afrikaner community shunned him. In public, National Party leaders made a show of ignoring him. Many of Naudé's staff at the Christian Institute had their passports withdrawn, and the security police raided his home and office. When he refused to testify against some liberationists, he was arrested. His father had, of course, long ago cut off all contact.

Naudé, who died recently at age eighty-nine, was beloved in postapartheid Africa. (He succeeded Archbishop Desmond Tutu in the South African Council of Churches.) On his eightieth birthday, Nelson Mandela said of Naudé: "His life demonstrates what it means to rise above race."

In the summer of 1994, a few things were happening in the life of carpet manufacturer Ray Anderson to prepare him for the "sudden" appearance of his burning spear. Environmental issues were becoming a factor in business that could no longer be ignored, and Interface's lack of an environmental plan was starting to make the company stand out like somebody's grandparent chaperoning at a dance, in a way a CEO ought to take personally. ("Interface just doesn't get it!" was a terse line duly conveyed back to Anderson after Interface lost a bid to supply carpeting for a new "green" building in suburban Los Angeles. To which Anderson replied: "Doesn't get what?"—neatly proving the point.)

But Anderson had also reached a transition point himself. It's fairly natural, when powerful people reach retirement age, for their thoughts to turn to "legacy issues"—and in some cases that's enough to prompt a shift in perspective: When all that remains to leave is a footprint, a life stands revealed in a new way. "I was sixty years old," he says. "I'd brought in a new management team and the succession plan was in place. But in my subconscious there was working away this question: What will this child of mine—this third child, after my two natural daughters—grow up to be? So Paul Hawken's book fell on fertile ground."

Late-in-life U-turns may defy the norm—even more than pre-age-thirty U-turns, à la Tom Williams, defy the norm. But they offer hope for the aging, the calcifying, the stuck. Ivan Ilych, the comfortably be-numbed functionary and tragic hero of the Tolstoy story, realizes, on his deathbed, "Maybe I did not live as I ought to have done," and that his life has thus been a fraud. The longtime Harvard professor of psychiatry and medical humanities Robert Coles used to assign his students Tolstoy stories, and "The Death of Ivan Ilych" was one of his favorites. "These stories tell of life's redemptive possibilities, remind us that those who, by secular standards, have a lot can be in terrible spiritual jeopardy, and fi-nally, insist that the time we have here is never over until the very end," he writes. "The book of our lives is open—even until the last breath."

THREE

The Likely Candidate

Is There a U-turn "Type"?

Basically, his whole life has been a series of re-creations
of himself in various forms.

**—Robert Soros, on his financier-cum-philanthropist
father, George**

In 1971, not long after the Apollo 14 spacecraft had lifted off the surface of the moon and begun its long trip back to Earth, Edgar Mitchell, the lunar-module pilot, allowed himself, almost for the first time in the mission, to relax. His mission duties were mostly behind him. He lay back in weightlessness and, through the module window, gazed at the blue marble of the Earth. He could see the little peninsula in Southeast Asia where he knew his younger brother was flying combat missions in a brutal civil war; the beauty of the Earth belied the strife and suffering contained within it, he thought. And then that thought—all thoughts—were swamped by a feeling. It was as if he had "tuned in to something incomprehensively big." He pushed away from the tempered glass, and the feeling subsided a little. But each time he returned to the window, it returned.

It was a bliss Ed Mitchell would liken to romantic love, and within it was a "flash of understanding," during which he perceived human life as purposeful in a way impossible to articulate in terms that don't sound spiritual and New Age-y. There was "an upwelling of fresh insight coupled with a sense of interconnectedness." He saw himself as a point in a kind of evolutionary continuum, the work in progress that is the human species—a species that is currently a mere piker compared to what it's on its way to becoming. "I was," he says, "part of a larger process than I'd previously understood." The universe itself is somehow conscious and alive, learning as we learn, he saw in a flash. Mitchell was a philosophical man by nature, but even his mind—honed by a doctorate in aeronautics and astronautics from MIT—was too blunt to grasp the precise meaning. It came to him that this was the "transcendent moment" so many religions speak of; that God, perhaps, is "something like a universal consciousness manifest in each individual."

Upon landing back on Earth, Mitchell wasted little time acting on the great change that had swept over him.

He knew, for starters, that his future with NASA was over; who he was and what the agency was no longer jibed. Mitchell had already been drifting from his early loyalty to hardheaded Newtonian rationalism above all. After graduation, he had helped develop delivery systems for nuclear bombs, and it was his growing misgivings about the implications of that work that had moved him to apply to NASA. (Basically, he had wanted to fly into space, and NASA was the only game in town.) His deepest impulses were communitarian rather than competitive. He was flirting with a view of the world in which mind and matter are not starkly separate things. Now NASA, too, collided with what he had come to believe life was about. The Apollo program, for all its achievements, was just one side of an extraordinarily expensive display of technological one-upmanship. NASA stood for logic without compassion; knowledge without wisdom, and "progress" improperly measured. It was this very view of the world that had to be overcome if the species were going to survive.

Within a year of splashing back down on Earth, Mitchell had quit NASA to found something called the Institute of Noetic Sciences (IONS), which works the seam between religion and science. He took up meditation. He has made statements about the power of intentionality and the material efficacy of prayer and the likelihood of extrasensory perception, the kind of talk that makes traditional scientists turn pale and grasp their temples. (NASA, predictably, has distanced itself from Mitchell.) What had happened to him in space, looking out at the stars, he concluded, was simply this: He had "fallen into resonant tune with the universe." That that experience is potentially available to all of us, and is far more satisfying than any material reality we can know, is a premise on which he has staked the last quarter-century.

Edgar Mitchell returned to Earth a profoundly changed man. But his astral epiphany was a solo one. Mitchell's Apollo 14 cabin-mate, the curmudgeonly Alan Shepherd, had no such moment of transcendence in space, and did not return demonstrably changed.

The difference is striking, considering how many variables were held constant. Both men experienced spectacular extremes of emotion up there: the mortal terror wrought by potentially disastrous technological glitches; the awe of stamping the fifth and sixth sets of bootprints into the lunar soil, and looking back on the Earth. Both had similar backgrounds as military-trained test pilots. They shared the cookie-cutter family profiles of American astronauts (who tend to be eldest siblings or only sons, middle class, politically conservative). Roughly the same age, they grew up in the same cultural petri dish. And yet only one of them "switched on."

As if the universe were replicating the experiment, the next Apollo mission produced a similarly startling discord between its two moonwalkers. Apollo 15's lunar-module pilot, Jim Irwin, was scouting around at the foot of a big crater when his eyes fell on an unusual rock. He picked up the rock—which would turn out to be the oldest object any human being has ever touched, a rock formed not long after the birth of the universe—and as he did so, *he* had an epiphany. Irwin, as he would later describe the moment, actually heard God's voice whispering to him. Upon returning to Earth, Irwin quit NASA and founded an evangelical ministry. (He would die shortly after one of his expeditions to Mt. Ararat in Turkey to hunt for remnants of Noah's Ark.) Meanwhile, commander Dave Scott, who had been roaming around in the same area on the moon, heard no voice of God, felt no life-changing *coup de foudre*, and did nothing more radically unexpected with the rest of his life than cowriting a book with a Russian cosmonaut.

In fact, five of the six Apollo missions produced the same story line: One returning moonwalker experienced a profound identity transformation and was launched on a new trajectory, while his partner—relatively impervious to any lingering effects of awe—stayed the course. On Apollo 12, for example—a terrifying mission in which the rocket was struck twice by lightning that knocked out its navigation platform and gauges—it was Alan Bean who experienced a moment of clarity about what life was about. Honoring a promise he had made to himself in those dire moments, Bean quit NASA in the prime of his career (at age forty-nine), repaired to a small room, and became a full-time oil painter.

There is a Web site devoted to explaining human behavior via the world's oldest joke: Why did the chicken cross the road? History's great thinkers weigh in (or so the site's creators imagine). Niccolò Machiavelli: "The chicken crossed the road so that others would view it with admiration, as a chicken which has the daring and courage to boldly cross the road." Jean-Paul Sartre: "In order to act in good faith and be true to itself, the chicken found it necessary to cross the road." Ralph Nader: "The chicken's habitat on the original side of the road had been polluted by unchecked, industrialized greed."

There are, it would seem, more possible motivations in the head of a restless chicken than we might imagine. But that's only half the problem of chickens and roads. The fact is, all chickens *don't* cross the road. Indeed, most chickens don't. We notice major life reversals precisely because they are not the norm.

Why do some people feel a tap on the shoulder and make a radical change in their lives, while others in precisely the same circumstances feel nothing? Why are "peak experiences"—which everyone feels at some point, whether watching a sunrise or running a marathon or playing a concerto—for some a gateway to transcendence and others a mere, pleasant passing chemical high, a postcard from the subconscious thrown out with the day's mail? Why is a miraculously synchronous event a directive from the universe to some, to be obeyed implicitly—whereas to others it is just coincidence? Why can some people hear Bob Dylan's album *Blood on the Tracks* many times and . . . nothing, whereas others experience the jolt that makes the world look a little different ever after (and turns them from agnostics to lifelong converts to the Church of Dylan)? Saul of Tarsus was not alone on the road to Damascus, but no one else in his group wrote much more in their journals the next day than "wicked sandstorm." Why do people exposed to the same stimulus respond so differently?

The Likely Candidate

The question certain social and cognitive scientists, sniffing for a causal link, might ask is this: Is there a type of person who is just more prone to "seeing the light"?

Someone who asked the question that way would be called a dispositionalist. Dispositionalists look inward for answers, to unique personality traits. Some people are just born "bad apples" or valiant leaders, is the theory. At the opposite pole, a more fashionable place to be if you had to choose, lie the situationalists, who look outward, at environmental factors. They maintain that circumstances are the more powerful determinant of behavior. ("You can't be a sweet cucumber in a vinegar barrel," as psychologist Philip Zimbardo famously put it. Or in Noam Chomsky's construction: "Any one of us . . . could be a gas-chamber attendant or a saint.") It's not who you are, but what has happened to you, and what continues to make demands on you, and how much.

Edgar Mitchell is a situationalist—at least on the topic of what happened to the Apollo astronauts. All the U-turners, as it happened, were lunar-module pilots. The astronauts who remained unmoved in any profound way were the mission commanders. "There were studies on this in test-pilot school," Mitchell says. "The guy flying the aircraft is focused on the job at hand. The guy in the back"—or in the case of the returning Apollo craft, the guy on the right—"is more open to the experience. I've talked with all the lunar-module pilots, so I know their mind-set. We all had about the same experience—we just describe it differently. I didn't respond like Jim Irwin or Charles Duke, who said it was like looking on the face of God. They responded according to that frame of reference. Myself, being a philosopher/scientist, I said, 'I don't know what's going on here: Let's find out.'"

That sounds like a plausible argument. But the rebuttal reveals its flaws. The astronauts were chosen to drive or to ride at least partly on the basis of their temperament. The commanders—Armstrong, Young, Cernan, and Scott—were all of a type, men of "maddening and amusing imperviousness," as noted by the journalist Andrew Smith, who interviewed all the living Apollo astronauts for his book *Moondust: In Search of the Men Who Fell to Earth*. The guy assigning Apollo moonwalkers to the right seat or the left seat—the former Mercury astronaut Deke Slayton—knew the candidates well. "What Slayton wanted was impregnability,"

Smith said. "Many of the commanders appear to be fine men, but it seems to me unlikely that they were ever going to become painters or preachers or poets or gurus, or have much to say about the metaphysical resonance of their journey."

Self-Made Saints

Jerome Kagan, the Harvard psychology professor emeritus, agrees with Andrew Smith's conclusion about those Apollo astronauts. "I think it has to do with the personality of who gets selected to be the commander," he told me. "The person in charge of selection knows who's cool."

Kagan has to be considered the definitive "dispositionalist" among living developmental psychologists (though the level of his commitment to nature over nurture has softened somewhat in recent years). He believes there definitely is a "type" of person who is more likely to U-turn. It is someone like James Joyce's Stephen Dedalus.

"In *Portrait of the Artist as a Young Man*, Stephen has given up his faith," Kagan says. "And at one point his friend says, 'Your mother wants you to go to Easter Mass.' And Stephen says, 'I'm not going—I'd be a hypocrite.' The friend says, 'Oh for God's sake just go!' And Stephen says, 'I can't go: it would violate my conscience.' Now, I know those types, and they're temperamental. They're prone to anxiety and guilt. They know that if they violate a personal and ethical standard, they're not going to sleep for a couple of weeks. The average person can transgress a little and sleep beautifully. Stephen Dedalus represents a type of person who can't do anything that's not consistent with their morals. There are people, who are prone to guilt, we call melancholic."

The Stephen Dedaluses of the world put tremendous pressure on themselves. They have a predilection for what Kagan calls "ruthless self-honesty." If they are depressive by nature, like Ludwig Wittgenstein and Leo Tolstoy—whom Kagan also includes in this group—they are likely to ascribe the crumminess they felt about themselves to not being virtuous enough. The psychologist Janet Landman compares Katherine Ann Power—the sixties radical who, accused of murder in a botched bank job, became a fugitive for two decades before guilt forced her to turn herself in—to Dostoevsky's famously guilt-ridden killer, Raskolnikov. Both "lacked the stomach to repress their moral emotions."

A whole category of U-turners fit this mold: Call them the "self-made saints." They are moral extremists really, dedicated to the pursuit of a kind of purity that verges on the impossible (but that they may have been raised to believe was their duty to show). When you delve into the past of a lot of apparently secular U-turners, you often find they were raised in a faith that they later rejected. They are excruciatingly hard on themselves, and exaggerate the need to atone through a wholesale change, rather than a mere adjustment of individual behaviors. The old belief system, whatever it was, is not simply an address to be vacated, but a house to be burned down. Their story is a redemption myth: They are trying not just to change, but in some ways to erase the former self that actually did damage in the world. The steel magnate–turned–philanthropist Andrew Carnegie would probably qualify. Carnegie had made his fortune through war—his empire growing with the demand for munitions. And he dedicated the second part of his life to financing what he believed was the only antidote to war: education. (Did Carnegie's spectacular generosity really have the deep psychological component typical of the self-made saint? The proof seems to be in a strange phobia he developed later in life, a condition called *chrometophobia.* Carnegie went George Soros's noted disdain for money one better: He would reportedly suffer anxiety attacks at the sight or even the *smell* of money—and so he refused to carry cash.)

But a penchant for feeling obligation acutely, combined with native restlessness, can set up the conditions for reversals of a slightly different kind. Numerous biographies of Gandhi concur that the great compassion he became known for was midwifed not by guilt but by a related emotion that's more acutely about identity: shame.

In 1893, when he was a young attorney enforcing British law in South Africa, Gandhi booked a first-class train ticket from Durban to Johannesburg, where he was scheduled to attend a trial. But soon after he had settled in the seat, he was confronted by a conductor, who told him he was in the wrong train car. The "coloured" section, with the "second-class Indians," was in the back. It was a humiliating moment. When he didn't immediately comply, he was thrown off the train, and forced to spend the night in the cold train station at Pietermaritzburg. Actually ex-periencing the discrimination he theretofore had known only in the ab-stract is credited with radicalizing Gandhi. You could say that on that day Gandhi's budding private beliefs—in *satygraha* ("the force of truth and love") and *ahimsa* ("nonviolence toward all living creatures")—resolved into a public fight for social justice.

It proved to be Gandhi's most public turning point. But there was a second reversal, toward an extreme, some would say irrational, puri-tanism and self-denial. By Gandhi's own reckoning, it had been set in mo-tion by a single incident in his youth. At sixteen, Gandhi was living at home in Porbandar, in western India, with his new wife, Kasturba, and his dying father. One night, overcome by lust, he left his father's bedside to go upstairs and make love with his bride. In the interim, his father died, alone. In that moment was born Gandhi's doctrine of celibacy. Only those who could conquer the most primal impulse could hope to aspire to loftier realms of Truth, he concluded. It was a self-punishment that be-came a creed, and a development with which Freud would have had a field day. The decision became entangled with Gandhi's desire to become wholly pure and chaste on behalf of "mother India."

Many consider Gandhi's life, looked at over its length, an insoluble puzzle. He seems to have been the ultimate chameleon, changing en-tirely, according to the slant of the light. "At one time he sounded like a socialist, and at another a dreamy conservative; or, again, a pacifist and a frantic militarist; a nationalist and a 'communalist'; an anarchist and a devotee of tradition; a Western activist and an Eastern mysticist; a to-tal religionist and yet so liberal that he could say he saw God even in the atheist's atheism," wrote the psychoanalyst Erik Erikson. "Did this polymorphous man have a firm center?"

Yes, Erikson concluded, he did. In fact, he was a type—even an ar-chetype. Erikson dubbed Gandhi *Homo religiosus*.

Risk-Plungers and Happy Carrots

If trying to ascertain, more or less scientifically, what a U-turn "type" looks like seems like a slippery proposition, it's probably no slipperier than trying to ferret out, say, a "terrorist" type—which teams of psychologists and sociologists working for the U.S. Department of Homeland Security are employed to do. So far, they haven't had much success, but let's run with the concept. If you scooped a couple of psychological profilers out of the FBI hive in Quantico, and asked them to produce a profile of a U-turner, it might look something like this:

> He is a forty-one-year-old American, raised middle class or better, stubborn, charismatic, optimistic, idealistic, sensitive, imaginative, and a little bit self-involved.

Where does such a profile come from, and how accurate might it be? Let's start with the *he*.

No doubt, you've noticed that most of the examples of U-turners so far have been men. Are men more intrinsically inclined to change radically, or is it the bias I'm picking up from the media, because more men than women tend to get their stories told, their dramatic tales confirming their roguish reputations?

In all cultures, quixotic plunges into the unknown are tolerated, even expected, in men. (We do not, as a culture, cut the "prodigal daughter" much slack.) Mythically speaking, men are yang, after all, to women's yin. The intrinsic tendency of yin is toward stability; the intrinsic tendency of yang is toward transformation.

But outside the realm of myth, we do know that, in general, men are more inclined to extremes. Young men in particular are given to what Piaget called a kind of "messianic morality"—spinning them out into extremist ideologies and cults and gangs in greater numbers. The proportion of men is higher at the far ends of virtually all distributions of human behavior and human traits, from height to sports participation to investment risk taking. ("More prodigies, more idiots," as this greater male variability is sometimes summed up.) The director Terry Gilliam was once asked to explain why engineers, who are mainly men, love Monty Python so much. Well, the troupe's popularity is explained by their being "very intelligent or very infantile while avoiding the middle ground," he explained. Engineers are, coincidentally, mostly men.

The comic novelist Mark Leyner weighed in on why this might be so, with his serious hat on, and reasonably convincingly. When you look back at your high school yearbook, Leyner noticed, the girls are perfectly recognizable as the women they became. Their personalities, their aspirations—they didn't change much at all. But the boys? Oy. Vast indeed is the disconnect between the self-contained lone gunmen boys *learn* to be—ask nothing, demand nothing—and the communal, cooperative family guys they are *asked* to be, and indeed eventually *yearn* to be as radioactive loneliness becomes unbearable. That's about the time when the men, "whose whole raison d'etre as Paleolithic punks had been being fierce and fecund and unattached, starts unraveling," Leyner writes. "The forces at work are too polar, too magnetically repellant. The center won't hold. So we lurch."

Of course, there may be another explanation for the preponderance of stories about male U-turners: It's not because women don't U-turn, but, conversely, because U-turns are no surprise to women. All women pull a U-turn, in terms of revising their identity (more so, I think, than men) when they have kids, even though different women react differently to motherhood. And then they U-turn again once the kids are grown.

The profilers in Quantico tell us our U-turner is probably middle class, at least. Why should that be? To the question, Why do some people enact a radical midlife change?, one answer is: *Because they can.* Certain elements of their life allow it.

To send forth new shoots requires a deep root system, decent support that allows you to explore. "What are the conditions for self-actualization: educational, sexual, economic, political?" asked Abraham Maslow, the pioneering humanist psychologist. His conclusion was that only the people who are pretty well provisioned with the basics are in a position to go for the summit. (Which is one reason U-turns are so much more common than they were even a century ago, when people tended to be poorer, less educated, and subject to a pretty inflexible educational/work path that was prescribed from an early age.) Choice is a modern phenomenon. And even now, people living close to the bone, with obligations that outstrip their savings, may not be able to afford the luxury *even to think about* radically changing their life. (I'm excluding, here the case of sudden, overt religious conversion, which can—and often does—happen to the poor. See chapter 13.

The Likely Candidate

In 1976, *Reader's Digest* published a story called "The Case for a Simpler Life," an early entry in the downshifting canon, in which the writer cited his family's view that waste is sinful. "Individually, people are finding that a simpler lifestyle provides greater satisfaction than the relentless pursuit of materialism." Who was the writer? None other than that son-of-the-soil Laurance Spelman Rockefeller, scion of John D. and brother of Nelson. He had, at the time of writing, pared down his existence to the basics: a number of large homes, a Bentley, a plane, a sixty-five-foot speedboat, priceless Chinese porcelains, paintings by Bonnard and Gainsborough, and so on. But by the standards of his own world, he was bucking the tide; among the five Rockefeller brothers Laurance was the quietest, the most conservation-minded, and perhaps just generally the most thoughtful—and so had the sensitivity, as well as the luxury of time, to really notice the cognitive dissonance a Rockefellerian lifestyle produces in an era of transparent global disparity. (You could say Laurance Rockefeller was ahead of his time, in that the dissonance he was feeling is what is said to drive the so-called "cultural creatives"—a cohort 50 million strong involved in a life-changing shift away from materialism into "creating meaning.") Those are the ingredients that can produce desperation and depression in people of means: Call it the Richard Cory effect.

"You have to come from a privileged enough background to feel guilty" about how easy your ride has been relative to others, Jerome Kagan told me. "The Palestinian bombers tend to be middle class. If you've had a harsh life, there's no reason to be moral: That would be stupid." The poor, by this reasoning, are cynics, and idealism of the sort we're talking about is the privilege of those in the middle class on up.

There's another reason that the better off are more inclined to make a radical change. As material wealth increases, life becomes more complicated, with interdependent parts, like a house of cards. Around the life you've created grows an infrastructure that must be maintained, a network of obligations, and it pretty soon happens that you can't change your circumstances just a little. Apart from superfine adjustments, shuffling the deck chairs a little, radical change becomes *the only kind of change* that's really possible: Sell the car, rent the house, fire the nanny, withdraw from the committees, liquidate the assets, call the movers, cancel the papers, and invite the neighbors for a farewell martini. If you really can't stand your life as it is, you have to cut and run.

The profilers down in Quantico have singled out Americans, which seems suspicious. Clearly, Americans have no exclusive claim on U-turn experiences. But you could say that committing strongly to one position is a rather American decision—or at least an American value. The boy does not grow to be president, nor does the poor immigrant laborer ascend to the executive suite, nor does the high school hoops player make it to the NBA by choosing balance. Narrow, sacrificial commitment is a founding American myth: Through it anything is possible.

Which sounds like a good deal, but there's a catch. The steep wage of that promise that you can be anything is that you must sacrifice everything else.

When a culture sets up extreme positions as models to aspire to, people can easily come to feel inadequate in the positions they currently occupy; then the desire to change becomes overwhelming. That's a state of affairs the psychologist Paul Watzlawick called *The Utopia Syndrome*—it's consumer capitalism's very engine, but its price is insecurity and dejection. "People blame themselves, rather than the unrealistic nature of the goal, for their failure to achieve it," Watzlawick said. "They think, 'My life should be rich and rewarding, but I am living in banality and boredom; I should have intense feelings but cannot awaken them in myself.'"

What about the profilers' epithet "stubbornly decisive"? For most people, beyond a certain point in life—an arbitrary age of forty is sometimes set—absolute truth tends to come in for distrust. Truth becomes contingent and situational as life clouds with nuance and paradox in the natural shift to "postformal" thinking. In other words, people go gray at the temples both outside and in, take up moderate positions somewhere near the mushy middle on just about every issue. But U-turners are different. U-turners are not postformal thinkers—or, if they are, their actions belie the nuances in the evolution of their thought.

Where most of us learn the habit of making incremental adjustments not only in our thinking but in our behavior, the behavior of

U-turners seems hyperdecisive. They have committed utterly to their position. The spiritual guru George Ivanovich Gurdjieff is a perfect example, as revealed in his teachings. For Gurdjieff (who came to his beliefs after a profound midlife crisis), the idea that people can agree to disagree, and both be right, did not compute. There is one truth, and you can get it now or get it later. "There can only be one understanding," Gurdjieff said. "The rest is nonunderstanding, or incomplete understanding."

Moderation—the way of softness and compromise—is the enemy of the U-turn sensibility. (There is a certain prudent practicality in this. "If you're in the middle," the opinionated broadcaster Don Meredith used to say, "you're going to get hit by cars going both ways.") When I tried to talk with the tree-sitter Julia Hill, through her foundation, the Circle of Life, I ran up against a coarse screening mechanism. Julia wanted to know one thing: Was the book going to be printed on recycled paper? I explained that that's not very common these days, so I didn't think so. Um, no. That was the dealbreaker. It didn't matter that I'd written for the alternative press, or that I was likely to tell her story sympathetically. She had simply drawn a line. It was a perfectly fitting response, of course: It is who she is, and it is why she was able to do what she did. "Living in Luna," she writes, "taught me that one of the best ways to find balance is to go to extremes."

"Nothing is more alien to her ideology than the notion of balance," wrote the psychologist Dan McAdams of Shirley Rock, the prostitute-turned-mob-connected madame, who turned her life around and became a pastor. "Her behavior on the streets, in prison, in church and in her own family is repeatedly characterized by extremes . . . Shirley swings wildly from 100 percent rebel to 100 percent criminal to 100 percent pastor and so on. Like Saint Paul, she throws herself completely into everything she does, and she believes strongly in everything she believes."

Like Shirley Rock, most U-turners have struggled mightily with their demons. Eric Hoffer liked to promote Blaise Pascal's notion that "We are made virtuous not by love of virtue but by the counterpoise of two opposite vices. It takes a vice to check a vice, and virtue is the by-product of the stalemate." In other words, apparently virtuous life turns *may* be driven by moral concerns, but they may simply be the conscience's strategic attempt to find a way out of a place of real trouble. Without Elsinore—the darkness inside our souls, as playwright Michael Frayn puts it—real virtue would never find expression, by this theory. If U-turners do indeed have more unacknowledged darkness in their souls, it would explain why their stories tend to be messy, with plenty of collateral damage: people hurt and people left behind. The Ned Flanderses of the world do not pull U-turns. But Pascal would say, the Ned Flanderses—all virtue—never produce the Big Virtues. They are steady. And steady never created a masterpiece.

It's tempting to add here that U-turners are uncompromising, but that's not quite accurate. Most people compromise, a little or a lot, moment by moment. U-turners do their compromising all at once. They move not at all, not at all, for months or years, and then—wham—they move completely. Instead of drawing one card each draw, they hold, hold, hold, and then trade in all their cards. (U-turners can live with the tension of internal contradictions for longer than most of us.) But they *appear* to be uncompromising. If you were scouting for candidates who might radically change their mind at some point, the best ones, counterintuitively, might not be the wafflers, but rather those with seemingly unerring confidence in their position.

U-turns rarely transform congenitally moderate people into extremists. That is, U-turners tend to be fairly extreme personalities to begin with. Che Guevara was a rebel from the get-go. It's clear from what Che's biochemist pal Alberto Granado writes in his own book that Guevara's violent revolutionism sprang at least as much from his own temperament as from anything this kid from the upper classes encountered along the road. Saul of Tarsus was an overzealous rabbi well before he became St. Paul. Whittaker Chambers remained a binary thinker, even after the scales fell from his eyes about Soviet-style Communism. "After his intellectual conversion, he still believed that one system was basically good and one was basically rotten," notes psychologist Howard Gardner, "but he reversed his position on which was which."

Chambers was a compelling guy—in part because conviction is an extraordinarily magnetic personality trait. Indeed, *intensity of conviction* is closely linked with what those Quantico profilers identified as *charisma*—it is part of the appeal of all successful leaders. Some have theorized about why recent converts often come off as particularly charismatic; the writer David Aberbach argues that charisma is released, like endorphins at the finish line of the New York marathon, at the exit end of a personal crisis—when, in the case of U-turners, uncertainty has resolved itself and a new identity is firmly in place.

(The conviction/charisma equation explains, I think, as an aside, why we Canadians are considered so dull. We are endlessly tolerant and provisional, and largely agnostic. We don't feel the need, when one belief fades, to immediately pick up a placeholder belief until something better comes along. We prefer, in the breach, to commit to nothing, accepting the perpetual vague unsettledness that comes with that decision.)

You want U-turners at your dinner party not because they are necessarily gregarious raconteurs, but because they so often seem unmalleable. Like the painter Paul Gauguin, who bridled against being typecast—he was a Christian who longed, in the jungles of Tahiti, to become a "savage"—they stand by their interesting and perhaps unpopular choice. They tend to be charismatic in the way good actors are—utterly inhabiting their part. They cannot suspect, and really aren't much moved to consider the possibility that, at the end of the run of that play, they will move on to a different role.

A final nod to our profile, and the character trait of imagination. U-turners are inclined to see the world as a story, rather than as a proof. The psychologist Jerome Bruner proposed that we can sort people according to how they understand the world in this sense: We are chiefly rational, or we are mythological. We are either people who lean hard on reason and observation, or we are invested in a narrative mode of thought, where "we deal with the vicissitudes of human intention, organized in time." To U-turners, life is dramatic and fraught and readily adaptable into a twisty M. Night Shyamalan script. That's not to say the lives of U-turners objectively *are* these things, but they are perceived that way. The research psychologists Robert McCrae and Paul Costa Jr., who have excavated the phenomenon of identity change, believe some people are disproportionately geared to "experience lots of crises, whereas others rarely, if ever, go through them."

The mythological imagination breeds a deep curiosity. U-turners are, by and large, questers. More than most people, they are interested in searching for meaning—a trait that, the psychoanalyst Marion Woodman believes, you either have or you don't. The incurious are not likely to examine their life, and therefore the U-turn process will never be initiated. Woodman calls the unexamining liver of life a "happy carrot." "They don't ask why. They live their life day by day, they don't question the meaning of things, don't think about coincidences. Those questions don't come up. They're not interested in the unconscious. They never pay attention to their dreams, so their dreams cut out," Woodman said. Exactly why some people are happy carrots and others strive for meaning is a question "Jung had no answer for," she said. "I don't know of anybody who has. I envy happy carrots, sometimes."

Happy carrots will never become U-turners.

The gulf between those who have an "appetite for meaning," as it is sometimes put, and those who don't would seem to be unbridgeable. In W. Somerset Maugham's *The Razor's Edge*, Isabel, the fiancée of protagonist Larry Darrell, stands dumbfounded before his sudden transformation from conservative would-be stockbroker to quester with a powerful jones for meaning. She admits that she can't understand his obsession with timeless spiritual mysteries. "If such questions could be answered," she shrugs, "surely they'd have been answered by now!" and you can be pretty sure at that point the relationship is doomed.

You could say that all U-turners share an intense drive to make sense out of the universe—that's a trait common to creative thinkers who have had aha breakthroughs, and to spiritual gurus. But where does that drive actually come from—what Daddy complex or fluke of genetics?

It's all but impossible, once you start gathering stories of U-turners, both religious and secular, not to be mightily seduced by genetics. (Hmm: Tristan Flora and her grandson, the painter Paul Gauguin, both pulled

U-turns. Could it be that U-turning is a heritable trait but, like male-pattern baldness, it skips a generation?) Might you or I, in fact, be genetically predisposed to standing against tomorrow what we stood for today, having "seen the light"?

It's hardly a far-fetched idea. There's good evidence that we do inherit unique neurochemistries that can predispose us to behave or think in certain ways. We know, for example, thanks to pioneering twin studies by a University of Minnesota scientist named Thomas Bouchard, that tendencies toward a particular kind of extreme commitment to a belief system—religious fundamentalism—appear to be at least partly heritable. There's also evidence that each of us has an innate, unique "set point" for things like anxiety and comfort with risk and even happiness. ("Trying to be happier," as one behavioral geneticist recently put it, "is like trying to be taller.") We might suppose that in U-turners the set point for risk-taking is high, and the set point for happiness is preternaturally low. Such people might then restlessly search for improvements in their lives where others, in the same circumstances, might be reasonably content to carry on carrying on.

It's widely believed, further, that certain people are simply naturally more endowed with certain kinds of intelligence, including the capacity for self-knowledge. With subtle and powerful introspective radar attuned to low chatter and minute shifts in mood and feeling—a dog's nose for cognitive dissonance—such people, it's fair to speculate, would naturally be more prone to about-faces when they found their actions diverging from their beliefs. By contrast, people whose neural truth-testing mechanisms were *under*developed would presumably be less prone to U-turns because they wouldn't detect the cognitive dissonance in the first place. Actually, such people exist—and lo and behold, they do indeed ferociously resist letting faulty belief systems go, because they are utterly oblivious to any sense that there's any problem.

In 1996, University of California at San Diego neurologist V. S. Ramachandran began working with patients with a rare neurological disorder called anosognosia, which affects roughly 5 percent of victims of a stroke in the right parietal cortex. The stroke paralyzed these patients' left sides. But, bizarrely, the patients were unable to perceive that they were paralyzed—and no amount of doctors' persuasion could convince them. Perfectly normal and cogent in every other way, these patients cooked up fantastical reasons why their left arm was just fine, thank you so much, even though they couldn't feel it or move it. Ramachandran developed a theory that, in terms of their role in the creation and revision of beliefs, the two brain hemispheres perform very different functions. The left brain is the rationalizer. It will do anything to protect a current belief system from attack—folding new information gracefully into it, performing gymnastic contortions to interpret the world so that the facts still fit the belief. The right brain sees the problem and does not flinch from it. Somewhere in those gray folds is a mechanism Ramachandran calls the "devil's advocate," whose job is to "question the status quo" and "look for global inconsistencies." When enough facts pile up that contradict the beloved belief, the right brain steps in and calls a halt to the charade, forcing a complete revision—"a Kuhnian paradigm shift." In the anosognosia patients, the "devil's advocate," the neural whistleblower just dying to stand up and expose an alternative "truth," seemed to have been knocked out. The result was denial and confabulation on a massive scale. Light simply could not get in.

If Ramachandran is right that, very broadly speaking, "the right hemisphere is a left-wing revolutionary that generates paradigm shifts, whereas the left hemisphere is a die-hard conservative that clings to the status quo," then we might suppose that there are countless gradations along the scale—from complete denial to complete and transparent sensitivity to alternative belief systems—depending on how developed the right hemisphere is with respect to the left, and how the two work together to determine the way we see the world. Anosognosics, essentially incapable of revising their beliefs, would define one end of the scale; at the other end would lie people with powerful devil's advocates, for whom the status quo doesn't have a prayer.

The theory that a "spiritual temperament" itself is a heritable trait got a boost not long ago when geneticists with the National Cancer Institute and the National Institutes of Health, in Washington, D.C., reported a genetic quirk that expresses itself more in some people than others. The quirk—a variation on a gene called VMAT2—correlates with a kind of skill that lead researcher Dean Hamer calls *self-transcendence*.

The Likely Candidate

It would seem to aid the ascension to the kind of altered state that accompanies epiphanies. The religious scholar Huston Smith had smoked out that personality trait long before the human genome was sequenced. "In studying the world's religions for fifty years I've come to the conclusion that there is a spiritual counterpart to Carl Jung's psychological personality typology—the temperaments Jung believed we're born into," he said. Jung proposed "intuitive versus analytical" as the polar ends of one key dimension of human personality. Smith believes there is a temperamental type who is "spiritually intuitive" in that way. So, where most people could be plunked down in even the holiest of circumstances—say, high in the Himalayan foothills at 3 a.m. on a full moon–bathed October night surrounded by chanting Gutana Tibetan monks and not feel anything but cold—the spiritual intuitive would be transported. (Smith would count himself among the latter group; it was, in fact, under these precise circumstances that he experienced an epiphany two decades ago.)

Faced, then, with the question, Why is it that two people may be in exactly the same circumstances, but one experiences a life-changing epiphany and the other isn't moved at all?, it's tempting to speculate they are just built differently. Throw together in the same person a lot of the qualities we have been talking about, and you have the ingredients for a big about-face.

It's tempting, in fact, to go down this road. Not just because genetic explanations for human behavior are all the rage. (And a handy out when we behave badly. Newsflash in *The Onion*: "Scientists Discover Gene for Eating Whole Goddamn Bag of Potato Chips.") Not just because there's quite decent support for them now: As scientists pull apart the human genome, personality traits like aggressiveness and gregariousness emerge in a new light—we're now told not just that they're heritable, but what particular gene they rode in on. Not just because we are forced to consider fairly bold claims, like those advanced by the philosopher and political scientist James Q. Wilson, that a *moral dimension* of our personalities may be innate.

It's tempting because it provides answers that seem so intuitively right: Some traits simply seem to defy environmental explanations. Why the extreme behavior in guys? No one has yet isolated a gene on the Y chromosome for radical midlife mind changes, but it does seem possible that sex differences may come into play in a roundabout way. (Women's double-X chromosome may serve to mitigate extremity: Exaggerated effects on one can be offset by the genes on the other.)

In midlife reversals, a determinist would not see too many cultural influences at play. This particular brain, they say, was going to detonate anyway. The instructions were prepared in the genome. As Edward O. Wilson famously put it in a photographic analogy, the negative was poised over the developing solution, waiting to be dunked.

Yet it soon becomes clear why this tempting road, if you follow it all the way, is mined. To go the distance is to accept the possibility, as sociobiologists do, that *everything* is heritable: intelligence, compassion, even criminality. In a world where everything is predetermined, ethical behavior would be fruitless. The idea of ethics would be nonsensical. The moral U-turn would be impossible, because no one could "develop" a social conscience they didn't have to begin with.

And certainly not everyone could find a faith. If the determinists are right, then, as Tom Wolfe put it, "The peculiarly American faith in the power of the individual to transform himself from a helpless cipher into a giant among men, a faith that ran from Emerson to Horatio Alger to Dale Carnegie—that faith is now moribund. It lives only in motivational talks by Fran Tarkenton." If the determinists are right, said Wolfe, "your soul just died."

There are all kinds of problems with determinism. If we are puppets of our genomes, then we must be unresponsive to what happens around us—which seems patently mad. What is innate—and a uniquely human trait—is the brain's capacity to adapt. We are nothing if not flexible.

How much of our behavior is actually a product of our DNA? Somewhere between a third and three-quarters, most cognitive psychologists now believe. That's a lot more than we used to think, but a lot less than you need to make the case that we are programmatically marching to our genetically determined fates. And while certain personality traits may make a midlife crisis more likely, we know there are cases that defy expectations. Plenty of U-turners would slip right past those profilers in Quantico without even being asked to open their bags.

The Likely Candidate

All of which pretty much quashes the idea that U-turns are the exclusive domain of gurus or CEOs or Rockefellers or moonwalking astronauts—or any other particular "type." This is a club that's open to anyone—anyone that is, with the chutzpah to *believe* they belong, and march right in through the gate.

FOUR

The Condemned Twin
Is There Only One Identity for Us?

A man's route back to himself is a return from spiritual exile,
for that is what a personal history amounts to—exile.
—Saul Bellow, *The Actual*

S idney Rittenberg sits drinking tea in a light-filled living room in a
hilltop house framed with pine trees a half-hour south of Seattle.
His shirt is buttoned to the chin. He looks a little like Jack Welch,
the titan of capitalism, and a little, somehow, like Jorge-Luis Borges, the
Argentinean fabulist. He has big eyebrows and, when he thinks deeply
about something, the wrinkles on his forehead make the symbol of pi.

Sidney, along with his wife Yulin, is one the most sought-after corporate consultants to China, advising clients like Microsoft and Intel and
Polaroid as they scramble for a grubstake in a market a billion people
strong. He is eighty-three years old. On some days he'd like to retire; but
he is so invaluable, now, at the dawn of the Chinese economic boom,
that he probably can't.

It's a position to savor, the denouement to a life story that is never far
from his mind.

As a young Stanford linguistics grad drafted into the army in 1942,
Rittenberg was sent to China for a brief tour of duty. But, idealist that he
was, he got seduced by Chinese Communism and stayed to join Mao's
Cultural Revolution. (Such a trusted soldier to the cause did he become
that Mao would write fondly of him in his memoirs.) And then, just

as abruptly as he had gained favor, Rittenberg aroused suspicion and was tossed into solitary confinement. He would spend the better part of twenty years in Chinese prisons, enduring systematic interrogations aimed to break him down and admit to being who the Communists believed he really was: a traitorous enemy of the regime. He remained stubbornly devoted to Mao, until the horrible truth of Mao's failings finally got the better of his denial (or, as he puts it, "the scales fell from my eyes"). When he returned to the United States in 1979—35 years after he had first planned—he was a changed man. But changed in complicated ways.

Conviction, as William James was among the first to understand, can be a kind of metaphorical survival mechanism. Sidney Rittenberg put the adage to a ferocious test.

During his first prison term—courtesy of pressure from Stalin on China to treat China-friendly Westerners as spies—Rittenberg suffered unimaginably. He was kept in darkness, awake, and so hungry he was forced to eat mole crickets and the plaster off the wall. (His wife, meanwhile, would wait three years for him, then give up and remarry.)

"The fear was not of being taken out and shot—big deal," he says. "The fear was of going mad. You're sitting there and the threat of your own madness is sitting there opposite you, and you know that either you get him or he gets you.

"You have to have a strategy to deal with that. Conviction works. Certainty works. Doubt will kill you." Was it possible that absolute, unwavering belief—that quality that the religious narratives tell us comes to the spiritually prepared in a lightning act of grace—could actually be cultivated, alone in the dark? For his sake, Sidney understood, it had *better* be possible.

He was a good Communist, he felt, but no puppet. The blind obedience to the party he'd seen in the young revolutionaries had deeply troubled him, and he had in fact openly scorned books like Liu Shaoqi's *How to Be a Good Communist*, which he'd read while hiding from the Nationalists in the high-mountain caves. But now he worked to eliminate any such cavils. Blind obedience was good. He'd been wrong to question it. It was only his selfishness that was preventing him from turning his whole will over to the discipline of the party. He tried to believe this. He did believe it.

In his prison cell he read *How the Steel Was Tempered*, a turgid revolutionary tract, and he tried to slip into the skin and thoughts of the young hero, to become a man who could "look back over his life with no regrets about time and energy spent in selfish pursuits."

He was creating a new identity. He thought of people back home he admired, ultracommitted labor leaders like the Quarry Workers Union organizer Homer Pike, and the Roanoke Rapids mill hand Old Man Mason. From these men he mentally harvested traits he could model. He scrutinized Mao's philosophical lectures, like "On Protracted War," learning them by heart. So deeply did he absorb the lessons that, one day when prison officials showed up to give him his grilling, he sprang from his chair and looked them in the eye. "I am a committed revolutionary and I will never, ever change," he said. "If you keep me shut up in here until I die, and you do an autopsy on my heart, you will find every fiber to be pure red. I will cling to my convictions no matter what happens."

When Stalin died, Rittenberg was released—only to be reincarcerated a few years later by a decree signed this time by Mao, who had changed his mind about Rittenberg and was now convinced he *was* a spy.

Prison conditions this time were even worse. Rittenberg was kept in the hole of a more dire prison known as the "ice house," so called for its unrelieved cold. "Counterrevolutionary scum"—that's what he was, according to prison guards who shouted the epithet through the door as they walked past. He heard people around him being tortured—and then, worse, silence. There were daily interrogations for three years. He could not give his captors what they wanted—his admission that he had networks in the foreign community—because, of course, he didn't. Daily he proclaimed his loyalty to the party, and was bounced back to his cell.

In the end, it was the same stubborn commitment to absolute faith that had saved his life that also delayed his exit epiphany. Across the world, the barbarism of the Cultural Revolution was now becoming apparent—nuclear scientists mucking out cow barns, classical pianists volunteering to have their fingers smashed. Mao had already brought more death to his people than any other leader in history. But cut off from any news or evidence of what was happening, Rittenberg could only assume that Mao was the shining proponent of social democracy he believed him to be. The only news Rittenberg got was the propaganda of the story he had written in his own head.

Eventually, toward the end of his second prison term, a new voice began to make itself heard. It came from a different place of conscience, an older place, and it grew more insistent by the day. It was not so much doubt as a new conviction, rising to replace the old one.

To stave off madness, Rittenberg had composed a mantra that he played in an endless mental loop: "My name is Li Dunbai. I am an American who of his own volition joined the Chinese Revolution and was accepted into the Communist Party. My aim is to turn myself into a genuine Communist, a noble, pure, and moral man, who lives to benefit the people, devoid of selfishness, devoted exclusively to the welfare of others."

Now the voice said:

"My name is Sidney Rittenberg. I am dedicated to seeking my happiness by contributing to the freedom and happiness of the human race. I am entitled to life and liberty, and no one can deprive me of those rights as long as I refuse to give them up. I will use my philosophy to realize as many of them as possible within the circumstances in which I find myself. I will never give up. The more they try to weaken me and break me down, the stronger I will become."

It was an identity that had, perhaps, been there all along, but buried; and now he summoned it again to replace the one he needed less.

"The self I had killed in the first prison," he says, "was coming alive in the second."

If you dig to any depth into stories of people who have had midlife reversals, a question that quickly comes up is this: On what level can this really be considered a reversal? Sidney Rittenberg's transformation seems as radical as they come. But you could say—and he himself says—he's very close to the person he was at age twenty: still committed and idealistic. It's just that at one point he realized that he had hitched himself to the wrong ideology. To what extent, then, can we say there was an "inner change of heart" to accompany his "outer change of allegiances"?

U-Turn

The question of "interior" versus "exterior" change is the anteroom to one of the biggest questions in philosophy: Why do we become the kind of people we do? Is it because we "discover" our true selves, a core identity that emerges when we ditch the costumes that got us past checkpoints and over borders to where we needed to be? Or do we, rather, "create" our true selves—because identity is provisional, dependent on what we've experienced, and what has influenced us?

The competing models of identity are a little like competing notions of a city. We are a metropolis like ancient Babylon, a proverbial "city on a hill" that "existed," as a vision of God, but had merely to be found. Or, rather, we are a city like Canberra, the product of guys with measuring tape and straightedges, planned and built from scratch in a geographically convenient spot. Some U-turn stories lend themselves to the first interpretation, and some to the second. The typical religious "conversion" seems to be more about the first—some spiritual catalyst ignites an innate flame of the divine. But you can explain it just as well through the second construct: Life's circumstances conspires to create a big problem, and God—or some God surrogate—proves the best-fit solution.

Meet the Wemmicks

There is a term scientists use to describe certain steep, snow-covered mountain slopes, or volcanic lava domes: They are *labile*, or "prone to slip." The word has migrated into the social-science literature as a descriptor of human beings. To the extent that we are *labile*, we are capable of *slipping* into another identity. This new identity is no "better" or "worse" than the previous one (just as *lability*, in the geological sense, is a value-neutral term). It's just different, one of many readily available to us. Sartre spoke of the self as "a project," that we are wholly created by our own choices and our habits, almost as if we could *make ourselves into anything we decide to be*. (You might say this is the very cornerstone of capitalist mythology. We *make something of ourselves*; we make a name for ourselves.)

To an extent this "slippage" between multiple selves, the making of ourselves into "anything we decide to be"—whether consciously or unconsciously—happens to us all. You are not, let's face it, the same person you were at breakfast. The playwright David Ives makes this point neatly in his one-act play *Seven Menus*. Diners preparing to chow down in the Restaurant of the Seven Menus are puzzled to find there aren't seven menus at all. There's only one. And it never changes. Ah, but you yourself are a different person each day, the manager explains, so you can expect a new food experience on every visit.

Cognitive scientists are inclined to point out that none of us can be fewer than two people—a left-brain consciousness and a right-brain consciousness, living contiguous but somewhat independent lives, a seamless entertainment duo: straight man and funny man. To be more accurate, we might complicate the picture by adding a forebrain consciousness and a hindbrain consciousness, butler and toddler, one trying to maintain order, the other reaching for the Thanksgiving turkey with his hands.

In Dickens's *Great Expectations* there is a character named John Wemmick with a strikingly dual personality. At work he is one person, cold and calculating as his job as a bill collector in a law clerk's office requires. But as soon as he leaves work, to go to his little home on an island, he is an altogether different person, sweethearted and generous.

If you were searching for a real-life John Wemmick, the British opera singer and literary journalist Mark Glanville is the closest you're ever likely to find.

The man who would become the principal bassist with the Lisbon Opera was a student of classics at Oxford, reading Euripides and Horace in the original Greek. But he was also a soccer hooligan, traveling with the notorious Cockney Reds, who barracked for Manchester United, ripped out bits of the stadium for trophies, and compared stitch counts of the victims whose heads they had staved in.

It seems impossible that that kind of base destructiveness could live in the same body with the sensitivity of the high artist. And it remains largely a mystery to Glanville, who reckons that he wanted so much to be liked that he was going to go with whatever group liked him back.

But there is a weird integrity to Glanville's double life. The hooligans were dark aesthetes in their own way, taking pains to get right their descriptions of the balletic deftness with which they kicked in the faces of scousers and Yorkshiremen. The Cockney Reds were dedicated to violence of all kinds—not just between football squads, but geographic and ethnic and sectarian—the distinctions between them (mods versus greasers, for example), deeply understood. It was a kind of art. Certainly a kind of deeply felt, tribal self-expression—which is one definition of culture.

Glanville's secret life as a hooligan unfolded slowly. Initially, he had been merely a hanger-on with this group, a spectator, enjoying the contact high he got from their approval. Around the hooligans, "I adopted a different persona," and improbably, he fit in with this bunch. They were a tonic to the friendlessness and sexual frustration that defined his life at a tough, lower-class school, where the other students, who neither understood nor appreciated his love of Latin and Greek and opera, routinely terrorized him. Glanville learned to feign toughness there, until the toughness was no longer an act.

Gradually, not just the camaraderie but the violence itself of the hooligan scene began to appeal to him. During the bottle-throwing uprisings in the stadium stands, he felt himself transforming, both physically (gone now was the velvet jacket of the academic; in its place were jeans and monkey boots and a Man U Fan Club badge) and internally—until one day he realized he had become a fellow traveler. During a day trip to Norfolk, he found himself threatening to "carve open the face" of a rival fan, and reveling in that private thrill of the moment.

He started to behave like a boor—swaggering and cussing reflexively—to the growing disgust of his father, the distinguished sportswriter and novelist Brian Glanville.

And then came a major turning point—or so it seemed at the time.

One day after a game in Coventry, he was leaving the stadium with a friend when three Man United fans were set on by a pack of rivals. One of the men managed to escape. The two who didn't were beaten senseless in front of Glanville and his friend as they watched. Glanville did not intervene. He rationalized: He and his pal were outnumbered—what could they do? There is a sort of code of ethics among soccer hooligans: The violence must be consensual. You don't take on anyone obviously weaker, and you leave your victim alone once he's on the ground. But the code here had been broken, and with it Glanville's illusions. Violence could not be contained within rules. He was peering into a world whose full dimensions he had never, in his eagerness to belong, fully appreciated. (And which he had miraculously escaped from without meeting a fate similar to that of these two poor Man U supporters, wrecked now, their eyes spinning like a compass near the North Pole.) He thought, "I'd never hurt or wanted to harm anybody in the way these thugs just had." He understood that there were gradations of savagery, and where he fell on the scale.

Glanville would write a gripping memoir about his days of running with the Reds, and the incident in Coventry stands as the moment of resolution. The bad-guy persona fell away at that point, when he no longer needed it, we are left to understand. But, in fact, things were not so tidy. The book ends, but for Glanville the dark allure of hooliganism did not.

"The truth is, I came back to it," he says. As he was parlaying the success of his memoir into a career as a novelist and cultural journalist, he found himself running with hooligans again, this time the even harder cases from Millwall, in southeast London, the most notorious soccer thugs in Britain. Glanville spent his days in the midst of serious street disturbances, and then headed off in the evening to host literary events at a local club. (How did he do it? "How does the SS officer watch Jews being butchered during the day before going off to enjoy Schubert in the evening?" he says. "The mind can easily be compartmentalized.")

In May of 2002 before a not particularly meaningful game between Millwall and Nottingham, a thousand Millwall fans attacked the police. Cars were set ablaze, and the searchlight from the chopper trying to film the scene from above caught the rising smoke, the police flares, turning it into a war movie. Four hundred people were hospitalized. It was the worst riot in Britain since the poll-tax uprising of 1990. And right there in the middle of it, somehow managing not to be truncheoned to the pavement, was Mark Glanville. It was, he recalls, "incredibly exciting."

It was here, though, that Glanville's hooliganism *did* officially come to an end—but for practical, not spiritual or emotional, reasons. Britons were so appalled that a strict judicial crackdown on soccer violence ensued. Those who did the most damage at Millwall were tracked down by photo evidence and slapped with jail sentences so harsh they sent the as-yet-unidentified perpetrators into hiding. "The people I used to go to the games with disappeared," Glanville says. "This wasn't worth going to prison over. I had a family to think of."

He can't help reading the state's harsh crackdown on soccer hooliganism as a symbol of something much more profound. It was the anarchy that the state was reacting to, the disorder that had to be contained. "It can't be entirely conscious, but the rational state is, I think, deeply afraid of its irrational underbelly.

"The best book ever written to explain this is Euripides's *Bacchanal*." Hooliganism—the drinking and drugs and physical release that accompany it—is a bacchanal. The bacchanal celebrates the whole catastrophe, the most profound joys and the most appalling excesses of being alive. "I came to see it as a microcosm of my own life," he says. These multiple identities are still within me, and they're still at war. I'm a rational person; but there's an irrational, dangerous element I love being in touch with.

"There's a wonderful thing Anna Freud said in a short essay: 'The child is afraid of the ghost in the hall.' And the way to deal with that is, You must pretend to be the thing you might meet in the hall. That's it in a nutshell. It explains a lot of my own behavior. I pretended to be the thing I was afraid of, and that sort of solved the problem."

Mark Glanville may be an extreme example, but many, many people grapple with reconciling private and public selves. (A Native American term captures the uneasiness. Trying to blend a traditional culture and values with a successful career in the market economy is said to be "walking two lives.") And the idea that those lives may be in polar opposition is less unlikely than you'd think.

Recently, a small group of academics, pioneers in a field we might call "happiness" studies, proposed a theory of psychic adaptation. It's based on the assumption that everyone's goal is to amass maximum happiness over a lifetime. And so everything we do is predicated on our guess about what the emotional consequences will be. We do things we predict will be emotionally fulfilling, and we don't do things we guess will be distressing. When we perceive what we're doing to be the "wrong" thing, and that wrong thing produces uncomfortable tension, and we have every reason to expect that we'll continue to feel as bad, if not worse, if we keep it up, then we're inclined to change. We're out of balance. The brain snaps into action and nudges us to come clean and do the "right thing"—not for any particular moral reason, but rather for the psychic repair we expect will follow.

The work has been greeted with excitement. (The truly surprising part of the findings is just how badly we predict what will make us happy.) But the basic premise of the mind as a kind of self-regulating system was Carl Jung's—indeed, it was one of his great contributions to psychoanalysis. Even those hard rationalists, who couldn't take Jung too seriously after he started conducting séances, tip their cap to one of his major insights: Just as the body itself is forever correcting its unbalances, so is the mind.

Here's a concrete example: "Every psychiatrist has seen cases of ambitious men who habitually overwork to the point of neglecting everything else which makes life worth living often break down in midlife with a severe depression," notes the British psychiatrist Anthony Storr. "This can be interpreted as the psyche's attempt at self-regulation. They are compelled by illness to slow down and reconsider their values."

All things contain their opposites, Jung believed, but rarely in equal measure at any given time. For the psyche to regain equilibrium, the one must eventually flow into the other.

Here, though, is the complicating element. Even though all things contain their opposites, "in the world of dogma, in order to avoid ambiguity" we tend to emphasize one pole to the exclusion of the other. We separate the opposites as much as possible, for "clarity of consciousness." That's natural: Everyone does it. We overlook nuance to sort people—from baseball players to war combatants—into opposing camps.

But when we move so far in one direction that we lose sight of the complementary opposite, "the blackness of the whiteness, the evil of the good, the depths of the heights, is no longer seen," as Jung put it. "The result is one-sidedness, which is then compensated from the unconscious without our help. The counterbalancing is even done against our will, which in consequence must become more and more fanatic until it brings about a catastrophic enantiodromia."

U-Turn

In other words, a violent compensation. A 180-degree flip.

The word *enantiodromia*—$35, on sale in the lobby—was coined by Heraclitis, but Jung found it perfectly apt for his purposes. When we deny the opposite side of an argument or ideology, when we push the extremes of any position, we are likely to U-turn, in Jung's view. The more purely *anything* we become, the more in danger we are of rebounding suddenly into the opposite camp.

More is implied here than simply the notion that "the pendulum must swing back," or to every trend there is a backlash: Those ideas suggest an external judgment about when it's time for a change. What Jung is talking about is a reversal in the nature of the thing itself. It is the very connection of opposites, Jung believed, that eventually tumble-turns them.

Not only that, but when the flip does occur, we must—according to the simple physics of the psyche—take up the new position with "equivalent psychic intensity," Jung believed. This does seem intuitively to be the case: The more jingoistic the soldier, the more committed the pacifist; the more convinced the atheist, the more passionate the convert.

"It seems radical," wrote the psychologist Bobby Matherne, "but if we want to effect real change, nothing else [but extreme overcompensation] will do. It is as if, when confronted with an intractable problem—we do not like the self we have become—changing the color of our shirt won't make much difference." The radical solutions that U-turners choose are, by definition, nontrivial. Not changing partners, but changing gender. Not changing from mutual funds to treasury bills, but bowing out of the money economy.

It's no doubt partly because radical midlife U-turns are relatively rare that many tend to assume it's only the foolish and impulsive who let themselves get so far gone in one direction that they end up bouncing wildly back. But Jung—who himself came apart in midlife—believed that some forces are simply beyond our control. Wisdom may never forget that all things have two sides, "and it would know how to avoid such calamities if it ever had the power," as Jung wrote. But it doesn't. And we don't.

The spiritual hairpin turns in the life of the satirist Tony Hendra are enantiodromia in action.

74

The Condemned Twin

As a teenager, for reasons involving guilt over an affair with another man's wife, Hendra concluded that he should become a monk. But instead—at the insistence of the very Benedictine monk who had heard his confession, and who had struck him as the perfect model of an honorable life—he went to Oxford to read English literature. And one night in a theater in Cambridge, watching a scandalous revue by the sketch troupe Beyond the Fringe, he was seized by a new calling: He would become a satirist. In this mission Hendra would find a mentor who was the kindly monk's exact opposite. *National Lampoon* editor Michael O'Donoghue was a man who strove for perfect sacrilege, "to save the world from people who wanted to save the world"—and soon, blasphemy became Hendra's "drug of choice," too. Years later, he would shed the cynicism and find his way back to God through his old friend the monk, Father Joe. Each move in his life seemed to counter the previous move, and precisely cancel it out. And each move, at the time, felt like the perfectly natural one to make.

"The power of paradox is that it proves, in a startling way, that opposites aren't," writes Paul Watzlawick. "The pairs are merely the two complementary aspects of one and the same reality. Things may be 'as different as day and night,' and the change from the one to the other appear to be extreme and ultimate, and yet, paradoxically, in the wider context, nothing may have changed at all." The physicist Niels Bohr liked to say that the opposite of a profound truth is not a falsehood, but another profound truth.

So not only should it *not* surprise us to see people transform into their apparent opposites, neither can we be sure that such an apparently radical change is even much of a change at all. It seems shocking when someone on the far right, for example, jumps to the far left (or vice versa). But if you don't pay too much attention to the content of what they're saying, the professional pundits who appear on opposite sides of a political or social debate on the big four American TV networks (especially Fox) often seem very much alike. That's because they're necessarily pretty radicalized in their views (too nuanced, and you won't be asked on). And people who are radicalized in their views tend to be ideologues—in the modern sense of the word. Just so, the temperament of the puritan is in many ways similar to that of the addict. In many addicts, there is an almost spiritual level of commitment to the very destructiveness that pushes them to the brink, from at which point a polarity reversal of that misguided energy saves them.

Atheist-into-fundamentalist is no more remarkable, in this light, than the converse. "Great believers and great doubters may *seem* like opposites," writes Jennifer Michael Hecht in her book *Doubt*, but they're more like each other than either is like the great mass of folks in the middle. "Both are preoccupied with the problem" of belief; they have just come down on different sides of the schism—whether the inanimate universe is in some way humanlike, or whether humans should just accept that we're part of an uncaring universe.

It's a testament to this concept that cop and criminal—maybe the most famous Jungian dyad—are perhaps not all that different when you consider that both can exist in the same man. Victor Hugo is said to have based both the dogged Inspector Jabert and his archnemesis Jean Valjean on a Frenchman named Eugene François Vidocq, who played both sides of the law.

Vidocq was a flamboyant and cunning French criminal who made something of a game out of routinely escaping from every jail where the constabulary of eighteenth-century Paris tried to hold him. But finally, tossed into a maximum-security prison from which his prospects of escape seemed slim, Vidocq struck a deal: In exchange for his freedom (it was "against his nature to be confined," he explained), he would work for them. Chiefly as an informant at first—plying his underworld contacts and smoking out criminals—all of whose tricks, like a master magician, he knew.

So successful was Vidocq in this role that he was promoted up the ranks and became, in 1911, the first chief of the world's first detective agency—the Sureté de Paris—eventually heading up a group of a dozen inspectors, all of them former criminals. Vidocq pretty much invented forensic detective work. The "anthropometric" tools of the detective trade he created—the plaster casts of footprints, the ballistics analysis—are still used by French police.

Vidocq was a delicious character—impulsive, Falstaffian, a slave to his appetites, and a mesmerizing raconteur. So charming that mere acquaintances often sent him money (which he promptly gambled away).

The Condemned Twin

An early master of what is now sometimes called social engineering—talking his way into, or out of, wherever he needed to go to or escape from. A man who had much to teach about how to live life fully.

He is the *ur* bad-guy-turned-good. But that label is in many respects bogus. Vidocq, it becomes clear when you look deeply into his story, didn't really change much. You could say he was still a crook with a fatter paycheck. "Among his detractors, Vidocq was and always remained a scoundrel and a criminal, a con man who emerged from the underworld milieu to become the kind of corrupt detective for whom dissimulation, extortion and graft are tools of the trade," wrote his biographer, Philip John Stead. But it might be more accurate to say that he was and remained a good guy all along—a man who, as a crook, helped the poor, and as a cop seemed at least as interested in freeing the wrongly convicted as he was in bagging the guilty. He never pursued anyone who had stolen for real need (or so he claimed).

What Vidocq's story tells us, should we choose to generalize from it, is that Walt Whitman was right: we *can* encompass multitudes. Opposing identities can live within us; external conditions determine which one will show its face. Vidocq was not a born criminal. He had the role of criminal thrust upon him when, at fourteen, he accidentally killed his fencing instructor and had to flee for his life. Every decision he made, thereafter, each pushing him further into criminality, seemed perfectly reasonable under the circumstances—generally, self-preservation—and given his nature.

The very qualities that made Vidocq a good crook also made him a good cop. It wasn't just his skills—his genius for disguise, his ability to worm out of any jam: It was more than that. It was his equanimity. His prison breaks alone were marvels of chutzpah. (Once he dived out the window of the prison into the river below; another time he simply walked out, in disguise, asking the watchman at the gate for a light on his way to freedom.) "His boldness," summed up the inspector general of the Gendarmerie, "makes him capable of committing the greatest of crimes."

You might be thinking at this point of the trope beloved by TV writers: that we all have within us an "evil twin" who sometimes escapes and runs amok with our credit cards and the garden weasel, perhaps while we are sleeping. The problem with the theory is that, except in rare cases, it's not so easy to tell which among our multiple personas is the bad seed. Labels of *good* and *bad* are, after all, often culturally determined. The difference between a feted, successful CEO and a gangster is a thin tissue of arbitrary laws. The difference between holding one political ideology or another may be one very bad day. The task becomes not to shuck the self—or selves—that are demonstrably evil, but the one that is not, well, *essential*.

We can assume Dickens's bill collector John Wemmick is not equally invested in his two selves; presumably his "home" identity is closer to his "true" nature—but the circumstances of his job prevent him from expressing it there. In other words, some components of "us" are more us than others. That's the view of psychologist Timothy D. Wilson, author of *Strangers to Ourselves*. Wilson suggests that we all have two "personalities"—an infrastructural one, a deep bedrock personality formed by the ceaseless glacial grinding of our adaptive unconscious for our whole life—and a more superficial one, a social construct that we *present* as us. The two may differ quite a bit. (The "true" us is more likely to emerge when we have to act quickly, without time for premeditation.) Like John Wemmick's, our job may demand that our constructed self be quite different from our "true" self. But if the gap between them becomes *too* wide, the pressure will build to leave the job—an easier proposition than trying to change our core personality.

Many of us, like Wemmick, are slaves to circumstantially prescribed roles that aren't us. The first step seems to be realizing the disconnect. How deeply would we have to meditate on our identity to get beyond the faith we grew up with, beyond the job we do, down, down, beyond even gender, to the level of something like the soul?

The Flitcraft Parable

In Dashiell Hammett's *The Maltese Falcon*, gumshoe Sam Spade recounts, to Brigid O'Shaughnessy, the story of a client he once had up in Tacoma. The man, named Flitcraft, was a middle-class real estate executive with a pleasant enough life. He had the house, the car, and "the rest of the appurtenances of successful American living, including a wife and two sons," Spade recalls. One day Flitcraft leaves the office and goes to lunch. When he doesn't show up for his 4 p.m. tee-off time, his golf partners are puzzled—Flitcraft had made the booking himself that very morning. Flitcraft doesn't come home that night. Or the next. He's gone. "His wife and children never saw him again."

It's a Spadeworthy mystery. Flitcraft seemed to be on good terms with his family, there was no evidence of secret vices or mistresses in foreign ports, his affairs were in order, though there were "enough loose ends to indicate that he had not been setting them in order" prior to disappearing. "He went like that," Spade said, "like a fist when you open your hand."

Five years later Spade succeeds in locating him; he has changed his name to Charles Pierce, as part of an attempted full identity makeover. It turns out that on his way to lunch five years before, Flitcraft had almost been hit by a falling beam at a construction site. The near escape from possible death shook him profoundly, made him feel "like somebody had taken the lid off life and let him look at the works." It occurred to Flitcraft—the good citizen-husband-father—that "in sensibly ordering his affairs he had got out of step, and not in step, with life." And so, a near victim of a random event, Flitcraft took his cue, and responded by doing something random, something rash, something midlife-crisis-y. He simply vanished. He felt no particular guilt, he told Spade: He'd left his family well provided for. What he had done had seemed perfectly reasonable to Flitcraft—"He would never know peace until he had adjusted himself to this new glimpse of life," Spade says.

But there's a twist. After a few years Charles Pierce became Flitcraft again—not in name, but in habit. Slowly, unconsciously, he began to duplicate his previous existence. He again became a successful businessman, and had a new family eerily like the previous one. His life was the same, right down to the habitual 4 p.m. golf games. When Spade found him, he had, after drifting around the world, settled in Spokane, less than hundred miles away from where he used to live. "That's the part of it I liked," Spade recalls. "He adjusted himself to beams falling, and then no more beams fell, and he adjusted himself to them not falling."

Flitcraft had his wake-up call. He understood that it was time to change his life, and he rebuilt himself from scratch. But, strangely, he rebuilt basically the same guy. The circumstances were different, but he wasn't. Once the catalytic event that had so rocked his world had faded into memory, all that was left was Flitcraft, back where he started, as if by some natural law.

A lot of the stories thus far make some sense in this light. On one level the U-turn of Arizona Cardinal Pat Tillman was less dramatic than it appeared: really just removing the metaphor from the game he was already playing, a shift to physically defending a value system whose benefits he had so richly enjoyed. It's a change, for sure, but it seems like an entirely understandable thing for the same core person who was Pat Tillman to have done.

The theory that we're pulled toward "home" is satisfying in part because it seems to mimic the symmetry of nature. An aging salmon that can't find its natal stream is doomed; it won't reproduce anywhere—if it can't close that particular circle it will die without heirs. A spruce tree knows "its place" in the narrative; if you try to graft a spruce branch onto its parent tree higher, say, than where it came from, it will reject that promotion.

Art, too, tries to come home. The symphony orchestra wants to end on the note it started on—and when that happens the audience is delighted, even though they can't *remember* the note it started on. The circular structure of a lot of classic scores—like Beethoven's Ninth, with its high beginning, its descent into grief, and then, at the end, its affirmation—pay off with a unique sense of satisfaction, like the novel that loops back on its first line with its last. (The classic example is *Finnegans Wake.*) Death is defeated, the existential anxiety of endings forestalled. The dream goes on.

From this perspective, a lot of what appear to be U-turns only look that way if you happened to walk into those lives, like latecoming moviegoers, in the middle. Those who knew U-turners from childhood can often see a symmetry to their supposedly out-of-the-blue transformation.

When George Soros started giving away his money, the disconnect was startling, if only because of the scale: Soros wasn't giving away millions; he was giving away *billions*. But again, those who knew him maintained that Soros was simply, after a long wander in the wilderness, coming home. Saving the world wasn't an utterly new impulse for

Soros—he had long harbored what he called "messianic fantasies." What was new, now, in midlife, was that he was finally in a position to make those early promises concrete.

You could argue that Smedley Butler—the decorated U.S. Marine general who subsequently published one of the century's most famous antiwar tracts, *War Is a Racket*—was merely returning to his roots after a short walk in the ill-fitting suit of a warrior. He was raised a Quaker.

These kinds of examples abound, once you start looking. And together they suggest a kind of rule of psychic consistency: people very rarely become idealists all of a sudden at age forty; they were idealists, however veiled, all along. Without a long view of them, our judgment of U-turners is likely to be flawed. A life that seems to be following a wacky parabola may in fact be coming full circle.

G. K. Chesterton liked to tell the story of how he once set sail on a boat from Dover. The ship sailed and sailed and encountered nothing. And then, after many months at sea, there came a cry, "Land in sight!" And looming into view were . . . the white cliffs of Dover. Chesterton said, "'I had to leave on an adventure. But then I discovered that the adventure was home.' It's a story that crops up in sermons more or less as follows: The whole mystery of human beings is to start looking outside of oneself, and then discover that it's inside of yourself. You go on an adventure and discover, after many months at sea, the white cliffs of Dover. And you come home."

But here's how a psychiatrist, rather than a mythologist, or an overtly spiritual person, might handle the idea of "coming home." A man begins by differentiating himself from his father—doing something pretty much the opposite of what Dad did, and then, as he matures, he drifts back toward the paternal groove, in a sense completing his father's life for him now that the father is gone or going. Ultimately, he lives his father's life, but a corrected version of it. He has addressed what he has discerned to be his father's shortcomings, but otherwise taken on the family business, completing his "hero's quest" in that roundabout way. So the legendary advertising man Stan Freberg, a minister's son, rejects his dad's line of work and goes in what looks like precisely the opposite direction. But he ends up creating a powerful ad campaign for the United Presbyterian Church. ("Is it lonely out there on a limb, without Him?") The American-religion scholar Randall Balmer rejects his minister father's plans for him to succeed him, and he goes in what seems like the exact opposite direction, into academia, that bastion of clinical secularity. But it turns him into a writer, and he pens a religious memoir that reaches more people than a lifetime of congregational sermons ever could. (One could guess that that's why people who have reacted extremely to their father, either emulating him precisely—that is, failing to differentiate at all—or rejecting everything he did, are often unhappy.)

Abraham Maslow maintained that people who change radically in midlife are, unless they are mentally ill, probably trying to "self-actualize," to fulfill the best promise of their true inner nature. But that inner nature, "what we were meant to be," is not obvious. "It's not strong and overpowering and unmistakable like the instincts of animals," Maslow said. "It's weak and delicate and subtle and easily overcome by habit, cultural pressure, and wrong attitudes toward it." Nonetheless, it's a force that, "even if denied, persists underground forever," pressing for expression.

Now we're in Aristotle's backyard.

Destiny, Aristotle said, is the plant that exists within every seed. An inherent purpose lies dormant in everything, and presumably everyone, and it exists only as potential until it is made real—if it ever is. He called the fruition of potential idea *"entelechy* (pronounced en-TEL-uh-chee), a word that derives from the late Latin meaning, literally, to "have completion." You'll still hear the term used in scientific, often botanical contexts; but the term has gained much more traction in the human-potential movement, where it has been adopted to mean the fulfilling, through action, of potential that has been dormant. It may be as simple as this: Something we used to know about ourselves, but somehow forgot, comes bubbling back into consciousness.

The great film editor Walter Murch, in a long, ruminative conversation with the novelist Michael Ondaatje, recalled how, as a kid, he had naturally gravitated to what would eventually become his métier. At age ten Murch picked up the strange hobby of sound editing. (The father of a friend of his had bought a tape recorder and Walter would go over and play with it endlessly, developing a knack for what we would today call *sampling*.) But young Walter, as he grew up, convinced himself that such a pursuit couldn't possibly be an actual occupation, that he needed to go into something practical—perhaps a career in engineering or architecture or oceanography or art history, and he drifted away from that essential passion. Only later did he realize that film offered an outlet that tied together his lifetime preoccupations, and that he derived as much delight from editing images as he had from editing sounds. Murch developed a theory that what we really loved doing when we were between the ages of nine and eleven—if we can remember it— may hold the clue to what we should be doing as adults. At that age we are old enough to have figured out what we like to do, but not so old that cultural and familial pressures about what we "should" be doing have stomped our innate enthusiasms down. "It's certainly been true in my case," Murch said. "I'm doing now, at fifty-eight, almost exactly what excited me most when I was eleven."

The importance of trying to do, as adults, what interested us as ten-year-olds has been expressed by many fulfilled, creative people who are, consciously or unconsciously doing it. (It dawned on the singer-songwriter Paul Simon one day in midlife that what he does for a living is "an idea conceived by a thirteen-year-old.") The precise age of that model young self is obviously somewhat arbitrary: C. S. Lewis maintained, in *Surprised by Joy*, that "most of our most important thinking is done before the age of fourteen." But indeed, if you look at the life of U-turners, many are not charting an utterly new course, but in fact returning to what they believed as kids or young adults.

"For the typical guy having a midlife crisis, the time he can most distinctly recollect that life was different was in his twenties," Tom Williams, the former venture capitalist and Michael Milken acolyte, told me. "For me, the time I can most distinctly recollect that life was different was when I was eleven, writing to McDonald's to get them to stop using Styrofoam. When you're eleven, it's all about heart. You do what feels right—and you don't do what doesn't feel right. The reason I'm successful now [in a philanthropic nonprofit venture] isn't because I've had experience at the hip of the best business minds in America. It's because I remember what I was like when I was eleven years old."

U-Turn

When Susan Orlean set out to profile the typical "American Man at Age Ten," for *Esquire* magazine, she found one close by, Colin Duffy of Glen Ridge, New Jersey. A kid whose enthusiasms and friendships and pet peeves were as crystal-clear as the future he saw for himself as an FBI agent. "The collision in his mind of what he understands, what he hears, what he figures out, what popular culture pours into him, what he knows, what he pretends to know, and what he imagines, makes an interesting mess," Orlean noted. "The mess often has the form of what he will probably think like when he is a grown man, but the content of what he is like as a little boy."

For those without the luxury of having been preserved in amber by a deft portraitist, the trick, then, is to remember who we were.

"When Shirley Rock was ten years old, her grandmother told her that God was going to 'call' her when she got to be fifty years of age," wrote the psychologist Dan McAdams. "Shirley assumed that her grandmother meant that 'God was going to call me home, and I was going to die.' But what she must have meant, Shirley now believes, is that God was going to call her to the ministry."

Her grandmother had seen in Shirley the congenital large-heartedness, empathy, and tolerance that would make her well-suited for ministerial outreach work. But she had also intuited that young Shirley's path wasn't going to be a straight one; between now and then she had a quest to undertake, and it would take her to some dark places. Her grandmother's hunch proved right.

A series of setbacks and bad decisions conspired to send Shirley Rock spiraling downward. She became a prostitute, then ran a brothel, got deeply involved in organized crime and addicted to drugs. Convicted of fraud for her participation in a confidence racket that bilked seniors, she found herself in prison in her early forties. And from that rock bottom she bounced. In prison, she decided to turn her life around. She joined a group run by ex-offenders to help cons get their heads back together. She started "paying back" to society, volunteered for various charities, ran a food bank for the church, provided counseling and language classes for new immigrants—all leading up to the actual "call."

Persuaded by a pastor friend and mentor, she found herself in church, alone. The previous night, also on his recommendation, she had perused the Book of Samuel, to no obvious effect—but on this day something was different. "I opened a book on church practice. And as I held the book, it just sort of fell open by itself and it went to prerequisites for the ordained clergy. And I said, Okay, if this is what you want, you've got it. And all of a sudden it was as if I could float. Every care, everything went off of my shoulders and out of my body, and my head was clear and the room was bright white. I mean it was just luminous, and I sat awestruck. I have never felt like that before, and I have never felt like that since, and from what I understand, I will never feel that way again. But I knew exactly what had happened, and I knew that I had been touched and that I was in the presence of God."

Shirley Rock became a pastor for an inner-city congregation, and went to work for a nondenominational group that runs shelters for the homeless and the poor. The ministry puts into action central beliefs and values about God and the world that Shirley held dear as a kid, but drifted away from. She had come home, that ten-year-old girl again, but with a world more experience and empathy now, and thus more deeply endowed for the work she had to do.

She was fifty-one years old. Her grandmother's prophecy had been off by a year.

It may be fashionably postmodern to claim that, in terms of intrinsic personality, there is no there there, but emerging research into personality flatly contradicts that notion. While we are carved and shaped by the environment, there appear to be certain core dimensions along which we remain stable—certain "basic tendencies" that have become plainly observable quite early on. The so-called "new science of human nature" puts heavy emphasis on the genetic component of certain key personality traits (like prickliness and religiosity), and one of its strongest pillars is the "five-factor model" of human personality, promoted by research psychologists like Paul Costa Jr. and Robert McCrae of the National Institute of Health. (The model is often remembered by the acronym OCEAN: Each letter represents one of the five dimensions that comprise a personality: the degree to which we are Open to experience; Conscientious; Extroverted; Agreeable; and Neurotic.) These personality traits—or rather the *propensity* for these traits—are largely encoded. Fixed. If we're anxious adults, it's probably not because we were overcoddled as toddlers, but that a particular gene on chromosome 17—one that regulates serotonin transmission—is quite different from the one found in folks who are preternaturally laid-back. That's the theory. And, in fact, the idea that "the core of our personalities does not change over time" is one of the two bedrock principles of forensic psychology and psychological profiling (the other is that the crime scene reflects the personality of the offender). This assumption allows detectives to construct a profile—physical, emotional, intellectual—of the perp from the crime scene.

So while people often describe U-turners—and they are likely to describe themselves—as a "different person" post-turn, if you bore in deeply, you will discover a consistency in these five major areas. These traits may develop quantitatively: We may train ourselves to be a little less shy, for instance. And they may be supplemented by new qualities. But they don't change qualitatively. There *is* a there there, it would seem, even though it may become more deeply buried as circumstances dictate the direction our life takes.

Some observers trying to solve the puzzle of boxer George Foreman's gentle and perpetual good humor—this from a man who once calculated the places on the human skull that convey maximum pain when you hit them, and then field-tested his theories with gusto—point out that he has always been deeply suggestible. As a kid, he took on the swagger and values of the reprobate punks he was running with. As a pro boxer, he refused to sign autographs until he discovered that Sonny Liston did, and then he did, too. "Liston was Foreman's only available mentor at the time, and so supplied him with all his cues for public surliness," *Sports Illustrated* noted. It's tempting to speculate that Foreman's early life, the surly-guy phase, was not authentically him, but rather a posture he adopted almost by chance.

People flounder because they get the search equation exactly backwards, believes the Quaker and activist Parker Palmer. They live from the "outside in," rather than the "inside out." That is, choosing a life path not because it's a good fit for who we are, but because it sounds noble or prestigious or just generally likely to win you a lot of approval—and then just forcing ourselves down it. "Vocation does not mean a goal that I pursue," he says. "It means a calling that I hear." "I must listen to my life and try to understand what it is truly about . . . *quite apart from what I would like it to be about.*"

Complicating things—or at least complicating things for Palmer when he tried to apply this insight to his own circumstances, and found himself comically overreaching—is that there is a moral dimension to the idea of vocation. At least according to the definition one learns in church, a *vocation* isn't merely a call, it's "a demand that asks us to become someone we are not yet—someone different, someone better, someone just beyond our reach." Palmer assumed that meant he must aspire to the loftiest ideals, the highest values and most noble truths, unremittingly. The result was "a distortion of my true self. I had simply found a noble way to live that was not my own."

At age thirty-nine, with a Ph.D. from Berkeley under his belt and job offers from Columbia and the University of Chicago, Palmer figured that the "noble" path that lay before him was the life of a college president. At age thirty-nine, he was being courted for precisely that job, and was very, very close to accepting one of those positions. Still an initiate to Quakerism, Palmer took advantage of a Quaker custom called a "clearness committee," whose purpose is to help confirm the chosen vocation of someone in the community. They do this not by giving advice but by asking questions, open and honest questions, no counsel, no judgments—in a session that takes hours—with a view to helping the interrogatee discover his own "inner truth."

"When you're in the middle of that two- or three-hour process, you start to realize how often in social interaction around this same question you've been faking it—coming up with answers that make you look good," he says. "But you realize, in this setting, I have no one to fool but myself. And why would I want to do that?"

The question that triggered Palmer's epiphany was simple: "What would you like best about that job?" The question left silence that Palmer could not fill. "*That* was very revealing. When I left that committee it was just so clear that I was interested in the job because the school had taken me on an ego trip. And on another level, I was imagining all these wonderful things I could do that had nothing to do with who I was.

In the middle of that committee I was, well . . . I was brought back to my nature. To have taken that job would have been a real catastrophe." (What he did was take a job that paid less than one-tenth the salary—an administrative post at a Quaker community near Philadelphia.)

"There's a story I've always loved about William Penn, after whom Pennsylvania is named," says Palmer. "Penn had learned about George Fox, the founder of Quakerism—this was in seventeenth-century England, and became interested in the teachings. And one day Penn met Fox. And he said, 'George Fox, I'm really interested in the teachings of this movement, and even to its pacifism. But the truth is that I'm a soldier in the King's army. So here's my question: If I'm to become a Quaker, when must I lay down my sword?' And Fox replied, 'Wear it as long as you can.' Which I think is a brilliant answer." Fox wasn't discouraging Penn from forsaking war for peace, but simply noting that no one could tell him when the time to make the turn had come. He would know. 'Wear it as long as you can.' Wear the sword, in other words, *until you can't not put it down*."

There are, you could say, two types of reversals. The first are those that follow a kind of redemption script—we "come clean" from a life we consider to have been somehow ethically wrong, answering a sense of duty to do the right thing. And then there are those that are more Platonic, more ethically neutral; we abandon a life that was "wrong" only in the sense that it was wrong for us, now. The distinction points out two definitions of morality: a fidelity to *goodness*, and a fidelity to who you feel you intrinsically are. There was nothing "wrong" with Parker Palmer's original option of becoming a college president or Julia Hill's business consultancy. It was only wrong in that it prevented some other "possible self"—one more deeply felt, and better fitting—from being born.

And in this respect his circumstances are more like the ones most of us find ourselves in—and his turn the kind most of us are more inclined to make. Tony Lowder, a young securities lawyer who committed a perfectly undetectable crime and then turned himself in after the guilt threatened to crush him, is the perfect example of the devil's disciple redeemed. But he is fictional, the product of Louis Auchincloss's novel *I Come as a Thief*. Most of us aren't faced with such clear choices. The "goodness" or "badness" of our life is rarely cut-and-dried. Most of us don't pollute watersheds or design weapons systems or pour solvents into the eyes of rabbits for a living. We sit at desks and move spreadsheets around. Most people don't change because they're doing anything obviously wrong; it's that they're not doing enough right. That's a big distinction.

But the effect, at the level of the psyche, is much the same. The body still flags a disconnect, of whatever kind. A big gulf between behavior and values, or perceived identity and observed identity, reads as a kind of systems error, as the Scottish psychologist Tim Carey puts it—and to fix it a fundamental "reorganization" is in order.

If there is a "true self" to come home to, why do we find it when we do? What initiates the homing sequence? Perhaps, some evidence suggests, we come to express that true self *when it's safe to do so.*

The British zoologist Alistair Hardy surprised his scientific colleagues with an apparent, William Jamesian midlife turn to the mystic. His work as a marine biologist was deeply respected, and he was already a fellow of the Royal Society and director of oceanic studies at Hull. He gave the world the earnest and definitive tome *The World of Plankton.* But in his inaugural address to colleagues at Aberdeen, where he had just accepted a professorship in natural history, the rationalist's Jungian shadow nosed out into the light. Hardy told the crowd that "mechanistic biology" was not true science. Biology, he said, must include a study of the spiritual needs of human beings.

This caused murmurs of the *What's the deal with this guy* variety among his confrères—although such talk as Hardy's was not beyond the pale for an eccentric scientist. But the lid came off the can when Hardy stood before a roomful of zoologists to give the presidential address at the British Association for the Advancement of Science.

Charles Darwin and Gregor Mendel seemed to have this evolution problem right as far as they went, Hardy told his audience, but the theory was missing a key piece: telepathy. Might not advantageous habits be passed among members of a species through ESP? Hardy would propose that members of a species shared a "general subconscious sharing of a form and behavior pattern—a sort of psychic 'blueprint.'"

Hardy, who became known as the "Unitarian Darwinian," went on to run the Religious Experience Research Unit at Manchester College, Oxford. But here, again, was a case where a midlife swerve seemed much more abrupt than it actually was, if you had the lifelong picture. As a youth, he prayed, and always believed that a higher power was responsible for his being able to spin gold out of his intellectual mediocrity. He had in his youth attempted séances and had wondered whether prayers to God were a form of extrasensory dictation.

And so, after all this, can we say which paradigm is correct? Do we find our identity or create it? Jung believed that we are constantly improving each day, by which he clarified that we are "becoming more of who we really are." He didn't say "finding," and he didn't say "creating." The paradoxical implication was that we are doing both at the same time.

There are U-turners whose stories seem to prove both theories.

In Sidney Rittenberg's story, there were two different types of epiphany. "The first [an idealistic young Rittenberg, drawn to a demonstration on the White House lawn, committed emotionally to the labor movement] was what you refer to as a resolution of one's core identity," Rittenberg told me. "The second [Chinese Communism and then the rejection of it] was on a higher level, based on the plateau arrived at in the first epiphany—it was simply about identifying the path through which to fulfill this identity and purpose."

The solution to the problem of "Who Am I?" lies, after keeping many identities aloft, in settling on one, a single self on which, as William James put it, "to stake your salvation." A choice, yes, but one that, if one listens deeply, seems so inevitable as not to be a choice at all.

One morning in the spring of 2005, Madeline Nelson sat down with a cup of coffee and a stack of newspapers and magazines, which was actually part of her job. A marketing executive at a big retailer, Nelson was conducting her regular press review, to check how the company image was being shot through the media lens into the kitchens of the republic. The answer was, spectacularly. Nelson was an ace at this job, her skills sharpened from a couple of years as head of communications for the investment-banking division of the French giant Société Générale, a company bigger than Nike.

She flipped open the current *New York Times Magazine*. And there was a photo of a priest, in robe and collar, commanding a downtown street corner. The story identified him as "Reverend Billy." But "Reverend Billy" wasn't a man of the cloth; rather, he is the the the alter ego of the New York actor Bill Talen—one of America's most provocative agitators for social justice.

Reverend Billy's mission is to drive the devil of consumerism out of shoppers, and, in his ecclesiastical getup, he will lay a hand on the forehead of bewildered people just as they get their wallet out to pay for a new toaster or a latte. The writer had caught Reverend Billy in full Jimmy Swaggart mien, his Church of Stop Shopping gospel choir swaying like aspens behind him in the chain stores of Times Square. Reverend Billy was performing exorcisms on cash registers and credit cards, and so ungluing staffers that, at the Disney Store, a manager raised his hands and exclaimed to the moving knot of shoppers, gawkers, and culture-jammers, "Anyone who isn't here to buy something will be arrested!"

Anyone who isn't here to buy something will be arrested.

Madeline Nelson set down her coffee cup. "Holy shit," she heard herself say. Her heart was pounding—and not from the caffeine. The story of Reverend Billy and his "retail interventions" had, somehow, undammed some deep spring within her. It was all there, and coming back: everything she used to value, everything she used to *be about*, thirty years ago—before she had incrementally slid off course.

The arc of Madeline Nelson, who came of age in 1970s Bellingham, Washington, is classic hippie-to-yuppie. A theater-school dropout, she had lived hand-to-mouth, organizing antiwar protests at night out of the print shop where she worked. But the Dickensian living conditions eventually ground her down. And so began what she now views as the long series of bourgeois compromises that pushed her down the slippery slope toward egregious materialism, but "so gradually that I didn't see the contradictions." She got a better-paying job at an educational nonprofit that organized technical conferences. Then the company, itself tired of being poor, started taking military-industry clients, who were flush with cash from President Reagan's Star Wars initiative. Nelson wanted to bolt but was persuaded to stay when her bosses offered to set her up with an affiliative job in France. And so it went, until, by the time she had been promoted up the ladder of the Société Générale, eventually heading communications for the investment banking division in Paris, she had thoroughly adapted to her corporate environment. Her friends were all senior-level bankers—nice folks, but so long immersed in the logic of corporate finance that they lived, really, in a world of abstractions. They turned the kind of investment deals, she noticed, "where the interest rates are so usurious, you know someone is getting seriously screwed down the line."

That night she found Reverend Billy's site on the Web, and called him up. She talked a lot; he listened pastorally. An "action" was coming up, he said, a bit of stealth performance art at Ground Zero that Billy called a cell-phone opera. She'd be welcome to come. So long had she felt detached from the need to "resist" that the invitation felt strange. It felt good. And, just as there had been in the early seventies, when she last felt this politicized, there was plenty *to* resist. America was engaged in a controversial war in Iraq. The Republican National Convention was looming. On the day of the action, Madeline Nelson headed down there, right from work, still in her "business drag."

Billy and his followers were consecrating the still-smoking ground, part of their weekly cosmic injunction against George W. Bush ever being able to use that space as a stage again. Nelson pulled out her cell phone as she descended the escalator, melting into the crowd rushing for the trains. She called her partner, Jim. They exchanged a few words about dinner plans, and then, on cue, Nelson launched into the "action" as Reverend Billy had conceived it: She began to recite, into the phone, in a normal speaking voice, the First Amendment of the U.S. Constitution.

She reached the platform and continued to circulate. And as she did, she passed other people in business suits muttering the same words. Slowly and organically, the reciters fell into step, and their incantations synchronized, until there were more than a hundred of them, a group now, *Congress shall make no law restricting the establishment of religion or prohibiting the free exercise thereof* reverberating in the underground vault.

It was pretty strange stuff, but remarkably powerful. When Nelson emerged back aboveground, she was breathless. "It was meaningful to me on so many levels."

Over the next couple of weeks, she got involved in other actions, including a mock group wedding—a Mini-Moonie affair—on Central Park's Great Lawn. The couples wove the First Amendment into their vows. Madeline Nelson spoke her lines with conviction, as police in riot gear hovered on the periphery of the action. And "that, for me, was the real turn," she recalls. "It wasn't quite St. Paul getting knocked off his horse, but it did feel like it happened in a sudden whoosh. It did feel like a conversion."

From there things happened quickly.

She would leave her job, she decided. There are so many more important things than to continue this cycle of hyperconsuming. The waste, she thought. And the waste of her own talents. "All the way down the line, it occurred to me that this was just wrong."

At lunchtime on November 30, 2004, America's busiest shopping day of the year (and not so coincidentally, "Buy Nothing Day"), Madeline Nelson entered Manhattan's Astor Place neighborhood. The Bermuda Triangle of Retail ("You can disappear in here," says Reverend Billy, "and they *won't even find your bones*")—McDonald's, Kinko's, Kmart. Evangelistically coiffed, she wore a tuxedo jacket, a priest's collar: a DoppelBilly. So thoroughly had she absorbed the values of her guru that she had become him.

There are three Starbucks within a few blocks. But the target today was the anchor café—the biggest Starbucks in Manhattan.

The action director gave the sign and in marched the DoppelBillys—Madeline Nelson and a half-dozen others similarly frocked. Nelson scanned the space: the couples leaning over their warm foam; the crisp young baristas—who, as Billy often reminds folks, have replaced the beautifully rude waiters from the Astor Riviera Diner, which once stood on this spot; the crowd of onlookers who had followed the DoppelBillys through the square and to the door, the bystanders who are always collaborators in this drama, if only by bearing witness; the police dismounting from their motorscooters outside and making for the door.

It suddenly occurred to her that this was the same Starbucks she used to come to regularly when she worked for the bank. It was midday; some of her former colleagues were probably here right now. For a moment, she froze.

The urge to balk came on; she fought it. Nelson and another DoppelBilly—they had divided into pairs—swanned up to a cash register and lay their hands on it and, looking heavenward—or at least earth-toned–ceilingward—to expel the spirit of corporate greed. "Send the money *back* to the people who sweated for it!"

The grip of the cop, when it came, was an oddly familiar sensation—though she hadn't felt it in thirty years.

"I did something then that was like a sense memory from my youthful antinuclear days: I let my legs go limp." The cop thought she'd fainted, and he let her slump, inert, to the tiled floor.

Three months later, she would be arrested—plucked off her bicycle on one of those critical-mass rides that block midtown Manhattan traffic, just one more nuisance protester amid a throng of civil disobedients too numerous to jail.

She went down to the site of Catholic Worker, the group founded by Dorothy Day, whose members pledge to live a life of "voluntary poverty." They settle among the homeless—a mission Nelson herself might well have dedicated herself to, had her childhood Catholic fervor not gone underground.

And then she moved on to things that made even Reverend Billy cringe.

"A couple of nights ago a supermarket threw out, among other things, four full cases of eggs. Dairy products, about to expire—out. Vegetables about to expire—out. A lettuce that comes in a fancy bubble box that's cracked—out." She scavenged the food from the dumpster.

To distribute, or to eat?

"Both."

When we last spoke she was putting the finishings on her exit strategy from her job. "My promise to myself is I'm out of there in October [2006]. It seems like a while, I know—but it took me fifteen or twenty years to get to here, so now a year to unwind it."

And then?

She has a certain set of skills as a professional communicator. A particularly transferable set of skills, which can put a magic aura around a bank or a superstore or a political candidate. But she would rather not use them at all. "What comes to mind to do is to try to keep things out of landfills. So to learn how to repair small electronics, how to repair appliances, seems a possibility. Maybe I'll go to a Vo-Tech for a year and learn those skills.

"There are moments when I think, Who Am I? It really does feel like all of the rest was like these barnacles that had built up all around me, and then I got this really good scrubbing, and what's underneath is who I am, which is who I've been all along.

"I don't feel like I'm making up a new person. Although I suppose I *am* going to make up how I earn my living now." The last I heard, Madeline Nelson was traveling across the country, taking part in theatrical actions in malls, crashing on the floor of other activists' homes. (Did I know anyone in Minneapolis who could put her up?) About this new identity—and its shoestring living—there appeared not a hint of buyer's remorse.

FIVE

The Revolutionary Evolution

The Speed of Change: The Ground for
Change Is Prepared

You can outdistance that which is running after you,
but not what is running inside you.

—Rwandan proverb

Max Weber believed that a life-changing U-turn could happen in a flash—in a sudden transformation of the spirit—
but it could also happen slowly, in a "gradual process of
purification." William James likewise thought that spiritual experiences come in two varieties: quick snaps and slow unfoldings. We
might call these two types of reversals *revolutionary change* and *evolution-*
ary change. They are different countries, but the border between them is
undefended.

Revolutionary turns are what we think of as the classic "conversion"
experience: nearly instantaneous changes of heart. "Basically, they have
come to a decision: 'That's it: I'm marrying her,' he decides; or, 'That's
it: I'm quitting my job,' " Karen Armstrong, the nun–turned–religious
historian, said not long ago. "It can be a moment of extreme drama."
When religious conversions happen this way, "all that has happened is
that someone who has been toying with the idea of religion has, for various psychological reasons—which are probably different in each individual case—suddenly felt, Now it's clear."

Epiphanic change, when you think of it this way, seems so tantalizing

96

a prospect that it shimmers in the imagination of just about everyone who's dissatisfied, or uncertain, or lost.

When my father-in-law, Bob Williams, was a newly minted physician, he traveled to Italy, hitting the hot spots with the kind of focused gusto of people who know they're not going to be traveling much for a long time. He went to Pisa. There was the tower, and, forgoing the obligatory gag photo, up he went—which you could do in those days. At the top was a little alcove on the leaning side, and he sat down there, by himself. "I looked out over the broad green lawn of the grounds," he recalls. "It was a beautiful day in May. You could see the baptistery in the foreground, the Duomo in the distance. I thought, Galileo stood here, almost exactly here, almost five hundred years ago, to conduct his experiment." Right on this spot our understanding of science is said to have changed. Science was based on logic and pure reason before he dropped those balls, and on mathematics after.

It occurred to Bob that if inspiration struck once at these coordinates it could strike again. Maybe the heavens were rent here, the forces aligned to nudge individual scientists a particular way. Bob had his own conundrum he was wrestling with: What avenue of research should he pursue? What would be a good project? He brought out a notebook. And literally waited to take dictation from God—or from Galileo. He sat there, slave to this uncharacteristically poetic fancy, all afternoon, until a security guy came around and told him they were closing the tower and would he mind, please, moving along home.

When Bob finally did make these decisions, it was by a series of methodical smaller decisions—with, no matter how he wished for one, not an epiphany to be found.

And no doubt that's the way change usually happens. It happens in the manner of philosopher Otto Neurath's metaphor of the way science proceeds: like repairing a whole boat at sea, rotten plank by rotten plank. Countless incremental adjustments, each of them a little fraught, a little dangerous, until eventually you sail back into shore on an entirely different vessel. Even though many big perceptual changes occur slowly, we *impose* a dramatic suddenness in the telling. C. S. Lewis's conversion to Christianity struck one day while he was riding his motorcycle to the zoo. ("When I got on the motorcycle," he would say, "I did not have this faith, and when I arrived at the zoo, I did.") But Lewis himself also described the creeping sense, many months before that moment, that a conversion was stalking him, like a pack of hounds, closing, closing. The hounds had been released the evening he took a long walk and had a fiercely wide-ranging talk by the River Cherwell with fellow Oxford dons J. R. R. Tolkien and Hugo Dyson (one of the most important walks in literary history, for many have traced to that extended conversation the genesis of both *The Lord of the Rings* and *The Chronicles of Narnia*), and these powerfully persuasive men planted the seed of *doubt in his doubt*. The hounds finally caught Lewis on his motor-cycle. (To stretch the image, and the time line, you could say the hounds were *born* many years earlier, in the trenches of World War I—which he was lucky to get out of alive.)

So a lot of so-called revolutionary changes are—when you examine them closely—more evolutionary than they appear. But evolutionary changes are also a little bit more revolutionary than they seem. Just as what we are calling revolutionary turns don't come out of the blue—there are always antecedents, things that led to things that led to insights—evolutionary turns are never seamless.

The mind works a bit the way stock markets do. From time to time, markets reverse their course, from bull to bear, or from bear to bull, in what may seem to novice traders like a sudden and completely unpre-dictable flip of the switch. But successful day traders operate on the premise that there are always precursive signs: Detect the first stirrings of a reversal and you can move your money and make a bundle. (Inter-estingly, the common wisdom holds that bearish reversal patterns form during uptrends, and bullish reversal patterns form during downtrends. Which suggests, if we can extend the metaphor, that things are neither as bad as we think in our times of despair nor as sunny as we think in our good days.) All the clues are there, in theory, if you know how to read them.

Not long ago a Canadian radio broadcaster named Mary Hynes was interviewing Jean Vanier, founder of the social services network for the mentally disabled called L'Arche. Vanier is a wise and gentle soul, whose own life describes a U-turn arc: He gave up his life in the navy to go live in a little community of mentally handicapped adults. He is, dispositionally, a quiet reflecting pool: in other words, a difficult interview. It is like playing tennis with someone who keeps catching the balls you serve and putting them in his pocket. Hynes had a list of prepared questions, and she tried to pin Vanier down on when, precisely, his epiphany happened. At what moment were his insights about the source of love, and our purpose on earth—the "This is why I'm here" moment—hatched? Vanier has in the past told the story that he had a mentor, a Dominican priest, who revealed to Vanier his "secret name," his mission in life. But when, precisely? She tried several times, and each time he gently steered around the question with metaphors about the invisible growth of embryos and flowers. Finally, his limitless patience hit an end.

"It's something that appears," Vanier said. "You can never say, It was Thursday that the flower grew. If you talk about growth you must talk about nourishment, and earth. You need a place to grow: community— that's the earth. You need the nourishment—the soil. You *need to know that you will never know the time.* So you can keep on asking me the time: What date? What happened? You will never know. You will never know what happened. Because it's part of the whole mystery of the growing person." (The best part of the exchange came next, as a throwaway. The interviewer was a little embarrassed: you could see her cheeks flare even over the radio. This "fetish for chronology," she admitted, was "a terrible occupational hazard that I have." "Well," Jean Vanier said, laughing, "you just have to grow up.")

There is wisdom in Vanier's response, but it's not the whole story. Growth—in plants, in markets, in species, in individual human beings—is rarely perfectly steady; there *are* decisive moments, nodal points that matter, disproportionately, to what that organism is on its way to becoming.

Just as we can generally debunk those who claim their epiphanies came flat out of the blue—can, in effect, "evolutionize" a revolutionary turn—so too can we almost always find breakthrough moments of insight in life changes claimed to be seamlessly slow and steady. That is, to "revolutionize" an evolutionary turn.

Evolution is discontinuous, Stephen Jay Gould theorized. Natural selection happens in fits and starts, with periodic bursts of frenzied activity—as mutations meet just the right environment for them, and those creatures thrive—and then, often for long periods, very little happens. That, a number of psychologists and psychiatrists have asserted, is more or less the pattern human growth follows at the level of individuals as well. When change happens, it happens abruptly. Often, the critical, nodal points are where change is circumstantially forced on us: The would-be convert is exposed to a persuasive influence just when he or she is most receptive to it.

And it's those, often emotionally charged, moments that we seize on when constructing what narrative psychologists call our *personal myth*.

All the other people we would like to be, or wish we were or even fear becoming, "exist," in some metaphorical sense, believes the social psychologist Hazel Rose Markus. These "possible selves" may make their way into our life, or they may not. They mill around backstage, waiting to be written into the play. They hover, awaiting their cue. For some, the cue simply does not come, and that possible self never materializes. But those for whom the cue does come enter abruptly. A character in a play cannot *phase in* to a scene. He is simply, suddenly, there, onstage. And not for no reason. Characters show up when the logic of the plot makes their appearance inevitable. (The new character arrives at a scene change in the play. But in our memory's reconstruction, it is a scene change precisely *because* the character arrived.)

Not long ago, the short-story writer Jaspreet Singh was passing through town on a reading tour. Jaspreet, who is writer-in-residence at the University of Calgary, holds a Ph.D. in chemical engineering, and he was comfortably employed in the field until he abandoned it all seven years ago to compose literary fiction full-time.

"Did it feel inevitable?" I asked him of the fairly sudden decision. "Like it was in the script?"

"It feels inevitable now," he replied. "But at the time it did not."

Jaspreet's graduate work at McGill involved phase transitions. He investigated the behavior of superabsorbent gels—the kind of material that's now being used in baby diapers and delivery devices for anticancer drugs. The gel materials have a very strange property: They swell or collapse dramatically, up to a thousandfold change in volume, in response to environmental changes too small to be perceived. The effect is of a trick of magic: a sudden bloom from a bud.

Why did he make the switch when he did, I asked, as we rode the bus through town. Why not earlier, or later, or not at all?

Had I heard of the word *metastability*? Jaspreet asked. On every continuum, there are certain *metastable* points, he explained, when things could go either way.

"Say I'm holding a kitchen chair like this, tipped back, balanced on the two back legs. For most of its range of motion I know which way the chair, if I let it go, will fall. But there is a narrow band in the middle within which the outcome can't be predicted; the chair could tip upright or bang down."

Outside the windows of the number 20 crosstown, it was night, and rain pounded down. We looked out at the street as the bus threaded its way through Vancouver's skid row district, past addicts standing in heroin contrapostos, victims of some unfathomable combination of chance, choice, and design.

A human life is a continuum, and on it there are metastable moments when the outcome can't be predicted. People who are not physicists recognize these intuitively, and call them by other names: *decisive moments*, say, or *teachable moments* or *moments of truth*.

"Let's say a father must choose between obeying the law and protecting his son," Jaspreet said. Two strong belief systems are suddenly in conflict. Cognitive dissonance is strong. The moment is metastable. That moment will have different outcomes for different people. One possible life materializes for one person; another for another. Two fathers in exactly the same circumstances head off, from that moment on, on different branches of an infinitely bifurcating tree.

Jaspreet has no answers to which father will act which way. Nor is he sure the physics metaphor properly applies to human behavior. He is a writer who builds elaborate scaffolding for his stories, then always—always—removes the scaffolding before the story is in published form, and never talks about it. If you knew that a short story began as a differential equation, might that not ruin it? If it were true that there is a script for us, that our actions are predestined, would we really want to know that? Wouldn't it, in some way, spoil the story?

The Crystallization of Discontent

When he was twenty-six years old, Anwar Shaikh, born in what is now Pakistan and raised a fundamentalist Muslim, experienced a moment from which his commitment to his faith would never recover. What is remarkable, given the details of his life, is not that this epiphany happened, but that it took so long. And that the disavowal came, when it did, not in a visceral surge of shame but in a cognitive snap—the pivot point of a scholar, not a warrior.

His early years, under the tutelage of his mother and his fundamentalist paternal grandfather and another family member who was a mullah, prepared him for the life of a jihadist, but he soon found himself on a collision course with this infamous concept at the heart of the hard-line clerics' interpretation of the Koran.

"We were told that murdering the non-Muslims, seducing their wives, and burning their properties was an act of jihad, that is, holy war," he said in an interview with the scholar and apostate Ibn Warraq. "And jihad is the most sacred duty of a Muslim because it guarantees him a safe passage to paradise where no fewer than seventy-two *houris*, that is the most beautiful virgins, and pearl-like boys wait for him. Such a reward is great temptation!"

It proved simply too tempting to a young man of nineteen, which Anwar Shaikh turned in 1947. In August of that year—amidst the violence that accompanied the partition of India—a period Shaikh now calls "the darkest of my life"—there came an incident which left him saddled with guilt and remorse. While working as an accounts clerk in the railway office in Lahore, he watched a train pull in from East Punjab, "full of mutilated bodies of Muslims: men, women, and children." That night he prayed to Allah, asking him not to forget the deal about the *houris* and boys. "And then I took up a club and a long knife, and I went out in search of non-Muslims.

"Those days were remembered for the curfew orders and everybody seemed terrified of everybody else. I found two men, Sikhs, a father and son. The father was perhaps not more than fifty, perhaps younger, and his young son. I killed both of them. Next day I did not go to work. I felt nauseated, but I wanted to kill some more non-Muslims. I encountered another Sikh at Darabi Road and I killed him too." These were people, the thought haunts him now, "who might have been alive even today, if it had not been for my fanaticism," Anwar told Warraq. But at the time that's not what caused him to turn away from his faith.

He was reading the Koran one day in Rawalpindi, in northern Pakistan, when something suddenly struck him as fishy. In the verse he was reading, Allah tells the faithful to behave well in front of the Prophet. "All of a sudden something struck me like lightning," he told Warraq. "I said, Why is it really for Allah to tell people to show reverence to Muhammad? Can't Muhammad tell the people these things himself? God was acting as a servant to Muhammad. This seems such a banal observation, but this is how my mind reacted to that: I came to the conclusion, all of a sudden, that it was Muhammad himself who was telling the people how to bow before him in the name of Allah, as though it were a command from Allah. By now, I felt that this veil of ignorance had been lifted from my mind.

"I was no longer willing to study the Koran through faith. I started reading it critically and rationally. And as I went through it, I realized the Koran did not appeal to me anymore the way it used to do, the way it had for the last twenty-five years." This new relationship to the text not as an object of devotion but as a piece of scholarship, open to questioning, set off all sorts of alarms. "The moment I started reading the Koran critically, it looked entirely [like] another book to me." Shaikh decided to subject the Koran to its own definition of infallibility—that "it must be a book from God, or it would contain many contradictions and inconsistencies." It came up so short that Shaikh was moved to write a whole book of his own, *Faith and Deception*, documenting those contradictions and inconsistencies as he saw them. He was now "out," not just a private questioner but an apostate, prepared to accept all that that meant. (What it meant was that a fatwa was promptly issued, and Shaikh, who has settled in Cardiff, Wales, has lived in its shadow ever

since. One writer who visited the author there in 2004, in a house fortified by burglar alarms, bars, and guard dogs, described his daily life as
"a state of near-siege.")

The psychologist Roy Baumeister coined a term for what happened to
Anwar Shaikh, and you can see it in the stories of secular and religious
U-turns alike. He called it the *crystallization of discontent*, and it works, in his
opinion, like this: A vaguely dissatisfied person suddenly connects the dots
of his or her various complaints and misgivings—which were previously
assumed to be unrelated. "The subjective impact can be enormous," he
writes. "A large mass of negative features may be enough to undermine a
person's commitment to a role, relationship or involvement."

So common a factor is disillusionment in big midlife changes that it's
almost synonymous with a *loss of faith*. But framing it that way makes it
sound more negative than it is.

"People who are disillusioned should be happy to lose their illusions,"
Sidney Rittenberg told me. Here, indeed, is the fortune-cookie version
of Sidney Rittenberg's adult life: Be grateful for your disillusionment—it
is a gift without which you might never have found the right path. It is
the way people break the trance of cults—which is to say all somewhat
irrational belief systems, from Maoism to consumerism to the social expectations laid on the stay-at-home mom. But disillusionment is slow to
deliver its payoff of liberty. Disillusionment is slow because stubborn
loyalty to the original belief system delays the moment of insight, even
as evidence piles up all around us that we are wrong.

Not long ago, crossing the street in downtown Vancouver, I noticed
a man pacing in front of the local office of the Church of Scientology.
He was short, with a neatly trimmed beard. He looked, from that distance, like the actor Jim Caviezel. He held aloft a sign that read,
"Thank God L. Ron Hubbard Is Dead Wrong," and on the flip side—
revealed when he spun toward the well-dressed but vaguely uneasy-
looking young Scientologists on the other side of the glass—"Scientology
Let My People Go."

The man's name is Gerry Armstrong. He became a Scientologist
more than thirty-five years ago, and he would spend a decade and a half
on the inside before disenchantment, a daring escape, and a commitment
ever since to bird-dog the church privately, publicly, and through the

courts that has made him, to the Church of Scientology, something like what Anwar Shaikh is to fundamentalist Islam.

As Armstrong tells the story today, the church was an entity that swallowed up "most of my adult life." As a young man of twenty-two, disenchanted by the workaday world (he'd been toiling as a logger) and searching for the Truth (this was 1969), he was enticed by a friend to join. And through a combination of natural aptitude and a string of co-incidences, he was promoted up the chain of command into an executive position within Scientology's pseudomilitary core.

Armstrong was everything a guru could hope for in a disciple: bright, an energetic apostle of the doctrine, and—his great strength—a brilliant recruiter. (According to Armstrong, for each new recruit he signed up he received a 15 percent commission fee, which he plowed back into the church.) He was extremely sharp. One of the things that had attracted him to Scientology was the promise that one could raise one's IQ a point for every hour spent "auditing" Scientology doctrine—which the church's literature claims can cleanse the mind of its habitual fog. Armstrong would log, by the end, well over a thousand hours of auditing.

Eventually, he rose to the top of the ranks of the Sea Order—the executive wing of the church. (This is a fairly large commitment: In the Sea Order, Armstrong says, you contractually pledge fealty to the church for "a billion years.") He became a personal public relations officer for Scientology founder L. Ron Hubbard. In that post, he was given the job of researching Hubbard's biography. "That was my great bit of luck," Armstrong told me. It meant he had access to Hubbard's entire archive, including both Hubbard's formal philosophy—thousands of pages on ethics and justice and economics—and his personal documents, from his old Boy Scout manual to letters to his father to the diaries he kept while traveling in Asia as a young man. Armstrong set to work gathering and collating this material, in what would become a two-year project.

It was a plum post. Armstrong got the use of a car and "almost unique come-and-go privileges" to travel widely in search of archival material. As he motored off the compound, "People would say, 'Oh, that's Gerry, he's working on this supersecret biography project,'" Armstrong recalls.

He soon realized that some things, in the World According to L. Ron Hubbard, didn't seem to add up. "The first clue I had was, we were to raise funds by promoting a movie called *Divebomber* that Hubbard said he'd written the screenplay for; well, I discovered he didn't write the screenplay at all. So we stopped promoting it."

Armstrong's reaction to this was not so much anger as, well, confusion. He figured there must be some sort of misunderstanding, rather than any systemic problem. An almost bone-deep faith in the man who aimed to purge the world of crime and disease, and to the principles he espoused, had been drilled into him.

"See, inside the organization, to have a critical thought about Scientology is considered almost a crime," Armstrong told me over a beer in Vancouver's historic Gastown—not far from the small town where he has ended up. "So, while I registered these contradictions, I didn't really bring them into my conscious mind for a long, long time."

Eventually, enough internal documents had come across his desk that, Armstrong says, he knew the Scientology story cold—well enough that, as he sifted through the material and the biographical sketches of Hubbard labeled "true facts," he recognized the ones that appeared to be in error. And, instead of reporting the problem, he simply corrected the documents.

Privately, if only to quell the niggling doubts, Armstrong had begun to get some second and third opinions about the church from outsiders—the most credible independent sources he could find. The outside picture of the church and its mission, he discovered, felt quite different from the "in-house" version: From the exterior perspective, it was less a church than a cult, and Hubbard less a saintly visionary than a megalomaniac. Which was the truth? He wasn't sure, but he began keeping a meticulous second set of records for himself.

By this time Omar Garrison had entered the picture. Garrison was the writer the church had hired to actually write Hubbard's biography, based largely on the archived material Armstrong had unearthed. Garrison wasn't a Scientologist; he was—for credibility—a "wog"—the in-house term for those who are not church members. Garrison insisted that he was going to tell the truth. ("This is not going to be a panegyric to L. Ron Hubbard," he told Armstrong.) Eventually, over many wine-filled meals, a trust developed between the two men. As they sifted through the reams of PR documents—not quite sure how to verify their accuracy—they grew more and more disenchanted with their mission.

By now, the very things that had brought Armstrong into the organization in the first place—"Hubbard's impressive claims of his personal achievements—his war victories, how he'd cured his own blindness through Dianetics, and so on"—seemed highly suspicious to him. Armstrong felt that Hubbard had exaggerated or fabricated his education, degrees, family, explorations, war wounds, and scientific results. (Omar Garrison corroborated this assessment in a 1985 interview with Mike Wallace on *60 Minutes*. A church spokesman, in response, explained that Hubbard's official military records did not corroborate Hubbard's claims because those official records had "been doctored.")

The bloom was now finally off the rose for Gerry Armstrong. Like a prospective car buyer who finds, in the trunk of the car he has been lent to test-drive, the sales manual containing the very pressure tactics that were used verbatim to seduce him, he felt a sense of shame and anger.

"Once I had enough facts, and became solidly critical, I also became extremely fearful," Armstrong says. He began planning his escape.

By now the church had moved its headquarters from the outskirts of Palm Springs to Los Angeles. Armstrong had been working in L.A. to get documents to Omar Garrison; with each shipment, he included a few of his personal effects—like a prisoner getting rid of the dirt from the escape tunnel a few pocketfuls at a time—until his belongings were all moved out. Eventually, he waxed the floor of the empty office, hung his uniform in the closet, and didn't come back.

In the Vancouver pub, Armstrong's wild hazel eyes had grown glassy, and his voice was beginning to wear thin. He never speaks this much these days; he spends his time, supported by welfare, working on his Web site with his partner (also an ex-Scientologist), rarely even coming into town unless he can cadge a ride.

The Church of Scientology has vehemently denied all of Armstrong's claims about its founder's mendacity, its treatment of members, its use of funds—it has made a habit of maligning the credibility of everyone who left. And in April of 2004, the church won a landmark half-million-dollar judgment against Armstrong for "breach of contract." (The contract was struck back in 1986, when Armstrong accepted money from the church in return for dropping his lawsuit and agreeing never to talk about Scientology in public.) Armstrong, unable to pay the settlement, declared bankruptcy and moved from San Francisco to Canada, where, as I discovered, he spends his days doggedly trying to dissuade others from falling into the trap he did. From a remove and on a shoestring, Armstrong works as hard against Scientology as he ever worked for it— a revalencing of passion, a kind of backlash dynamic, that's typical of people who have lost a strong belief. When those who have given their all to their object of devotion fall, they fall hard—having realized, as Erik Erikson once put it, that they have "fatally overcommitted to what they are not."

Groundhog Day

One way to think about the idea of being receptive to a transforming insight is like this: There are a lot of lightning strikes in an evergreen forest, but relatively few forest fires. That's because those big firs and hemlocks, insulated by bark as thick as a phone book, resist igniting. For a whole forest to go up, conditions must be perfect. Saul walked right past Jesus without recognizing him, just as the wandering ascetic Upaka walked past the Buddha, because neither was "ready" to see them for what they were. The idea that we are presented with opportunities for enlightenment, and only recognize them when we are receptive—have *earned* that receptivity—do we engage the truth, is a trope common to both religious and secular descriptions of how enlightenment works.

Karen Armstrong evokes T. S. Eliot's image of the spiral staircase to describe her own spiritual journey, from a teenage Catholic nun to a staunch disbeliever (and, indeed, scathing critic of religion) to a scholar who found her way back to faith—albeit of an inclusive, ecumenical kind. A faith really unlike either of the two extremes it was born from, but encompassing them. Our progress up the spiral staircase of life moves us along two vectors at once: We pass the same points again and again, but at higher levels of understanding.

The Revolutionary Evolution

That's pure Sartre. Or Bill Murray. In the film *Groundhog Day*, the lessons of life are lost on the callow weatherman with the fiery libido. They are offered again and again, but they do not take, and so his life does not change. He remains stuck. Only when his maturity and courage reach a certain threshold do those lessons mean something. On the morning that finally happens, nothing is different . . . except him. He is finally ready, and so, exposed to the very same opportunities, the same cosmic sparks, that have rained down every day previously, everything changes. This idea that we are condemned to encounter the same lessons over and over again until we "get it" also echoes Freud: "A thing which has not been understood inevitably reappears; like an unlaid ghost it cannot rest until the mystery has been solved or the spell broken."

Gandhi maintained that the truth always came upon him "as if from a voice that had spoken before he had quite listened." He often told of his inner narrator, which would pipe up unexpectedly in the preparatory calm of silence—but then with irreversible firmness and an irresistible demand for commitment.

Even Friedrich Nietzsche, Gandhi's philosophical opposite, claimed that the truth always approached "on the feet of doves. That is, the moment of truth is suddenly there—unannounced and pervasive in its stillness. But it comes only to him who has lived with facts and figures in such a way that he is always ready for a sudden synthesis and will not, from sheer surprise and fear, startle truth away." Only when we're ready to do so, as the Buddhists say, will we stop sucking on the pointing finger, and look up and see that it is pointing at the moon.

In 1927, Bluma Zeigarnik, a German psychologist, was sitting in a busy coffee shop in Vienna, marveling at how the waiter was able to remember all the orders he had on the go. She asked him about this and he replied that, yes, he could hold in his head an almost limitless number of orders—but only until he'd filled them, and then they were gone. At the end of the workday he couldn't tell you what kind of coffee anyone had had. Zeigarnik did some experiments of her own, and discovered that we tend to remember an uncompleted task better (roughly twice as well) as a completed one. Outstanding needs cause a kind of tension, she concluded, and the brain, to relieve it, churns away until the needs are satisfied. The mind won't rest until it has resolved a conflict—and then it lets go.

Most of us—except for the very few for whom everything has gone perfectly swimmingly up to this point—might be said to have unconsciously framed the "problem" of our life thus: "I want to be maximally happy and challenged and fulfilled, but I am not. (That is, I can imagine feeling more happy and challenged and fulfilled than I am now.) So I am hunting. Every day I am on the lookout to improve my circumstances." To the degree that that mantra moves like a CNN breaking-news crawl through our subconscious, we are receptive to change. We are incubating a solution, trying to find the missing piece of the puzzle that is the problem of our life. The subconscious scans, looking for the *inert knowledge* that is always there, but hidden in a blind spot. The U-turner is thus primed to find a solution he had no idea was in him, but which, when it comes, seems to have come out of nowhere.

The Philosophical Friend

In his book *Changing Minds*, the Harvard cognitive psychologist Howard Gardner recounts how, over the course of a single afternoon in the fall of 1969, he completely changed his mind about his life's work. That day he had met the charismatic Harvard neurologist Norman Geschwind, and had come to realize the dead end he was on in his current line of inquiry in developmental psychology, and the vast possibilities that pursuing a new line of work under Geschwind promised. But on reflection Gardner concluded that that out-of-left-field insight was not so sudden at all. "What seemed to be a Geschwindian moment—a sudden dramatic turn—was masking a more gradual change in intellectual allegiance," Gardner recalls. With a little thinking, he managed to ferret out the precursive stages to that "sudden" insight. He had always been interested in biology. He'd been wondering "what kind of postdoctoral fellowship might rescue me from embarking on a standard teaching trajectory that held little appeal." Subconsciously, he had been looking for a brilliant mentor figure who could limn some new corner of the sciences with more of a future for him, a "fluent, mature" artist who could school him a little on how to organize material, and how to think. The student being ready, the teacher appeared: Geschwind. "While the decision to work with Geschwind erupted almost instantly into consciousness, this 'change of mind' had long been in the works in the recesses of my mind."

The philosopher and ethicist Jacob Needleman calls the Norman Geschwinds of our lives, who seem to be there for us just when we need them (or are ready for them) "philosophical friends." It's the Geschwinds whom Albert Schweitzer was talking about when he said, "In everyone's life, at some time, our inner fire goes out. It is then burst into flame by an encounter with another human being.'" And in fact there's evidence that it's the Geschwinds who are more responsible for catalyzing U-turns than anything else. If you boiled down to a single line psychologist Chana Ullman's comprehensive study of conversion experiences, it would be this: Ideas don't convert people—people convert people. "The discovery of a new truth," she concludes, "was indistinguishable from a discovery of a new relationship, which relieved, at least temporarily, the upheaval of the previous life."

Ideally, Jacob Needleman believed, such a person respects you enough to treat you not as you are *but as you have the potential to be*. And therefore he or she can take you somewhere you never expected.

When in the mid-1990s, after the release of his album *The Future*, the singer-songwriter Leonard Cohen dropped out of sight, and word filtered out that he had gone to live in a Zen Buddhist center atop California's Mt. Baldy, thence to shave his head and settle in for a seven-year stay so ascetic that weeklong meditation sessions were sometimes broken only when the singer stepped outside to pee in a bucket, many people wondered what was up. Where had *that* particular turn come from? The answer was a Zazen monk named Joshu Sasaki Roshi, whom Cohen had met and befriended years before, and been captivated by as he added Buddhism to his hopper of Drugs Worth a Try. "Old Roshi," crowding ninety years old then, was a resource he was foolishly failing to appreciate, it dawned on Cohen one day, and he decided to "take the opportunity to hang with him while he's still around." And so up the mountain he went. Roshi (who is still alive and, as Cohen recently put it, "in top form" at age ninety-eight), who taught Cohen how to drink and how to think—or rather, how not to think—now taught him how to be in the world. It was who Roshi was, and not what he did, that so attracted Cohen; in this case, the man dictated the path.

"If he'd been a professor of German in Heidelberg, I'd have followed him there," and become a professor of German, Cohen told an interviewer not long ago. But Roshi happened to be a Zen master, so Leonard Cohen became a monk. ("I learned later that anxiety fades, naturally, on its own," he later remarked. "I wish I'd known that: I could have saved myself the suffering of the monastic lifestyle.")

The service rendered by the philosophical friend is not one he has necessarily offered, but one we have imposed on him. Indeed, a "philosophical friend" need not be more than figurative; not a friend, per se, but merely someone bearing timely news and perspective, another intelligence coming in hard and fast on a different enough angle, so that when it hits we're knocked left, right, or back.

In April of 2000, Bill Joy, the then forty-six-year-old cofounder and chief scientist of Sun Microsystems—a man *Fortune* magazine dubbed the "Edison of the Internet" and long regarded as an Apostle of Tech—disclosed his unease with technology's implications.

"I was sitting with John Searle, a Berkeley philosopher who studies consciousness," Joy recounts in a mini-memoir he wrote for *Wired* magazine about his crisis of conscience. "While we were talking, Ray Kurzweil approached and a conversation began, the subject of which haunts me to this day."

The subject was how flesh and metal, already codependent, were going to integrate to a degree scarcely imagined, and sooner than anyone might think.

Kurzweil handed Joy a partial printout of his forthcoming book *The Age of Spiritual Machines*, outlining a future "in which humans gain near immortality by becoming one with robot technology."

Joy scanned the text. This was real dystopic sci-fi stuff, and dead serious at that. It could easily be the fate of the human race to cede decision-making control to machines. Or else machines would simply wrest that control away.

There followed a long exegesis, warning of the unintended

consequences of technology. Joy found himself being pulled along. He didn't disagree. In fact, it was a compelling argument.

He turned the page to discover that this section was not Kurzweil's prose. It was an excerpt from an essay, and Joy saw the byline now: Ted Kaczinski. The Unabomber. It was part of the manifesto the *New York Times* and the *Washington Post* had controversially published, caving in to Kaczinski's demands. Ted Kaczinski, a man who almost killed with a bomb one of Joy's best friends, David Gelertner. A murderous lunatic—and yet one who had climbed into Joy's brain and made a seductively persuasive pitch that Joy now "felt compelled to confront."

Joy performed the same thought experiment on friends: showing them the passage without the byline. He became a little obsessed with the future conjunction of flesh and metal. He delved into other books on the subject, and sought out other friends for heart-to-hearts. One was the futurist Danny Hillis, who told Joy, yes, it was probably true: The surrender of our will to machines would probably happen; but it would happen gradually and we'd get used to it. (Joy had dreaded having his own fears corroborated, but Hillis's existential shrug was even worse.) Joy knew this much: He designed computer network systems for a living. The horrors of self-replication had direct applications to what he did every day. He knew how it might unfold. He understood the problem at the intuitive level. In his field, such a runaway train could do physical damage to hardware and software and royally gum things up. But the same principle, applied to genetic engineering or nanotechnology, would be lethal.

"Our most powerful twenty-first-century technologies—robotics, genetic engineering and nanotechnology—are threatening to wipe out human beings as a species," Joy wrote in his cri de coeur in *Wired*. Suddenly, Joy was the village Cassandra, espousing a bracing new outlook on life, and all set in motion by that chance meeting with Kurzweil.

Just what is it this so-called "philosophical friend," whom we chance to encounter, is actually providing? Simply put, something we lack—a bit of information, an odd but somehow apt non sequitur, a piece of the puzzle that nudges us closer to coherence—and which we aren't likely to have come up with on our own.

That's why this person, if indeed it is a person, is probably not going to have been a boon friend since high school. She is going to be a stranger—or at best a very casual acquaintance. This seems counter-intuitive, but it was proven, more or less, by a phenomenon called the "strength of weak ties." The Stanford sociologist Mark Granovetter discovered that the less well we know someone, the more likely she is to provide life-changing opportunities. Why? Because, unlike our closest friends, who probably share our views and interests and social network, people we barely know inhabit a slightly different universe: They've read books we'd never pick up, been to places we'd never venture, know people we don't. These people are the pattern-breakers, the ones who are likely to kindle the profound insights. (The moral of Granovetter's theory: Always talk to the passenger next to you on the airplane.)

The great function of the philosophical friend, you might say, is the precise inverse of that of our closest friends. They aren't our great cheerleaders, mirroring our values, supporting us unconditionally; on the contrary. As Kurzweil did for Bill Joy, they unsettle us, destabilize us, create tensions in our lives that we must face—when we're ready.

Receptivity

The editor of the leftist magazine *The Partisan Review* once described the gradual shift of the magazine's politics to the right during the 1980s as a "slow-motion brain transplant." That's a good term for the gradual ideological reversal, which is the most common kind. We deal with new information by assimilating it into our understanding of the world and our stable sense of who we are in it—a painless, subconscious process, like putting things in a shopping bag. As we face information that can't be easily assimilated, we accommodate to it, gradually stretching the bag. What can happen, over time, is that the bag stretches so much that it has effectively become a different bag. Our belief system has changed.

But very occasionally, as we're moving right along, merrily assimilating, we encounter some novel piece of information utterly alien to our identity and our belief systems and yet so irresistibly compelling that it can't be ignored. The bag won't stretch far enough to fit it. The evidence contrary to our belief system has unfolded before our eyes, and, overpowering even our heroic ability to rationalize, it breaks the bag.

That was the strange fate of John Mack, an esteemed Harvard psychiatrist and polymath (he won the Pulitzer Prize for nonfiction in 1977 for his biography of T. E. Lawrence), whose career took a fantastic turn in 1990. That was the year a middle-aged man approached him in Cambridge, Massachusetts, and asked Mack, somewhat tentatively, if he might take him on as a patient—or at least hear his story. The man believed he had been abducted by aliens.

Now this is a not-terribly-uncommon story for psychiatrists to hear, one widely assumed to be a kind of media-fed delusion. But this fellow was obviously suffering, so Mack agreed to meet with him. As the patient spooled out an increasingly bizarre tale, involving an intergalactic breeding program he had apparently been recruited into, Mack listened sympathetically. Word soon got out that there was an apparently nonjudgmental Harvard psychiatrist willing to hear the stories of abductees and not immediately pronounce them flat-out nuts—so other members of the "experiencer" community began filtering through Mack's office. Mack gave them all a hearing.

Something about this group surprised Mack. They had no obvious psychopathology, no evidence of childhood sexual abuse. Yet they had obviously been traumatized by *something*. As he listened to story after story, remarkably similar variants on a theme, something shifted inside Mack. He allowed himself to imagine something utterly heretical: What if what they're saying is true? Or, if not literally true, what if they had indeed experienced something paranormal, something science can't measure?

"I could not account for these experiences by anything I knew as a psychiatrist," Mack told me when we met in 2003 in his stately home near Harvard Yard. "My psychiatric background did not equip me really to explain this, except to see that something traumatic had happened to these people, but it wasn't like the usual things that traumatize people."

The stories seemed to fall into a kind of unmapped space.

"The issue is the definition of epistemology," Mack said. "Science is a certain piece, a certain method, a certain way of knowing, but only one way. And it's one way that is subsumed within a much larger field of knowing. The larger way of knowing James called *intuitive* or 'knowing that comes from intuition and the heart.'

"The fact is, these people are having mysterious experiences. Virtually all have been through the gamut of searching for other explanations by doctors or therapists. They sometimes spent years with therapists who were looking for psychodynamic explanations of sexual abuse or childhood traumas that were displaced onto aliens. And none of that ever went anywhere." He would have been remiss, Mack suggested, not to entertain other theories. "If this does not yield to conventional explanation, then it begins to erode the worldview that says it's not possible."

But Mack did more than entertain this unthinkable alternative. He bought it. In 1990, he published the book *Abduction*, in which he lent his imprimatur to the theory that the phenomenon is very real, and widespread, with portentous implications for humanity. (What Mack read into them was that Earth as a "living system" was under threat, and the abduction phenomenon was a kind of outreach program from the cosmos.) Mack would later soften his position on alien abductions somewhat—suggesting that the stories may be less literally true than metaphorically true—but the damage to his professional reputation had been done. He was briefly suspended, then reinstated. He was a source of mirth to former colleagues, but all the more loved by the "experiencer" community who saw him as having fallen on his sword for them. When he died in 2004, he was deeply mourned by this group.

Mack's turn took a lot of people by surprise. But there were incidents in his past that prepared the ground for the reversal. In the 1970s, his life had, like William James's, veered toward the mystic, and he had become involved in the est movement. He was receptive to "alternative realities" by the time the mother narrative of all alternative realities landed on his lap.

* * *

The Revolutionary Evolution

The basic equation of conviction + cognitive dissonance + catalytic event = a potential change of mind or heart, seems to be universal, holding across time and across cultures. And, in fact, you can break the process down into its elements.

It's useful to think of U-turns as the product of a two-stage process, marked by two discrete beats. The first beat is an unexpected event—it could be a tragedy like 9/11 or a more personal matter. It challenges our deeply held assumptions, breaks down our resistance, and makes us, perhaps for the first time, vulnerable to change. Something has now happened to us. We have been bumped onto an inexorable path to transformation, though we may hardly be aware of it. All we may feel is that creeping uneasiness, that sense that things have fallen out of balance.

The second beat is another event that, because we are now vulnerable to change, actually pushes us over the line. The first beat has caused us to doubt what we believe is true. The second, to accept an alternative truth. If the first beat is the tinder, the second beat is the spark. The first beat often has an emotional component; the second—like the banal, kitchen-sink moment that ignites an epiphany in a fictional character—need not. (Because the emotional work has already been done.)

"Emotional occasions are extremely potent in precipitating mental rearrangements," writes William James, in *Varieties of Religious Experience*. Those mental rearrangements aren't the same as a conversion; rather, they're the initiation of the search that makes the eventual spiritual experience possible, he contends. James sees conversions as a kind of subconscious maturing process, a ripening of the soul that the initial questioning set in motion. "Some hidden process was started in you by the effort, and made the result come as if spontaneously."

James speaks of the soul, but Beat 1 needn't be understood in spiritual or metaphysical terms. It simply marks the moment we become receptive to alternatives. Very often it's because the event—whatever it happened to be—had the power to shift our perspective, to somehow allow us to see our life more objectively; and from that new angle the flaws in our position are clear.

This is what happened to William Kunstler. We think of him as a flamboyant, radical, civil rights lawyer, defending social outcasts of all

117

stripes (and angering Right and Left alike by taking on clients like John Gotti and the 1993 World Trade Center bomber). But Kunstler was once a sleepy suburban tax lawyer in New York, raking the lawn on weekends, "bored out of my skull." It was one week in Jackson, Mississippi, in 1961 that got the turnaround started. He had popped down to lend a hand in the defense of hundreds of black activists who were trying to desegregate bus terminals in the South (in so doing, the so-called "Freedom Riders" nationalized the civil rights struggle), who were moldering in prison on outrageous charges. Kunstler ended up staying for months, and helping out in other civil rights cases. By the time of the trial of the Chicago Seven, he realized he "had found [his] place in the world."

The Princeton philosopher emeritus Harry Frankfurt (best known for his recent book *On Bullshit*) hatched a metaphor that has been embraced by certain helping professionals, whose job it is to help turn around the lives of people nose-diving into the abyss. To be struggling in life is like being addicted to narcotics, Frankfurt posited. There are three kinds of drug addict: the "wanton addict," the "willing addict," and the "unwilling addict." The wanton addict craves the drug and gives no thought to his addiction. The willing addict *has* thought about it and, pleased with the thoroughly delightful high, has decided to keep using the drug. These two are probably beyond rescue. But the third kind of addict, the unwilling addict—the one who wants the drug but, full of shame and anger, wants *not* to want it—is a good candidate for a turnaround.

To have reached that spot is to be standing over the proverbial frozen sea with an ax. Twelve-steppers would just call it admitting the problem, but in the context of life U-turns it's more than that. It's genuinely wanting something different for yourself. Once you want something different, you have become like Frankfurt's hypothetical unwilling addict. The internal struggle that will ultimately power the turnaround has been set in motion. The brute addiction is what Frankfurt would call a "first-order desire," and the wanting not to be addicted is a "higher, second-order desire." For the wanton addict and the willing addict, that show's already over, because there is no struggle. (One or the other desire has already won.) But the unwilling addict is at war, and the struggle itself has a fair chance of destabilizing the first-order desire and sapping its strength.

At the end of the interval between Beat 1 and Beat 2 comes a kind of reckoning, as the internal tension of a life spent doing the wrong things well comes to a head.

SIX

The Crying Baby
Is There a "Natural" Direction to Turn?

A conservative is one who admires radicals centuries after they are dead.
—**Leo Rosten, author, 1908–1997**

The world, ideologically speaking, is a vast, multivalent freeway system, people urgently driven toward what they're urgently driven toward. And it's tremendous fun to stand on a bridge and watch them pass in opposite directions.

As the environmentalist David Suzuki became politicized and veered left, he did not fail to notice that his former student and protégé, Greenpeace cofounder Patrick Moore, had become a paid spokesman for various biotechnology interests. Suzuki, who has become very leery of corporate plans for biotech, made it clear that he would not be inviting Moore over for tofurkey anytime soon. "Let's expose this guy for what he is," said Suzuki. "A paid industry hack."

As Ronald Reagan went right, he passed Gore Vidal heading left. The young Reagan was an idealist who tried to join the Hollywood Communist Party in 1938; the young Vidal, born into privilege, was fairly conservative. In the 1950s, they switched valences. Both were starting to make good livings (Reagan from acting; Vidal from his plays), and the larcenous tax rate for high-income earners sparked different reactions in the two men. Reagan found it profoundly unjust, but Vidal saw an opportunity for the creation of a decent welfare state. Then came McCarthyism,

120

and the gulf between the two men grew, as Vidal became increasingly radicalized. (Vidal takes credit, tongue only partly in cheek, for Reagan's eventual place in history. Reagan had gone out for the lead in Vidal's play about a presidential candidate, but was turned down on the grounds that he just wasn't believable in that role. The rejected Reagan quit acting and went into politics. "I like to say that had it not been for me," Vidal writes in his memoir, "Ronald Reagan would never have been president.")

John Mack, the late Harvard psychiatrist, met his opposite number in a young Harvard psychology professor named Susan Clancy—when her work investigating repressed memories of trauma pulled her into the abductee community. If Mack had had an epiphany of sorts— What if it's true?—Clancy had had one in the other direction. Her own upbringing—feminist, lapsed Catholic, blue-chip liberal education— prepared her to believe the recovered memories of childhood sexual abuse that she started documenting when she began her career. But as her interviews with survivors of abuse went on, she realized that many of the most elaborate, terrifying tales she was hearing had the air of confabulation about them. "There was a moment where I said, 'Oh my god, I'm not sure this really happened.'" Ever after, she leaned hard on the scientific method, and when she found herself interviewing "abductees," she doggedly rooted out rational explanations for what Mack was now labeling paranormal.

In the last part of their careers, John Adams and Thomas Jefferson, the second and third U.S. presidents, changed each other's minds, as Howard Gardner points out. They had begun their political careers as fast friends, but then differences in temperament and political views became more and more apparent, and they became enemies—gravitating to opposite poles in just about everything, and calling each other some very bad names. In the end, a chance event caused conservative Adams to write democratic Jefferson a letter, and a détente was brokered—to the relief of both men. ("You and I ought not to die," as Adams had written to Jefferson, "before we have explained ourselves to each other.") As they rekindled their friendship, each conceding the areas in which they had been wrong and the other right, their trajectories began converging again. (One likes to think they were on their way to roaring past each other in the other direction—each so persuasively conciliatory that the other bought the arguments, with interest. But old statesmen are sometimes content with compromise.)

It's safe to say that there are predictable patterns in the way people change in the expression of their views, the intensity with which they hold their convictions, their desire to hold them close or scatter them widely. "The most distinguished persons become more revolutionary as they grow older," said George Bernard Shaw. (Which leaves the rest of us undistinguished schlubs doing the opposite.) It does seem true that most of us get less zealous as we age. (Headline: "Ice Cube: From Angry Young Rapper to Lovable Hollywood Dad.") Many are the once-criminally radical types who turned, in later life, in more socially acceptable directions, trading up in the factory-outlet store of Jungian archetypes, from warrior to statesman.

To suggest that traveling in one ideological direction is more "natural" than another, however, seems like a rigged game. So much of what we decide to do, think, and believe is circumstantial—whether the liberal gets mugged, or the conservative gets downsized—that broad conclusions about "natural" directions pretty quickly get us into trouble. But since it's a game people have been playing forever, why don't we just wade in.

The Berkeley cognitive linguist George Lakoff tells this story of a conversation he had in his garden a few years ago with his mathematician friend, the late Paul Baum. "I asked Paul if he could think of a single question, the answer to which would be the best indicator of liberal versus conservative politics." Baum thought about this, and came up with the following:

"If your baby cries at night, do you pick him up?"

The response got Lakoff thinking long and hard about the fundamental differences between the essential *liberal* and *conservative* sensibility—and ultimately prompted him to write a book on the subject, *Moral Politics*.

The anecdote is almost guaranteed to get parents applying the test to their own child rearing. In our own household, the answer to Baum's question would be: Yes, we picked our crying daughter up—at first. The no-cry "attachment parenting" school of thought has an undeniable hold on insecure new parents; but over time we came to believe in the wisdom of the rival school, Ferberization: That is, let 'em cry. In other words, we started as liberals and became conservatives.

And that is the pattern for almost every other couple we know.

Which raised the inevitable (and, to us, troubling) question: Is liberal-to-conservative just generally the default direction that human beings go?

"If you're under thirty and you're not a liberal you have no heart; but if you're over thirty and you're not a conservative, you have no brain," Churchill allegedly said—and the adage does *seem* to describe the statistical norm. "How many former Leftists, Socialists, Marxists, Trotskyites and Democrats have moved right? Literally hundreds," wrote the conservative commentator Jonah Goldberg not long ago. "If you count normal, non-pointy-headed people, millions. Generation after generation of the Left's best minds have decided they like things over here more. From Max Eastman to Eugene Genovese, Whittaker Chambers to Ronald Radosh, intellectuals migrate from left to right almost as if obeying a law of nature."

True enough, there is no shortage of examples. You could hardly swing one of P. J. O'Rourke's Brooks Brothers neckties without hitting a public intellectual whose ideological life followed that path. Writers particularly spring to mind—possibly because members of this tribe have a biological need to inflict their opinions on people, all the more so if their opinions are newly acquired. The late Michael Kelly, alternative-press reporter turned liberal sacred-cow tipper, and the feminist-turned-feminist-scold Christina Hoff Sommers both fit that description. But there is no more vivid example than the journalist and editor David Horowitz, who morphed from hard-leftie to hunter of the left.

Horowitz had impeccable leftist bona fides. The son of lifelong Communists, he was chummy with Eldridge Cleaver and Huey Newton, and he edited and wrote in the 1960s for the influential *Ramparts*. He remained a committed leftie until age forty. But gradual disillusionment (at one point he and a friend decided to vote for Reagan, then sat down and tried to figure out why they'd made that decision, and it wasn't immediately obvious) set up a tipping point that came when his old buddies, the Black Panthers, murdered a close friend. It was a punch in the gut that punctuated, with emotion, a conclusion he was coming to intellectually. "I had believed in the left because of the good it had promised," he would write. "I had learned to judge it by the evil it had done."

Horowitz has since completed the turn. A conservative pundit and strategist, he has come not only to denounce the hard left in whose circles he once traveled, but has spent plenty of energy ferreting out their alleged crimes. (Horowitz has published the names of academics whom he claims are mere liberal propagandists, and to promote his most recent book he traveled around the United States visiting campuses to expose "liberal bias.") He calls his shift a "conversion," and it's tempting to try to read it as the story of the ideological journey of his generation. But it could just be one guy's grasp for a solution to a private life that was in turmoil.

Former hippies gone right are also thick on the ground in the environmental movement. Earth First! cofounder Dave Foreman came to denounce radical action; former Sierra Club director Ron Arnold became the environmental movement's worst nightmare. (Among his recommendations: cut down remaining old-growth forests on public lands, and open all national parks to mining and oil drilling.)

So, too, does a left-to-right move seem to accord with people becoming Christians. Now there's nothing *inherently* conservative about Christianity (there's a good case to be made that Jesus would be a Democrat, or even a Naderite)—but many Christians, especially those who settle near the fundamentalist end, stake a clearly conservative position on the main social issues of public debate—gay marriage, abortion, monogamy, and so on. In a rapidly polarizing America, the born agains, swinging right, have passed the secularists going the other way. And the two sides are out there beating the bushes—the right looking for converts, to paraphrase the writer David Reiff, and the left looking for victims to enlist to the cause.

There's even a fairly compelling argument as to *why* left-to-right should be the natural way to go. Human beings resist uncertainty. The philosophies of secular liberals are all about uncertainty—about trying to hold competing opinions in the brain, nonjudgmentally, without your skull exploding. Eventually, that becomes impossible, and the former liberals drift toward religious and political orthodoxy to resolve the tension. Several high-profile post-9/11 political swings seemed to have been catalyzed by a feeling of vulnerability that left the turners searching for stronger Daddies than the ones heading up their side. If that's true, we might expect more turns to the right, in an age when the bogeymen can no longer be thought of as "over there," but, rather, have breached the walls and entered the building.

But hold on. There are other ways to think about ideological turns that cast quite a different light on the issue. For one thing, let's get the facts straight on the numbers. Jonah Goldberg's assertion that, on life's turnpike, there's no ideological traffic to speak of from right to left is patently untrue—as evidenced from the apparently increasing incidence of defections from neoconservatism.

Two prominent former neocon authors, in particular, have described a moment of clarity akin to waking up in a strange hotel room next to someone they neither feel any attraction for nor, frankly, recognize. In both instances, the moment came as they listened to speeches by people they thought were fellow travelers.

For Michael Lind, a former editor of the neocon journal *The National Interest*, which helped map the course of Reaganism—and just generally a baby-faced Conservative It Boy—the wake-up call came inside the Houston Astrodome, at the 1992 Republican National Convention. Lind stood listening to the concession speech of Pat Buchanan, who had been the pick of one of Lind's favorite mouthpieces, *National Review*. A true conservative. But Buchanan's words were bracing, and not in a good way. It was a hateful speech. Buchanan called for a "cultural war" and a "religious war." He came down hard against homosexual rights and abortion on demand and women in the military. He stood against "the amoral idea that gay and lesbian couples should have the same standing in law as married men and women."

As he listened, Lind felt a creeping revulsion—and a deep sense of foreboding about the party whose colors he was flying. If this was the guy of Lind's people, what did that say about Lind's people? What did it say about Lind himself? Minutes later President Bush invited Pat

Robertson to join him in the presidential box, and Lind's epiphany was complete. There, before him, was the proud alliance of "callous plutocracy and crackpot fundamentalism." Then and there, at field level in a kitschy sports arena, Lind concluded that conservatism, so promising in the '80s, had now been co-opted by far-right "kooks," by "cultural and religious extremists." The implications for public policy were profound. Lind saw, in a new way, the Religious Right as a puppet of the Republican Party—and, it seemed, vice versa. None of this was anywhere he wanted to be.

Lind had moved in his heart, you might say; now he had to formalize the shift. He attacked Buchanan in the lead op-ed of the *New York Times* the next day. Then he pecked out a long essay he called "The Death of Intellectual Conservatism," marched over to the leftist journal *Dissent*, and dropped it over the transom. The moment it left his fingers, Lind became, for all practical purposes, a different man. Because now he was publicly yoked to the views of this essay, which, upon its publication, almost immediately plucked the strings of the zeitgeist. (The essay is still talked about as a turning point for a generation of disillusioned neocons.) Lind called Pat Robertson an "energetic retailer of anti-Semitic libels," the overclass a huge problem, and neoconservative leaders morally corrupt. He would go on to write a book called *Up from Conservatism*, which predicted that "for the foreseeable future . . . the honorable name of conservatism is likely to remain the property, in the United States, of shifting coalitions of libertarians, racists, medievalists, Protestant fundamentalists, supply-siders, flat-taxers, isolationists, gun fanatics, anti-Semites and eugenics theorists." So cleanly did Lind break from his former self—his affiliations, his passions, his roots—that he roasted conservative stalwarts William F. Buckley Jr. and Irving Kristol—two men who once gave him jobs.

Francis Fukuyama's moment came much more recently. It was February of 2004, and this time, playing the role of Pat Buchanan, was Charles Krauthammer. The political columnist (known widely for his longtime back-page byline in *Time* magazine) was delivering the keynote address at the American Enterprise Institute in Washington. Fukayama, the respected author of *The End of History* and darling of the neocons, listened as Krauthammer not only defended the Bush administration's lone-wolf, kick-butt-then-take-names foreign policy toward what he (Krauthammer) called "the new existential enemy, Arab-Islamic Totalitarianism." Krauthammer framed it as a kind of moral duty to bring this evil enemy—really no different from Fascist Germany and Japan—to the ground.

Fukuyama was appalled by what he heard—and then more appalled still when the lecture was greeted not with the stern silence he expected, but with hearty applause. These were his people? He left with his head in a whirl. And, almost immediately he began writing a book that publicly announced his recantation, and a certain low-level dread for the immediate future: *America at the Crossroads: Democracy, Power and the Neoconservative Legacy*.

(If there's a pattern here, it's that the new generation of neocons are using the return portion of the ticket their forebears bought. The original neocons all started out on the left, became disillusioned, and traveled over to the right.)

These two gentlemen are by no means the lone wagons in the leftward migration.

Consider Edward Luttwak, the former Republican military strategist who so convincingly preached the philosophical wisdom of massive arms buildup that Ronald Reagan would come to call him his "most trusted advisor" (and liberals would come to call him "crazy Eddie"). Luttwak delighted in goading lefties, peaceniks, Communists, and generally anyone opposed to an unfettered free market as naïve and stupid. But his guns are now pointed at the right. He has savaged European left-centrists like Tony Blair for betraying their socialist roots, and called the United States "a capitalist nightmare, a grim warning to leaders seeking to unleash free-market forces in their own countries."

David Brock, a young conservative author who was commissioned to do a literary hatchet job on Hillary Clinton (as he had done on Anita Hill), found he couldn't when he got to know her. Brock wrote a hymn to Hillary instead, and then, in case anyone missed his reversal, published a book called *Blinded by the Right: The Conscience of an Ex-Conservative*.

And there are plenty more. More than simply the odd exception that proves the rule. It *could* be that, as Howard Gardner suggests, we notice *all* the right-to-lefters because each of them is a Man Bites Dog story, whereas the left-to-righters vanish into the wallpaper because their turn is the expected one, the cliché—so the apparent parity between the sides is deceiving. But there certainly *seems* to be healthy representation from this tribe. A whole passel of disaffected neocons, once-rising stars of the New Right.

You could say that neoconservatism lends itself to flips: It's a well-defined position that has an almost exact analog on the left. The political scientist Shadia Drury calls neoconservatism the "new Marxism." Both are "made up of a set of very simple ideas that can be understood by people who are non-professional, non-philosophers, and that explain everything that is wrong with the world." That certainly makes neoconservatism sound like something one grows *out of*, not *in to*.

Just so, liberals would say. And they might even invoke a classic argument of John Rawls, which we will explore further in the next chapter, to support the idea that right to left is the natural direction to move. Rawls believed that "a communitarian concern for the economically disadvantaged should take precedence," and indeed is a kind of moral impulse. "Given the uncertainty of life, you will be inclined to want a society in which the lot of the worst off—of the poor, of people defeated in war, of women, of servants—is as good as it can be," said Martha Nussbaum, a professor of law and ethics at the University of Chicago. "Self-interest itself, via thought about shared vulnerabilities, promotes the selection of principles that raise society's floor."

And out you go into the world to vote for Nader or tithe to Oxfam or protest the more heavy-handed rulings of the WTO.

To the Berkeley linguist George Lakoff, conservatism and liberalism represent opposing paradigms: the Strict Father versus the Nurturant Parent. These are metaphors we ourselves deploy, he believes, but unconsciously and reflexively, and in good faith. (Each side thinks its strategy is the way to promote moral behavior.) To Lakoff, a move from left to right, from liberal to conservative, isn't a natural evolutionary step; in fact, it goes *against* the natural grain of things. Conservatism is about discipline and denial, the morality of punishments and rewards; liberalism is about empathy—a human emotion of the highest order. The conservative model "contradicts what we know about how the brain works." As most people grow older, wiser, and better informed, our thinking becomes *postformal*—more nuanced, less inclined toward absolutes. Which suggests we should drift toward, not away from, liberalism as we see through conservatism's false economy.

It's no accident that Lakoff assigns a male gender only to the conservative character, which embodies the traditionally male trait of the ruggedly individualistic conqueror. The liberal character, what the psychologist David Baken calls a "communal" archetype, is more traditionally female, embodying the lover, the caregiver, the friend, the ritualist. You could say that the move from right to left is the shift from a more localized concern—for oneself, one's family, one's immediate community—to a more universal concern for the species, which some developmental psychologists would say *is* the natural order of things. In time, the rugged individualist matures, learns empathy, and joins the human race.

If the left-to-right migration tends to be a gradual turn—that familiar, decades-long softening of the hard ideologies of youth—right to left is more likely to be a true reversal, a relatively sudden change resulting from the changer having seen the light.

The screenwriter David Milch once made the analogy between this kind of shift in perspective and the breaking of an addiction. The U-turn performed by addicts who come clean is that they, in effect, stop looking in, and start looking out.

"The first time I shot up, the guy who was my dealer said, 'Heroin's gonna give you everything, but you're gonna have to give everything to heroin,'" Milch said. "That's true. The precondition of the addictive sensibility is you're alone; it's you and the dope. So it's a constricting perspective. And it's a great blessing to be released from that." Milch reflected on why addiction counselors advise the newly clean to take the message into the community. "The reason is not to get people into the tent. It's because the act of generosity is what keeps you fit against the distorted perspective of disease, which is isolation." (And, of course, a biologically necessary one: A species can't survive without a fair degree of interdependence among its members. "Communities of loners," as writer Mark Singer put it, "tend not to be around very long.")

There is a school of psychology that holds that men, as they mature, become less libertarian and more communitarian. Less concerned with the right to be left alone (the "morality of noninterference") and more concerned with the responsibility to help others—to perceive suffering and alleviate it. Less wedded to a rigid code of moral conduct and more flexible and situational in their moral judgments, as morality becomes less a rule book and more a story.

Men become, in other words, more like women.

Supreme Court judges in North America, it has been widely noted, seem inclined to drift leftward in their jobs. When the ostensibly wisest among us just naturally become more liberal as the odometer turns, it's inviting to conclude that some basic law of human development is at work. That liberal compassion is the natural product of a judge's job—prolonged exposure to the world's injustices, and the required habit of squeezing into the shoes of folks on all sides of every dispute. The buck-stops-here nature of the job of a Supreme Court judge is an interesting crucible for a level of truth, as demonstrated through action, that most of us could never approach. If you knew your vote was the last hope for addressing some persistent social inequality, wouldn't you at least lean in that direction? (Of course we cannot make these claims without picking a fight. One popular, somewhat cynical theory is that isn't because there's anything inherently wiser about liberalism that Supreme Court judges go left; it's because none are so independent-minded as to escape the need for approval and even love, especially from the liberal opinion-makers they might find themselves passing the vinaigrette to next Saturday night.)

It becomes clear why the game is rigged. You can always build a case that your new tack is the morally correct one, the best for all concerned in the long run—and even keep a certain appearance of continuity and consistency. The crying baby solution, in our case, seemed to expose a problematic conservative drift in a couple that always considered itself pretty liberal. But we could reconcile it like this: Letting the baby cry is a shift toward thinking of the needs of *the family as a system.* The circle of moral consideration expands from one tired person to three. The aggregate level of happiness increases, Mom and Dad can function in the morning, and the baby, who will learn within a couple of nights to soothe herself back to sleep, pops up like toast the next morning blissfully unaware that there was ever a problem.

And maybe there never was.

SEVEN

The Change of Heart

Emotion as a Turbine of Transformation

Compassion is a two-way street.

—**Frank Capra**

Abe Bonowitz, director of Citizens United for Alternatives to the Death Penalty—a grassroots abolitionist group—was once militantly *in favor* of the death penalty. He reveled in the chance to debate the issue from the pro–death penalty side, in being a thorn in the side of the abolitionists. Bonowitz was by nature strong-willed and opinionated, and he was sure he was right on this one, for a couple of reasons.

Growing up Jewish in Ohio, he learned about the Holocaust when he was a young boy, and developed the gut-level belief that people who commit horrific crimes ought to suffer the same fate: an eye for an eye. At the same time, he was being taught that the American justice system, perfected over a couple of hundred years, *is* just, its principles sound, its outcomes largely defensible—and those ideas together created a powerful cocktail. (Bonowitz remembers one day when he was about ten watching TV with his dad. "There was a story about a guy who'd just been sentenced to death. And they came back to the anchorman, who said: But of course he won't be executed for years. And I remember saying to my Dad, That's crazy. They ought to take him out and shoot him in the morning.")

It was not an opinion shaped by any personal experience (even into young adulthood "My only connection with the legal system was getting the odd traffic ticket, which I deserved," he says), but it was deeply felt, and he carried it through into early adulthood, where he was known to stand in public forums and opine that the death penalty was eminently practical: both necessary and fair. "The United States has the best justice system in the world," he'd say, "and if that includes the death penalty, fine with me. I'll pull the switch myself."

But then one day a member of Amnesty International challenged Bonowitz to make his case. Prove the abolitionists wrong—don't just weigh in with opinion.

Bonowitz had no professional interest in any of this (he worked in the graphics department of AT&T in Columbus, and had attended his first Amnesty meeting out of curiosity only), but he took up the challenge and began carefully building something like a professional brief: reading the pro-death-penalty literature, speaking with fellow supporters on the issue, boning up on the intractability of certain psychoses, the economics of executions versus lifetime incarcerations, the deterrence research.

And then something happened that knocked him sideways. At an Amnesty International conference in Minneapolis in the late-'80s, he took a seat in a lecture hall to hear a man named Michael Andress speak about the death penalty. And Andress, Bonowitz recalls, "dropped a fact that blew me away" "He said, 'If you're planning to kill somebody in Ohio, just don't do it in Franklin County, Cuyahoga County, or Hamilton County, where the urban centers are. Those are the only counties with a big enough tax base to afford to pay for a death-penalty prosecution.'" (Which is much more expensive than a non-death-penalty prosecution.)

"That shook me," Bonowitz says. "It made me realize it's not about the severity of the crime, it's about geography and money and politics and race." Suddenly, the big plank on which his argument rested—the justice system is sound—seemed to give way. "In that lecture hall I literally jumped from one side of the fence to the other *on the question of practicality*," he says. "I realized, okay, I can no longer agree with the system as it presently exists." Bonowitz amended his position. "If we can improve the system so that it's fair and equal, then I'll still pull the switch myself; until then, we can't be killing anybody." It was still not a moral issue to Bonowitz, and not really an emotional issue.

That would soon change. Bonowitz's real epiphany—the event that completed his U-turn—came when he attended a workshop put on by a group called the Journey of Hope from Violence to Healing in Indiana in 1993. The group is made up largely of the families of murder victims, and one by one he heard their stories. A man named Bill Pelke described how he watched his grandmother die a hundred times. She had been murdered, and her accused killer, a fifteen-year-old girl named Paula Cooper, was on death row—and every time the news came on, he saw his grandmother's body being wheeled out of the house. Others spoke plainly about how no amount of killing was going to bring back their loved ones, so why put others through the same pain they had come to experience?

"That's when my heart changed," Bonowitz said. "My head had already told me, there's a problem here, but I hadn't really come to understand the collateral damage. Meeting these people, seeing the pain in them, I realized it was no longer about the numbers or questions of fairness—the death penalty creates a whole new set of victims, and that is not right."

Not right. Not "not practical," but "not right." The discourse had shifted onto moral ground.

"And that's when I began to call myself an abolitionist. That's when, for the first time, I could in good conscience say, I believe the death penalty must be abolished, worldwide. Government can't be trusted with the power to kill."

Bonowitz's conversion was twofold. An intellectual shift started the turn, and an emotional one completed it. When we most recently spoke, he was walking the talk—or at least driving it. He was on a cell phone half an hour outside of Bryant, Texas, in a 2000 Dodge Grand Caravan towing a trailer that said No More Killing on one side and Stop Executions Now on the other, on an endless speaking tour of the gymnasiums and churches of the heartland of the killing states.

U-Turn

The Ten-Billion-Nerve Knot

In the hierarchy of mind shifts there lie, at the bottom, simple decisions: quickly made judgments—the bus instead of the car one morning, the cabernet with the fish—that won't bring down the roof if you get them wrong. And then, higher up, there are the kinds of cognitive transitions the novelist Nicholson Baker describes as more like the slow accretion of conviction, the abandonment of something you used to embrace under the weight of a million "nearly insignificant complaints." There is feeling in these cognitive shifts, but it's amorphous and twinkly and weak and swamped by the surging of the neocortex as you assimilate, and accommodate to, new beliefs.

At the top of the pyramid lies something different. Something swifter and grander and more completely transformational. At its core is a strong emotional component that makes the phenomenon as least as much a change of heart as a change of mind.

The Hindu word for faith, *sraddha*, means "almost without equivocation, *to set one's heart on*," notes Wilfred Cantwell Smith, the late Harvard professor of comparative religion. One commits to the position, in other words, and, thus committed, "lives loyally, with life and character being shaped by that commitment." Fierce devotion to a position you have arrived at by faith sometimes produces a *credo* that, whether silently repeated like a prayer or shouted from the rooftops, serves as a sort of moral guide. The word *credo* "is a compound of *cor, cordia* (heart), plus *do* (put, place, set, and also give). Literally, then, again: 'I set my heart on.'"

In Charles Baxter's novella, *Believers*, the hero, a Catholic priest named Father Pielke, is exposed to some things that defeat his spiritual resolve, and he turns in his collar; he becomes a teacher, marries, has kids, and never feels God move in him ever again. (The story is told from the point of view of the son, who is essentially trying to investigate why his father's U-turn occurred.) It becomes clear that the catalyst was a trip to Weimar Germany, where Father Pielke witnessed events that kindled his animal passions in different ways. He saw a woman publicly beaten and humiliated for having slept with a Jew, and then he himself, Father Pielke, was the victim of a seduction attempt by a beautiful,

134

conniving American woman. These events brought him down to earth and made him vulnerable to the priesthood-breaking romantic advances of the woman—the narrator's mother—who was waiting for him on his return.

The son tries to piece together the actual mechanism of the turn. "My father had now seen a woman beaten. He had heard her cries for help . . . This woman, now, was all he needed for an image of the soul."

Without emotion, a lot of U-turns simply wouldn't happen. Emotion brings to the U-turn equation the necessary, irrational leap of faith. Because, on paper, at least—if you simply weigh the pros and cons of reversing course, disavowing your old life and burning bridges behind you—performing a U-turn often looks like madness. If our left brains ruled exclusively, no one would act on a radical impulse to turn; we would talk ourselves out of it. The lawyer Clarence Darrow was once asked why he persisted in taking on clients who, while probably innocent had little hope of beating their rap. He replied, "Because my intellect hasn't caught up with my emotions yet."

The Harvard psychologist Howard Gardner calls this sort of thing— the impulse to accept a certain course of action, even knowing, perhaps, that it flies in the face of one's better judgment—*resonance*. An idea or plan resonates "to the extent that it feels right," it "seems to fit the current situation, and convinces the person that further considerations are superfluous."

Of all the reasons we change our minds, reverse course, construct ourselves anew, resonance is one of the least understood. But it is arguably a more powerful lever than reason. You could give a logically watertight speech, but if it doesn't have that intangible emotional component, if it doesn't strike some intuitive chord, you'll likely bring few skeptics around to your point of view. But the opposite happens all the time; people are routinely persuaded to change their minds by resonance without logic. If I told you at a dinner party that in the next century tobacco will kill a billion people, you still might not think twice about quitting smoking. But if I brought along to that dinner party my pal Murray, who had survived throat cancer, and you watched Murray drink his wine via a straw through a hole in his throat, you might go cold turkey on the spot—and pester every smoker you know to do the same. (Even though one poor guy's fate ought not to be as logically persuasive as sheer statistical probability.) One theory for why conservative American judges appear to go soft during their tenure on the bench more often than conservative European judges is that the American judges find themselves staring into the tears and woe of real people. Many European countries allow decisions to be made—the constitutionality of this statute or that to be tested—based on theoretical principles alone. But U.S. law says federal courts must decide on actual disputes. So American judges, day in and day out, face the bald facts of true stories of suffering by folks who put flesh and blood to abstract social injustices. What judge in these circumstances could be entirely dispassionate? And maybe more to the point, would we really want one who was?

In religious conversions, and religious deconversions, emotion—not reason, not research—is almost always the direct catalytic agent. "The promptings of one's own heart convince one person to return to her faith, another to shift to a new one, a third to become an agnostic or atheist," says Gardner.

But to some degree secular U-turns, too, operate on the principle of a leap of faith. Just about all the U-turns discussed in this book have some element of resonance. At some point, no matter how much hard cogitating on the matter has occurred, the turn simply "feels right" to the turner. This is one of the things that distinguishes a U-turn from a run-of-the-mill revision of one's thinking. Eventually, the heart kicks in.

Where exactly resonance comes from isn't well understood. But the idea of "gut knowledge" that your life must change isn't an empty expression. Scientists sometimes refer to the knot of nerves in the stomach, a couple of inches below the navel—the densest concentration of nerves outside the brain—as the body's "second brain." Many Eastern cultures depict this little bundle of nerves as a kind of spiritual organ. The Japanese refer to the region as *hara*, the place where, during meditation, energy and awareness conjoin, the body is gentled into equilibrium, and tremendous life force is generated. You could think of it as the place where what the Harvard theology professor and Presbyterian minister James E. Loder calls "convictional knowing," or "conviction beyond reason," is ignited.

The Change of Heart

Not long into his practice as a clinical psychologist in Fife, Scotland, Tim Carey began to be struck by a similarity in the language his clients used to describe their problems. When they talked about the specific conflict—they wanted to be able to go shopping without a panic attack, say, or cut down on binge drinking—they conveyed a sense of being impeded. What was impeding them was another side of themselves. "It's very common for people to describe struggling or arguing with themselves or being involved in a 'tug of war,'" Carey told me. "People have also told me it's like they have two sides or two different parts of themselves that are fighting." A self trying to win social approval and another self trying to be "true."

Carey came to believe that perceptual conflict—the various sorts of "living a lie" that so many U-turn stories exemplify—is at the root of just about all enduring psychological distress that prompts people to consult guidance counselors, life coaches, and psychiatrists. That's why such people seem to be resistant to pure cognitive therapy, which tackles problems rationally to reveal the faulty logic at their core, he thinks. For these, the toughest nuts to crack, when people are truly *stuck*, Carey concluded that a purely rational approach won't work, no matter how impeccable the logic the therapist deploys. And that's because, for people juggling both a private and a public self, John Wemmick–like, "there's no logical way to gain approval and speak your mind at the same time." For as long as this situation exists in the head of an individual they will feel torn.

Because we cannot simply reason our way out of this kind of trouble, the only way forward is by adopting a solution that *bypasses the intellect*, he believes. (The technique he came up with is called the Method of Levels, based on the premise that all of us, all the time, have things we're aware of and things we're processing only semiconsciously at best. A therapist alert to the cues that a "background thought" just hovered on to the periphery of awareness can seize the moment, ask the right question, and step down into the heart of a client's real concerns.

"I just had a feeling," we say, when responding to what our gut is telling us, but what we really mean is, "I had an emotion"—for a feeling is just a label we put on the emotion that came first, reflexively. Emotions happen; we can't stop them any more than we can call off a flinch. They're simply our body reacting to the environment via a complex set of chemical and neural responses. Feelings are our *interpretation* of those signals. (My heart is racing and the context is ominous, therefore I *feel* scared.) Feelings are the brain churning to turn inchoate emotion into "images"—the whole process happening just at the threshold of consciousness. (Emotions don't directly cause behavior. What they do, as the psychologist Roy Baumeister once put it, is "push and pull the mental apparatus around, so that people notice what is important and adjust their behavior so as to function more effectively." More precisely, Baumeister added, "emotion operates by directing attention to important issues and problems.")

"Like geological upheavals," writes Martha Nussbaum, "emotions mark our lives as uneven and uncertain, prone to reversal." It's that very quality of emotions, indeed, that long tagged them as hindrances to sound judgment: Emotions can lead to prejudices, some charge. In general, you'd really rather have your heart surgeon or a bomb defuser's work unclouded by worry or depression or even joy.

But that notion has been radically revised in recent years, as emotions are now coming in for a fairly profound reappraisal and are gaining renewed respect. After decades of dominance by behaviorism, and the ascendance of evolutionary psychology—the premise that we are all robotically following genetic and neurochemical instructions that benefit the species—emotion, once considered purely noncognitive and thus too primitive to be worth much study, is elbowing its way back into the scientific discourse.

"It's clear that a lot of time, people make decisions on gut feeling," says Edward Bowden, one of the Northwestern University psychologists who mapped the "aha!" moment. "A friend of mine, some years back, was trying to choose between these two careers, and he was sort of waffling between the two. So he methodically made a checklist of the pros and cons of each. And the idea was to get a mathematical weighting and then make a rational decision. And he did the math, and figured it all out. And then he switched careers—to the one that had *fewer* pros and *more* cons. His rational weighing didn't matter much, in the end. He went with his gut."

"Brain science is increasingly appreciating the centrality of emotions as guides to life," said Cal Tech neurologist Steve Quartz, "and emotions are typically more in line with one's wishes than rational deliberation." (Quartz calls this the "law of primacy of feeling.") "The upshot: Deliberation is cheap, emotions are honest."

In his book *Descartes' Error*, neurologist Antonio Damasio describes a group of patients who suffered damage to a particular part of their frontal lobe—the orbitofrontal cortex, behind the eyes—that governs a certain class of emotions but has little role in cognitive function. Patients who have suffered damage there, making them purely rational beings, become not better at decision making, as you might expect, but worse: in fact, useless. They couldn't make even the simplest of decisions.

Damasio's better-known confrère, Oliver Sacks, recounts the story of a judge who suffered brain damage that stripped him of all emotion. It might seem as though this would make him an ideal judge: His rational thinking was unimpeded. But he himself didn't see things that way, and he resigned from the bench. He realized that he "could no longer enter sympathetically into the motives of anyone concerned—and that since justice involved feeling, and not merely thinking, he felt his injury totally disqualified him."

What emotions do, as the neurologists are now proving, is "provide [us] with a sense of how the world relates to [our] own set of goals and projects," as Nussbaum puts it. "Without that sense, decision-making and action are derailed." That's why the emotional component of a U-turn shift seems so important. It's the activation of emotion that gives us the big-picture perspective, helps us prioritize what's important—and *then* we can act.

You could say that emotions are themselves a kind of judgment. When we hear from them, they are reporting some kind of deficit, a "neediness or lack of self-sufficiency"—in a way that our logical left brain is not nearly as well equipped to handle.

The neurologist V. S. Ramachandran's work with his anosognosia patients—the ones who, because of damage to part of the right neural hemisphere, refused even to acknowledge bald facts about their own circumstances—suggests an extraordinarily important role for the right hemisphere in insight-driven change. For Ramachandran, what began as a localized investigation of a quite rare affliction grew into something much more profound: an unexpected trip "right into the heart of human nature." His patients were living embodiments of denial. True, it was cartoonishly exaggerated in these patients, but the denial was unmistakably the same force that all of us battle daily, whether we are just ignoring our in-tray or "denying the finality and humiliation of death." (Or keeping at bay nagging and unsettling doubts about the course our life has taken.) The right hemisphere, the steward of emotion, is also the keeper of an important kind of global intelligence. Clearly, the intuitive mind is not to be trusted with the *only* set of housekeys (neuroeconomists have determined, for example, that gut instinct, trying to protect us, makes us more averse to risk than it is strictly rational to be). But we lock it out at our peril.

All this amounts to the biggest revision of the theory of emotions since the Stoics weighed in. Emotions do not "push," blindly, like mole rats moving dirt. Instead, they "pull." There is intention and direction and purpose to them—and, according to Martha Nussbaum and others, that purpose is relatively lofty. Emotions concern themselves with human potential, "one's own flourishing or one's important goals and projects"— the living of a complete life. In other words, emotions are trying to tell us something about *what we ought to be doing*. Gandhi spoke often of how, at important moments, his "inner voice" would pipe up, with its decisive counsel. His strategy, writes Erik Erikson, was to make that inner voice "'hold its breath' for a while," to give him time to study the facts. More often than not, the facts bore out what the intuition knew all along.

Early Christians often distinguished between "conversion of the intellect" and "conversion of the heart." The implication was that conversions preceded by a lot of plodding intellectual spadework (St. Augustine's, for example) are somehow less touched with grace and therefore less powerfully authentic than those that happen suddenly and blindingly to doubters on the road. But epiphanies, of whatever sort, involve both intellect and emotion. It's *how* that particular gin and tonic is mixed that's up for debate.

The Change of Heart

To hear some U-turners describe their experience, it would seem that the head precedes the heart.

Conservative senator John McCain pulled a couple of surprisingly abrupt policy turns in recent years—most notably on the environment. For years he maintained his steadfast skepticism that the environment was in much jeopardy—though he continued to gather research on the subject. As incoming data began to paint a progressively darker picture, he held the line, routinely earning a failing grade from environmental groups, whom he stonewalled. Then a few things happened in his life: He moved to the Southwest, to a ranch near Sedona, where the desert sunsets moved him to announce he had stumbled on "the most beautiful place on Earth." He struck up a close friendship with a liberal Arizona congressman and staunch environmentalist; he got to know some of those mosquito-in-the-tent activists; and at one point, while attending a rally at Dartmouth during the presidential primaries—McCain's "coming out" moment as an environmentalist—he invited one of them up onstage, raised the man's hand overhead, like a boxing referee pronouncing the victor, and pledged to act on climate change. (He did.)

But more often, as U-turners describe their journey, precisely the opposite seems to happen: The heart precedes the head. They feel, first and foremost, and then the rational mind gets involved as the arbiter of which among those powerful instincts and emotions to honor, and what they might mean.

Michael Ignatieff, the former Harvard professor turned Canadian political aspirant, had just such a moment. On a trip to Ukraine (his heritage is Ukrainian and Quebecois), Ignatieff went to visit his grandfather's grave, only to discover that a butcher had been using the slab to cut meat on. The desecration hit him in the gut.

Up to that point, Ignatieff, as befits a coolly detached modern intellectual man of the world, had scorned the small-minded, internecine tribalism that nationalism represented, championing instead a kind of postnationalism, a borderless humanitarianism where ideals are important but things—possessions, land—aren't.

But in that moment he became a defender of nationalism. He understood why people were willing to die for their land: to keep strangers from tramping on their ancestors' memories.

"Land is sacred because it is where your ancestors lie. Ancestors must be remembered because human life is a small and trivial thing without the anchoring of the past. Land is worth dying for, because strangers will profane the graves," Ignatieff says. At his grandfather's cryptside, he realized that coolly detached academic magnanimity was, in fact, the luxury of privileged Westerners from stable democracies who had never been oppressed or threatened with the erasure of their past. "Looking back, I see that time in the crypt as the moment when I began to change, when some element of respect for the national project" crept in.

(Ignatieff is scorned by many leftists who see him as a turncoat, having become hawkish on a couple of important fronts: support for the Iraq war and an apologist for torture under some circumstances.)

The critic Terry Teachout experienced a similar about-face, not on a point of moral philosophy, but on a piece of art. The work was *L'Allegro, il Penseroso ed il Moderato*, a stage version of Handel's oratorio, and widely considered to be the masterpiece of the modern-dance choreographer Mark Morris. But it did nothing for Teachout when he saw it performed at Lincoln Center, and he panned it in the *New York Daily News*.

A few years later, Teachout ran into one of Morris's dancers, and he sheepishly admitted that he just didn't *get L'Allegro*. She nodded, without malice, saying, "Don't worry: You'll experience it fully in the future." The gall!

But she was right. When *L'Allegro* came to the Brooklyn Academy of Music a couple of years later, Teachout saw it again. And this time, he was astonished. Sitting there in the dark, a question occurred to him about that first exposure to the piece: What was I thinking?

Of course, that was just it: He was *thinking*.

Teachout had written that first review from his head, which was not quite equal to the job. And then his heart checked in.

The next time *L'Allegro* returned to New York, Teachout reviewed it for the *Wall Street Journal*. His piece, this time, was really a mea culpa, explaining that he'd been wrong in just about every possible way about *L'Allegro*, before the scales fell from his eyes. "I was too dense to know a masterpiece when I saw it." *"L'Allegro,"* he would conclude, is "a whole world of dance in a single evening." In the piece, Teachout talked about other mistakes he'd made in the past, when his powers of comprehension were not up to the work he was charged with judging, and an essential paradox of the job of the critic emerged. The critic is asked to pronounce, in a newspaper of record, on a perhaps-ageless piece of art. The target is fixed, but the critic is moving, growing more mature, his perception sharpening. He may have an entirely different response in a year's time. But the paper goes to bed tonight.

The critic needs to marshal her most astute judgment; and one thing is clear: If she relies on her rational mind alone, she's going to be sorry.

Kurt Andersen, who had Teachout on his public-radio show to discuss the aesthetic about-face, said he thought leading with the heart is the instinct of good critics: "They respond emotionally to something, and then they try to figure out why they like it."

"Right," Teachout replied, and he told a story about Hans Keller, the Austrian musician and musicologist. There was a term Keller liked to invoke, a term coined by the jazz musician Thelonious Monk: *ugly beauty*. "As soon as I detest something," Keller writes, "I ask myself why I like it." It's ugly beauty that's present in many true chef d'oeuvres— off-putting at first and then finally, once you struggle and punch through—more beautiful than anything you could warm to immediately. Before the highest of art, it would seem, the heart is somehow a more reliable guide than the head. It's only through the heart that you *get* "ugly beauty."

The conscious mind is the last one in the room to know: That seems to be the story with most U-turners—and it corroborates a theory of emotion hatched more than a century ago and still widely accepted. The James-Lange theory, named after the two scholars (William James and Carl Lange) who stumbled on it, independently, in the 1880s, says that in matters of emotion, the body precedes the mind—not the other way around. In other words, we spontaneously react, and then look for contextual clues to put a name to what it is we're feeling. (William James came to his insight after running into a bear in Alaska, and his aha moment boiled down to this: "I am running from this bear; therefore, I must be afraid.")

Communication between the "two brains"—the one in the head and the one in the gut—moves both ways, but the conversation is so complicated we haven't yet begun to understand it. What we do know about emotion is that its role is ancient and elemental, designed to keep us alive. When it detects that it needs to take action—because a radical adjustment is required in a system that has fallen out of balance—the body releases hormones and neurotransmitters, and we *feel* something. What we experience as "feelings," then, are our wake-up call to a problem, writes Antonio Damasio, *"that the body has already begun to solve."*

Of the almost unlimited palette of emotions human beings are heir to, scientists have singled out six as the primary, or "universal" emotions—and each of them is a candidate to catalyze a U-turn in people who are prepared for one. (The emotions are happiness [or awe], sadness, fear, anger, surprise, and disgust.) But it would appear that, as far as U-turners are concerned, the mother of all emotions is one that doesn't make the short list—perhaps because it is not so much a primary color as a complex blend. That emotion is compassion.

The Empathic Shift

Ancient Buddhist philosophers—who *did* put compassion near the center of the mandala of virtues of the "noble-minded man"—called it *Jen* (sometimes translated as "human-heartedness"), and they defined it thus: The ability to identify with the joys and troubles of others as if they were one's own.

"Compassion is the natural response of the heart unclouded by the specious view that we are separate from one another," writes the American Buddhist teacher Sylvia Boorstein in *It's Easier Than You Think*. It is an emotion strong enough, she believes, to effect "permanent character change [in those so prepared]."

Buddhists obviously have a heavy buy-in to compassion. But even the hardheaded atheist philosopher and neuroscientist Sam Harris allows that love—compassion's close relative—when deployed, creates a huge ripple effect of social benefit that simply cannot be dismissed. "There is a circle here that links us to one another: we each want to be happy; the social feeling of love is one of our greatest sources of happiness; and love entails that we be concerned for the happiness of others," Harris writes in *Faith No More*. "We discover that we can be self-ish together."

Compassion is connected to suffering in the following way: The more we ourselves have suffered, or anticipate suffering, or are able to identify with the sufferer, the more compassion we will feel. Martha Nussbaum makes the point by evoking Rousseau's *Emile*: "Why are kings without pity for their subjects? It is because they count on never being human beings."

It is in the shift from feeling invulnerable, like those pitiless kings, to suddenly feeling vulnerable that's at the heart of many U-turns—and it's one of the reasons major catastrophes like the 9/11 attacks or South-Asian tsunamis tend to trail U-turns in their wake: Those who have been spared feel connected to the victims by virtue of a newly kindled sense of common vulnerability. What follows from *that* realization—or should follow, according to Aristotle—is that we're inclined to help people in the future.

"Where there would be room for guilt," in such an instance, "is if we *didn't* make an adjustment," said Nussbaum recently. "If we just went on buying our SUVs," carrying on our reflexive consumerism. That is, if we didn't allow ourselves to be moved, and changed. Moved to, as Nussbaum put it, "do something to make people less vulnerable in fu-ture." That might mean a change in our own life to reflect this new level of outward-lookingness, this new level of compassion.

Aristotle believed compassion is generated in a three-step process. Without all three components compassion cannot be ginned up, but *with* them compassion is inevitable.

It begins when we notice someone in distress.

The first condition is to recognize that the distress isn't trivial. (Or, as Aristotle put it, the suffering has "size.") This person before you is really hurting.

The second condition is to believe the distress is undeserved. That is, nothing they did, no action or even character flaw, provoked it. It seems to have just been terrible bad luck. (This, as the sociologist Candace Clark has pointed out, is related to the idea of "belief in a just world," which is thought to be a prerequisite to sympathy. You must perceive that bad luck has happened *to a worthy person.*)

The third condition is to understand that the "possibilities open to the sufferer are also open to us." We must, in other words, be able to identify to some extent with the sufferer's life. You might call this the "There but for Fortune" effect. Once you can feel, with the late folk-singer Phil Ochs, that "There but for fortune may go you or I," you have developed the skill to climb to a different level of morality. ("Misfortune is the great leveler," the Jewish mystic Simone Weil once said. It's not that all of us are miserable, but that each one of us might be.)

A classic example is what apparently happened to Che Guevara: A privileged medical student traveling cross-country unexpectedly becomes a class traitor and joins the revolution after seeing the way the lepers lived. In a stroke, he flips from Stoic—in the classic sense of unattached and self-contained—to fiercely, hopelessly engaged.

The story of Dave Dellinger, the Chicago Seven member who became one of the most prominent activists of the twentieth century, offers a more contemporary example. When Dellinger, in later life, pondered what had brought him to where he was—just where a life born of privilege and apparently destined for conventional bourgeois success went awry—he concluded that a pivotal moment occurred during his stint at Yale, following a football game. The students and the "townies" frequently clashed at these events, and on this night Dave and some friends were swarmed by some local toughs. Dellinger drove his fist into the face of one of them—and then, as he looked at the guy lying on the ground, experienced almost overpowering revulsion at what he'd done. At the animal violence that the heat of this tribalistic moment had provoked. What had just expressed itself there, shockingly involuntarily, was a part of himself that must not be allowed to get loose again, Dellinger understood. It was in him, as it was in everyone, but it must be tamed. This was not an intellectual decision. The emotional impact of the moment was so strong that he could hardly do otherwise.

"The lesson I learned," he would later write, "was as simple, direct and unarguable as the lesson a child learns the first time it puts its hand on a red-hot stove. Don't ever do it again! But the pain I felt was a spiritual pain, as if I had suddenly emerged from a fit of anger and realized that I had pressed a child's hand on to the stove. I knew that I would never be able to strike another human being again." (Dellinger didn't walk away from the man he'd clobbered. He stayed by his side, apologized at length, and then walked him home.)

Of Aristotle's three conditions, number 1 is fairly straightforward; we might expect that pretty much everyone who saw the survivor of an accident or misfortune deal with the fallout would recognize that the victim's distress was real. It's easy to be persuaded that another person's suffering, even if it's trivial to you, has "size" for them. (Personal-injury lawyers routinely move juries in this direction, by bringing them into the world of the sufferer, whose—Nussbaum's example—minor lip injury has killed his career as a professional flutist.)

A few more potential compassionistas will fall away at condition 2—the question of whether the sufferer "deserved it." In America, particularly, there is luck culture and blame culture, and little gray in between. Americans, Nussbaum suggests, can't be a little bit deserving or undeserving. They are blameless and therefore pitiable, or they are at fault. So there's a fair chance that this condition—blamelessness—won't be fulfilled.

But the chain breaks for many observers at condition 3, what Aristotle called the *judgment of similar possibilities*. Simply put, the observer just can't empathize with the sufferer. They can't imagine suffering a similar fate themselves. (And there are many ways to imagine that one might be immune.) As we gain empathy, as we learn to take others' perspective—to view them not just as body but soul, appreciating their desires and feelings—those people are drawn into our "moral circle." And once that happens, social scientists have repeatedly shown, we become more likely, when we see those people in distress, to step in and help. Conversely, the circle shrinks when we fail to consider the internal life of a person or people—when we "dehumanize" them.

In November of 1960, Amnesty International founder Peter Benenson conceived of a new way of thinking about human rights protesting. He had long been an activist at an abstract level, defending particular philosophies, crusading for particular issues. He was a politician, really. And then, almost overnight, his focus shifted to the fine grain. He started to see—really see—the individuals at the heart of the causes he was championing. And he understood that his former perspective—the view from space, essentially—was never going to gain much ground on the world's problems. The answer lay in the faces of these individuals.

The moment of insight came one day while Benenson was riding the subway in his native London, and reading the *Daily Telegraph*. He came across the story of two Portuguese students who had been dining privately in a Lisbon café, and had raised their glasses to liberty. Someone at a nearby table saw and overheard these two men, and reported them, and they were jailed. The little scene was so vivid that Benenson could see it, could feel it—and the specificity of this particular injustice stirred him in a way he had rarely been stirred. (It "produced a righteous indignation in me that transcended normal bounds," Benenson would later write.) He got off at the next stop and went straight into the Church of St.-Martin's-in-the-Fields, there to sit for an hour in a pew pondering what to do. How to organize individuals who might feel the same kind of indignation he was feeling, and effectively channel that wrath. He put together a protest to get the Portuguese students freed—even as he began more broadly to formulate a World Year Against Political Imprisonment. Benenson's relatively newly discovered need to serve had found an outlet. The protest became a movement—one extraordinarily effective in drawing attention to human-rights abuses by organizing campaigns around individual prisoners of conscience.

The origins of the poet Gary Snyder's activism can be traced to a hike one day in August of 1945. He had climbed Mt. St. Helens, reveling, on the summit, in the thin-air high. When he descended back to Earth, he landed with a thud. The bulletin board in the lodge was plastered with the news that atomic bombs had just been dropped on Hiroshima and Nagasaki. There were numbers—an estimated 150,000 dead in Hiroshima alone—and there were pictures: aerial views of the blasted city, captioned with a scientist's blunt estimate that "Nothing will grow there again for 70 years." It did not take a poet's soul to inhabit, in that instant, the world of the survivors: The moral circle of everyone who read the news that week no doubt swelled, if only for the time it took to read and digest the information. But Snyder turned the feeling into a commitment, to force the circle open.

"I swore a vow to myself," Snyder would write of that moment. "By the purity and beauty and permanence of Mt. St. Helens, I will fight against this cruel destructive power." And he did.

To say that the Peter Benenson who got onto the subway that November day was a different person than the one who got out off it, and the Gary Snyder who came down from Mt. St. Helens was different from the one who went up, sounds true only in the figurative sense. But the kindling of compassion is a concrete shift, a *measurable event*.

Specific things happen in the brain when our moral circle widens. So-called "mirror neurons" fire; these neurons respond to the imagined suffering of others, generating actual feelings of suffering in ourselves. (The Clintonian "I feel your pain" is less platitudinous than it seems.) What has been called the "empathy circuit," a particular pattern of neurological firing that snakes through several brain regions and amounts to the very signature of compassion, comes alive. Not long ago the neuroscientist Richard Davidson and his team of researchers at the University of Wisconsin's W. M. Keck Laboratory for Functional Brain Imaging and Behavior provided the best-ever look at the empathy circuit at work. Davidson recruited as research subjects Tibetan monks hand-picked by the Dalai Lama. The monks were instructed to meditate themselves into a state of what Buddhists sometimes call "loving-kindness"—a nonspecific love-spam to the whole sensate world—while sensors on their scalp recorded micromovements of blood flow, closely linked to brain activity. (One of these monks graced one of the more striking covers of *National Geographic* in recent memory.) What was most interesting about the brain scans, to those who knew what they were looking at, was the surge of activity in an area of the cortex where "behaviors associated with obtaining goals" are born. This is an area very sensitive to emotion—in this case the urge to help. "It is," as the science writer Sharon Begley put it "as if the monks' brains were itching to go to the aid of those in distress."

It's worth noting that compassion—a deep, painful emotion—is not the same thing as empathy, which might be described as "thinking yourself into the skin" of the one who is suffering. The key distinction is this: Compassion consists not in imagining *yourself* suffering, as a Method actor might, but in imagining *the other person* suffering. In other words, when it's not about you, and you still feel it, that's compassion. But empathy and compassion are related in the sense that the first is almost a prerequisite for the second. It would be rare to have compassion without first having empathy. And empathy often begins with a sense that this person is like me—the third tumbler in Aristotle's lock. (Jesse Jackson, who was famously sympathetic to drug addicts, partly attributed his strong feelings to having suffered a brief addiction himself—to prescription painkillers following surgery. "Why am I so sympathetic and empathetic?" he said. "Because I was trapped for a moment myself.")

Perhaps the most important of what Sidney Rittenberg calls the "nodal points" in his life came in 1942, mere weeks after he landed in China with the American forces. Rittenberg's language skills—honed in the labs of Princeton—enabled him a more intimate involvement in the local culture than most American soldiers, and he soon found himself involved in the life of a poor rickshaw driver named Li Ruishan.

Li's only daughter had been killed; a drunk U.S. Air Force sergeant, returning with a hooker from a nightclub bender, had run her down in the night. It was Sidney who was charged with delivering the compensation check to the family. Li's wife, it turned out, had actually watched the jeep drive over her daughter; after that night, she never spoke again, and died soon after. "She was all we had," the small barefoot man told him in a barely audible whisper. "Our life is nothing."

The compensation check was for a mere $26—the amount the army deemed appropriate for the loss. Li accepted it with deep gratitude, and only reluctantly. Not long after Rittenberg had returned to the barracks, the rickshaw driver appeared, having made the trip on foot. He had $6 he wanted Sidney to take, "for all his help."

Something inside Sidney Rittenberg shifted then. To him, Li represented a whole vast underclass that needed saving. Arriving in China, he had had no particular investment in the cause of this country or its people—he had frankly hoped the war would end soon so he could travel a little and come straight home. Now he knew he wasn't going home. He couldn't. He had passed through a door from which there was no going back.

"When human beings are born, they're not yet genuinely human, I believe," Rittenberg told me. "They have to go through a kind of transformation. When suddenly—or gradually—we become aware of the fact that you are responsible, for our own life and, as far as we are able, for the best interests of others. There has to be a point at which we *commit to being a member of the human race.*"

You could think of that particular point, that shifting instant when we "join the human race" as a change in the way we measure our own progress.

In the "before" condition, we measure our flourishing against others in our tribe: How am I doing compared to my neighbor? We are as oblivious to the larger context, the implicit costs to some foreign stranger of our every lifestyle decision as "a tall pine tree is oblivious that it flourishes at the expense of smaller trees in its shade."

In the "after" condition, we come to measure our progress against the progress of everyone, everywhere—or else we stop "measuring" progress altogether.

Rationalizations "consist in lies that the privileged tell themselves," the British philosopher Simon Blackburn writes. "And we have already conceded that a life lived amidst lies, or in a fool's paradise, is not a flourishing life. So the ingredients are all there to suggest that real flourishing or true human health implies justice. It implies removing the oppression, and living so that we can look other people, even outsiders, in the eye."

I thought I understood the story of Michael Allen Fox, the philosopher who wrote the book defending animal experimentation until a logical conundrum forced him to overturn his own conclusions nine months later. But there's a dimension to Fox's turn that didn't become clear to me until our third or fourth correspondence. Fox's recant was not as clinically rational as I'd first thought. It was at least as much a change of heart as a change of mind.

As soon as *The Case for Animal Experimentation* hit the shelves, a couple of philosophers Fox deeply respected pounced on an inconsistency. Fox came off in the book not as a scold at all, but as generous-spirited—toward both the animal-rights side and the experiments that were the book's central argument. He seemed to be trying to have it both ways, which discredited him, in his colleagues' view, as an advocate for either the scientists or the monkeys.

The charge of hypocrisy forced Fox to reverse-engineer his arrival at his conclusions, back to where the idea for *Animal Experimentation* began. It began, interestingly enough, where it ended—with Peter Singer.

A decade earlier, when Fox was the editor of the university magazine *Queen's Quarterly*, Singer's own book, *On Animal Liberation*, had come across his desk for review. The book set forth the case that a new social-justice struggle had emerged, in the tradition of feminism and abolitionism. This struck Fox as bizarre, and misguided. He panned the book in an editorial. Singer wrote a rebuttal, to which Fox responded. And the jousting match that ensued became the heart of Fox's book, with Singer acting as the foil.

But now, the criticism forced Fox to reexamine with fresh eyes those original thought experiments he had initially dismissed. This time around, they had the effect Singer had intended.

There had been another powerful critic of Fox's book: The woman he was seeing at the time, a staunch feminist, "pretty much trashed it," he says. Fox claimed in the book a kind of native dominion for man over animals. Well, didn't men used to claim the same prerogatives over women? The whole thing had become quite personal at a difficult time in Fox's own life, when his defenses were pregnable, his heart vulnerable.

Fox now hauled up into full consciousness something of which he had only been vaguely aware. "There is no such thing as looking at something in an emotionally detached way," he thought. "It became increasingly clear that I had been untrue to myself, that I had been playing the philosopher's game of supposing I was a rational being above all."

He felt chastened. And at the same time, oddly free. Free in something like the way Sartre talked of the kind of "inner freedom" that follows radical conversion and a major life change. In that low moment, light really did get in. "I was reminded that being true to oneself is the

The Change of Heart

most important task," Fox told me recently, when I asked him to try to reconstruct his thinking in that moment twenty years ago. "Perhaps that sounds trite and shallow, but it is accurate, so far as I can tell."

Fox has now moved to Australia, home of Peter Singer—the strict libertarian who, ironically, helped Fox's compassion jump the species barrier. As the scriptwriters would have it, Fox's apparent nemesis turned out, in the third act, to be a "philosophical friend" who had the greatest impact on his view of the world.

EIGHT

The Kandinsky Decision
Why People Don't Turn When They Really Should

Like a man restored from death, there stood Henry Jekyll.

—Robert Louis Stevenson, *The Strange Case of Dr. Jekyll and Mr. Hyde*

"Why did the chicken cross the road?" is a good question. "Why *didn't* his companion cross the road?" is a better question, if only because it's less predictable.

If you're asking the first question, then you belong to what's known among change theorists as the "persistence" school of human development: Inertia reigns, stasis is the norm—indeed more and more so as we calcify into middle age. The persistence school forces us to explain why those who change do so. But a competing school assumes that change is natural, and that it's persistence that's the real puzzler.

How is it that latter-day Jobs, caught in war zones or natural-disaster sites, beset by wave after wave of misfortune—enough, you'd think, to turn any believer into a doubter—hold fast? What accounts for Traudl Junge, Hitler's secretary, remaining loyal to her boss until the end, and indeed failing even to perceive that there was reason to question his judgment? Yasir Arafat, in the face of overwhelming, and apparently quite natural, pressures to do so, never made the necessary shift from guerrilla to statesman—arguably at great cost to his people. The demonstration of the power of the atomic bomb turned a number of scientists who had been committed to developing nuclear weapons into peace activists on the spot. ("It should have ended war," said one such scientist,

154

the Canadian nuclear physicist Norman Alcock.) Under the circumstances, *not* to have undergone such a shift was, you might say, abnormal, even dysfunctional. But plenty of people didn't.

Why not? "If you said to me, what's the single reason that people fail to change minds as often as we would like, it's underestimating the power of resistance," says the Harvard psychologist Howard Gardner. "Changing your mind about anything significant by the time you are middle-aged is difficult because you have had decades of practice in thinking another way." In order to overcome that old, ingrained way of thinking, "we really have to undo those neural networks and move them in another kind of way." Which explains why children are much more likely than adults to change what they think about the world. It's not entirely because they're impulsive, or immature, but because they can: Their brains, plumbed with billions of connections that neural Darwinism has thinned in the rest of us by adulthood, are just more "plastic."

That most of us would really rather not change our minds is, then, something of a design flaw in the human brain. Basically, we tend to agree with what we already believe—no matter what the facts say. We feel better believing what we already believe. The economist John Maynard Keynes's cold-blooded declaration that "If the facts change, I'll change my opinion," *sounds* reasonable, but in actual fact if someone has a deep conviction, showing him bald evidence that his belief is faulty serves not to weaken that belief but, paradoxically, to strengthen it—a phenomenon psychologist Leon Festinger famously discovered in the 1950s. (Festinger was studying how members of doomsday cults behaved when their prophecies failed. After the deadline passed without incident, Festinger observed, the members rationalized away the apparent refutation of their belief, and, in fact, stepped up their proselytizing.) Festinger, who coined the phrase *cognitive dissonance*, observed that when our beliefs collide with the objective facts, we're overwhelmingly inclined to throw out the evidence. Or at least to reinterpret the facts so as to protect the belief system. "Human beings engage in the most amazing mental gymnastics to justify their hypocrisy," Festinger said.

Indeed, the ability to confront one's own hypocrisy honestly, and subsequently to be prepared to trash a faulty belief system, is assumed to be so rare that people who possess it are too few and far between to make a decent sample to study. "We don't have any data on such people," Elliot Aronson, the social psychologist, told the writer Lauren Slater when she asked him about that. "The vast majority of people," he said, "hang on to their beliefs until death." (The eminent UCal Berkeley psychologist Jack Block told me more or less the same thing. "The individuals who suddenly change the structure of their lives are a rare lot," he said. "Even rarer are those who reverse what they have done so long. The personality transformations in which you are interested cannot really be scientifically studied.") That, then, places U-turners—the ones who didn't drink the Kool-Aid in Jonestown, so to speak—in the minority, but it doesn't quite get to the reason why. Neural design flaws and the human need to save face are obviously only part of the answer, since, as we've seen, some people do manage to surmount them, and change their beliefs radically in adulthood.

Know Thyself

To burrow more deeply, it's important to consider that there are two distinct components to the enterprise of turning a life around: The first is perceiving a need to change, and the second is, having perceived the need, actually carrying out the act of changing. The first, you might say, is an internal shift, and the second is an external shift. If either component is missing, nothing happens that the world can observe. The scoreboard does not change.

In an essay about George W. Bush, the writer Philip Gourevich cast light on the process. "Because Bush does not appear able to recognize his own errors, much less admit them, he is incapable of self-correction." Gourevich was talking about Bush's use of language—those magnificent malapropisms known as Bushisms that continue to issue from the presidential mouth. But the same point holds more broadly. The president, whose chief political strategy has been "making a virtue of rigidity," in Gourevich's estimation, has a hard time changing his behavior not because he lacks the courage to do so, but because he doesn't see the problem. The equation never even gets to phase 2.

The two constituent parts of a morally driven U-turn—self-awareness

156

and the royal jelly, once you have perceived what needs to be done, actually to do it—are analogous to the two main components of an authentic "conversion," according to the early Christian church's sacrament of penance. That first phase, the self-awareness, was what was sometimes called *contrition of the heart*. The second phase, the actual moral "reform," was *contrition of the mouth*. (Originally, that meant taking your confession to a priest, but now generally means taking it to the media.) According to Christian doctrine, a strange alchemy happens when those two components are in place; it becomes a spiritual event.

It's appealing to look at the first component, the perception of a problem with the life we're living—radar for cognitive dissonance—as an innate trait. But that's not necessarily right. While some of us seem more sensitive to our shifting internal landscape, there's evidence that we *all* got a good set of moral radar at birth. Each of us has an intuitive ability to make "strong evaluations" of which ideals and goals are most noble, as the philosopher Charles Taylor put it. If that's true, then each of us has the capacity to intuit that something is wrong—the first step in U-turning, and maybe the most important step. "You can't get out of jail," as R. D. Laing put it, "until you know what you were in for."

But such self-knowledge doesn't come easily—especially during the times of crisis when it's actually needed. In such moments it's hard to be objective about our own shortcomings—because our judgment is too clouded to know if our judgment is clouded. The prepared mind will presumably be more receptive to a catalytic moment, will "get" it, where others will miss it—or where we ourselves would have missed it at an earlier time in our lives.

Some people are plainly more introspective than others. But self-knowledge can be cultivated. In general, says Taylor, the more self-knowledge you acquire, the stronger "self-evaluator" you become, the more likely you are to cobble together a life that aligns with your "true nature."

Without self-awareness, the gears of a potential U-turn don't turn, even when we are wildly off-track. (When hypocrisy is unconscious, it isn't really hypocrisy, because we aren't even aware of our faults.) The moment self-awareness dawns is when the cognitive dissonance kicks in. Now you, the U-turner, have become the proverbial adulterer stoning the adulteress—the hypocrisy as yet undisclosed to others but known to yourself. What has happened, says William Ian Miller, is that you have crossed the threshold from fool to knave—which is to say, from self-deception to deception. Now, Lucy, you have some 'splainin' to do—to yourself.

At some level the U-turner in such a position realizes that the life he's living, while not without its payoffs, is not sustainable. He is in what David Perkins, who studies creative breakthroughs, calls an Oasis of False Promise. An oasis is a resting place, not a destination—but leaving it, once you've decided you should, takes real courage on the follow-through.

Joseph Conrad called this quality of courage "facing it": the degree to which we are able to stand there looking at an almost unbearable truth about ourselves is, Conrad believed, "the very nature of integrity." George Orwell was profoundly moved by Conrad's idea of "facing it," as distinct from denying a painful incongruence or even merely acknowledging it intellectually: The resolve that such a response takes, the *power* it requires, explains its relative rarity. (Orwell had himself been in circumstances—notably cracking down on dissent as a member of the Indian Imperial Police in Burma—where "facing" the contradictions in his own character was required, and he recalled how difficult it had been.)

Andrei Sakharov, the father of the Soviet hydrogen bomb, began to have deep misgivings about nuclear weapons after seeing the horrible health problems suffered by people in the test zones. He also knew that publicly expressing these misgivings was going to bring all sorts of grief down upon him. After much deliberation (history shows that the catalyst to this decision to go public—to shoulder the consequences come what may—was his wife, Elena Bonner), he came forward and began to actively campaign against nuclear weapons. For his candor, he ended up imprisoned for seven years in Gorky.

The Quaker writer Parker J. Palmer calls these "Rosa Parks decisions." They say, in effect, what Rosa Parks says she came to understand on that Montgomery bus: "I will no longer act on the outside in a way that contradicts the truth that I hold deeply on the inside. I will no longer act as if I were less than the whole person I know myself inwards to be."

The Kandinsky Decision

The two branches of the decision tree, in a Rosa Parks–style U-turn, are "go-along to get along" versus "hang-it-out-there-come-what-may."

Going Public

Clearly, our beliefs aren't like light switches that toggle on and off. There are gradations in the degree of commitment with which we believe in things. You could say that simply agreeing with something binds you to it less strongly than believing in it—since belief implies that something more than simply the intellect has been engaged. And private belief, in turn, binds you less strongly to it than some public declaration of it.

It's about the point when people start proselytizing that they tend to get dubbed fanatics. (Eric Hoffer, indeed, called proselytizing a "hallmark" of the fanatic.) But by the standards of some ancient philosophers it's incumbent on you, if you really believe in a cause, to proselytize—the idea being that *We have a duty to prevent unnecessary suffering, once we understand that we can.*

This progression of commitment into a sense of social duty is common among artists and scientists when they become politicized. The shift is one from small-picture thinking—literally necessary for someone whose life is lensed through a microscope, and must make order from the world found there—to big-picture thinking, and the obligations that come with thinking of yourself, and everything you do, as part of that bigger system.

In 1955, there circulated within the scientific community a document often called the Pugwash Manifesto. It had been hatched at a conference in the Nova Scotia town that gave it its name, where concerned nuclear physicists from East and West had convened to discuss how to rid the world of nuclear weapons. (Pugwash might well have saved the world. Out of those talks would eventually come all the important test-ban treaties of the next decade.) The manifesto's principal author, Polish nuclear physicist Sir Joseph Rotblat, anchored it with one impossible-to-forget injunction to his fellow scientists: "Remember your humanity and forget the rest."

What Pugwash called on the signatories to do was repudiate the legitimacy of the very thing they had devoted much of their life to creating. Effectively, Rotblat was asking his colleagues to make the turn that he himself had made. Rotblat was part of the British team on the Manhattan Project, and few in Los Alamos had a more personal motivation to see the Allies develop the bomb than he; when the Nazis invaded Poland, they took his wife away to a concentration camp, and he never saw her again. But Rotblat struggled with the implications of the work he was doing, and, late in the war, quit the Manhattan Project on moral grounds.

At the time, high-level atomic physicists and academics tended to live and work in a bubble of pure science—blindly devoted to research, living and breathing equations—an utterly interior, amoral existence. Pugwash challenged that notion; Rotblat's argument was that precisely *because* scientists understood the technical implications of their work they had a social duty to take a public stand.

Over the following years and decades, the spirit of Pugwash seemed to inspire ostensibly apolitical groups to consider the broader impact of what they were doing—to join the human race in this new respect. Even if you weren't building nuclear weapons. Even if you were only, say, making advertising.

The signatories of the First Things First Manifesto were graphic designers who had become increasingly uncomfortable with the direction their profession was heading, given its growing power. (If poets are the unacknowledged legislators of the world, graphic designers are the unacknowledged behavioral scientists, for whom the whole world is a Skinner box.) They called for radical change in the way graphic designers think about what they do, who they do it for, and why. Published in 2000 (actually as a more relevant update of an original document written thirty-seven years earlier), the manifesto sliced to the heart of a key debate: Is advertising value-neutral as many claim—simply the long-haul cab that hitches to any freight company that will pay the way? Or do ad professionals—writers, graphic designers, filmmakers—have a moral obligation to be concerned with the underlying political questions? To take a stand by not promoting "harmful" industries like cigarettes, arms, and so on.

The Kandinsky Decision

"We propose a reversal of priorities in favor of more useful, lasting and democratic forms of communication—a mindshift away from product marketing and toward the exploration and production of a new kind of meaning," stated the First Things First Manifesto. The signatories included industry heavyweights like Milton Glaser, Jonathan Barnbrook, Rick Poyner, and the late Tibor Kalman. (The manifesto, it must be said, did not produce the hoped-for mass mea culpa in the industry. Either because it came off as too preachy, or because it pushed buttons designers were not ready to have pushed, it seems not to have been taken all that seriously.)

The progression in commitment of Howard Lyman, a fourth-generation cattle farmer from Montana, was typical of U-turns that involve social justice. After Lyman was diagnosed with a cancerous tumor in his spine, and he became convinced that meat was the culprit, he simply stopped eating meat—at first. But when explored the issue further, and came to conclude that factory-farmed meat was exposing the world to a potential new pandemic of disease, a simple private commitment no longer sufficed. With a newfound moral imperative—*We have a duty to prevent unnecessary suffering, once we understand that we can*—a quiet man was compelled to take his message public. (He went as public as public gets, appearing on *Oprah*, and so moving the host that she was prompted to say, "I will never eat a hamburger again.")

In this context—if you genuinely believe you can prevent suffering—full commitment is a virtue and dragging your heels almost a vice. Recently, the neuroscientist Sam Harris made the argument that well-meaning people who take moderate positions in the face of harmful extremism are, in their apparent tolerance, only promoting intolerance, and thus deepening the suffering of others. He was talking about religion—specifically, those religious pluralists who defend religious fundamentalists of all stripes, imagining, as Harris puts it, "that the path to peace will be paved once each of us has learned to respect the unjustified beliefs of others." (Of course, the people who hold those fundamentalist beliefs look upon their own proselytizing as moral, since it is aimed at preventing the unnecessary suffering, and possible damnation, of others—and thus they have a duty to prevent it, if they can.)

As U-turners experience an escalation in commitment, two different

161

tipping points come into play: The first concerns one's own change of mind, the second the willingness to announce that change of mind publicly and live with the consequences. They contain, between them, some of the most difficult work of a lifetime.

"To face ourselves, that's the hard thing," says the con-man imposter, Paul, in John Guare's *Six Degrees of Separation*. "To make the act of self-examination bearable, we have imagination." He is standing in the Upper East Side apartment of a self-absorbed couple called the Kittredges, in front of their big Kandinsky painting, which turns out to be double-sided. One side is unbridled and wild and flamboyant, the other muted and contained. One side is chaos; the other control. The Kittredges have been hanging the Kandinsky chaos-side down. Paul, an utterly charming liar who has passed himself off as the son of Sidney Poitier, turns the painting dark-side out.

The great fear at the heart of all excavations for the Truth is that we might not like what we find.

This is what the psychoanalyst Marion Woodman may have been getting at with her answer to the question, Why are some people spiritually curious and some not? Those who aren't may simply be, congenitally, disinterested. But it's equally possible that they're avoiding the whole issue out of fear—or at least prudence. They may understand, at some level, what work lies ahead, what difficulty and risk lie on that path.

Assuming that a moral dilemma about our life has penetrated our consciousness, that it's sitting there in front of us like a fish on a plate, the decision to turn or not to turn often comes down to weighing our reputation against the truth. When our reputation becomes more important than the truth, we become, in the psychiatrist M. Scott Peck's phrase, "people of the lie"—and that tag has been applied to whole communities (like the Catholic clergy in the eighties, largely ignoring the pedophilia problem in its ranks). The poison, in these circumstances, Peck used to say, "is in the culture, but it's in all of us."

John Gabriel Stedman, an eighteenth-century British seaman, worked as a crew member on the slave ships plying the West African Coast. To the ire of his employers, Stedman reversed his allegiances and, in sympathy with his captives, wrote a book outlining the appalling treatment of African slaves by Western Europeans, a book that became a cornerstone of abolitionist literature. But it took Stedman a long, long time to wake up to the injustice happening all around him.

Stedman had joined a military expedition to quell a slave rebellion in Surinam. The diary he kept during that time reveals a hale, hard-drinking fellow, possessed nonetheless with a sharp eye and great sensitivity, as well as a grasp of the Creole tongue of the slaves, which he took it upon himself to learn—all in all, a credible, effective, and persuasive bearer of witness. But the culture of cruel, husbandrylike containment of slaves had become so engrained in the culture that it was hard even for someone as obviously compassionate as Stedman to see anything particularly wrong with it. Stedman's diary itself is almost surreally matter-of-fact about astonishing cruelties. Here is an excerpt from the entry from April 17, 1774:

> A Negro infant lately drowned for crying, and a Negro forced to jump into boiling sugar, who died. A Negro was lately shipt to death on this plantation. I beat a negro for deserting. I mess along with the officers.

Stedman would often interweave detailed descriptions and sketches of local plants, berries, and fish with accounts of crippling brutality: The effect is one of almost autistic emotional detachment. Over the five years of his slave-ship missions, Stedman began to more deeply grasp the full perspective of the dehumanizing injustice (toward that end, he even cut his hair short and expressed pride, with his bronze skin, in looking like a mulatto)—and the damning memoir he eventually wrote attests to the moral U-turn he made. But slavery was so deeply entrenched that people resisted seeing it as anything but a turbine of the economy.

In the years since his release from prison in Communist China, Sidney Rittenberg has thought long and hard about what delayed his rejection of Maoism. Why did it take him so long to figure out he was on the wrong road?

"There were two reasons," he told me. "The first was a kind of 'I told you so' pride." He could hear a little voice in his head, his mom's, saying, *You'll grow out of it*—a phrase she had deployed, hopefully, when he joined the radical student movement as a teen, and again when he started working with trade unions and cotton-mill workers. *It's just a stage he's going through.* And he would be damned if she was going to be able to say the same thing about the cause he had committed his adult life to, which was not the kind of thing you grow out of, like a pair of pants.

The second was another kind of pride. He didn't want to be thought of as a traitor. He knew he stood accused, by his fellow Communists, as the kind of kid (comfortable, middle-class background) who was likely to sell out the cause. To sell out was the worst thing you could do, in Sidney's mind, and he vowed never to do it. Even though others were.

"I knew at the time that many prominent intellectuals who were in or close to the Communist movement in the States, when the going got tough—like after the Soviet-German nonagression pact—the prominent intellectuals began dropping off one by one. And on a lower level, in our school, these kids who were very active one minute, when they became frightened or angry and dropped off, they suddenly didn't believe in racial equality or civil rights. They lost it all." Sidney wasn't that kind of kid—he was *consistent*, come what may. He'd literally gnash his teeth at the thought of selling out. "My hatred of turncoats prevented me from being able to examine my own basic premises," he said. "I could be critical of everything else, but I never allowed myself to have the slightest doubt."

Sidney Rittenberg's ideological stubbornness was grounded in deep emotion. And the paradox of the role that emotions play in change is that, while they often trigger a moment of insight in the end, at first they delay it. And delay it. "The more one has emotional attachment to a view, the harder it is to change," Howard Gardner told me. "I would have a much easier time changing my mind about the origins of the universe than about child rearing or financial planning or the existence of God."

If Isaac Newton hadn't been so committed to a belief in God, he might not have been stumped for so long by the problem of gravity, many now believe. Newton was flummoxed by how celestial bodies manage to exert such influence on each other from such great distances. He could only reckon (having previously thrown out the theory of a sort of "interstellar ether") that God Himself must be pulling strings up there. Newton's conviction "that God could and would intervene in the running of the universe," notes Anthony Storr, "prevented him from considering other possibilities and thus brought his enquiries to a halt." Similarly, had Darwin not abandoned his Christian faith (after the death from tuberculosis of his beloved ten-year-old daughter, Annie,) the same thing would very likely have happened to him—he might have resisted the idea of evolution. As it was, the overturning of faith made room for the full play of his mind.

John Clausen, the late sociologist from the Berkeley Institute of Human Development, boiled down to three factors what determines to what extent we're likely to change our lives (for the better): circumstances, motivation, and resources. What's in our way, how much we want out, and who's around to help.

Sometimes the people who are around to help aren't helping very much; in fact, they're part of the problem. In other words, the behavior we're trying to break is socially sanctioned. It's considered "normal," while the behavior we have a strong feeling we should be doing is strongly discouraged. "You're not allowed to experience the sky as gray," as R. D. Laing put it, "if others view it as blue."

In a famous experiment undertaken in 1959, psychologist Solomon Asch proved how strong the pressure to conform is. So powerful is the desire for the approval of "the group" that we will often overturn the verdict of our own senses—what's right before our eyes, what our heart says is true—when the people around us believe the opposite. (Asch called this a "distortion of perception," as distinct from the distortion of action that can occur when you know your behavior doesn't accord with your beliefs, but you do it anyway to fit in.)

This noses around the edges of perhaps the most profound issue of the twentieth century. The point of Asch's work—and if you missed it, the point of the more explicit "obedience to authority" experiments of Asch's student, Stanley Milgram—was to try to understand how perfectly decent people could be persuaded to act, against their better instincts, in the most monstrous ways.

One of the most indelible figures in the Roman Polanski film *The Pianist* is a man who appears only briefly toward the end. Wilm Hosenfeld is a high-ranking Nazi officer and prison-camp commander who discovers the Jewish pianist Wladyslaw Szpilman hiding in the attic of a bombed apartment house in occupied Warsaw. To prove he is who he says he is, Szpilman slowly opens a dusty piano in the corner and plays Chopin's *Nocturne*. Whereupon Hosenfeld, his face kaleidoscopic with emotions resolving themselves, lets him go. Hosenfeld supplies Szpilman with enough bread and cheese to keep him alive till the end of the war—an act of generosity that's really an act of contrition by a changed, broken man. It's a deeply moving scene.

Hosenfeld was an actual historical figure. He had indeed been a committed Wehrmacht officer, loyal to Hitler; he did meet Wladyslaw Szpilman under pretty much the circumstances portrayed in the film; and he did perform a full about-face, scorning Nazism and rescuing Jews in ways more commonly associated with Oskar Schindler. Szpilman's piano solo may have hastened Hosenfeld's enlightenment, but it wasn't the reason for it. By the time he met the pianist, Hosenfeld had already nearly completed the turn.

His diary, written in a crabbed hand in two notebooks, and stored carefully away from the family until its publication in German, tells the story of the slow breakdown of his resistance to the truth, and the evolution of his shame.

Hosenfeld initially believes the Nazis' National Socialism is the only antidote to "Bolshevik chaos," and as late as 1939, when he is sent to Poland to run the prison camp at Pabianice, he has expressed few doubts about der Führer's vision. What he observes in occupied Poland begins to test his devout Christianity—and his ability to believe, at the same time, in both the legitimacy of his faith and the legitimacy of war.

By April 1942, Hosenfeld has a pretty good idea of what's happening at some of the camps. He has heard of mobile gas chambers, clothing stripped from the dead and sent to textile mills for reprocessing. There are rumors that "somewhere near Lublin, buildings have been constructed with rooms that can be electrically heated by heavy current, like the electricity in a crematorium. Unfortunate people are driven into these heated rooms and burnt alive."

It is simply too much to take in, so he doesn't. He can't.

"It is hard to believe all this, and I try not to, not so much out of anxiety for the future of our nation, which will have to pay for these monstrous things some day—but because I can't believe Hitler wants such a thing and there are Germans who will give such orders. If it is so, there can be only one explanation: they're sick, abnormal, or mad."

From time to time, Hosenfeld creeps up to the truth and then, unable to face it, backs away.

"If what they are saying in the city is true—and it does come from reliable sources—then it is no honor to be a German officer, and no one could go along with what's happening. But I can't believe it."

But the more credible the information Hosenfeld gets, the harder it is for him to dismiss it. The Polish greengrocer who sells Hosenfeld vegetables tells him what he has seen: Gestapo agents moving through the Jewish maternity hospital, plucking babies from their cribs, dumping them in a sack, and throwing them in a hearse.

Hosenfeld tries to circumscribe the damage: Perhaps it is "just a few lunatics" behind this casual brutality. "Have the criminals and lunatics been let out of the prisons and asylums and sent here to act as bloodhounds?" No, he concedes, "it's people of some prominence in the State who have taught their otherwise harmless countrymen to act like this."

The nation-shame that he has been experiencing evolves into a kind of species-shame as a scary truism asserts itself: There is nothing in any of us that isn't, to some degree, in all of us. "Evil and brutality lurk in the human heart. If they are allowed to develop freely they flourish, putting out dreadful offshoots, the kind of ideas necessary if the Jews and the Poles are to be murdered like this."

"Why did this war have to happen at all?" he asks in September 1942. "Because humanity had to be shown where its godlessness was taking it."

(It's a little astonishing that Hosenfeld's Christian faith has held up through all this. The familiar "Where is God?" question provokes the familiar answer: "God allows evil to come about because mankind has espoused it, and now we are beginning to feel the burden of our own evil and imperfections." If anything, his faith has grown stronger, as one belief system—in German Nationalism—has been replaced by an older, more powerful belief system—in a Christian God.)

Eventually, Hosenfeld observes a couple of Gestapo agents with whips returning from the ghetto, and has to restrain himself from pushing them under the wheels of a tram. His thinking has evolved from, "This can't be true" to "This is terrible" to "This *cannot stand.*" There is the sense from his diary entries now, in late 1942, that to do nothing would itself, at this point, be criminal. Hosenfeld is, or feels, alone with his conscience. And one thing emerges as most important: integrity. You have to live with yourself.

"Lying is the worst of all evils," he concludes. "Everything else that is diabolical comes from it. And we have been lied to; public opinion is constantly deceived. Not a page of a newspaper is free of lies, whether it deals with political, economic, historical, social or cultural affairs . . . The liars and those who distort the truth must perish and be deprived of their power to rule by force, and then there may be room for a freer, nobler kind of humanity again."

And so Wilm Hosenfeld moves, by late 1942, into the final phase of personal transformation: trying to find the avenue to change. How can the Nazis be stopped? He is convinced that an internal revolution can't work because "No one has the courage to risk his life by standing up to the Gestapo"; a military coup won't happen because the military has been decimated, "the army is willingly being driven to its death." Only individual acts matter.

Wilm Hosenfeld's diary was never meant for publication; there is no do-good impression management; it is simply the record of one man processing his emotions. Writing it took real courage: If it had fallen into the hands of the Gestapo, they would have, in the words of Wolf Biermann, the German poet and essayist, "taken him apart."

Rabbi Sheila Peltz once visited Auschwitz. As she stood before the gates, she wrote, "I realized that I never want to be as certain about anything as were the people who built this place." In that phrase is the kernel of a lot of complicated insights. (It is essentially where pragmatism came from, as a backlash against the horrors of Fascism and Communism.) It can be marshaled to defend U-turns: Behold the tragic consequences wrought by such utter, steadfast commitment to our current vision, philosophy, or belief system. On the other hand, a common criticism of U-turners is that they take up their new position with such unbending zeal that they seem as dogmatic as those "who built this place."

168

The Kandinsky Decision

Are U-turns more about certainty or uncertainty? I think they're more about certainty, but still more about faith. They say: I was fairly sure of my original position, it took a lot of bomb strikes to weaken and finally erode my position, and now I stand by my current position as the best possible fit.

A certain kind of philosopher would argue that U-turns could be prevented—that is, the *need* for U-turns could be eliminated—if people learned to fear uncertainty a little less. In other words, the kind of incremental drifting off center plumb that forces an eventual radical redefinition of ourselves could be prevented if we developed the skill of "facing" the uncomfortable tension of not knowing, and taking it apart for clues. The writer David Foster Wallace popularized the term *democratic spirit*, a combination of rigor and generosity whose ideal is simply the willingness "to look honestly at yourself and your motives for believing what you believe, and to do it more or less continuously." The ideal is something like pure intellectual integrity—which is not very realistic (more than that, it suggests a life spent in fear like the Zen initiate living in vague, perpetual fear of being knocked on the head with the monk's cane if ever he loses the plot and falls asleep in the meditation hall). But as an idea, not necessarily something to aspire to but something to consider, the democratic spirit gives shape to another way of living. A way that involves asking ourselves, at regular intervals, throughout our whole life, before things ever come to the point of the Big Required Correction: What if I'm wrong?

NINE

The Road to Damascus
Are Some Secular Turns Really Spiritual Events?

By night an atheist half believes in God.
—**Edward Young,** *Night Thoughts,* **Night 5**

L ee Strobel was an award-winning *Chicago Tribune* reporter who became the paper's legal-affairs editor. Almost as central to his identity, Strobel was an atheist. On the autumn day in 1979 when his wife, Leslie, announced, out of the blue, that she had become a Christian, Strobel's world got a lot more complicated. "I rolled my eyes and braced for the worst, feeling like the victim of a bait-and-switch scam," he would later write.

Strobel half expected his wife to morph, before his eyes, into a kind of distaff Boy Scout; it would be all community service and soup kitchens from here on in. He waited, silently furious. But it didn't happen. Leslie seemed, well, happy. At peace. More at peace, actually, than he himself. Clearly, she was not "content" in the way most of the Christians he used to know seemed to be content—benightedly, ignorantly so. She remained her brilliant self. And so what Strobel had felt as resentment began to change into something like envy.

He found himself scissored by competing forces. To accommodate his wife's new direction would mean, it looked like, recanting his current lifestyle and value system, the cynicism that had served him so well. (Plus how could he be sure that underneath the cynical guy there was anything at all? It would be like stripping away the paint from an original Robert Motherwell because you believe there's a long-lost Picasso beneath—a risk of everything.) On the other hand, his wife had gone *somewhere*, somewhere very much like oblivion; if Strobel made the leap as well, he'd get to see her again.

Strobel undertook intensive research. "I launched an all-out investigation into the facts surrounding the case for Christianity." It was the start of a spiritual journey that would last two years. He picked the Bible apart, verse by verse. He recalled, "I plunged into the case with more vigor than any story I had ever pursued," marshaling his Yale Law School training. And over time an unsettling feeling took root. He was like the proverbial juror a hairsbreadth away from voting the accused into the electric chair, who experiences a sudden rush of doubt. "The evidence," he says, "began to point to the unthinkable."

He laid out the "case" in the style of a legal apologetic, which would eventually become a book, *The Case for Christ*.

In retrospect, Strobel breaks his conversion process into three components: Believe, receive, and become.

Having convinced himself, on the historical record, to believe that Jesus is the Son of God who died for his sins, he next had to look for his own sins. They were easy to find. "The truth is that I had been living a profane, drunken, self-absorbed, and immoral lifestyle. In my career I had backstabbed my colleagues to gain a personal advantage and had routinely violated legal and ethical standards in pursuit of stories. In my personal life, I was sacrificing my wife and children on the altar of success. I was a liar, a cheater, and a deceiver."

Thus chastened, Strobel was ready for part 2 of the equation: Receive. Unlike other faiths he had examined, which required would-be converts to "do" something (pay alms, go on pilgrimages, work off karma from past misdeeds), Christianity "was based on the 'done' plan." The work, that is, has been done by Jesus on the cross. What is left, simply, is grace. And grace is "available to anyone who receives it in a sincere prayer of repentance. Even someone like me."

What followed, on that day of reckoning—November 8, 1981—was what Strobel describes as a "rush of reason."

And he slipped into the third stage: Become. "I knew from John 1:12—'The old is gone, the new has come'—that I had crossed the threshold into a new experience. I had become something different."

Strobel quit journalism. He became a teaching pastor at Willow Creek Community Church, near Chicago, and then joined the mighty Saddleback church in the same role. (The constituency for the new message is a lot hungrier than the constituency for the old. Where Lee Strobel the atheist reached perhaps tens of thousands through his newspaper column, Lee Strobel the believer now, through his books and Web site, reaches millions.)

As he deconstructs the process of his own conversion, Lee Strobel sounds a lot more like superattorney David Boies than pugnacious rabbi Saul of Tarsus—the paradigmatic Christian convert. And indeed, in its almost forensic attention to the workings of the machinery of the heart and mind, Strobel's story sounds utterly contemporary, a transformation tale for the age of reason. But, in fact, the story could have been ripped straight from the biblical scriptures. All the classic elements are present: the radical, 180-degree shift in perspective. The newfound beholdenness to the people you once, in a roundabout way, persecuted. The period of "blindness"—during which you are in a kind of nonperson limbo while your software is getting rewritten. The zealousness of the commitment to the new position. And perhaps, too, a vague sense of terrified awe at the magnitude of what just happened, as if the implications of the turn are too big to be grasped all at once and won't be known for a long time. "It is hard not to suspect that most of us who are converts," writes the academic and born-again Christian Elizabeth Fox-Genovese, "do not initially grasp the magnitude of what we are being chosen for."

What's interesting, though, is that all these components tend to be present not just in religious conversion tales—Christian or otherwise—but in secular U-turns as well. In fact, the more you compare spiritual and secular U-turns, the more alike the two seem. People who have undergone big transformations—religious or secular—almost invariably resort to metaphors to convey some sense of what has happened to them, and often these metaphors are quite beautiful and seem perfectly apt. It is a play where the actors change scripts; it is a geological event; it is a chemical reaction; it is a rebirth. But the overwhelming impression one gets is that this is the same black dog being looked at in the night.

The Buddhist teacher Sharon Salzberg has written of how she believes we muddle through a spiritual problem—and the description could easily be transplanted to how a veteran art critic suddenly "got" the genius of Mark Morris; or a police detective suddenly realized you could think about crimes in epidemiological terms, and came up with the concept of geographic profiling; or a frustrated Johan von Gutenberg finally arrived at the insight, after visiting a vineyard, that wine-crushing technology was the answer for his printing press.

The Neuroscience of the Aha Moment

Whether you understand that sudden snap of new understanding in spiritual or secular terms—and there is a whole field, called "insight theory," that aims to do just that—the thing, the actual neurological event, boils down to a perceptual shift. A second ago you saw the two faces in profile, now you see the chalice; a second ago you were heading for premed, and now you know you're going to be an artist; a second ago you had no feeling for a god, and now you do. Somehow, in a single instant as dense as a collapsed star, your understanding of something changed. And whatever just happened must have left a neural signature. Only in the last couple of years has imaging technology been sophisticated enough to produce maps for the purposes of comparison. And the early returns are as provocative as the phenomenon they're studying.

At least three teams of neuroscientists have been stalking what might loosely be called spiritual transcendence. In Montreal, the neurologist Mario Beauregard and his research assistant Vincent Paquette have been trying to isolate the *"unio mystica"*—the sense of mystical union with God that holy people of all faiths have described following moments of religious ecstasy. In this case the holy people were fifteen Carmelite nuns whom the scientists had recruited from the local community, and who proved to be exceptionally good sports. For the pilot experiment, each, in her turn, sat in a padded office chair in a sound-proof, electromagnetically neutral room, donned a swim cap fitted with electrodes and a bundle of colored wires maypoling out the top—and they prayed. (Each of the nuns had experienced the unio mystica in the past, and the idea was to try to climb the flank of that mountain again, as high as they were able.) The leads from the swim cap snaked, unseen, to an electroencephalogram machine in the next room, which recorded a kind of movie of the type, location, and intensity of the women's brain waves—a rough record of the where and what of communion with God. A *very* rough record. Using an EEG to determine what's going on in the brain, I have heard it said, is "like a man away on business in New York using a seismograph to tell if his wife in Los Angeles is cheating on him." So researchers Mario Beauregard and Vincent Paquette repeated the experiment using functional magnetic resonance imaging (fMRI), which records microscopic changes in blood flow—a close correlate of electrical activity in the brain in real time. The machine recorded that, as the nuns ascended toward a state of mystical union, different regions of their brains came alive.

Meanwhile, other neurologists were claiming a neighboring—and perhaps overlapping—neurotheological grubstake: Eastern-style "enlightenment." Andrew Newberg, a professor of nuclear medicine and a director of NeuroPET research at the Hospital of the University of Pennsylvania, ushered Tibetan monks into his lab at Penn, lit some jasmine-scented incense, injected them with a radioactive tracer, scanned them with the SPECT (single photon emission computed tomography) machine as they reached the height of their meditative trance, and produced a "snapshot of the brain in the moment of spiritual transcendence." Not long after, in Wisconsin, the neuroscientist Richard Davidson and his team conducted their research with those compassionate Buddhist monks. (The point of Davidson's work wasn't to pinpoint a "god spot," per se, but to demonstrate that the brain can be *physically modified* through training.)

At the same time as these neuroscientists in North America were triangulating on the seat of the soul—or at least the seat of the *manufacture of soulful experience*—in Chicago, yet another team was using much the same technology to test for something nominally quite different: the moment of cognitive *insight*.

Where the first group was trying to diagram, neurologically, the "ah" experience, Marc Jung-Beeman and his colleague Edward Bowden were trying to diagram the "aha" itself. Jung-Beeman, a psychology professor at Northwestern University, set up an experiment whereby subjects did word puzzles while changes in brain activity were monitored by EEGs and MRIs. *Pine, crab, sauce.* What do those words have in common? It took subjects a few seconds or minutes to come up with a word that pairs with each of them. But the moment the answer popped to mind, researchers in the next room, reading the scanners, observed a crackle of activity in the right temporal lobe. It took about a third of a second for the insight to emerge as a word: *apple.*

What the researchers saw on the screen during that "eureka" moment was a signature of fast waves unlike anything they had observed before—very different from the brain at rest, and very different, too, from the signature of a brain that's crunching numbers or otherwise doing its workaday heavy lifting. It turns out that when you "get" a solution, a joke, a connection—that is, when we make an intuitive leap—it *shows*, neurologically, as an event as singular as a fingerprint. The research scientists were extremely excited about this, for it seemed to suggest something with implications far beyond a simple word problem. The researchers believe it's a hint of what might be at work in larger life change. "You've heard these stories where someone's working in a business, making a lot of money, and they realize that it's not their purpose in life and they go work in an inner-city school," Bowden says. "I think that could work the same way."

James Austin, a Harvard-trained neurologist who specializes in brain disorders, admits that while that assumption is a leap, he thinks the insight researchers are starting to get warm. The work of Austin, in some ways the *eminence grise* of the neuroscience of consciousness shifts, stands as a bridge between the two camps. Since 1974, when he himself had a profound experience while meditating in Kyoto, Japan, Austin has explored a phenomenon that seems to tie together the contemplative component of mystical union with the sudden apprehension of the "cognitive snap." Zen Buddhists call it *kensho*—awakening. In a fugitive moment of existential comprehension, "the essence of things" is briefly glimpsed. (Such a moment of clarity might come, for example, when the student, grappling with why a Zen master responded to his question "What is the basic truth of Buddhism?" by removing a shoe and putting it on his head, suddenly *gets it.* Ha! The response suddenly makes sense—and he can never see the world in quite the same way again.) Austin determined that kensho consists of a sequence of phases, or "flashes," each of which seems to recruit different parts of the brain.

Here, though, is the really interesting thing about the early results of all this heady neuroscience: the studies, each ostensibly measuring something unique, seem to overlap quite a lot. If each scientist were asked to submit a sequence of pictures of the brain around the particular moment of departure to another plane that they studied, and those pictures were hung in an art gallery, a casual viewer filing past them all would probably be struck more by the similarities than the differences. In each case, there is a kind of changing of the guard from one brain region to another; as one part powers up, another dims. The first "flash" of kensho is marked, Austin suggests, by an initial spike of activity that fades before the next phase, "insightful knowing," kicks in with an entirely different signature of activity; the process seems remarkably similar to what Marc Jung-Beeman observed in the "gatekeeper" spike that occurs before the test subject smacks his forehead and shouts, "Aha!"

The Buddhist monks and Franciscan nuns in Andrew Newberg's studies had quite different descriptions for the transcendent state they achieved (or approached, or at least aspired to): To the monks it was a kind of universal consciousness, an egoless melding with the cosmos; to the nuns, it was union with God. But their neural activity was quite similar. As the prefrontal cortex gets humming as subjects bear down and concentrate, the OAA in the parietal lobe backs off—neglecting its job of maintaining the boundary between where we end and the world outside of us begins. And into the ether the subject ascends.

One region of the brain that seems to be actively involved in these phenomena—both the ahs *and* the ahas—is the right temporal lobe. It's no surprise why, in the popular imagination, a mysterious nuclear glow surrounds that bit of gray matter below the right ear. Within the folds of the right hemisphere—the "truth-telling" hemisphere, as V. S. Ramachandran's work suggests—it is where the muse lives, where art comes from. But, practically speaking, it is where *we* live; where—in the medial and lateral temporal cortex—we write our autobiography. It's what recognizes our mother, our spouse, our children. It is where those vaguely supernatural déjà vu experiences are produced, and also—in the event of illness or injury—the rarer "jamais vu" experience, where what ought to be familiar, isn't. The right temporal lobe functions as a kind of switching yard, blocking interference, recruiting other parts of the brain to integrate information in new ways, the better to solve problems. What kind of problems? Puzzles, riddles, practical problems—and even, perhaps, "spiritual emergencies."

When insight—call it revelation, epiphany, enlightenment, or peace—finally comes, it comes spontaneously, in the view of every one of the neurologists studying it. "No top-down impulse sponsors it, no person injects a self in there, nobody pauses to think over what's going on," writes James Austin about the onset of kensho. In Jung-Beeman's experiments, that early, pre-"aha" spike of activity, the figurative finger that reaches for the light switch, is a thoroughly unconscious process—which explains why insight seems, when it comes, as if it had appeared "out of nowhere."

But *seems* is the operative word. Those bolt-of-lightning solutions—obviously correct when you "get" them—are, in fact, the product of sustained work by a brain toiling, testing new connections, linking existing knowledge in new ways, beavering away below the threshold of consciousness. Even though you yourself may give up on a problem, declaring yourself "stuck," your brain never does.

It soon becomes hard to skirt the question: Are all these researchers simply taking different paths to the same waterfall? Does all this brain work—all this convergence on certain circuitry that's installed in everyone's head and activates in pretty much the same way, whether the input is a powerful spiritual memory or a peak meditative moment or a leap of insight (or even an epileptic thunderstorm)—prove that we're looking at a universal neurological event? And is that same circuitry activated in *any* sudden moment of clarity—from discovering God to perceiving the moral indefensibility of eating meat?

Commitments and Confessions

Religious conversion is almost definitively accompanied by some altered, mystical state, Max Weber believed. That mystical element would seem to differentiate it from the secular turn; yet secular turners often describe an otherworldly component to their transformation that loads it with spooky import, making it feel quite unlike anything they've been through before. Most everyone agrees that it is not rational. Much hard cognition may have preceded it and followed it, but in the moment itself, the neocortex is mugged and silenced as the thieves of id and intuition steal through the house.

Religious converts sometimes describe their new life as the role they were born to play in a script that predated them. (This idea is closely associated with Calvinism, but it's by no means exclusively Protestant, or even Christian.) Secular turners often speak of the decision as a powerful compulsion—which made it feel less like a choice than a kind of obedience to operating instructions. (Like the answer to a question, as Julia Hill put it, that you didn't know you were asking.)

Religious (particularly Christian) converts often describe a sense of relief and peace, postconversion, in having returned "home." (Or in Wordsworth's more explicit phrasing, having returned "to God, who is our home.") But this metaphor crops up often in stories of secular transformation as well. In 1996, the economist Donald McCloskey sent a letter to his colleagues preparing them for a big change. He was no longer answering to "Donald"; he was, in fact, in the process of altering his appearance to align with his true identity, and "Deirdre" had taken Donald's place. "You cannot imagine the relief in adopting my correct gender," McCloskey said. "Imagine if you felt French but had been raised in Minnesota."

Post-turn, U-turners typically feel a powerful, subjective sense of confirmation that they did the right thing. What the psychologist Howard Gardner calls *resonance*—the sense that *this just feels right*, that it makes sense in my gut even if I can't articulate it—marches under plenty of different banners. Descriptions of "nonfactual" ways of "knowing" abound, and a lot of them sound a lot like faith. The New Testament scholar William Barclay distinguishes the two in this way: Knowledge is the acceptance that something is factually true (it's the chlorophyll in them that turns leaves green), but if it has no direct impact on your life, there's little reason to be *committed* to that particular fact. Faith is a kind of knowledge that you're highly motivated to commit to because it does have an impact on your daily life. A dollar will buy me a cup of coffee. Or: following this new path will invest my life with meaning.

Upon cracking open Paul Hawken's book *The Ecology of Commerce*, "The scales fell away from my eyes, and in a flash I decided that we should lead the way," the carpet manufacturer Ray Anderson told me. The language is striking, as if, to capture the ineffable moment of clarity, secular descriptions just aren't up to the job. Some describe a kind of conscience-cleansing (the element of "coming clean"—an unabashedly spiritual metaphor—is one many U-turns share), a drive to persuade others to do likewise that seems nakedly, evangelically religious.

That's clearly the case with John Perkins, whose life arc, as he describes it, was less a rise-and-fall than a blastoff-and-bail, muttering a thousand Hail Marys on the slow glide back to Earth. An idealistic former Peace Corps volunteer from Vermont, Perkins became an economist and, not long after was hired by a secretive Boston-based consultancy with both corporate ties and connections to a U.S. government intelligence agency. He soon found himself lured into the clandestine métier of what he calls the "economic hit man." Effectively, he was an international loan shark. His job, as he describes it, was to help arrange financing for developing countries to build big public-works projects they couldn't otherwise afford. The price estimates for these projects were grossly inflated, and extortionate conditions were set on the repayment of these loans, conditions the countries couldn't possibly meet. When the governments ran out of money and inevitably defaulted, big, U.S.-based multinationals—chiefly engineering firms and petrochemical companies—would seize control of the countries' natural resources. The whole purpose of the enterprise was to enable the United States to take over other countries' economies under the radar and with minimum bloodshed.

This was black-helicopter stuff, seductive but, as you might expect, spiritually corrosive. For years, Perkins lived with the hypocrisy of maintaining two identities: One was of a decent, liberal guy helping the poor (he did work pro bono for a number of aboriginal groups) and the other was a high-flying opportunist who directly oppressed the poor. Eventually, a budding crisis of conscience overcame him, he crashed into something very close to what used to be described as a nervous breakdown, and sat down at the computer to finish something he'd started years earlier but had never been able to carry through: a tell-all memoir.

The express goal of *Confessions of an Economic Hit Man* is to explain to average Americans the "truth" about foreign aid: how its goal is, almost always, to bring more of the pie to America. But the book is also a personal call to atone. Perkins wrote it to convert people, as he himself had been converted—and implore them to make a commitment to lead a moral life.

"Now it's your turn," Perkins writes, summing up. "You need to make your own confession. When you come clean on who you are, why you are here during this time in history, why you have done the things you have—the ones you are proud of, and those others—and where you intend to go next, you will experience an immediate sense of relief."

I got that same feeling talking to Tom Williams, the wunderkind philanthropist. An almost religious air of self-abnegation hung over the conversation. He remembered how executives at Rupert Murdoch's Newscorp had tapped him like a maple. ("We want your brain," they had said. "We need to understand how you think.") And how he'd let them, let himself be used, for a lot of money, "by one of the world's biggest, and sometimes tawdriest, corporations so they could increase their profits." He remembered his own rationalizations. Sure, he'd started out with an honorable plan: to generate big ideas and surround himself with incredibly smart people who could execute them. And, yes, by the time he was in the venture-capital game he had already drifted away from it. But, hey: Wasn't he still *supporting* big ideas, following the honorable tradition of the patron funding the arts? He was Guell to their Gaudi, Guggenheim to their Gehry—underwriting the magic. And the expensive suits? The nightlife? Well, there's no shame in wealth: You're pumping cash into the economy, raising all the boats. Spend and make money freely, for your actions were long ago sanctioned by God.

Yeah, right.

You get the sense, speaking to Williams now, that he did not so much shelve those Armani suits as *shed* them. "Today my old skin has become a dust. I will walk tall among men and they will know me not, for today

I am a new man, with a new life." The protagonist in Og Mandino's slim novel *The Greatest Salesman in the World* breaks out of a long slump in one crackling moment of truth. The book is a Christian parable—but Mandino's description of the born-again experience strikes such a common chord that it could be thumbnailing just about any of the secular turns described in this book. In fact, if you replace the word God with the word *hope* in any religious rhetoric, you can see how easily the religious and the secular interchange. Read figuratively, much biblical scripture could easily be the narrative of secular U-turns. The "kingdom of God" might simply represent "an inner spiritual change in the hearts of men," as the psychiatrist Anthony Storr puts it. (The more orthodox Protestants, of course, find such loose interpretations crazy-making, and a slippery slope at the bottom of which lies . . . well, flat-out secularism.)

The word *conversion*, as it commonly appears in English translations of gospel passages, actually has a secular root. It comes from the Greek *epistrephein*, a rich and loaded word with multiple meanings—all of which resonate for those who have made a sudden life change. It really just means a "turning around," as in "turning one's back upon someone," or "turning from ignorance to knowledge," as William Barclay points out. Or, somewhat more subtly, turning a ship on a new tack when the captain suddenly realizes he's made a terrible mistake.

There's another sense in which the word can be understood. It is the "idea of doing again," of returning to some previously performed action and, this time, getting it right.

When the army lawyer James Kennedy was living briefly in Germany on a training course, he received a letter from his father. What Dad needed to tell him was that he had seen the light. He had become born again. And he beseeched his son to do likewise. Kennedy's father laid out the six steps to salvation: Acknowledge, repent, confess, forsake, believe, receive. Now, Kennedy had no intention of becoming a Christian. But the Christian template, like any good story, works on a number of levels. And Kennedy realized that it was a useful guide for the big, secular transformation he was making in his own life—from closeted prosecutor of homosexuals in the army to openly gay defender of gay soldiers. The same story became a fixed star two people could navigate by, from opposite ends of the earth.

U-Turn

Tests and Trials

Dennis Miller did not exactly hide his transformation—from left-leaning, dadaist wisenheimer to right-wing scold—when he took to the air in 2004 with his new cable show. The "New Dennis" was the lede, the theme, the very moral of the show. It was time for some long-overdue truth-telling: about the joke that is the UN, the hysteria of animal-rights activists, the pantywaist ineffectualness of liberals just generally. The tone was pure Gurdjieff: There's Dennis's opinion, and then there's the opinion of those who will eventually share it.

Miller's shift was unmistakably a kind of conversion, and the nature and intensity of conversion is such that the convert often has trouble keeping the moment to himself. The message seems to cry out for expression, in the general direction of those who haven't yet woken up— which is, of course, a familiar, and sometimes derided, component of the born-again experience: "As no roads are as rough as those which have just been mended, no sinners are so intolerant as those which have just turned saints." And so on. (As one critic noted of Miller's new agenda: "If only this were funny.") After Damien Hirst's transformation from the drug-and-booze-addled Bad Boy of British art to clean, upstanding citizen seemed to prompt a whole group of celebrity ex-addicts to go public with just how the new virtuousness has improved their craft, *Guardian* writer Zoe Williams had seen about enough. "Tee-totalitarians!" she huffed of this group as a whole. "The state of being rehabilitated is akin to a monotheistic religion. Its *sine qua non* is that any other way can only be the wrong way."

But the impulse is not purely egotistical bluster. The Spanish poet Solomon ben Judah ibn Gabirol calls "propagating" what you've learned an essential step in the general process of being wise. (Another way to look at it is that we're obliged to teach what we have learned.) The compulsion to spread the idea that has changed your life is the same one, whether it results in stumping for a particular faith or for a particular kind of social justice. The "awakened" spirit and the sparked social conscience are kissing cousins.

The imperative to spread the word is actually part of the job description of Judeo-Christian converts. ("The Christian is called upon to be the partner of God in the work of the conversion of men.") But spreading the word is only one of many duties. There are ethical obligations as well—perhaps chief among them, to "respond with love." Hebrew law makes clear that Jews have obligations to respond to others' misfortunes. One cannot ignore one's neighbor's wandering ox, one cannot hide from people in trouble.

But secular turns carry many if not all the same sorts of obligations—it's just that they aren't formal; they're implicit, understood as private, personal injunctions. A duty to relieve the suffering of animals, for example, or reduce one's ecological footprint, or donate money without the possibility of the recipient feeling indebted, or just simply to do no harm.

In Deepa Mehta's film *Water*, Gandhi, just released from prison, passes through town by train and a crowd gathers on the platform to get a glimpse of him as he stops briefly for a public prayer. "I used to believe that God is truth," Gandhi tells the crowd. "Now I believe that truth is God." Among the throng is the nun Shakuntala, the heroic center of the film, whose faith has been tested by the unnecessary suffering she has seen women face because of strict adherence to ancient religious texts. Her face registers the discord of the two sets of instructions. *Follow your religion.* And *follow your conscience.* "What," she asks, "if your conscience conflicts with your religion?"

Søren Kierkegaard would have called that a false choice. Follow your conscience, he would have advised, for conscience-driven behavior *is* religious behavior. When you obey the calling of your conscience and make a moral U-turn, he insisted, you're on God's payroll, whether you know it or not. The philosopher C. Steven Evans moves the ball a little further upfield: Conscience is a vehicle through which "ordinary individuals"—as opposed to prophets or otherwise "chosen" individuals—can hear a divine call. An active conscience conveys a sense of one's moral obligations (a social, not religious, construct, he believes)—and builds a sense of one's "true" self.

The most consistent part of the U-turn experience is probably what happens after the decision to change has been made. The public blowback faced by U-turners often has the feel of a kind of public trial. The suffering that follows—in the form of humiliation, social rejection, and just plain inconvenience—makes it seem as if the turner is satisfying a formal requirement of the religious conversion, no matter what precise form the turn takes.

In 1976, after William Powell converted to Christianity, he tried to tie up un-Christian loose ends his life had created. One big problem was the book he had written as a godless nineteen-year-old, the infamous monkey-wrenching guide, called *The Anarchist Cookbook*. The book was still out there, selling steadily year after year, just waiting to put subversive ideas into the heads of kids, oh, about his son's age. Powell called up his publisher and asked that it be taken out of print.

Sorry, he was told—that wouldn't be possible.

But it's my book, Powell said.

Actually, no, we hold the copyright, Powell was told.

It was true. In what seemed like a trivial detail at the time—one whose repercussions he couldn't possibly have fathomed—the copyright had been taken out in the publisher's name and not the author's.

Powell was stuck.

There was only one thing to do, short of renting a bullhorn and roaming the streets, disavowing his own book. He went onto Amazon .com, called up the book, and posted a letter. In a kind of combination mea culpa and warning, Powell laments that he did not have a more censorious editor to save him from himself, and enjoins folks not to buy the damn thing—"a misguided and potentially dangerous publication which should be taken out of print."

It's hard to believe that the author of the sober, as–told–to–Joe Friday Amazon posting and the author of the spirited *Anarchist* posting are the same guy. And in a sense they aren't.

"The book, in many respects, was a misguided product of my adolescent anger at the prospect of being drafted and sent to Vietnam to fight in a war I did not believe in. The central idea to the book was that violence is an acceptable means to bring about political change. I no longer agree with this," Powell said.

The most interesting part of the posting is the reaction of readers. They do not, many of them, like this William Powell who is posing as the man who wrote their beloved guidebook. Not one bit. Many of the letters suggest that the author of the book might have a strong libel case against the author of that disparaging letter on Amazon.com.

"It is unfortunate that we lose our sense of outrage and angst as we grow into adulthood," writes one reader, in response to Powell's diatribe.

Another: "Religion claims another victim."

And: "You are a liar William Powell. You thought you knew what was right and saw that was true. Yet now you think you know what is right and see that it isn't true if we still need to publish your fine book. Times really haven't changed, man—you have."

The irony is, the most vexing problem for religious converts is not that they have changed, it's that people sometimes refuse to accept their transformation.

You could see the wheels turning in anticipatory dread for author Naomi Wolf after her most recent hairpin swerve following a midlife crisis. Wolf had had to fend off criticism of shape-shifting before. Once the new face of feminism—her book *The Beauty Myth* was lavishly praised by Germaine Greer as the best feminist book since *The Female Eunuch*—she had publicly tried on other selves, including advising Al Gore on his wardrobe palette during the 2000 presidential election. Her crimes against identity stamped her as a lightweight. ("After too many tacks and jibes," one critic put it, it became clear that "she suffers from the opportunist's lack of intellectual coherence.") But in early 2006, during a self-imposed writing retreat in the woods of upstate New York, Wolf had a full-blown spiritual conversion, a mystical experience that made her certain the universe was full of benign purpose, guided by a caring God; that love, as Mary Tyler Moore intuited, is indeed all around, and we have each been put here to fulfill a spiritual mission. It was, she says, "the most profound moment of my life."

Even bringing this up, she knew, would expose her to ridicule. "It's very embarrassing," she told a reporter for the British *Sunday Herald*, to whom she came out of the closet with her newfound religiosity early in 2006. "We're intellectuals, we're on the left, we're not supposed to talk like that." She worried that her experience would demean her feminism somehow, or crush her intellectual bona fides. Her vision of Jesus during a "light meditative state" induced by a hypnotist to help her deal with writer's block would surely bring knowing nods. She *really* worried that this new twist in her narrative would be co-opted by the Religious

Right. "I want so much to distance this from Christianity," she said. "It has nothing to do with any religion whatsoever."

In some ways the fallout is less severe for traditional religious converts than for those whose transformations are even more, well, freestyle than Naomi Wolf 's.

Kevin Rowland, founder of the British band Dexy's Midnight Runners, had a rollicking career in which his own identity seemed to become a casualty. Rowland was the Marlon Brando of '80s pop, an emotional white guy trying to keep it real, constantly on the hunt for other "young soul rebels" like himself to call over to the campfire. A couple of monster hits ("Come on Eileen") made stars of the lads. Rowland moved to New York, did a lot of shopping, and, when success proved an empty experience, grew depressed. The commercial pixie dust vanished, and, by the early '90s, all but broke, Rowland descended into drug hell and eventually twelve-step rehab.

The man who emerged from that trial was a different Kevin Rowland. He was eager to make a new album, consisting entirely of covers of songs that helped him get through those dark days. He already had a name for it: "My Beauty."

The problem was that the lyrics, which had once found their mark in his wounded heart, no longer reflected his "healing" view of the world. He contacted the creators of those songs and asked if they wouldn't mind if he brightened them up a bit. Many, unsurprisingly, said no. But one band that said yes was Squeeze. What Rowland did to their exquisite 1981 ballad "Labeled with Love," about a nostalgic alcoholic, is almost grounds for federal prosecution.

Original: Home is a love that I miss very much / So the past has been bottled / and labeled with love.

Sweetened by Rowland: "Home is a place I don't know where that is / So the pain has been bottled / I'll stay with my dreams."

In his first public performance after rehab, the reborn—and reinvented—Rowland sang three songs from the album at a 1999 concert in Reading, England. He was pelted with fruit, which stained his sarong. (The album reportedly sold fewer than five hundred copies. One online reviewer said simply: "Poor confused guy.")

The Road to Damascus

Ricky Williams, the prized young running back of the Miami Dolphins, suddenly quit football in 2004, at age twenty-seven, to embark on a pilgrimage and find himself, hanging teammates and fans out to dry. Then he returned to the team a year later—insisting there was nowhere he'd rather be picking himself up from than the astroturf of Tropicana Field—and ran into plenty of furious teammates, coaches, and fans, demanding an explanation. Who walks away from his commitments, and then *walks away from the walking away*? At the press conference announcing his return, a sweet-natured Williams shrugged and said, "My loyalty is to the truth, not to consistency."

But Ricky Williams's "truth" is complicated. The truth is—and maybe this is the most accurate thing you can say about his story—that the world sometimes imposes consistency even on people who fight mightily to file their own flight plan.

Williams's turning-point moment—the second one, marking his return to football—came in the airport in Bangkok. Williams and his new best friend, a wandering seeker he called Mystic Steve whom he had befriended in Australia, were about to board a plane to India. They planned to meditate and study and plant a garden in the alpine meadows. But when Williams's flight was called, he balked. When the final boarding announcement came, he waved good-bye to Mystic Steve. Williams had recently learned that he had been successfully sued by the Dolphins owner for $8.6 million in back pay—a punitive settlement for deserting the team. Williams understood that the debt would follow him to the ends of the world—to the most remote Indian ashram, to the lemon-tree orchard on the farm he planned to buy in Australia—until he faced it. In the Bangkok airport, he decided to return to the United States. He watched Mystic Steve board the flight to New Delhi alone—sailing off into a future Ricky Williams might have shared, but that had just been foreclosed on him.

During his hiatus, Williams apprenticed himself to an Indian guru named Swami Sitaramananada, and devoted himself to Hinduism to the point where he almost changed his name to Riodan. And then, at the last minute, he didn't. It was a strong signal that the incipient self that was developing had been stillborn. When Williams returned dutifully to the practice field, he had the look, writer Chris Jones observed in *Esquire*, "of an inmate who had made it over the wall, only to be dragged back to prison."

Left Behind

For U-turners, the social repercussions ripple out in two directions: You suffer, and those in your life suffer. The ones who get collaterally sacrificed, in the case of many U-turns, are family, friends, and professional acquaintances. Old colleagues may feel betrayed. Left reeling by this new direction her beloved has taken, a spouse confronts that classic choice: *Would I rather live in his world, or live without him in mine?*

Jincy Willett's short story "The Haunting of the Lingards" exposes what must be a secret fear of many agnostic couples: not that they will find God, but that *one of them* will. In the story, the wife, Anita, sees a ghost. She elects not to tell her husband, "who has a pure contempt for the mere idea of ghosts." But a friend spills the beans. Now the event is something that must be dealt with. The husband, Kenneth, is coolly patronizing in his skepticism. "If there was a ghost in Giddings' attic it existed independently of all known physical laws, and probably in violation of fundamental theory," he says. The sighting—well, the withheld secret of the sighting, too—confirms for this couple their irreconcilable difference, and the apparently bombproof marriage blows apart. (*Apparently* is, of course, the operative word. The incident merely exposes a rift that was already there, unacknowledged. An old Lillian Hellman line neatly captures the dynamic: "People change and forget to tell each other.")

If you're about to cross a bridge, there's obviously no guarantee your partner will join you. It could go either way. Which may help explain why new converts to a cause are often such zealous proselytizers: Saving the marriage may take the best sales job of their lives. What philosophers call a "mimetic drive" may be at work here. U-turners seem almost biologically compelled to sell this new idea, on which so much is at stake for them. Just as born-again Christians will invest furiously in converting their loved ones, highly motivated to save their kin's eternal souls, many secular U-turners believe the new meme they have adopted has, in some hard-to-explain way, "saved their life." Now the job is to prevent it from severing their connections to loved ones.

When Virgil Butler walked off the kill floor at the Tyson chicken-processing plant and went public with his "conversion" to vegetarian-ism so that he'd be accountable ("I wanted to make sure I never had that option again"), a few things happened. He got his life back and saved his relationship with his vegan girlfriend—continuing at the slaughterhouse would almost surely have been a dealbreaker. But he es-tranged himself from just about everyone in town in the bargain.

"Some of my family who still work at the plant won't talk to me any more," Butler told me. "The people I knew who I considered to be my friends don't have anything to do with me publicly. Even the ones who will come over to the house, if I meet them in a store or something, they'll just walk by like they don't even know me. They're scared of Tyson. Tyson would fire them in a heartbeat if they were seen talking to me. I couldn't even go up to the sawmill and get a job because I'd have to use Tyson as a reference, and they've pretty much blacklisted me around here."

When Jeffrey Wigand, the chemist and a former top executive of Brown & Williamson tobacco company, blew the whistle on the tobacco industry's knowledge of its product's deadly effects, he became a hero, immortalized in the Michael Mann film *The Insider*. He also received death threats, and, watched his marriage fail. And once the glow of righ-teousness died, where was he left? His salary dropped 90 percent, and he started schlepping his antitobacco crusade from school to school.

I asked the Apollo astronaut Edgar Mitchell about the impact of his epiphany in space on his personal life, his relationships with the people who never made that trip. "I've had *three* marriages," he replied, and left it at that.

The Belief Engine

In the biblical telling, after Christ is crucified, and appears back on Earth as a mortal, he takes an unrecognizable form. After Mary Mag-dalene discovers the rock rolled away from the tomb, there is general confusion. She sees Jesus, there in the half-light of dawn, and mistakes him for the gardener. She is in tears. The "gardener" asks two questions of her: "Woman, why are you weeping?" and "Whom are you looking for?" The two questions—the first full of compassion and the second a call for clarity—are enough to spark the shift of perception, so that when he next says her name—"Mary"—she cracks open and sees him anew. He is not the gardener at all (his shape-shift guise) but her Jesus. One common interpretation of that story is that the only way you will recognize the Messiah is if you yourself change, and learn to see things as if for the first time.

That's the point of a lot of Bible stories. One sometimes gets the false impression that converting to Christianity is something done in active, rather than passive, voice. That is, one is less likely to convert to Christianity on one's own as one is to *be* converted—by someone or something. It could be by the oratory of the priest, or by apparent evidence of something miraculous, or by some vividly understood promise of salvation, or by personal testimony of others who have "seen the light." But, in fact, the scriptures suggest, the oratory of the priest or the promise of salvation or the power of another convert's story would fall upon stone deafness if the convert hadn't done much of the intransitive work first.

The idea that the grace of God comes only to the receptive isn't exclusively a Judeo-Christian one, of course. Islam is founded on such a notion as well. Islam is said to have begun when the archangel Gabriel appeared to the prophet Muhammad and brought the first revelation of the Koran. But such a revelation is not dispensed like the morning newspaper. Only someone particularly spiritually endowed is in a position to receive it. "*The soul has to be prepared*," said Seyyed Hossein Nasr, a professor of Islamic studies at George Washington University (and author of, among many books, *Knowledge and the Sacred* and *Ideas and Realities of Islam*), "or has to receive that particular grace which makes this possible."

While the religious convert hears a directive from God that cuts through the noise of his life and becomes an operating instruction, few secular U-turners describe a sense of taking dictation in this way. Yet it's common, looking back on events, to view a U-turn as a kind of "happy accident"—some unexpected hardship that looked, at first blush, like a curse, but without which the new understanding could never have been found. (That view of the world mitigates the inevitable suffering a life-change produces.)

What the religious call *grace*, and the aspiritual *coincidence*, meet in a term coined by Carl Jung: *synchronicity*. It is the notion that chance events—especially incredibly unlikely coincidences—weren't chance at all: They carry meaning, and perhaps a message.

In 1967, Helen Palmer had a series of premonitions that were so powerful that she thought of them even at the time as "visions," and they proved eerily prophetic. Among them was the strong feeling— more than that, an *inner knowing*—that a friend fleeing to Canada to dodge the draft ought to change his route. She contacted him, and he did so—thus avoiding being arrested with others trying to cross the border in the planned spot.

This was mighty unsettling, for she had always thought of herself as governed by rationality and evidence-based rigor—and indeed was studying in New York at the time to be an experimental psychologist. Like Jung's famously stuck patient who made progress only after a rare beetle flew in the window of the therapist's office and landed on her at the precise moment she was describing last night's dream about that very same rare beetle, it took an impossible event to knock Palmer off her perceptual moorings. "A direct jolt of inner knowing is especially startling to people like myself, whose confidence previously lay in intellectualism, because it urges us toward a way of life we might never have rationally chosen," she writes in *Inner Knowing*. Palmer moved from New York to California to become a writer (and a noted interpreter of the Enneagram personality test).

Steve Hassan, a Boston-based "exit counselor" who helps detach people from cults, was fully ensconced in the Unification Church, apparently beyond rescue by friends or family, when a road accident radically changed the script. Hassan was driving a van early one morning, to pick up a fellow Moonie who'd been out all night fund-raising. He fell asleep at the wheel. The van slammed into the back of an eighteen-wheeler, landing him in a local emergency room—in the hands of non-Moonies for the first time in years. "The accident subtly began breaking the Moonies' hold over me in several important ways," Hassan said. "I could eat, sleep, and rest. I could see my family. I could slow down and think." Hassan's father organized a deprogramming team of ex-members to meet with his son, and, despite fierce resistance, he was wrested away from the church—thence to devote his life to counseling others away from the same fate.

It's easy in retrospect to impose an explanation of synchronicity on utterly chance events that changed the course of human lives, so that their biography invariably contains the line, "And the rest is history." The great evolutionary biologist Ernst Mayr had set his sights on med school when one day, while out walking near his hometown in German Bavaria, he spotted a couple of unfamiliar-looking ducks on a lake. It turned out they were red-crested pochards, a species so rare they hadn't been seen in Central Europe in seventy-seven years. The report stirred such interest from biologists and ornithologists that Mayr found himself plunged into their world. He shelved his plans for med school, devoted himself to zoology, and did not look back.

For born-again Christians, it's a standard trope that certain people are put in your path. In the retrospective telling, they seem to show up in your life just when you need them—as Billy Graham did for a drifting, semialcoholic George W. Bush, or the Reverend Philip Benham did for "Jane Roe" (aka Norma McCorvey). Bill Joy met Ray Kurzweil by chance. Paul Hawken's book landed on Ray Anderson's desk at just that propitious moment when he had to come up with a new truth for the shareholders to whom he didn't want to lie. "And you tell me," he says, "that there's not a hidden hand in all of this?"

The Paul Hawken moment turned Ray Anderson into a quester, investigating potential explanations for what happened to him. "I've read a thousand books, I'm sure, since reading Hawken's," Anderson says. "Who ever has had something serendipitous happen to him has to wonder: God almighty, how did that happen? There may be a more profound explanation than any of us understands.

"Did you ever read any of David Bohm's work? He hypothesized something like an implicate order underlying all reality. You look at an ocean and you see the choppy waves on the surface: that's where we live. We live in the choppy waves. And underneath it all deep, deep water."

192

Many who would vigorously distance themselves from the idea of predestination nonetheless accept that something like what Jung called synchronicity is at work in the world. Because so often it seems to ring true. Life seems daily to deliver brown-paper packages so apt in their content and timing that we can only laugh. It becomes very difficult not to at least entertain the thought that the order was phoned in before we were born.

That's precisely the note that John Irving struck in *A Prayer for Owen Meany*—and it's one of the things that gave the novel its energy, and its broad appeal, even among people without a "religious" bone in their body. (It is, I think, Irving's only really great book. And it clearly tapped the deepest springs within Irving himself. The novel seemed to possess Irving while he was writing it. "For weeks John would walk around the house, he'd come to dinner, speaking in Owen's voice," Irving's wife Janet Turnbull once told me.) The story of the quiet, funny-looking boy who becomes a kind of unwitting prophet, tips its cap to predestination. In Owen Meany's world, nothing is useless or inexplicable, theologian Eugene Peterson notes. There are no accidents.

The world of Owen Meany—where people, places, and things catalyze epiphanies that change lives; where our script is chosen, and we are merely following it; where we're meant to discover our identity, our purpose, our mission—is a kind of theological midpoint. In one direction there's but a short step to the scientific principle, an aspect of chaos theory as properly understood, that pretty much everything is connected; every thought and action has a vast chain of consequences that we can't possibly anticipate or really comprehend. And in the other direction, it's a fairly short step to accepting a contention like Rabbi Lawrence Kushner's in *The Book of Words*: "You are where you are *supposed* to be." (From *there*, it's only one more step to calling God by name: "Before you were born, God planned this moment in your life. It is no accident that you are holding this book. God longs for you to discover the life he created you to live . . ." That's, you guessed it, Rick Warren, in *The Purpose-Driven Life*.)

If you step back from the question of whether such beliefs are in fact "true," whether such signs and portents and philosophical friends have indeed been put in our path to nudge us toward our destiny—and there's no way to prove the case either way—looking at the world this way serves a function. The brain is a "belief engine," says Michael Shermer, the former *Rational Enquirer* editor. A machine designed to solve the riddles of existence. Hungry for order and meaning, the mind discerns patterns. It sees constellations in randomly scattered stars and deities in plates of spaghetti, formulates conspiracy theories out of random malfeasance, and sees portents in coincidences. It is akin to a biological drive, this search for unity, for integration.

But this "belief engine" has two very different modes. Under certain conditions it leads to scientific thinking and under different circumstances it leads to magical thinking—a different form of pattern making. The anthropologist Bronislaw Malinowski, who studied New Guinea tribesmen on the Trobriand Islands in the 1920s, discovered that those who lived by the peaceful lagoon tended to harbor few magical thoughts: They were as close to "scientific" thinkers as you could imagine in that time and place. But those who braved the open sea routinely were extravagantly magical thinkers. The more jeopardy a particular group of Trobriand Islanders put themselves in, the more they turned to magic.

Those Trobriand Islanders, Shermer suggests, are all of us. The more difficult the environment/enterprise we're engaged in, the more likely we are to resort to magical thinking. The less control people have over their lives, the more meaning they invest in luck and fate. Superstitions are part of the modern belief engine. We're more likely, in the heat of the moment of ecstasy to see "signs" as confirmation. Certainty—of a faith, ideology, or anything—settles on us because we really, really need it.

Conversions tend to happen within two years of a "bottoming out" in one's life, studies have found. It's in that deep trench where the division between secular and religious tends to blur. In the nadirs of human lives, there are few flat-out atheists. And few, too, who aren't willing to throw in their whole hand for a new draw—to change themselves wholesale. That trench is a place we're all drawn to, the psychologist and theologian James E. Loder suggests. Eventually, if only briefly, loneliness, absence, or fear of death seizes us and takes us that way. And the void starts engulfing us. It happens, generally, in midlife. The person in that circumstance is like a scuba diver starting to descend: The deeper he goes, the faster he sinks. "The corrective," Loder writes, "is the intentional turn inward and the renewed search for the lost face." That's a midlife crisis. Or a major U-turn. Or a spiritual emergency. Jung insisted he never met a client over thirty-five whose problem wasn't spiritual in nature.

For those who have suffered deeply, the great function and solace of God is that He brings immediate relief. He is a tool for restoring the psychic imbalance that chaos engenders. By William James's lights, it's not as if we take our problems to God and He answers them; rather, it works the other way around: Whatever answers our problems we *call* God. (Blow this notion up to the scale of a whole culture and you have Nietzsche's idea of religion as what serves the needs of the group.) Not lots of problems and one God, then, but lots of gods and, at root, only one problem, one question: "What is the meaning of my life?"

The psychiatrist M. Scott Peck has noticed remarkable consistency in the "conversion" experiences of some of his clients, be they atheists who find organized religion, or fierce individualists who cave in to the strictures of the military or a highly regimented corporation. "Something astonishing happens to that person and it is usually totally unconscious," Peck writes. "If it could be made conscious, I think it would be as if that person said to himself or herself, 'I am willing to do anything—*anything*—in order to liberate myself from this chaos.'"

There are two ways to interpret the fact that U-turns are generally preceded by crisis. One—the one we've been talking about—is what you might call the "crutch" paradigm: At sea and buffeted by problems, the U-turner is just grasping for some way out of the existential morass. After interviewing close to nine hundred people who perceived themselves to be at a crossroads, Po Bronson concluded that "Self-questioning isn't something we do naturally—we're forced into it by a change in circumstances." (Bronson's subjects, given voice in his book *What Should I Do With My Life?*, had been wrong-footed by setbacks until many of them teetered on the edge of emotional collapse.) When you canvass people who have hit bottom, you find shame, despair—and very often a kind of slow-boil fury, born of a sense of being unfairly dealt out of the game, known as indignation.

It was this last emotion the playwright Arthur Miller seized on to investigate why U-turns come at low points in life. Call it the "restoration of dignity" theory. The tragic figure has been knocked out of what he considers his "rightful place" in society—and he is trying to recover some scrap of dignity, at whatever cost. This partly explains the motivations of some whistleblowers.

"Most people find ways to feel good and moral," Jerome Kagan says. "They are good mothers, good professors, good writers, good plumbers." A common trait among U-turners is that they tend not to have had that outlet, that way of reassuring themselves of their goodness. One reason the U-turner turns, then, is because something has threatened her sense of goodness—and she is, temperamentally, not the kind of person who will just quietly swallow that humiliation. She will act on it.

"Remember Mark Felt, the guy who was revealed to have been Deep Throat?" says Kagan. "He thought he'd be the next director of the CIA, and when he was passed over, he was mad as hell. His competence was threatened. He felt, I am competent enough to be the next director. And, goddamn it, you didn't think so. You threatened my conception of myself. So then I do a moral act—and it *was* a moral act— and he felt good about himself again."

That unquenchable little flame of dignity was evident in the men and women who were nearly broken by the Great Depression, and who yet struggled on, against hope—a group that profoundly affected Miller, and shaped his sensibilities. But Miller realized the trait was also at the heart of many of the great mythic characters, from Hamlet to Macbeth, who find themselves similarly on the outside looking in. Either they have been displaced from their niche, or they are madly trying to get there for the first time, Miller noted. Either way they are lost and demoralized, and "the fateful wound from which the inevitable events spiral is the wound of indignity, and its dominant force is indignation." If you peer through Miller's lens, you can find the "restoration of dignity" motive in just about all doomed human activity, from police-informing to suicide-bombing. The theory helps explain why some

196

people pull major life reversals despite the expected catastrophic consequences of doing so. The poignancy is in the commitment, and the commitment comes from the almost innate need to restore the self-respect they feel they lost when they bottomed out. Looked at this way, U-turners of this sort may be tragic figures, but U-turning itself isn't a character flaw at all, but rather a noble character trait. It is the mind-set of the revolutionary. In the moment of questioning what has gone unquestioned, the character gains "size," as Miller puts it. "The commonest of men may take on the stature of a king, "to the extent of his willingness to throw all he has into the contest."

The "crutch" paradigm no doubt contains much truth—but it's not the whole story. The unfortunate part of the crutch paradigm is that it reinforces the notion that U-turners are in some sense wounded or broken, their behavior symptomatic of some deep problem they are attempting, through this radical behavior, to adapt to.

Many theologians saw Martin Luther's midlife unraveling as a necessary spiritual battle, God entering his flesh like chemotherapy. But the prevailing opinion among nontheological biographers is that Luther wasn't sick in the soul: He was frankly psychotic. The chess master Bobby Fischer's radical midlife politicization inspired many on the left, until his volcanically provocative anti-Americanisms just seemed nuts, and his venomous anti-Semitism a little sad (and bizarre: His mother is Jewish). Arthur Conan Doyle's flip, from rock-ribbed rationalist into a man who publicly stated that he believed in fairies, had a local newspaper asking openly in sixty-point type: "Is Conan Doyle Mad?"

Today many would-be U-turners, who explained their symptoms to a psychiatrist—stress, confusion, roiling conscience—would likely receive a diagnosis of Borderline Personality Disorder, a catch-all term that has become one of the most popular diagnoses in psychiatry. "It's a kind of diagnosis for our age, this complex, changing, fluid society in which young people are not allowed to internalize a coherent picture of who they are," Dr. Theodore Milton told the *New York Times* recently. Dr. Milton is a psychiatrist who helped revise the *Diagnostic and Statistical Manual on Mental Disorders* (DSM), the bible of modern psychiatry, to include borderline personality. "There are too many options, too many choices, and there's a sense of I don't know who I am—am I angry, am I contended, happy, sad? It's the scattered confusion of modern society."

But are those symptoms really pathological—as it is customary for science to assert in the face of existential problems—or just possibly a keen awareness of cultural paradoxes, no-win choices, the obligations to take on multiple roles that almost always conflict with one another, at least a little? "Insanity is a perfectly rational adjustment to an insane world," said R. D. Laing, pressing the point a bit—or maybe not. Gregory Bateson famously described a kind of psychic trap he called the "double bind"—the problematic situation in which a person believes he cannot do the right thing, no matter what he does. What ensues, eventually, is that the person has a "nervous breakdown." The identity fractures, the "I" comes apart, and he emerges as someone else entirely. (Bateson's original research was on children who received mixed messages from their mothers. But you could say that the "mixed messages" we all receive from the culture might pull at the psyche in a similar way.)

The psychiatrist Robert Coles once wrote to Anna Freud to seek her opinion about Malcolm X. What, he asked, did she think "accounted for the sudden shift in his life—from 'confidence man' and jailed 'psychopath' or 'sociopath' to fiercely obedient and articulate Muslim, and then, to gentle and loving person who urged decency and charity upon all of us?"

"Dear Robert," Anna Freud wrote back. "We know, more or less, how to account for what goes wrong in people," but we don't know how to account for what goes right. "We don't know about the miracles that take place, and I don't only mean the big ones." Anna Freud worried that, seen through the traditional lens of psychiatry, Malcolm X's hairpin turns looked pretty dysfunctional—perhaps even like evidence of psychopathology. (Which is how religious conversions have typically been viewed.) She was wary of such a diagnosis. "Maybe in time we'll understand more about these matters—what makes some people so much more impressive (not only psychologically, but as human beings in their behavior with other human beings) than we understand now."

That letter prompted a kind of paradigm shift in Coles himself; Anna Freud's open-mindedness urged him to take a much more expansive, less prescriptive and judgmental view of the spiritual life.

In 1994, a new category of affliction was added to the most recent edition of psychiatry's *Diagnostic and Statistical Manual:* the "religious or spiritual problem." (It would seem on the surface that this inclusion would pathologize religious experiences, the way homosexuality's inclusion pathologized *it* until the category was removed from DSM in the 1980s; but, in fact, the point is to depathologize them, to make people consider them a "spiritual quest" rather than a "psychic disturbance.")

"Spiritual crises can be mistaken for psychiatric disorders, and this can lead to tragically unnecessary hospitalizations and stunting of the growth potential for persons integrating a spiritual emergency," wrote Stanislav Grof, the psychologist who coined the term *spiritual emergency,* which was the basis for that DSM-IV category. A *spiritual emergency,* as Grof defined it, is a specific kind of psychological difficulty, or crisis, in which individuals experience episodes in which they "may feel their sense of identity is breaking down, that their old values no longer hold true, and that the very ground beneath their personal realities is radically shifting."

Descriptions of the symptoms of "spiritual emergencies" sound a lot like the internal landscape U-turners inhabit when their cognitive dissonance becomes too great to bear.

A reasonably strong case can be made that U-turners are people who were temperamentally inclined to remake themselves in midlife— and it was circumstances and social pressures that dictated the remake's form—religious or secular. But what if it's not a personality trait at all, but rather a phenonomen of epiphanies themselves? Once it happens— once we've had some of our most fundamental assumptions shattered, the personal universe turned on its axis—it becomes easier for it to happen again. We know what it feels like, we know we can survive that particular storm (because we did once), and we know, or believe, that we emerged as wiser people. So there's actually incentive for it to happen again. In some intangible way, it's an adaptive response. In a surprising number of cases, I discovered, U-turners remade themselves radically in more than one area (faith, job, ideology). It's almost as if the psychic adaptations that rejecting one orthodoxy require build the muscles of questioning orthodoxy *as a matter of habit* that serve us later in life.

Epiphanies are, perhaps, adaptive in the following way as well: Some psychologists have raised the provocative possibility that we develop in life by climbing a succession of small epiphanies. In terms of depth and complexity, the insights are progressive. They're sequential. You must stand on one to reach the more rarefied level of the next. In other words, a U-turner could not have had the subsequent, more profound insight without the earlier more superficial ones.

This, then, is the alternative way of looking at the U-turn experience: It is not a crutch at all, but a ladder.

TEN

The Good Hypocrite

*What If Fairly Radical Change Is Not Only
Defensible But Inevitable?*

Half the time, I don't even agree with myself.
—Marshall McLuhan

In Defense of Hypocrisy

The novelist Mark Helprin is generally thought of as a conservative writer: When he's not producing fiction, he pens commentary for the unflaggingly right-wing editorial page of the *Wall Street Journal*. But you can count Helprin among the writers for whom 9/11 rearranged the furniture a little. It made him a pessimist, and the Bush administration's behavior after the attacks—its zealous commitment to meddlesome "nation-building"—made him increasingly uneasy. When the United States invaded Iraq, Helprin had seen enough; he openly opposed the war—and became a dogged Bush critic. Now those who had known him since he was a kid might have traced the post-9/11 recalibration to his past: He'd grown up liberal, voted the Democrat line in college—in fact, he had opposed the Vietnam War and dodged the draft—so perhaps their boy had merely come (back) to his senses. But those who didn't know Helprin were befuddled. What the hell just happened? "Hey," they asked, "where's the consistency?"

"If you're consistent and the road turns," Helprin replied, "you'll crash."

Hypocrisy is often defined as behaving differently today than you did yesterday (even though that's a distortion of the word's actual meaning—saying one thing while doing another). If you accept that definition, then hypocrisy can pretty easily be defended thus: to flip-flop is human. It is one sign of a truly adult mind. The ability to nimbly adjust your views as new information comes in is a necessary evolutionary adaptation. Because new information is always coming in, faster and faster, laying siege to your well-considered opinions.

The marketers and pollsters who divide the world into types predicate their economic calculus on your behavior being absolutely predictable (if you are a churchgoing suburbanite, you are a Republican; if you are a gay urbanite, you are a Democrat, and so on). They would really rather you stay perfectly still, so they can lock in on your position. But staying still is not an option, because, since everything around you is moving forward, doing nothing is the same as moving backwards. "You've got to make decisions," said the British climber Joe Simpson, who unaccountably survived his fall into a crevasse, alone, on a mountain in Peru, as a storm closed in, by deciding to go *down*, deeper into the void. "You've got to keep making decisions, even if they're the wrong decisions. If you stop making decisions, you're stuffed."

With every new insight you chalk up, you become a different person, "the person you previously were, plus understanding," as the psychologist Bradford Keeney puts it. "This new you cannot necessarily perform what worked for the previous you. This means you must always learn to do something different." Doing something different leads to a fresh experience. And the cycle of renewal continues. So consistency, that much-vaunted value whose violation used to carry the most grievous label of all—"sellout"—is really not possible, for it demands the condition that you be "as ignorant today as you were a year ago."

When John McEnroe began hosting a nighttime cable TV talk show a couple of years ago, a *Los Angeles Times* columnist pointed out that McEnroe's understanding of himself seems constantly to be under revision. Before joining the talk-show wars, he had been a "tennis player, rock star manqué, sometime art dealer, father of six and husband of celebrities." As a chat-show host, McEnroe was almost embarrassingly unpolished, yet oddly appealing, and you could tell that he desperately hoped network executives would let him ride up the learning curve until he gained his balance. (They didn't.) But the *Times* writer was feeling generous. "McEnroe might be a bit of a dilettante," he wrote, "but there's nothing wrong with being that. It's a sensible response to the fact you only live once."

To circle back around to the slippery question of "authenticity" and "honesty," then: Is it more honest to be faithful to your old vision of the world—of who you used to be—or to be faithful to human nature?

No one behaves entirely consistently, not even—perhaps not least— the seemingly noblest among us. The environmentalist Edward Abbey is widely beloved for his principled defense of nature, but one biographer couldn't help noticing that he threw beer cans out the window of his truck. The singer Leonard Cohen, as he has grown older, has dealt with being a lot of contradictory things at once, and holding mutually abrasive opinions, by trying to stop worrying so much about it. "It becomes more and more tiresome," he said not long ago, "to defend an opinion you probably never really held in the first place."

"Modern life is just too full of contradictions for people to claim their behavior is always in line with their ethical aims," says the University of Toronto cognitive scientist Keith Stanovich. We all wrestle, more or less constantly, to reconcile the two. But—and here is the big, heartening point—we don't have to succeed in aligning them to be ethical human beings. We can live with a certain amount of hypocrisy, as long as we've thought the issue out thoroughly. (The irony is that it's those folks who are struggling with moral questions at the highest level, constantly subjecting their thoughts to scrutiny and reevaluation, who tend to be the ones accused of hypocrisy. "Those who are frankly self-serving but consistent," Stanovich notes, "escape the charge entirely.")

Some sorting out of the big issues from the little ones happens at every stage of everyone's life. Ideally, we strive to reconcile the big inconsistencies and let the smaller ones ride. The question the U-turner is confronted with repeatedly, then, is: *Is this a bridge I'm prepared to die on?*

U-Turn

The Leap of Faith

There's a three-blind-men-and-the-elephant quality to the lives many of us live—the continual making of pronouncements on the meaning of life and the true nature of our identity from what we think is big-picture information, but isn't. Since we can never really be certain, taking a firm position, on anything, can seem unwise. Chess players are familiar with a circumstance in a match called a zugzwang, where any move they make is likely to hurt them. If they had the luxury of more time, they could construct a more considered decision. But they don't. The would-be U-turner is frequently in a kind of zugzwang bind. He'd make a better move tomorrow, but he has to move now.

And here is where something more than simple logic is required.

Just as one can't come to a belief in God through reason alone—to try to is to be like those mythical, two-dimensional Flatlanders trying to perceive a third dimension—the leap from fashionable academic agnosticism to damn-the-torpedoes, full-commitment belief in something or some idea isn't one that can be made by reason alone. Because, *logically*, a leap like that doesn't make much sense.

Agnosticism has on its side, as noted, a powerful historical argument: totalitarianism. *I never want to be as sure of anything as the people who built this place.*

It's also supported by the seemingly bulletproof integrity of the scientific method, whose essence, as Thomas Huxley put it, is that "It is wrong for a man to say he is certain of the objective truth of a proposition unless he can produce evidence which logically justifies that certainty." Agnosticism is an evidence-based credo. It says: *Prove it. Prove it with double-blind tests in peer-reviewed journals, and then I'll believe it.*

But if we only made decisions based on unchallengeable proof, there would be no Precautionary Principle. We wouldn't take steps to reduce our carbon emissions, since the case that humans are contributing to global warming is strong but not definitive. No one would be vegetarian on moral (as opposed to health) grounds, since we can't know *for sure* that animals suffer the way we suffer, or that their emotional life is much like ours, and there's no sensible reason to grant intellectually inferior species moral equivalency. No one would give a second thought to their kids being perpetually plugged in to the entertainment grid, since there's little definitive evidence that consumer culture is detrimental to the "soul" (if there is a soul), that violent video games have any impact, that advertising has any impact. (Sure, there are correlations between, say, levels of depression and television watching in a culture, but we cannot infer causality.) It makes no sense to devote two years to saving a single redwood when the forest around it is mowed down, and when the old tree is going to fall anyway. It's not rational for a chemical engineer to throw his whole career over the side to write short fiction: Literature, after all, as the poet said, "makes nothing happen." James Joyce has no measurable impact on the economy, or even on human happiness.

And, of course, by strictly logical criteria, spiritual agnosticism is the only way to go, since both belief and nonbelief are equally indefensible: You can no more demonstrate that God doesn't exist than that He does.

But strict logic is not always the right tool for the job.

In the film *Contact*, written by the late Carl Sagan and his wife Annie Druyan, a radio astronomer played by Jodie Foster gets lured in a philosophical discussion with a spiritual young man, played by Matthew McConaughey, who believes in extraterrestrial life. Scientifically, the notion is what Stephen Jay Gould would call a "bad theory," not because it's unlikely but because it's not testable. That's Jodie Foster's take, too. How can you believe in something for which there is no definitive proof? McConaughey knows enough about her to push a big button.

"Did you love your father?"

"Yes," she replies, "very much."

"Prove it," he says.

This is what the U-turners discussed in this book ultimately have in common. Virtually all the things that they took a leap of faith and committed to wouldn't have happened if they had relied on reason alone. They might well be wrong, and they know it. They might not believe tomorrow what they believe today, and they know that, too. They know that the costs of failing to commit aren't strictly calculable, but they have intuited that those costs are higher than the cost of doing nothing, until a doctor slides their eyes closed and they finish there, in the equipoise of perfect academic equivocation.

Some of the criticisms leveled at John Walker Lindh, the jug-eared young "American Taliban," centered on the naïveté of the man, more specifically the naïveté of the idea of the search for the fool's gold called "authenticity." At root, Lindh's mistaken assumption was, as the essayist Ron Rosenbaum puts it, that "Authenticity must always be found not in otherness but in oppositeness." But consider the other extreme to Lindh's reflex to push against the perceived evils of his own culture by trading himself in for his opposite number. It is blind self-assurance that the way you already are—your values, your system—is correct, so there's no need to investigate alternatives.

Not too long ago, one ad-industry veteran expressed his frustration with the new, creeping self-righteousness he was seeing among a certain breed of graphic designer, who insisted that the adman's power be used solely for the good. Anti-consumerist design was already becoming the rage. "Doing graphic design that's anti-consumerist is a bit like fucking for chastity," he said. "Graphic design has always been used for both good *and* evil, so stop being nostalgic—it is the very nature of the beast." The human soul can't be bifurcated like that, he was implying; we can't cut away the dark parts, pretend they don't exist, and embrace the light—any more than Dr. Jekyll could develop a potion that kept Mr. Hyde at a restraining-order's distance.

But U-turners aren't necessarily guilty of that error. You can still believe the soul contains light and dark, that we are made of multitudes, but choose to let the strongest voice in the choir speak. To jump the gap is not to deny the existence of the part of you that you are repudiating, but to choose not to back it. It's like a lawyer's strategy: The moment you are hired on and agree to advocate for this new client—your new identity—even though you are only 51 percent persuaded of the legitimacy of this character, that's enough. You argue the case as if it weren't 51/49, but 100/0. The tipping point came the moment you decided, consciously or not, to take the case.

Commitment need not come from naïveté. "The test of a first-rate intelligence is the ability to hold two opposing ideas in the mind at the same time, and still retain the ability to function," wrote F. Scott Fitzgerald famously in *The Crack Up*. One should, for example, "be able to see that things are hopeless and yet be determined to make them otherwise."

The Good Hypocrite

U-turners are often accused of being idealists, which is sometimes just shorthand for "fanatics." But the difference between the two is clear. The fanatic is absolutely sure; the U-turner need not be sure, only moved—enough to make the required leap of faith.

A Developmental Step

There are some fairly strong arguments that certain kinds of U-turns are maladaptive and destructive. But, in general, I think, a lights-out case can be made that major life changes of the kind we're talking about are by and large *con*structive. That, as we've seen, the emotional turmoil that precedes it, which looks a lot like a mental health problem, might in fact be an adaptive response.

An authoritative-sounding theory, advanced by Eric Hoffer and others—who have observed that extremely low self-esteem correlates with big life reversals—holds that only people who think of themselves as total losers would be willing to throw themselves on the discard pile and change utterly what they stand for. But the rebuttal to the theory is bracing. Yes, U-turns may correlate with low self-esteem—but they also appear to correlate with extremely *high* self-esteem. Ironically, it's people at the far ends of that measure of mental health who seem similarly equipped to take that drastic step. Both types, Elliot Aronson, professor emeritus of psychology at UCal Santa Cruz and an expert in dissonance theory, recently noted, have "nothing to lose by saying, 'Geez, I guess everything I invested in doesn't make much sense.'"

"Some sort of epiphany or transformation, I believe, is a natural feature of genuinely human, as opposed to animal, life," Sidney Rittenberg told me. "The more people are aware of this, and the more they learn to lean into it rather than away from it, the better off and the happier they may be." At any given moment, you are either on the right path or you are on the wrong path, C. S. Lewis believed, and, if you are on the wrong path, "you're getting farther from your true self with every step." Not to take what we intuitively believe is the correct course, some of the humanistic psychologists hold, is a failure of will that will come back to haunt us—not in some future lifetime but in this one.

"The serious thing for each person to recognize vividly and poignantly, each for himself, is that every falling away from species-virtue, *every crime against one's own nature,* every one without exception, records itself in our unconscious and makes us despise ourselves," wrote Abraham Maslow. Martin Luther, who could get away with making pronouncements in Latin, was fond of saying, "*Semper oportit nasci, novari, generari:* We must always be reborn, renewed, regenerated." The rebel's crises of identity are, apparently, the price of the ticket to the grown-ups' table.

As he compiled the results of the thirty-five-year-long Grant Study—a pioneering tracking of a group of men from college to midlife—the Harvard psychiatrist George Vaillant noticed something surprising. The subjects he calls the "best outcomes"—the men who moved into later life with the most happiness and success and general mental health—were the ones who had had a midlife hiccup. They did something different. They moved into new territory, often taking on responsibility their life to that point hadn't prepared them for. They needed to take something of a blind jump. "Instead of delving progressively deeper into their specialized careers and acquiring progressively more competence, in middle life the men's career patterns suddenly diverged and broadened; they assumed tasks that they had not been trained for," Valliant reported. Conversely, the ones who fared less well, in the long run, were the ones who, in midlife, held steady as she goes.

"Some of the men in the study, the majority of them lawyers and business vice-presidents, ignored the rising sap of the forties," and they paid for it. They paid for it by getting stuck in a single-minded career focus—a stage that, Erik Erikson believed, healthy people outgrow on the way to the more richly personal, human rewards of later life. Failing to rebel—that is, failing to chart some fairly novel new course—during this midlife "second adolescence" may be as harmful as failing to rebel during the original adolescence was. An essential developmental step is skipped—and when that happens, there are always consequences. That, at least, is the theory, and the fear.

The midlife rebellion the U-turn represents is like a middle manager parachuting back to high school to correct some mistakes. It looks like a step backward, but some theorize that it's actually a leap forward to a higher level of moral functioning, where rules of principle supersede the rule of law. They look similar, the first adolescence and the second—both preceded by crisis and involving acute questioning of identity, intolerance of hypocrisy, challenging of orthodoxies, and bad decisions about pants.

Why does it take U-turners so long to go back and graduate? William James believed that if no "definite crisis" happened during the first adolescence, then issues of identity remain unresolved until midlife, when a spiritual dimension of life surfaces. That heretofore missing element works like an oxytocin drip at the bedside, hastening the rebirth.

Albert Schweitzer was in the middle of setting up a little hospital in French Equatorial Africa when he developed the metaphor of how the soul becomes imperiled when we live superficially. "You know of the disease called sleeping sickness?" he wrote. "There also exists a sleeping sickness of the soul. Its most dangerous aspect is that one is unaware of its coming. That is why you have to be careful. As soon as you notice the slightest sign of indifference, the moment you become aware of the loss of a certain seriousness, of longing, of enthusiasm and zest, take it as a warning.

"It is tragic that most men have not achieved this feeling of self-awareness," Schweitzer wrote. As a consequence, "When they finally do hear the inner voice, they do not want to listen. They carry on as before so as not to be constantly reminded of what they have lost."

Maslow had a slightly different theory of what causes this state of psychic tension. He spoke of the stress that can build up if one senses an *evasion of one's destiny*. If we believe that we were put here to do great, important, socially constructive things, and find that we are instead underachieving—perhaps, out of fear, we turn our backs on what we believe, deep down, we *should* be doing—our whole body lets us know, in Maslow's view. This is a moral argument at its root; it resonates with Aristotle's notion that we *must* become the kind of person we *can* be.

The notion of avoiding one's moral destiny is what some psychologists have called the "Jonah Syndrome." The name comes from the biblical story, in which God asks Jonah to carry a warning to the people in his morally decaying city to shape up, and Jonah just can't do it. He does everything to duck this responsibility, until finally he is forced to face it. In the end, Jonah does carry out the request, and a great odyssey of transformation and repentance comes to a close. (It's interesting that, like so many U-turners, Jonah does not change on his own. He embarks on this journey only when he's forced to; it's only after some sailors literally haul him up from below deck, in the teeth of a storm, and involve him in a debate about who is responsible for the storm, that Jonah volunteers to be tossed overboard to calm the waters. It's in the amniotic belly of the whale that he experiences his "rebirth.")

"You must tell yourself the truth about where you seem to have been placed and why," said Rabbi Harold Kushner, who frequently teaches the story of Jonah as a parable of responsibility and atonement. "I guess I'd have to say you learn what that feels like by trial and error. Your destiny looks you in the face, and you know you've got to do something. If you don't do it, it's going to be real hard looking in the mirror the next morning."

When Nathaniel Kahn, director of the Oscar-nominated documentary *My Architect: A Son's Journey*, began investigating the career of his father, the great architect Louis Kahn, he discovered that, until surprisingly late in life, his father was pretty much adrift. "He was about fifty years old and still hadn't found himself," Nathaniel said. True, he had settled on a métier, which puts him ahead of most of us who are lost, but he was lost within it, an emerging modernist style that escaped Lou when he tried to emulate it. It was only when he accepted an architect-in-residence post at the American Academy in Rome, and traveled for the first time to the ancient world, that the dawn came. "What he saw, in the remnants of the ancient world, changed his life." Now he had a mission: "to build modern buildings that had the feel of ancient ruins."

All this resonated for the son, for before chasing his father's ghost, he, too, felt lost. For years a kind of dogsbody in the middling tiers of the media industry, he decided, as he approached forty, that he needed to make a feature film. He woke up just in time.

"It always frightens me to think you could go through your entire living having capabilities within you that you don't use," he explained to the journalist Simon Houpt. "To me that's the scariest thing of all.

The Good Hypocrite

Everything else you can kind of deal with and negotiate and we all have to die in the end and that's the way it is. But the idea that you have cards left in your hand that you haven't played and things you haven't done—it's terribly torturous to have talents and either not be able to use them or find a way to use them."

Surely the decision to play our best cards is a personal one. And failing to do so can quite clearly cause tension or depression or worse. But is it actually unethical?

Erik Erikson thought so. "Whenever and wherever man abandons his ethical position, he does so only at the cost of massive regressions endangering the very safeguards of his nature." And because every decision made by every individual redounds down the generations, Erikson liked to point out, what's at stake isn't just whether one person finds happiness or torment, but "the collective life of mankind."

That's a lot to lay on anyone's conscience—but the Buddha more or less said the same thing: *Only by finding and acting on our true calling*, he said, *can we save the world.*

The Moral Imperative

If he had lived in the computer age, Jean Piaget might explain U-turns this way. We chug along, quietly assimilating new information into our worldview; then we confront something too big or radical to assimilate "into the present structures of knowing," as he liked to say. The hard drive crashes. A new one is installed in its place, a "new structure of knowing." The new hardware is an upgrade, better able to handle the volume and kind of data it's going to encounter. A crisis, resolved by a life change, has landed the U-turner back into the world powerfully, exquisitely rewired.

George Vaillant evoked the image of a twisted old seaside tree to represent someone who has adapted successfully to his conditions—its beauty is appreciated eventually. That's a good working definition of the evolutionary U-turn, but the metaphor holds true for more sudden conversions as well. These were trees that were growing one way, and then—crisis!—the earth slid out from under them, and they ended up disoriented; but their genetic instructions continued apace, and, in that new attitude, they grew as before. Those are the trees that make you stop and look.

We want to feel moral and virtuous, to feel "ethically worthy." So strongly do we want that feeling that when the normal avenues to express that ethical worthiness are closed off, we're inclined to take a radical lunge in a new direction—religion or social justice or animal rights—to feel good about ourselves again.

William Kunstler, the drowsy suburban tax lawyer turned radical crusader, arguably got way more from the civil rights activists in the South than they ever got from him: He got a life-changing sense of purpose and virtue. In some ways, it assuaged the guilt he felt about the privileges he had had bestowed on him, the investment his parents had made in him—Yale and Columbia Law school—that had mostly gone unrealized. "Coming from a family that had provided me with a childhood of comfort and security, I felt that in order to validate my life, my time on earth had to count for something," Kunstler wrote in his memoir, *My Life As a Radical Lawyer*. "I felt a need to justify the air I breathed, the food I ate, and the water I drank." During the trial of his most famous clients, the Freedom Riders, "The media attention, and ego gratification, added to my feeling that I was doing important work." Kunstler's view of himself changed. "I began to see myself as someone who had a real contribution to make."

Kunstler's motive may have been self-serving in these respects. Indeed, he admits, "At first I felt like Lord Bountiful succoring the masses: I would help these poor people, represent them in court, save their lives, help them regain their liberty." But the motivation for continuing on the path he had found was nobler. Deeper, less self-centered. As the years passed, especially after the Chicago Seven conspiracy trial, "when I learned that the government would stop at nothing to win its case," Kunstler became increasingly involved in representing people who could not stand up for themselves.

And that's how it often works with U-turners. A turn initiated for fairly superficial—or at least inarticulable—reasons ripens into real moral conviction.

The Good Hypocrite

Because ethical behavior isn't something we casually pursue to alleviate the insecurity of living without limits: it's something, evidence suggests, we are *driven* to pursue, because it is hardwired. The human moral sense, evident in kids as young as two years old, Jerome Kagan points out, is a motive so powerful that it is trumped only by protecting ourselves from harm. It's a product of evolution that ensures our survival. (That doesn't mean moral behavior is easy, for, as we've noted, our values and desires are frequently at odds.)

At issue with U-turners, in the phase of crisis that precedes their turn, are two of Immanuel Kant's essential questions: "How do I be good?" and "What should I do?"

And it's around this point that the U-turner, if he really is being honest about his motivations, must perform some tricky calculus. The relief of suffering is not a zero-sum game. How should we weigh the relief of our own suffering that a U-turn provides against the suffering to family and friends and colleagues that a sudden embrace of a new, "true" life can bring?

On the night of August 20, 1995, the night the "dam broke" for Donald McCloskey, the respected professor of economics and history had been driving alone on a toll road in Illinois. McCloskey's private trope was that he was a man who sometimes played at being a woman, cross-dressing a little, "just a hobby." But there in the dark that night, amid the hum of five-axle traffic, an epiphany had landed. He was not a man who sometimes played at being a woman. He was not a man at all. This recognition made him suddenly burst into tears. And so, where a few miles back in Aurora, Illinois, Donald McCloskey—married thirty years, with two grown children—had gotten in the car, in Dekalb, the woman who was to become Deirdre McCloskey would momentarily get out.

About what happened there could be no doubt. "People have moments," he would later explain it, "when self-knowledge becomes more than a swirl of facts. A singular truth of character stands in front of you. Secularly speaking, *it is knowing yourself instead of knowing about yourself*."

But the epiphany was the easy part. Having "woken up" to his true

213

nature, it fell to McCloskey to decide what, practically, to do about it. This was not an easy choice. He was still, in body, a man. Intellectual honesty compelled him to come clean and act on his moment of clarity in the car. But the consequences seemed monumental.

And so, as economists do, he drew up a cost-benefit analysis. He wrote it down just so:

"The Costs and Benefits of Womanhood."

Among the costs:

- My wife would leave me. This would be the loss of my best friend.
- My daughter would reject me, though my son I think would continue to love me.
- My birth family would be appalled. My mother in particular would be unable to handle it.
- I'd lose all my casual friends, and many, many of my professional friends.
- The transition is impossible in my occupation. A woman would not be allowed to have the intellectual style I have.

On the plus side, well, "I get to be pretty."

On paper, the positives were mightily outgunned. But in a move that did not make what economists would call "utilitarian" sense, he elected to go forward.

Donald told his wife about his epiphany. Not unexpectedly, she had some trouble with it. More than some. She cried, she withdrew, she became angry and depressed; his fears for the marriage seemed well-founded.

What followed was a series of events you would not wish on anyone. The trauma was comprehensive, and spread equally between family members, with the biggest portion reserved for Donald-cum-Deirdre McCloskey.

Not long after he revealed the news to his family, two deputies showed up at his door and took him away in handcuffs to the psychiatric unit of the state hospital, on the grounds that he was a "danger to

himself." (It was his psychologist sister who had initiated the commitment, only out of the purest love for him, she insisted. And clearly his
son thought he was doing a compassionate thing when, at his father's
mental-fitness hearing, he testified against him.)

Because he would not sign the consent forms to be "treated" by the
hospital (a wise move, since he would have been agreeing to be committed for up to three years), his Blue Cross coverage had been voided.
Hospital bills started piling up. One bill alone, for a single day—
actually six hours—as an outpatient in that Graduate Hospital in Iowa
City, where he had been sent, came to $18,461. McCloskey would bat-
tle the hospitals for years over these bills.

The community of neoclassical economists reacted predictably—
neoclassically. As the initial shock wave spread, Deirdre found herself
dropped from the roster of conferences where Donald had been scheduled to speak. When she returned to academic life, Deirdre found
herself the target of scorn by a small group of feminists who view
gender-crossers with disdain—men who do not belong in this world
they have infiltrated. (Deirdre has since reestablished a strong reputation as a historian and "feminist economist.") Looking for a church in
the community she finally settled in, she found people avoiding her, unable to deal with her—in a way that suggested to her what it must be
like to have a fatal disease.

At one point, she tallied up the strictly numeric costs: roughly
$90,000 for the basic surgeries—including cosmetic and voice surgery
from good doctors—plus "a lot of surgery to fix their surgery." But
more significant costs are often the ones that don't make it on the ledger.
The real cost of making a crossing like McCloskey's isn't money, she decided: "It's what you sacrifice by taking the path." McCloskey had lost
a wife, a son, and a daughter.

And what *they* had lost, well, that was the kind of collateral damage
economists call "externalities," and these can be incalculable.

As far as Deirdre could surmise, the loss of Donald to Deirdre was,
to Deirdre's wife, a loss "worse than a death." "Had Donald died of a
heart attack at age fifty-three, as his father had, the wife would have acted
the widow for a while, sad to see her life's companion leave, dignified in

her grief," Deirdre said. But he was gone and not gone. Murdered, but there across campus sat the murderess, alive and happy and unpunished. "She felt," Deirdre imagined of her wife, "that the crossing made thirty years of her life meaningless." She divorced and moved to another town and never came back to Iowa City.

After several months of exchanging e-mails with him, her son, a Chicago businessman now, broke off all contact. Deirdre received one last e-mail after a year of silence, informing her that her son had been married the week before. "You were not of course invited. That is all I will say." Deirdre was reluctant to give up on her daughter, a college student in Lawrence, Kansas, who had also severed all communications. She tracked the daughter down and ambushed her with a visit, which did not go particularly well. The daughter promptly moved and got an unlisted number. Previously, when Deirdre was still Donald, this daughter had sent a letter pleading with him not to go through with what he was intending: It would be a failure of his duty as a father. How far does duty extend? Deirdre asked herself then. "To avoid their self-defined hurt from embarrassment, am I to refuse my life?"

Not long ago the *New York Times* ran a story about a woman who, after her wealthy executive husband suddenly announced he'd had an epiphany and was entering the priesthood, sued him. Her argument was that she had, essentially, been sold a bill of goods. Had she known this impulse was in him, she might not have married him. By her way of thinking, there is an implicit clause to the marriage contract. You cannot change. You cannot change because your life is not your own, as long as you have attachments.

Your family may imply that, because your decision hurt them, it was not entirely yours to make. Twenty years ago, Chuck Collins, a great-grandson of Oscar Mayer, decided to give away a half-million-dollar inheritance to charity. It wasn't easy. As soon as he made his intentions known, he was guilt-tripped about how his crazy decision would unfairly punish his children, and their children, who had done nothing to merit getting booted off the gravy train. (Collins *had* no children at the time, but the argument lost none of its provocative philosophical sting. What do we owe, to whom, and in what measure?)

Even U-turns made for the most ostensibly selfless reasons can seem selfish to those who get sacrificed for the "greater good." Gandhi stands as the paragon of compassion of the twentieth century. Yet, like many social activists, his compassion toward the faceless hordes did not quite extend to the people closest to him. (His wife, Kasturba, bore the brunt of this devotion to chastity. And, in fact, Gandhi's testing of his own resistance to temptation—he slept nude with young women— had a callousness about it that complicates the picture of the man of ultimate compassion.) Charles Dickens had a term for the practice of big-picture do-goodism at the price of friends and family: *telescopic morality*.

From Denise Ryan's perspective, the story of her mother's sudden abandonment of the fifties matriarch role to move to the tropics to paint, can be summed up in a sentence: "My mom found her bliss and we were left to struggle." Inarguably, the decision destroyed the family as it was. The marriage almost immediately began to unravel, and her mom's abrupt transformation, Denise notes, left her father perma- nently changed. "After the divorce he became very conservative," she says. He left the field of law reform and went to work for a big oil com- pany, eventually managing the tax department, a Cadillac filling his private parking stall. (He died of a heart attack at age fifty-four.) On grounds of pride, and principle, her mom refused child support, which left the family in a strange spot—inhabiting the family house in an up- scale neighborhood, but too poor for the kids even to go on class field trips. Left largely alone as their mother threw herself into her painting downtown, the kids went lawless and when they briefly stopped going to school, nobody much noticed. One day her dad took her aside, Denise recalls, and said: "Your mother ruined her own life, and then she ruined her brothers' lives, and now she has ruined you." (As for Denise's mom, Angeline herself, well, the decision left her suddenly isolated—"I quickly realized I was the only one who knew who I was"— and into psychotherapy. It sent her plunging about five tax brackets. For years, she almost literally lived on peanuts, and she grew gaunt—a true starving artist.)

Denise is quite candid about the effect it all had on her own life. For many, many years, she delayed any kind of traditional attachment—marriage or kids—since it appeared that this is what had undone her mother. "I thought, This is one of the things that made her snap."

And this is the point in the story where a jury asked to render a verdict on the U-turner would almost have heard enough.

But it's not so simple. It is never so simple.

"What the kids didn't understand at the time was that I was in a crisis," Angeline says. "I had no option." Her own father's death had foreclosed on the possible self he had always longed to become—for he, too, had been a talented painter, but the hardworking life of a new immigrant allowed no time for it. "I don't know if the understanding was completely conscious," she says, "but I knew I had to live the life he never got a chance to live." It was her life, too: That much Angeline Kyba knew. She wasn't about to let another possible self evaporate. She couldn't.

"It was a life-or-death situation. The kids didn't believe it at the time, but I think they do now."

Some years ago Denise came into chance contact with an old childhood friend from the neighborhood. The friend, too, had had a similarly perfect June Cleaver of a mom. In the same stifling circumstances, the friend's mother had found a different way out. One day, while the rest of the family was away on a car trip, she walked into the garage and took her own life. Angeline's solution was ragged and unwelcome, but ultimately less tragic. In some ways it was not tragic at all, for it played out, in the end, in unexpected ways.

There was an almost vaudevillian affection between Denise and her mom when I saw them in the back garden of Denise's home one scorching summer evening, as her funny husband turned souvlaki on the grill and her five-year-old, Alexander, did flying dives into the wading pool. Her mom would recall an incident from the past and Denise would flatly contradict the memory, but in a way that suggested she conceded a truth behind it, a bigger truth. In the larger picture, honoring her wake-up call did no great disservice to the kids, Angeline believes. On the contrary. "I think," she said, in a quiet, vaguely Faye Dunaway-ish voice, "that it showed them there are other ways to live."

The Good Hypocrite

I asked Denise what she thought her life would be like today if her mother hadn't performed her big midlife U-turn. "Probably I'd have become a lawyer," she said. "That was always the plan. My father hoped I would graduate from West Point." Today Angeline Kyba's grown kids are spread out across the landscape. One is a professional skier living in a charming mountain town in British Columbia; a second lives in Berlin, a composer of some hit pop songs and a guitar player in Nina Hagen's band. Denise, on leave from a newspaper job, is finishing a novel. All are living their bliss in ways traditional career counselors tell you never to count on.

The immediate feeling of those "left behind" by a U-turner's decision is often betrayal—but perhaps less by the turn itself than by its suddenness, which implies that feelings were hidden. In social groups there is that need for truthfulness, Nietzsche believed, the obligation to show, "by clear and constant signs," who we are. It is an issue, at its core, of communication.

"This kind of thing can be managed more or less well," the University of Toronto cognitive scientist Keith Stanovich says. If you're taking on water, engaged in a private struggle to reconcile belief and desire that seems to be approaching some tipping point, "then it seems to me you have some moral obligation to be telling people." The would-be U-turner, typically, feels the disequilibrium but keeps a lid on it, believing stoicism to be the best course. Until the big discrete shift comes about. "Discrete shifts can often look sudden, and selfish in their suddenness. But they may not look so selfish if the person had been revealing the struggle all along. If people came out of the closet with their small worries earlier, as they built up, we might be able to avoid these big, precipitous turns."

But duty goes both ways. Once the person starts articulating these struggles, people around her may have a kind of moral obligation to meet her halfway.

"We have this tendency to freeze people into the original roles we have for them—and of course families do this all the time," Stanovich continues. "Who you are as that seventeen-year-old kid is who you must forever remain. So the role that families can play is that when someone announces that they're wrestling with changes, they restrain themselves from slamming the lid."

The question of what is ethical behavior, in a given circumstance, is, of course, endlessly debatable. But the issue of *whether* to act ethically, once we've figured out what the ethical course is, is somewhat clearer. Evolutionary psychologists suggest that we are *inclined* to act ethically. If we truly don't believe that carrying a sword is ethical, there will come a point when we *can't not put it down.*

The idea that we are innately ethical—that, as Steven Pinker puts it, "Evolution makes you the kind of person others can trust"—makes sense, in social terms, as an explanation for moral U-turns. And at the same time it doesn't. Can a phenomenon that brings so many negative social consequences really be said to be adaptively advantageous?

The best way to answer that question is to turn it around: What harm can come of continuing on the wrong path?

In his speech of April 13, 1968, in Memphis (the "If I Had Sneezed" speech), Martin Luther King evoked the image of the three travelers on the road to Jericho, and their respective responses to the stranger in distress at the roadside. The priest and the Levite first passed by the man and didn't stop. Perhaps, King mused, they were fearful of a trick: *If I stop to help this man, what will happen to me?* "And then the Samaritan came along," King said, "and he reversed the question: 'If *I do not* stop to help this man, what will happen to me?'"

If we do not stop, and act to relieve suffering when we know we can, what will happen to us?

Paul Medlow, a young man from Indiana, was one of the 90 or so soldiers of Charlie Company who, on March 16, 1968, were placed in an impossible situation. They had been sent in with two other companies to the North Vietnamese village of My Lai 4 (which the soldiers knew as "Pinkville"), believed to be a fortified stronghold of enemy soldiers. Under pressure and demoralized from having recently lost men in their company, they were not in a position to marshall their strongest ethical beliefs when their commanding officer, Lieutenant William

Calley, ordered that all 550 men, women, and children in the village be herded into ditches and shot.

All the soldiers of Charlie Company were asked to participate in the killing. Some of the soldiers found ways to stop being soldiers on that day—at least the kind of soldier they had been asked to be. Some improvised schemes to get out of the impossible situation. Some did not openly defy orders, but surreptitiously shot into the air. One soldier, quickly sizing up what was being asked of his platoon, "shot himself in the foot in order to be medevaced out of the area so he would not have to participate in the slaughter," as Seymour Hersh, the investigative reporter who broke the My Lai story in the *New York Times*, recounted recently. But these "ethical" soldiers were the outliers. Under the circumstances, a reversal required both the courage to defy a direct order and a kind of trust in one's own independent, intuitive judgment—and most of the members of Charlie Company weren't up to such a leap. They did what was expected of them on that day, killing everything in their path. Their conscience remained suppressed and their conscious mind, at least, relatively untroubled.

Among the saints and the sinners, Paul Medlow fell somewhere in the middle. Paul Medlow's conscience kicked in eventually—but by then it was too late. Medlow was among those who followed orders. He did, as Hersh recounted, "an awful lot of shooting."

The next day was mop-up duty. "One of the mothers at the bottom of a ditch had taken a child—a boy, about two—and got him under her stomach in such a way that he wasn't killed. The boy crawled out of the ditch while the soldiers were having lunch. Calley looked at Medlow, and said, "Kill him." Medlow shouldered his machine gun . . . and then he lowered it. "Plug him," Calley said. Medlow couldn't do it. "So Calley ran up as everybody watched, with a rifle, and shot the kid in the back of the head," Hersh said.

"The next morning, Medlow stepped on a mine and he had his foot blown off. He was medevaced out. As he departed, he cursed: 'God has punished me, and he's going to punish you, too.'" (What happened to Medlow devastated his family. The soldier's mother, when Seymour Hersh later tracked her down at the family chicken farm in New

Goshen, Indiana, said of the army: "I gave them a good boy. They sent me back a murderer.")

Medlow, tormented by what had happened, came forward as a whistleblower. But he is remembered, thanks to his testimony, and his documentors, as a good man with an asterisk by his name. He was, and remains, the soldier whose epiphany missed the train.

ELEVEN

The Thought Experiment
Can a U-Turn Be Willed?

Long stretches of silent meditation in bare cells bring monks
to the sort of visions non-believers can achieve only with
expensive pills or perhaps a mishap with a bad clam.
—Randy Cohen

I t just happens," says Ray Anderson of the light that comes at the
end of the long tunnel of cognitive dissonance. "It can't be willed, I
don't believe."

He is speaking from his own experience, but the point makes
broader intuitive sense. How can you will something—like sleep, or a
proclamation of your spouse's love, or an epiphanic mind shift—that's
supposed to happen spontaneously? William James believed that, ultimately, true conversions must be unwilled, because the last, necessary
link in the causal chain is giving up the will in the form of self-surrender.
"The very last step must be left to other forces and performed without
the help of the will's activity." You can't voluntarily cause an epiphany
any more than you can will a sneeze.

But you *can* voluntarily walk into a grain silo or an abandoned house
full of cats—*thereby setting up the conditions for a sneeze.*

If there were no basis for the idea that the conditions for a U-turn moment could be created, no missionary among the "heathen" or the psychoanalyst with a stuck patient would bother to make the effort. No one

223

would pray, or smoke peyote with a shaman, or try to lead a rigorously clean life, or go live in a peat hut. It is the very basis of religion that you can *do* things to enlarge your sense of compassion and connectedness to the world—to take the altruism toward kith and kin that is instinctive and, through hard work, widen its scope, until not a living creature is omitted. In the Tunnel of Love at the Reality Theme Park, the attendant hands you a shovel and says, *You gotta dig it yourself.*

Artists routinely reach for catalysts to inspiration. Composers listen to Mozart, writers read William Faulkner or Joseph Mitchell. And many kinds of therapy depend on the client being willing to meet serendipity halfway.

In the sciences, the case has steadily been building that breakthrough thinking is not so much a slave to numinous "inspiration," but an actual skill that can be cultivated because it's a lot more systematic than most people realize. ("Most 'inventions' that we often assume came in a flash," as the writers of a 1987 book called *Scientific Discovery* put it, "in fact evolved over years or decades or systematic thinking about the problem.")

Yoga was invented not for physical health but as a spiritual discipline—a rigorous and precise ladder to transcendence.

The idea that intense study and scholarship can bring on epiphanies is central to the tradition of Jewish mysticism.

The notion that "imaginative contemplation" can "aid the believer's spiritual progress toward the goal of salvation" was at the heart of St. Ignatius's enormously influential *Spiritual Exercises.* (The exercises were specifically aimed at projecting yourself into the sandals of Christ—What might He have been seeing, hearing, smelling, thinking about?—until you eventually come to inhabit Him, or He you. But you could say that many more modern, New Age-y visualization techniques are an extension of Ignatius's strategy—adapted and popularized by the self-improvement gurus to turn the meek, middling sales representatives who diligently employ them into bulletproof masters of all they survey.)

Eastern spiritual traditions are rich in intellectual exercises designed to engineer the kind of cognitive dissonance that, as we have seen, often precedes big eureka moments. This is the premise of Zen koans, so cryptic and paradoxical they force the mind to make a quantum jump.

And it's roughly how the *I Ching* is supposed to work. For three thousand years the *I Ching* has been a tool of divination for people who need to make a decision that "rational knowledge" has failed to equip them for. Tapping the *I Ching* is seen as a way of gaining access to the spiritual engine room from which, supposedly, your life is being run.

It works like this: After a lot of soul-searching to articulate the problem precisely, you put a question to the universe. Then you throw coins or yarrow stalks and, in the way they fall, the answer is revealed—not in so many words, but in a kind of symbolic language that supposedly does an end-run around the mental block. The main thing to understand about the *I Ching* is that it doesn't provide answers; it helps *you* come up with answers, by recasting the problem. Of course, the very fact that you are consulting the *I Ching* means that something is out of balance. You're searching, therefore you're halfway to change already.

(Some modern Christian theologians view the Bible as a device of divination, God's Magic 8-Ball. Such people, in the tradition of John Robinson, urge us to look into the Bible as if it were a mirror. Embedded in the biblical stories, they believe, is our own personal story, which will become clear the moment we open ourselves to seeing it.)

Western mental health professionals are likely to call their divination system something like reframing. The idea is to try to help the client see things in an entirely different way—to encourage the "cognitive snap," a shift in perspective.

The late psychoanalyst Milton Erickson was famous for penetrating the intellectual defenses of reluctant clients. He did it by wrong-footing the intellect, and then zipping into the breach. Actually, Erickson stumbled upon this strategy, what he came to call his "confusion technique," by accident.

"On a windy day . . . a man came rushing around the corner of a building and bumped hard against me as I stood bracing myself against the wind," Erickson writes. "Before he could recover his poise to speak to me, I glanced elaborately at my watch and courteously, as if he had inquired the time of day, I stated, 'It's exactly ten minutes of two,' though it was actually closer to 4 p.m., and walked on. About half a block away, I turned and saw him still looking at me, undoubtedly still puzzled and bewildered by my remark."

Erickson had injected "confusion" into this interaction with the stranger, and there being no new information forthcoming to resolve it—because Erickson had promptly marched on his way—the man was left to put the puzzle pieces together on his own. Erickson would come to the opinion that this is how effective therapy always works; he often admitted that he couldn't *create* a sudden shift in perspective, but he could "seed" one. It's in that moment of confusion that doors of perception are opened. It's in that instant when someone is pumping for meaning that he is ready for a big paradigm shift.

Erickson's strange, Delphic response ensured that the stranger, who had snapped out of his daydream by crashing into Erickson on the street, did not slide immediately back into his habits of thoughts, but was destabilized. Hyperalert now. Hungry for the next piece of information—rather like the way a hypnotized patient is highly receptive to suggestion. What Erickson had discovered that day was a new method of hypnotic induction.

Erickson would incorporate the confusion technique into his therapy. Often it took the form of hitting the client with an observation or an anecdote that subverted her expectations, left her puzzling and grasping. Some of Erickson's "teaching tales" have this quality to them. The cryptic nature of these stories means they can't be processed rationally; instead—and this is what some psychologists have deduced about why they work—these little stories communicate directly with the right brain, the seat of symbolism and emotion. "Transformation," as Erickson's disciple Sidney Rosen once put it in his collection of Erickson's teaching tales, *My Voice Will Go with You*, "is more likely to occur when the recipient is in a receptive state." "In such a state, a story, or a single word in a story, may trigger a mini-satori: enlightenment."

Kalle Lasn, publisher of the anticonsumerist magazine *Adbusters*, has never to my knowledge been overly influenced by Milton Erickson, but he is intellectually indebted to the Situationists of the Sixties, who pushed some of the same buttons. Those prankster-*philosophes* believed that, many times a day, each of us comes to a fork in the road, at which point we can do one of two things: We can act the way we normally, reflexively act, or we can do something a little risky but genuine. We can choose to live our life as a "moral, poetic, erotic and almost spiritual refusal" to co-operate with the demands of a consumer culture.

You might say that the whole point of *Adbusters* is to induce a kind of intellectual U-turn, a mind shift. The magazine tries to engineer a se-ries of "gotcha" moments. The first one is to make you notice; the next one is to make you think; and the final one is to make you change.

Lasn often used to speak of his magazine, in its early years, as a "Tro-jan horse" on the newsstand. It was glossy, it was slick, it looked like all the others. But you start flipping through and, hold on, the ads weren't real. They looked real, but they were spoofs. The text was satirical, wickedly hard-hitting. What *was* this magazine? You pumped for meaning. That's what culture-jamming is all about: It tries to initiate this moment of brief, temporary, intellectual vertigo. There's a group called Public Works, closely affiliated with the Media Foundation, which undertakes guerrilla "subvertising" campaigns. They do things like "editing" billboard mes-sages, and randomly inserting screeds against the encroaching monocul-ture inside books in bookstores. They are trying to create epiphanies.

The Media Foundation is predicated on the idea that a U-turn can be—to mix a metaphor—catalyzed. Or at least, by the idea that people can be moved, emotionally and quite suddenly, by what they see and hear, to change their degree of agency in the world. To shift from a noun to a verb, so to speak, from a passive dealer in ideas—like an aca-demic or a researcher—to an activist.

(People who hate *Adbusters* really hate it: "Facile, didactic, bumwad!" they say. "If I want a sermon, I'll go to church!" And so on. But it's hard to imagine many other magazines that get as many e-mails from readers saying, "You changed my life.")

If our current belief systems are faulty, then we aren't in a good posi-tion to think ourselves into a position of greater clarity, since the instru-ment of that investigation—our brain—is already biased, unobjective, in a sense corrupted. (It's like looking for glasses that you misplaced; you'll never find them without your glasses.) So we need tricks or tools to force objectivity on us.

The psychologist Bradford Keeney has an exercise he sometimes does with groups of clients: Throw a dinner party where no one is allowed to tell the truth.

"Sometimes I request people never to tell anything true about themselves for an entire weekend we are working together. What takes place is often remarkable. People are more likely to express their deepest desires, dreams, and unconscious longings when they try making it up. In this sense, their lies reveal more profound truths about their life than anything that would be uttered in an effort to be purposefully true.

"When you discover that your lie is more true to your self than your truth, that realization chips away at the reliability of your conscious efforts to understand your life." The ingeniousness of Keeney's falsehood exercise is that it forces people to scrutinize their lives in a way that approximates objectivity.

C. S. Lewis once created a technique he called "lived dialogue," which aimed to marry intellect and emotion. If the Socratic method is about attacking what's wrong, through fierce and continuous questioning, until you're left with what's right, then Lewis's technique is a kind of spiritual corollary: You investigate the truth of each thing you desire by actually trying it, and then asking whether it satisfies the hole in your heart. You test the earthly pleasures each in turn. By process of elimination, you arrive at the best candidate, and your whole life, in this way, becomes an "ontological proof." His technique, Lewis believed, exploited the best elements of Socratic dialogue and a "lived" dialectic. Where your intellect and your intuition converge lies your answer.

It sounds like a lot of work. The philosopher Mark Kingwell realized he could get the same effect just by going fishing. This works for him because he finds fishing crushingly boring, and "Boredom is the beginning point of all philosophy. When do we get bored? When we find ourselves engaged in an activity with no obvious utility. And when that happens, the mind opens up." When Kingwell explained his theory to his friend, the philosopher Bob Gibbs, Gibbs told him that he himself had a similar conduit to the higher planes. Not fishing, but baseball. Baseball is the Sabbath, Gibbs explained. "It's time outside of time. There's activity, but there's no work. So meditation can happen."

"We think boredom is the enemy of stimulation," Kingwell says, "so we go to squash it with stimulation." Which just foils our escape from boredom, "which would actually have been the way out."

Enforced solitude has been a traditional way to get in touch with "the kingdom of God [that] is within you." Hence Tibetan monks' retreat to caves.

But simply *pretending* you are in isolation can sometimes be enough.

"Nobody going into solitary confinement is going to have enough resources," says Sidney Rittenberg, who ought to know, having spent the better part of twenty years in Chinese prisons. "Everybody is going to have to rebuild in order to survive. I've given a lot of thought to how, when I teach, to bring young people to the point of conscious transformation without locking them up in solitary. How can you create the circumstances?

"I always ask my students, 'What is the picture in your mind of a happy life, for you, personally, twenty years from now?' Stops the conversation. But if I ask, 'What would you do if you were going to buy a new car?' they say, 'I'd test-drive it, I'd read the literature, I'd talk to people who own them.' I say, 'Well, does it make sense that you pay less attention to where your life is going than you do to buying a car?'

"When I was locked up in solitary, immediately the issue came up: What are the things I absolutely can't live without? They're not the things I used to think I couldn't live without. It all comes down to a word—integrity. I used to recite every day, 'This, above all: to thine own self be true, follows as the night from day . . . to any man.' From old Polonius in *Hamlet*. Integrity means you are who you say you are. And you do what you say you will do. And that's more important in isolation than anywhere else, I suppose, because you have to live with yourself. Who you are is all you have."

How many of us really examine, rigorously, deeply, the consistency of our beliefs? A technique often used in Jesuit training is for a student to be given an ethical question to ponder. He's then led into a room and, before a small panel of inquisitors, he is obliged to make a case for one side. He's then led into the next room and must defend the opposite position. When you have to argue both sides, the theory goes, you're in a good position to expose the flaws in your current position.

Socrates called this the Elenchus. It's a kind of consistency test that he felt one's beliefs, under cross-examination, must pass, and it's a cornerstone of the Socratic method. Under such scrutiny, a faulty belief system can easily be shattered. The method demands the following sequence of reasoning: You figure out what you believe (at least on subjects of any importance to you). Then you determine which other beliefs these are logically related to. Then you accept only those beliefs that are compatible with one another. And, finally, you try to live your life accordingly.

This is hard, hard labor. "To examine the logical consistency of [our] beliefs, when undertaken correctly, is to examine and mold the shape of our self," writes the philosopher Alexander Nehemas. It is a whole life's work, and part of what makes it so difficult is what's so terrifyingly at stake: it means, or it might mean, "a basic change of life."

This is, of course, the point of the thought experiments of Peter Singer: They push buttons most of us would rather not have pushed. Singer's little stories are designed to conjure a particular kind of moral change—what the philosopher Kathryn Pyne Addelson calls "moral passage." What they do, if they succeed, is kick us up to the next level of moral development by forcing us to confront moral problems where we *didn't even know they existed.*

Here's another example from the Peter Singer hopper:

Meet Bob. Bob is a car nut whose prize possession is a vintage Bugatti roadster. One day, while out walking, Bob sees a train bearing down on a toddler who has wandered onto the tracks. Bob can save the child by throwing a switch and diverting the train onto a siding. But parked on that siding is . . . his beloved Bugatti. If he throws the switch and saves the child, his car will be crushed. The kid or the car—which to choose? Nobody with any heart or soul would fail to save the child, Singer has us acknowledge. But wait: Aren't all of us in the developed world, in effect, in the same position as Bob? We know there are kids, in Africa and India, in the path of the speeding train of starvation or disease. With only a few dollars—a tiny fraction of our disposable income—we could save them.

Here, Singer provides the toll-free numbers for UNICEF and OXFAM.

"Now you, too, have the information you need to save a child's life," he writes. "How should you judge yourself if you don't do it?"

Peter Singer's thought experiments derive their power from the same source as John Rawls's famous thought experiment in his *Theory of Justice*. If we could set up a model where we didn't know what station in life we'd end up in—we could be a billionaire or a beggar—we would naturally become more liberal in our thoughts about how to shape society, Rawls argued. The uncertainty about our own fate would force us to pay special attention to the least well off, and to favor an economic system that reduced inequity, or tolerated it only if it ultimately raised all boats. We could not intellectually wall ourselves off from the poor, because we could be them, so Rawls's game teases out our empathy, and possibly actually our compassion.

Writers who are attracted to the personal essay form often say they like the scope it gives them to explore, with as much latitude as nonfiction allows. That's actually the meaning of the verb *to essay*. In this context, literally "To make an experiment of oneself." From time to time, you run across people who have, effectively, turned their life into a study of how to live. And the experiment rarely leaves them unchanged.

Mark Stuyt's Truth Experiment

Mark Stuyt (rhymes with "loot"), a senior sales executive for the software giant PeopleSoft, had just led his sales team in a presentation to a big government client, and he could tell by the expression of the guy in charge—a grizzled, seen-it-all department head—that it hadn't gone well. The guy was shaking his head.

"You people don't know what you're talking about," he said. "You're just here to sell more software we don't need."

Now Stuyt knew that wasn't true. His team had spent six months studying this client's problems, which were copious. The accounts were a mess. No one in the whole department was using the very expensive system they'd already bought. If they invested a couple of million dollars in some new software right now, as Stuyt was recommending, it would save them between $50 million and $60 million over the next five years.

But the department head was having none of it. "You people are all liars," he said, nodding to the door. "Now get out of my office."

"That," Stuyt says, "is what put me over the edge."

The "edge" was a social experiment he had been mulling for some time. The guy who called him a liar to his face seemed to have formed an opinion based on some generalized notion that software salesmen aren't to be trusted. What really rankled Stuyt was that the guy wasn't entirely wrong.

Experienced high-tech reps like Stuyt get to know pretty quickly what problems a client is going to run into down the road, and, very often, they're big problems. Multimillion-dollar problems. "But if we told them that upfront—that to implement this properly you're going to have to spend millions of dollars—we wouldn't even get in the game," he says. "So instead we move forward with the sales campaign, knowing internally that they're in for a shock down the road.

"That has never really sat very well with me."

The experiment was this: Stuyt vowed that, for a full year, he would tell customers the truth. Not the "Your-hair-looks-like-it-was-cut-by-beavers" kind of truth—which no one really needs to hear—but the truth about their software needs. No fudging, no prevaricating. If his company didn't have the right tool for the job, as best he could tell from their description, he'd say so. If he could see them making bad decisions, because they were naïve or ill-informed—decisions that would cost them in the long run—he'd tell them that, too.

And he did. For a full year, Stuyt did his due diligence, divined the company's problems, and then told senior management, "You've got a train wreck coming. You can't possibly accomplish what you want to accomplish in a given time with the money that you have. You're doomed."

Stuyt had wagered that his obvious honesty and sincerity would work in PeopleSoft's favor ("Companies lose way more money in mistrust than they gain short term by lying," he believes) and that, in the bargain, would translate to more money in his own pocket. "I come from the position that the truth works in relationships, so it should work in business relationships, too." It was, he now admits, a naïve assumption.

The Thought Experiment

Over the year of the experiment, Stuyt worked harder and longer than he ever had. And in the end, he found himself "far short of my revenue target for the first time in many, many years." The invariable response of folks being told that they had an impending disaster on their hands was, "Look, Mark, don't tell us how to run our business—just show us how your software works." And then, their ego wounded, they'd roll up the blinds.

It seemed a pretty irrefutable result: The truth doesn't work—at least in this business. Maybe in *any* business with publicly traded companies. The whole megillah is "fatally flawed by a greed and deception that's built into the business model," Stuyt says. "Trust-based relationships take time to develop. But the bulk of us operate in a business cycle driven by the financial quarter. And producing quarterly results often comes at the expense of doing the right thing."

Of course, none of this was news to Stuyt's colleagues. "We've been trained by the buying community to appeal to their egos rather than their business needs, and to do otherwise is too costly," one colleague—an exceptional salesman—summed it up to Stuyt in one particularly candid lunchtime exchange. Not only does it not pay to tell the truth, others rationalized, but customers *don't want to hear it.*

The disillusionment that had been growing before the experiment was now cemented. Not with PeopleSoft (whose leaders, it must be said, were pretty tolerant of his eccentric methods), but with the culture of sales. "It's salesmen who have created this problem by lying to people for decades—for centuries—and it has conditioned people not to believe," Stuyt says. "If PeopleSoft had a mandate, Thou Shalt Tell the Truth, I guarantee you sales would get cut in half. There'd be massive short-term suffering. Over the long run, I do believe it would work, but [with publicly traded companies] there *is* no long run."

Stuyt realized that the only way he could maintain his current income level—not "get ahead" but simply maintain the status quo—was "to adapt my own values to my clients' beliefs." The options seemed to be these: Adapt or die.

Or leave.

So he left.

Stuyt and his wife—herself a technology executive—and their three kids, hopped a plane to Puerto Vallarta, Mexico, that place of mojito-filled denouements. And new beginnings.

And this is where the story takes a strange twist.

There was always a backdoor option in Puerto Vallarta—which is one of the reasons they chose it as a destination. Stuyt's sister-in-law lives there, and works in the time-share industry—which is perpetually looking for new salesmen. And at a certain point, when the mortgage payments on the house back home began to weigh heavy on the mind, the job started to sound quite good. Hey, these guys only work four hours a day. "I'd still have eight hours to spend with the kids," he reasoned.

There was, of course, no earthly reason why the Truth Experiment, if it hadn't worked in one of the more upright industries, would work in one of the sleaziest, but Stuyt—the new man in the time-share boiler room—dutifully put it into action.

For two full months, working every day, Stuyt sold nothing at all—for the simple reason that, as he explains it, "If you tell people the truth about time-shares, they will never buy. Ever. Ever." He was the worst performer on the sales team, worse by far than guys being fired around him. Yet his sales manager refused to fire Stuyt, because he was clearly a hale fellow of good character (translation: He was one of the few hires who wasn't obviously running from the law, or alimony payments) and, well, the manager knew Stuyt had it in him to do better. All it would take would be a little . . . attitude adjustment.

In the end it wasn't the money that made Mark Stuyt abandon the Truth Experiment. It was his ego. A top-rung tech salesman who can't move a lowly time-share? That was tragic. *What are you doing?* he asked himself in a low moment. *Either suspend this completely or get in the game.*

It was easy enough to make the turn. "You just flip a switch: *boop*," Stuyt says. "And I don't mean that you outright lie, but you turn on the sizzle."

Almost instantly, things changed. Under the Truth Regime, he'd had two barren months and then, in December, found a little of the old mojo and made $2,500. In January, besizzled, he earned $17,000. February: $25,000. Quite literally, *bags* of money: The salesmen were paid in cash, which they then cautiously carted home. (Stuyt, who looks a wee bit like that actor who used to play Doogie Howser, and was not so much bronzed from the Mexican sun as smoked like a ham, seemed to flush a little from a complicated nexus of emotions this memory called up.) He became expert at subtly, relentlessly, breaking down the pact that husbands and wives strike in the parking lot before these sales presentations, that they *will not cave*, no matter what. Where before he had closed none of his clients, now he was closing almost half.

Negotiating the morally ambiguous ground surrounding all this was a challenge he addressed with some concrete strategies. He tried to make the judgment of who could really afford this, and who couldn't. And, like all good salesmen, he did a pretty good sales job on himself.

"The only way I could get behind it is—I really do believe that if you're going to go on vacation, there's no better way in the world to do it than to do it in a time-share. If you're committed to vacationing every year, and you like to stay in nice spots, it's actually a pretty good system.

"If we stayed, I'd have earned far more, working four hours a day, than I could ever have made back home," he acknowledges. "But finally, it didn't sit right. So now we're back."

Back and pounding the pavement for another job . . . in software sales. "It's not by choice that I'm getting back into high-tech," Stuyt says quietly, heading out into the dappled downtown sunlight. "I'm not excited about it. But I think this time I'll have a less idealistic approach. I won't use the truth like a club. You know: 'You're doomed, your business processes are dysfunctional, you don't have enough funding for this project.' You can warn people about where they're going in a lot of different ways.

"But at the end of the day, the truth is the truth. There are only so many ways of saying it."

And so, in spite of everything, the truth experiment goes on.

"You can't undo that learning," Stuyt says. "If I were to stop telling the truth now, the universe would kick me in the bag so hard you'd hear it from the North Shore. It was an experiment to begin with. But I've come to realize it's part of who I am."

U-Turn

John Freyer's Life-for-Sale

"I am a collector of junk" is how the artist John Freyer described himself, back in his grad-school days at the University of Iowa. He was one of those guys whose apartment is full of stuff picked up in church basements and in charity auctions: the plundered bounty of other people's dreams. He had a fascinating archive of artifacts—from heart monitors to Iranian bowling shirts—all of which sat as quirky inventory back home in Iowa City when he spent a mind-clearing summer in New York in 2000.

It was on the road, not to Damascus but back to Iowa City that fall, when he had his epiphany: "I started to think about how unnecessary the items in the apartment that I was driving back to were to my daily living." It didn't feel good to be going "home." The sheer tonnage of accumulated stuff that constitute, by some measures, a home, weren't a source of comfort to Freyer; they felt like a burden. He really just wanted to turn the car around, head back to New York City, and stay there. But to make a clean break from Iowa City—and the insular life of self-involvement he had acquired like a habit—would require disposing of everything that kept him there.

The initial plan was simple: He'd have a big yard sale and pare the inventory down to the essentials: no more than could fit in the trunk of his car. He'd use the Internet to do it.

And this is where chance turned a straightforward housecleaning project into something far more profound.

He needed a Web site to coordinate the enterprise. But all the sensible-sounding names he could come up with (yardsale.com, junksale.com) were taken, so he noodled around until he typed in "allmylifeforsale.com." *That* was available. *All* my life? Now, the difference between thinning the inventory and torching the inventory is one not of degree but of kind. It was almost too radical to comprehend. He certainly hadn't planned it. But maybe it was meant to be.

Over the course of one long night with fifty people, some of them friends, some of them strangers who had responded to an ad, he tagged, sorted, and put everything on the block. People tagged Freyer's CDs and his pants. They tagged his spoons, and his sideburns, which he'd saved in a baggie. They got a bit conceptual, expanding the scope beyond physical objects to routines and rituals. Somebody tagged the opportunity to have a sit-down meal of a cheeseburger. "They tagged all the things that I did in Iowa City." Freyer says. And then, sale by sale, he watched his "life" get carted away. As he got closer to the bone—gone the blender, the backpack, the winter coat—he was forced to adapt his lifestyle.

And so what had first become a simple practical decision, and then almost a goof, grew into an experiment involving the nature of identity ("I wanted to find out what happens to me when I no longer have the things that supposedly define me") and even the very nature of consumer society. The virtual marketplace was different than the physical marketplace, in that what gets bought and sold isn't just goods that have been in someone else's home, but goods that have been part of someone else's life. It's the *story* that's the real value; and by "participating in the cycle of lost and found," as Freyer would later put it, "we perpetuate the possibility of anonymously becoming someone else's story." Really, why else would someone from Des Moines be interested in his toothbrush?

He began corresponding with his buyers. They all had their own reasons for participating. Some saw Freyer's project as a cool, conceptual art piece. Some wanted "to be part of the goal—to help me rid myself of these things and see what happens."

When everything was gone, Freyer set out to realize the full, unanticipated potential of the experiment: In an old ambulance he'd acquired, he criss-crossed the country, visiting the folks who had bought his stuff. A divinity student from California who had purchased a T-shirt said Freyer's project put him in mind of "another man who gave up his possessions and traveled: Jesus." Freyer found this a bit bemusing. "I wasn't on a spiritual journey." But then again, Freyer says, thinking aloud, "I did put myself into the hands of anyone who would take care of me. My route was determined by people's generosity. I was fed and clothed by people who participated in the project." It sounded, when you framed it that way, a little bit like a spiritual journey.

At one point the kinds of conversations he was having made him think of the way commerce happened half a millennium ago: It was as much an exchange of culture as of goods. It reminded him of the spice trade (with a few differences: You were more likely to come home with a new favorite band, and less likely to come home with slaves).

Freyer had transformed from acquisitor to divestor. And, in the process, from a loner-ish art student to a communitarian connected to a global network of strangers. He had commodified himself, but in a good way: You could say (oh, it'd be pushing things, but you could say it), that he himself became, to all his buyers—and maybe even to himself—a found object.

Zell Kravinsky's Moral Extremism

At least in the way it starts, Zell Kravinsky's story appears a bit like John Freyer's. But as became clear to his friends and family, Kravinsky's evolving philosophy of a life properly lived goes far beyond giving away your material possessions. Indeed, Kravinsky would develop his notion of "total divestment" to a degree that would test the boundary between the provocative and the pathological.

Kravinsky, a fifty-year-old from Philadelphia, is a charismatic, dramatic man, a former teacher of transcendental meditation and a professor of Renaissance literature at the University of Pennsylvania who amassed a small fortune in real estate before a series of Peter Singer-esque thought experiments led him to redefine his ethical obligations to society. As Kravinsky was becoming rich, he started thinking about giving some of his money away. "Zell gave away money because he had it and there were people who needed it," a friend recalled. But with that simple gesture, that interruption of the pattern of his life thus far, something happened to his perception of himself.

"I used to feel that I had to be good, truly good in my heart and spirit, in order to do good," Kravinsky confided to *New Yorker* writer Ian Parker. "But it's the other way around; if you do good, you become better." At this point Kravinsky was still, in many people's eyes, dining with the saints. But friends' and colleagues' feelings toward his generosity took on more complicated shadings as he pushed the limits of his new philosophy. Kravinsky became the proverbial fellow who gives until he literally has no more to give.

The Thought Experiment

He donated almost all of the $45 million he had earned in the buy-
ing and selling of commercial properties. But he remained restive. It
occurred to him that "the reasons for giving a little are the reasons for
giving a lot are the reasons for giving more."

Failing to help others when we know that we could, he was coming
to believe, is psychologically corrosive, a kind of disease. He sometimes
mused about the logical apex of a moral life: days of abject poverty,
perhaps spent handing out pamphlets in the subway.

One morning he disappeared and his wife, who had thus far been
remarkably sanguine about his dispersal of the family fortune, was horrified to discover that he had donated a kidney—to a stranger. Such a
"nondirected" organ donation is an extremely rare gesture, which
made it seem, to some, all the more admirable. It was when Kravinsky
started talking about donating his *other* kidney, and living on dialysis,
that eyebrows shot up.

To Zell's mind it made perfect sense. "What if someone needed [my
last kidney] who could produce more good than me?" he told a *New
York Times* reporter. "What if I was a perfect match for a dying scientist
who was the intellectual driving force behind a breakthrough cure for
cancer or AIDS? I'd be a schnook not to give it to him. He could save
millions of lives, and I can't."

When Kravinsky later suggested that the only thing stopping him
from giving his whole body to science (one man would die, yes, but
many—the recipients of his harvested organs—would live) was that he
wasn't sure it'd be fair to his family, well, that's when some people
started questioning his motives, and even his sanity.

But, again, Zell was unapologetic. "I think in terms of maximum
human utility—not in terms of my own life," Zell would later tell
CNN's Paula Zahn. "Everyone who said to me that you have given
enough, why don't you stop, why do you need to give an organ—I think
they're missing the point that all of us are morally and logically duty-
bound to give all we can in either direction."

Whatever the complicated Freudian interpretations the giving-spiral
of Zell Kravinsky lend themselves to, it's clear that the underlying
driver is a spiritual one. "What I aspire to is a kind of ethical ecstasy: Ex
Stais: standing out of myself, where I'd lose my punishing ego."

The problem with this life experiment in moral absolutism—utilitarian philosophy made flesh—is that there was no good way to end it. "Having redefined his life as a continuing donation, but having given away everything that came immediately to hand, Kravinsky was not sure how to proceed," noted Parker. "When his thoughts migrated to rhetorical extremes, the choice seemed to be between life and death."

Kevin Kelly's Six Months to Live

There is an experimental theater project in New York called "The A-Train Plays." The premise is that participants write a play in the time it takes the subway to travel from Coney Island to the Bronx and back. Some pretty vital work is often produced, surely in part because of the crushing deadline. To the degree that all drama is autobiographical, you can imagine the playwrights harvesting their experiences and compressing their own lives into that span of time. The conceit creates a natural, almost Aristotelian pressure of events. The gun you introduced in Harlem must go off by lower Brooklyn. The dramatic reversal has to happen before you die. Everything, even the most mundane thing, is freighted with meaning. We can conceive of our end; and so the driving force is, rather than expectation, a kind of Hitchcockian suspense, which is a darker energy.

Kevin Kelly made of his life an A-Train play—but with a somewhat less pressing deadline. Instead of two hours, he gave himself six months.

As a young man of twenty-seven, a wandering freelance photographer, Kelly experienced a dramatically transcendent moment in Israel, on Easter Sunday, as dawn broke and the sun shone on the tombs of old Jerusalem. Kelly was not a very religious guy; he hadn't made a pilgrimage to that spot: He was just passing through, on his way to Yemen. Yet in that instant he became a Christian. And "the tension of trying to figure things out was resolved. It was as if you'd been working on a problem for a long time and suddenly the answer was there, and it was very clear that it *was* the answer. I believed Jesus Christ had risen from those tombs."

The Thought Experiment

Well, that was interesting. But the "answer" raised a thousand questions. What was Kelly to *do* with this knowledge? What did it mean? Was it a kind of directive to carry something out, and if so, what?

He returned to the hostel, which had now opened for the day, and flopped down on the bed. As he tossed and turned, mulling, the "meaning" of the moment he'd just passed through came to him: *You need to prepare to live for another six months, and then die.* This second moment was almost as sudden and strange as the first.

"Nothing like that had ever been in my head before," he says. "I'm not one of those people who habitually gives himself tests to see what he can handle. I'm very, very cautious. I'm scared of heights. So this was very . . . foreign. It didn't feel like a test I was giving to myself." The sense that it was something he'd been given, rather than something he'd cooked up, led Kelly to give the directive a name: "the assignment."

Was it true? Was he really going to die in six months' time? Kelly didn't know. "As a rational, scientific kind of adult, I said to myself, Look: I'm twenty-seven years old. I'm in great health. There's no history of psychosis in the family. This is so, so unlikely to be true. *But,* given that the way it came, and the importance of the place where it came, it could also be true. Statistically it's unlikely, but there's no way to disprove it. The only thing I feel is that I should follow through with this assignment, and embrace it as if it was real."

And so Kevin Kelly began preparing to die. "I was praying that I would not, but I was preparing to. On every level, I was acting as if this were my fate."

He made a will, settled his affairs, wrote letters to the people with whom he had unfinished business, righted what wrongs he could; he took his remaining money and divvied it up into cashier's checks, which he mailed anonymously to various people who had been kind or important to him ("the first true act of charity I had ever done"). When Kelly asked himself where he most needed to be, the answer surprised him a little: with his parents. He flew home to New Jersey. "My mom was coincidentally in bed with a bad back, so I was actually able to help out with chores," he recalls. He washed dishes, pruned shrubs, took out the trash. It was almost definitively mundane time, but the kind of time that memories, of the sort we are said to grasp and hold just before we

241

die, are made of. And then he decided there was time—just—to visit all of his family members. But since they were spread out across America, and he had no money, he decided to make the trip, five thousand miles all told, by bicycle. The plan was to arrive back home at his parents' house in New Jersey just as the actuarial clock struck midnight, "to die" the day after Halloween.

Assuming that the prophecy of his impending death was true forced upon Kelly a kind of ruthless questioning of the value of things in his life that had become habit. It compelled him to make decisions he couldn't otherwise have made. The most difficult was to put away his camera, which had become a part of him, the means through which by reflex he viewed the world. "The thought of riding my bicycle across the country and not bringing my camera—I didn't think I could do it," he says. But if he really was going to die, there wasn't much reason to take photographs; better to just look at things unmediated. (He decided to bring a sketchbook instead.)

As the six months unspooled, Kelly's great struggle involved the notion of living in the moment. Certainly, having no "future" put enormous pressure on Kelly to savor each passing instant, and eventually he found—because he had so thoroughly convinced himself that this was the end—that he was able not to think of his life beyond Halloween, to let go of any plan or notion that fell beyond that horizon.

At the same time, the Buddhist emphasis on the eternal present did not strike him as the secret of life, not at all. Something like the opposite insight bloomed instead. He came to understand that "having a future is part of what being human is about. It's not actually a very good thing to live entirely in the present. One needs to have a past, and a future, to be fully human."

In the days leading up to his death, he had felt great spiritual torment, and he found himself praying for delivery from his burden. But then he was home, at a welcome-back meal with his family, having a pleasant evening. He was exhausted. And so, with tiny pirates and angels still streaming to the door, he went to bed, having told no one of his "assignment" to die that night. He closed his eyes, "as prepared as anybody could be prepared" to die that night. "I'd done all that I could."

And then he woke up. It was morning. He was still here. "It was if I had my entire life again." When Kelly told the story on National Public Radio's *This American Life*, his voice broke at this point. He tried to start again and couldn't. Dead air continued for some seconds as he tried to compose himself. (Archived on the Web, it's an extraordinarily moving piece of radio.)

"There was nothing special about the day. It was another ordinary day. I was reborn into ordinariness. But what more could I ask?"

He could become whomever he wanted to be. What he became was the first executive editor of *Wired*, a magazine devoted to the frame of time he once thought he'd never get to see—the future.

The kinds of questions Kelly's experiment raises—If you knew, or could convince yourself you knew, exactly when you were going to die, how would you live the intervening days? And what, when your expiry date passed, would you discover you had become?—touch on Albert Camus's notion of the "apprenticeship in death." Camus believed that a brush with mortality can bring on the kind of epiphany, the kind of clarity Kevin Kelly discovered. It doesn't really matter if imminent death is real or imagined.

Certainly, Ludwig Wittgenstein, the turn-of-the-twentieth-century philosopher and the father of language theory, believed that the fear of death could be a potential passageway to transformation—which is why he continually put himself in harm's way. Volunteering for the army in World War I, he angled for the most hazardous assignment, and seemed gratified to be assigned to an observation post exposed to enemy fire. As a habit, Wittgenstein "consistently sought any job that would put his life at greatest risk," the psychologist William Todd Schultz notes. The aim was apparently spiritual growth "of the sort only achievable via confrontation with, as [Martin] Heidegger put it, no longer being in the world." ("Perhaps nearness to death will bring light into my life," he wrote to a friend.)

But Wittgenstein's relationship with death was complicated. What made his risk-taking all the more courageous—and fodder for psychoanalysts—is that for him this experiment with mortality was like an agoraphobe being dropped off by cargo plane at the North Pole.

U-Turn

The philosopher was in fact *terrified* of death, obsessed with it. He believed that it was stalking him (even when he wasn't stalking it). Wittgenstein once frantically called up Bertrand Russell in the middle of the night and tried to explain all his work in progress to him—fearing that he might expire at any moment, leaving academic question marks for posterity. But he seems, too, to have understood that while facing death could open transformative vistas, his own outsized fear of death was getting in the way of his progress. If he could break through it, he would not only be a better philosopher. He would be a free man.

TWELVE

The Parole Board's Dilemma

*True Turns and Bogus Turns, and How to
Tell the Difference*

So let us begin anew, remembering that civility is not a sign of
weakness, and sincerity is always subject to proof.
—John Fitzgerald Kennedy

The subject of U-turns is, like the lives of U-turners themselves,
spring-loaded. There comes a point when the weight of dramatic stories and their big emotions—all that tragedy and
courage and redemption—triggers a kind of corrective response of
doubt. Nagging questions and credibility issues arise.

Almost as old as the notions of enlightenment and rebirth themselves is the notion that one ought to be suspicious of apparent enlightenment, because, most likely, it is self-deception. (This is what Lin Chi
probably meant by the line, "If you see the Buddha on the road, kill
him." Mortals couldn't even perceive a true agent of the divine—so the
fellow you think is the Buddha is an imposter, a manifestation of your
own *wish* for enlightenment—and he's doing you no good.) By this reasoning, we should approach not only our own, but others' supposed
U-turn moments with a healthy measure of skepticism. And critics
have been quick to oblige.

In his book *My Goodness: A Cynic's Short-lived Search for Sainthood,* the savage Joe Queenan decides—in an epiphanic moment one day—that he
doesn't necessarily have to be mean. He will try to override his reflex for

snark, he decides, and be a better man. It is a six-month odyssey, with the requisite twists and turns and frustrations, the botched attempts at benevolence, and the final twinkling realization that he is who he is—a son of a bitch. Beware the professed U-turner—that's the message: Sinners always slip back. The image of those poor schlubs trying desperately to be something they're not, something they will never be, recalls the proverbial Type A man's dogged attempt to transform himself into a Type B, dutifully mapping out the strategy in his Day-Timer ("7:45 to 7:47—smell the flowers").

To some critics, the antipodean flip that U-turners seem to make— the whole *idea* of an antipodean flip—seems just a little too pat. People don't simply switch cognitive tracks like railcars, goes the argument. Things are almost always less binary, and more subtle, than they appear. Left or right, introverted or extroverted, faithful or faithless—surely we don't cleanly sort out along such lines. (Even sexual orientation—one of the easier distinctions to figure out, you'd think—is murky; Kinsey himself assumed that we are all to some degree bisexual, as witnessed by his famous scale of gradations.) In this light major identity shifts seem less like crossing a river than drifting from one place to another on the same lake, perhaps following the fish.

The change in linear direction that we often describe lives as taking midcourse is a randomly chosen metaphor—and it's inexact as a representation of what's going on when people evolve, or transform themselves. Language isn't quite up to the task of conveying what we are pulling away from, and drawn to. It becomes clear that each of us is talking about something different, even though we may be using the same words.

It's also true that actual lives lived are rarely as inspiring as the myths that grow around them. And rarely as straightforward. Many of what have become classic U-turn stories in the popular mythology don't hold up, under scrutiny, as such tidy narratives.

Adam Hochschild, author of the abolitionist history *Bury the Chains*, had started out intending simply to write the biography of John Newton. "Here was a slave-ship captain who became an abolitionist and wrote this beautiful hymn, became a preacher, and wrote many other

The Parole Board's Dilemma

hymns as well," Hochschild said recently. "But then I found that his life didn't really fit the script that I had imagined.

"He was indeed a slave-ship captain. He sailed for more than ten years, about five or six of them as a captain. He kept the most detailed log that has survived of any British slave-ship captain. Also, his letters to his wife described things that he witnessed on his journey. He never questioned slavery at all. However, he left the trade not out of belief, but for medical reasons. Then he entered the ministry and began writing hymns. And all this time he continued to have all his savings invested with his former employer, the slave-ship owner, and that relationship ended only when the man went bankrupt. Newton said not a word against slavery for more than thirty years after he left the trade. Until suddenly this movement erupted around him, and a man whom I had never heard of named Thomas Clarkson came to see him and said, 'Newton, you really must speak out about slavery.' And at that point Newton wrote a pamphlet." Hochschild started wondering about this fellow Thomas Clarkson—and he was off in a new direction, with a new hero.

While he *was* actually aboard those slave ships, Newton never really identified with the ill-treated slaves. "He did not have, there, surrounded by suffering, the compassion-based moment of enlightenment, the moment of Amazing Grace, that turned him into an abolitionist," Hochschild noted. "It wasn't until many years later that his own conscience was awakened about it. All the more striking because he'd been, for several years at that point, a clergyman—whose very business is the awakening of conscience."

The stories that unraveled under fact-checking were in some ways the most interesting part of the research for this book. One of my favorites involved Paul Mulvey, a hockey player for the Los Angeles Kings, who was the team's designated goon. Late in a lopsided game that was threatening to get really ugly, the coach turned to him and told him to fight the toughest guy on the other team—who happened to be the most penalized player in league history. "Get out there, and don't dance!" the coach said. Mulvey shifted his weight forward, about to report for duty. And then something occurred to him. His eight-year-old son was in the stands. Something made Mulvey, in that brief prelude to mayhem, think about his son, and the boy's growing apprehension of what his dad did for a living. Mulvey hesitated. He saw himself through the eyes of a kid for whom he was the most important role model on Earth. He remained seated. The coach told him again: *Get your butt out there*. He remained seated. A third time the coach shouted his command. Mulvey refused. He was promptly benched—as he knew he would be. He was immediately placed on waivers, and no other team picked him up. He was effectively blacklisted, and he never played in the NHL again. He now lives in Reston, Virginia, where he coaches a minor-league team and runs clinics for kids on sportsmanship.

This was great stuff. But when I reached Mulvey, and asked him, How old is your son now, he replied: "I don't have a son. Unless you know something I don't know."

Oh. No young charge in the crowd that night through whose trusting eyes you saw yourself anew? "Nope." Then why the abrupt reversal in behavior? Well, Mulvey said, he'd never actually been sent out specifically to fight before. When this coach—who was brand new—tried to force him to do something he felt was wrong, it irked him. "I hadn't been getting much ice time, and I kind of felt I had more talent than I was being allowed to use. I think a lot of athletes who get pigeonholed into certain roles feel that way." That makes Paul Mulvey, who runs a chain of hockey rinks now, a good guy. But he's not a U-turner.

History sands down nuance. The collective desire for great stories of redemption produces tales that fall into the category of "too good to check." So much do we love and need U-turn stories that if they didn't exist we would have to write them ourselves—and, of course, we do: compulsively. Rumors persist, especially in the Christian community, that Charles Darwin recanted on his deathbed; that John Wayne converted three weeks before he died, after reading an inspirational note sent to him by the crippled daughter of an evangelist; that the British mathematician Alan Turing, who broke the Nazi enigma code and conceived the computer, found God in the months before he committed suicide. Whether or not they contain kernels of truth, such spiritual urban legends endure because they serve a purpose. Like all great myths they have—at a time when literal truth seems slippery and elusive—a somewhat comforting element of intuitive truth. They are, as more progressive Christians sometimes say of the stories in the Bible, "the way things never were but always are."

"I feel some responsibility through the years for urging readers to look upward," Robert Bly once wrote. "I love ascents—who doesn't love ascents?" But, of course, what we love and what is true aren't always the same thing. Not all transformations turn toward the light. Not all reversals are for the good. Not all lives are noble or heroic. There is an alternative to the twin heroic arcs of the slow climb and the quick rise from a bounce. It is the fall with a thud. A guy of privilege and happiness is corrupted by bad or immoral choices, falls onto hard times, or just generally self-destructs. The psychologist Henry Murray called this the "Icarus Complex," naming what he believed is a self-destruct mechanism inherent in some people, perhaps all people. You don't hear as much about the about-faces in the other direction—hero to zero—for some pretty obvious reasons. They're shameful stories to tell. They get recounted to psychiatrists in dim rooms, not to the media, or even much to friends. But there's nothing to suggest they're any less common.

When you root deeply into the heavily publicized epiphanic U-turn stories of public figures, they come apart reasonably often. John Kerry's so-called "life-changing Christmas in Cambodia" was a nice idea, but it's now widely disputed. Bob Dylan's plunge down the rabbit hole of drug culture in the sixties that instantly transformed his songwriting from mundane to ethereal makes perfect sense as an explanation for suddenly revealed genius; but, in fact, as Dylanologists proved, the drug use was not a magic new element—Dylan had been using drugs on and off since childhood.

What about those who have an epiphany that *their epiphany itself* was false? What does that tell you about the trustworthiness of the experience of "finding one's true self"? In the novel *The Mackerel Plaza*, by the late Peter DeVries, the protagonist, Reverend Andrew Mackerel loses his faith. He is surprisingly sanguine about this, declaring it "not such a tragedy—like losing a wooden leg in an accident." This is almost the definition of the counterfeit conversion. *Like losing a wooden leg in an accident.* In other words, less a sacrifice than it appears, because what is given up is not the essential self. The essential self is long gone.

There are grounds to at least argue the sincerity of some of the U-turns described in this book. Michael Lind's swing from right to left? Pure expediency, claim some critics. ("It has long been known that the surest route to journalistic stardom in Washington is right-wing apostasy: Establish yourself as a devout political conservative for a few years before renouncing all things conservative, and the inexorable result will be copious kudos.") David Brock? "The consummate creature of our times," writes one observer, "constantly morphing himself from road warrior to sacrificial lamb, star witness and finally rumormonger, so as to keep pace with the rollicking zeitgeist."

Certain types of U-turns raise immediate alarm bells, and high on the list is the jailhouse conversion.

Consider Barry Minkow. A phenomenally driven young entrepreneur, Minkow built a franchised carpet-cleaning company into an empire worth some $300 million, before he was convicted, at age twenty-two, of massive accounting fraud and found himself in solitary confinement at Terminal Island near Los Angeles. Minkow tells a stirring tale of his epiphany on Thanksgiving Day, when the guards shoved his sad dinner under the cell door—the Jell-O and salad nuked beyond rescue. He looked around his environs—the bars, the toilet, his tattooed cellmate—and something suddenly clicked and he saw himself clearly. "Maybe it's me. Maybe there's something wrong with me. Maybe when they go to all this trouble to put you in a place like this, you'd better do some changing." (Minkow, forty now, is a San Diego preacher to an evangelical-church congregation 1,400-strong.)

It's an American trope, with familiar plotlines. You do an egregious wrong and then you make amends. There follows the book (*Cleaning Up: One of the Greatest Wall Street Comeback Stories of All Time*, by Barry Minkow), the Web site, the consultancy, and the show you take on the road. Through his "Fraud Discovery Institute," as his Web site puts it, Minkow now "lectures business students, law-enforcement officers, and corporate executives on white-collar crime." Badda boom.

The former hacker Kevin Poulsen—aka "Dark Dante"—was a virtuoso teen cyberpunk who specialized in breaking into government and military systems designed to be impenetrable. Poulsen was a mythic figure in the hacking community in the 1980s—think Matthew Broderick in

WarGames—because of his preposterously young age and his pop-cult chutzpah. Poulsen routinely hijacked PacBell—once tapping the calls of a Hollywood actress he aimed to blackmail. He used his skills as a "phone phreak" to run escort services and hack into contests sponsored by TV and radio stations. (His most inspired con victimized a Los Angeles radio station. On the day of a high-profile giveaway, Poulsen and some hacker pals jammed all 250 phone lines, and Poulsen casually dialed in, the "lucky" caller, wouldn't you know, and drove away with a Porsche.)

Poulsen's cyberjoyride ended when a slip-up—he attacked the phone lines of *Unsolved Mysteries* during an episode devoted to him, and inadvertently left some crumbs—sent federal investigators to his bedroom, where they discovered an arsenal of electronic devices that, as one FBI agent put it, "would have put James Bond to shame." Poulsen was arrested for fraud, conspiracy, wiretapping, trespassing, and, unprecedentedly, espionage.

Which was when the outlaw myth really began to take root.

While on bail and awaiting indictment, Poulsen escaped, and remained on the lam for seventeen months. During which time he tapped into the phone lines of judges and prosecutors, and broke into the databases of the Department of Justice to erase evidence against himself. "He even," according to the online publication *Cybercrime*, "conspired to steal classified military orders and went as far as to crack an army computer to snoop into an FBI investigation of former Philippine president Ferdinand Marcos."

And what has become of the first hacker in the United States ever to be charged with espionage?

He is now an industry consultant, of course. After serving less than half of a fifty-one-month sentence, Poulsen walked out of prison, into the light of a world wired with Ethernet cable and full of opportunity. Announcing himself "fully reformed and penitent," and making noises about "repaying his debt" to society, Poulsen was soon offered the job of "editorial director" at the big Internet Security firm Security Focus, and his Second Act as upright citizen, covering developments in cyberspace from the lawful side, was off and running.

The narrative of hacker to computer-industry executive is a fascinating arc, for if ever there were a rite-of-passage U-turn it's this one—as anyone who first knew Apple founders Steve Jobs and Steve Wozniak by their phone-phreak handles "Berkeley Blue" and "Oak Toebark" will attest. Former hackers are in demand by security firms for obvious reasons—the robber knows the bank best. (There can be few other jobs where your employer conducts a criminal-past check, hoping to find one.)

But the wisdom of hiring former hackers remains hotly debated in the tech community. Ethics aside, the question looms: Can a former criminal be trusted? How could an employer be sure that a Kevin Poulsen had matured beyond the famous adage of tinkering cyberpunks that "There is no right and wrong; there is only fun and boring" and was ready to join a world governed by some sense of morality?

"Let me explain why it's a BAD idea to hire hackers," the IT consultant Dana Epp posted recently in a technology discussion group. (He had just received a résumé from a "reformed" hacker who wanted Epp to hire him, and he—Epp—thought the reply was worth sharing.) "When you hire a hacker you don't just get his or her amazing talents. You also get their ethics. And ethics are NOT something you can turn on or off on a whim."

Not long ago, after a young German man named Sven Jaschen—who is believed responsible for nearly three-quarters of the virus infections that plagued Internet users in 2004—was hired amid great fanfare by a security company. Brian Martin, an ex-hacker who's now a security consultant, put the whole issue in blunt perspective: "The industry is full of criminals."

That's no doubt true. But it's an error of logic to label reformation testimonies of all former hackers as snow jobs, just as, more broadly, it's an error to discount all changes of heart that happen in prison. Because these are precisely the conditions in which genuine reformation happens—enforced solitude during which soul-searching is inevitable.

Standards of Proof

The conversion experience would seem to be such a private, subjective event that there's no way to know which ones are authentic and which aren't. But there are groups whose job is to do just that. Parole boards must make a call on whether the murderer really has been reformed; physicians handling sex-change candidates administer batteries of personality tests to make sure their client's decision is bone-deep; Scientologists use a specialized lie detector to test new recruits' commitment to the church's principles.

Think, for a minute, about the army's mechanism for assessing the commitment of conscientious objectors. Unless they were drafted, these are folks who, almost by definition, had a moral crisis, a "wake-up call" after enlisting that changed their views entirely. (If they had qualms from the get-go, the assumption goes, they would not have enlisted.) The category of *conscientious objector* exists because governments acknowledge, at least on paper, that, as the former marine-turned-*Jarhead* author Anthony Swofford put it, "The young soldier who enlists is not a fully formed man. His reasons for joining up are often not very good ones, often attempts to patch up other psychic deficiencies he hasn't had time to become aware of, let alone work out. And therefore he shouldn't necessarily be held to his pro-war view once he comes to his senses in the war zone."

Conscientious objectors tell powerful U-turn stories, and many of them are proof that C.O. status is a lot messier in practice than in theory. Young men like then-nineteen-year-old Stephen Funk of California and then-twenty-four-year-old Mike Hood of Illinois had torturous rides through the system—they were either jailed while waiting for their application to be processed or faced the prospect of being sent to the front lines with a dummy weapon—and ended up becoming outspoken critics of the army's recruiting process. These men had a sort of double epiphany: a personal reckoning ("I cannot kill") and the awakening of a broader politician conscience. ("This is a poverty draft. It's a class issue. It is deeply not right.")

Lawyers who take on conscientious objectors as clients say they are almost never faking. ("That's not the easiest way out of the military," says one.) But, of course, that isn't good enough for the army. The sincerity of the conversion must be demonstrated.

The key word the army's legal arm leans on is *crystallize*. "You have to show that your beliefs"—religious or moral convictions *that are the primary controlling force in your life*—"crystallized since you joined the army," said

Bill Galvin, head of the Central Committee for Conscientious Objectors in Washington, D.C. Further, "The applicant must show that expediency, or the avoidance of military service, is not the basis of the claim." How? There are procedures that allow for a hearing, at which a number of experts submit evidence on the candidate's behalf. Typically, the applicant is interviewed by three people: a chaplain, a psychiatrist, and an investigating officer. Getting through all three hoops is not easy.

Parole boards work in somewhat the same way, in that they demand a similar kind of "proof " of change. When the panel mulls its verdict on an inmate, a chief consideration is this: Will this person's release constitute "an undue risk to society"? Which boils down to, How likely is this person to reoffend? Since, under most circumstances, the best predictor of future behavior is past behavior, members of the board must be convinced that something profound has happened to the parole candidate while in prison to override that rule. They must believe that the person applying to come out of prison is a qualitatively different person than the one who went in.

The board looks deeply into the applicant's past. Was his upbringing so poisonous that even with the best-faith efforts to modify his behavior, he stands little chance of avoiding slipping back into that hard old self? Is there, in the opinion of professionals, evidence of a change of attitude and behavior as a result of the prison time itself, treatment and healing programs, violence- and anger-management classes, educational upgrading, religious counseling, and so on? Psychologists and psychiatrists look for consistency in patterns of behavior. In a sense, this is a measure of the integrity of the turn.

The board tries to assess whether the convict has repudiated that old self by gauging the degree of his remorse. A showstopper for parole boards is "evidence of an attitude of indifference to criminal behavior and the impact on the victim." An absolute must is "evidence of, or commitment, to change." The board's job is to distinguish mere regret—"I'm sorry I got caught and am paying a price I didn't anticipate paying"— from true remorse. (Regret is amoral; remorse, moral.) They look for some overt and heartfelt acceptance of responsibility, which is a little like the Christian criterion of a public declaration of the new faith, verbally or ritually.

The Parole Board's Dilemma

In fact, a parole board's criteria overlap a fair bit with the criteria of the early Christian Church's sacrament of penance.

Is the repudiation of the old self real? The test is the quality of the contrition and remorse.

Judging remorse, the parole board itself makes a kind of leap of faith. It's impossible to know for sure that you aren't getting gulled.

Every major religion has criteria for sifting the "true" religious experience from the counterfeit. Every religion's God chooses His exponents carefully: You can't bluff your way into the club of the saints. So an investigation of the authenticity of a vision begins with an investigation of the character, or state of spiritual readiness, of the receiver.

"The Christian message provoked different reactions in different hearts," writes the religious scholar William Barclay "What, then, is the saving reaction of real and true conversion?" There must be repentance. There must be a purification ritual, a public declaration of the new faith. There must be genuine belief in the truth of the new path. And there must, finally, be the taking of the new faith out into the community and spreading it around.

No one has yet established criteria for secular U-turns, but the psychologist William Miller is in the ballpark.

Ten years of studying the phenomenon of what he calls "quantum change" led Miller and a graduate student to single out four traits as the true life-changing epiphany, the hallmarks of quantum change. The epiphany must be "vivid," "surprising," "benevolent," and "enduring."

The element of "benevolence," from what I've observed, often takes the practical form of someone making a public declaration of reform, donning a white hat and dedicating her life henceforth to "doing good." But the exercise can sometimes recall Dr. Jekyll's excitement over the invention of a potion that separates the light and dark aspects of his nature. One is tempted to ask: How likely are some of these folks—whose sin of hubris is thinking they can, like Jekyll, hive off the two parts of themselves—to snap back to their Hydes?

I once interviewed David "Jelly" Helm, a fairly high-profile art director who had created some award-winning TV commercials for big international clients. Not long after he did a big Nike soccer spot featuring World Cup players, he experienced an apparent damascene moment, publicly denounced the advertising profession as immoral, and quit in disgust. That was the news hook. He seemed serious about the decision. But fairly soon after, he was back in the ad game with big, blue-chip clients, as if the earlier declaration had been a midnight shout from a bad dream that he had already forgotten by morning.

Backsliders make up a big percentage of any group that tries to change its habits radically. (Banner at the prison gate: Welcome back, Recidivists!) And false saints are always smoked out eventually—because no one can pretend to be something he isn't indefinitely. No matter how confidently erected the false front, over time and especially under pressure, our core personality will seep out—a phenomenon psychologists call "leakage." This is why police interrogations of suspects sometimes last for days, and why the producers of reality shows shoot so much footage—they do not want to be manipulated by contestants who are "in character," misrepresenting themselves to advance some agenda. In time, the Truth will be revealed.

In the late '90s, singer Courtney Love undertook orthopedic work on her image. The former heroin junkie whose addiction almost pushed her to follow her husband, Kurt Cobain, into suicidal oblivion, cleaned up her act. Remade as an antidrug spokesperson, she hit the speaking circuit. At the launch of some public-service antidrug TV spots (cosponsored by Partnership for a Drug-Free America and the Musicians' Assistance Program), Love called drugs "dumb and self-indulgent." She smiled broadly to the mostly young crowd—some of whom had been bused in to fill the house. At one point she nodded to a blue-haired girl and said, "Drugs make you make bad fashion decisions."

Things looked good. Until October 2, 2003, when Love had a very bad day. She was arrested for breaking into a Los Angeles home, overdosed on drugs, and ended up in the hospital. It was enough to make kids think twice about being inspired by, say, Art Alexis of the band Everclear, who himself appeared on a TV antidrug spot boldly pronouncing, "I used to be a rock-'n'-roll cliché."

(There ought to be a support group for the families of athletes and politicians who quit in the prime of their careers to "spend more time with the family"—and then a year later are back pursuing their careers in earnest. The conclusion the public is left with, which tends to go unspoken in the press conferences announcing the return: "Turns out I didn't really like my family all that much.")

Which brings us to William Miller's fourth and final hallmark of true transformational change. It is "enduring." By *enduring*, Miller means that the transformation seems to be permanent, "a one-way door through which there is no going back."

That element of durability makes just about everybody's list, from the army's to biblical scholars' interpretation of religious conversion. In a "real" conversion—be it religious or secular—all oscillation is supposed to have stopped, and the convert stands fast in the new attitude, presumably forever. "Durability," writes the psychologist William Todd Schultz, "may represent the one true hallmark of a legitimate turning point event."

But is that reasonable?

Jung didn't think so, and neither did William James. Both maintained that backsliding doesn't diminish the "truth" of the original conversion.

"What is truly important in a conversion," according to James, "is not so much the duration as the nature of these shiftings of character to higher levels. Men lapse from every level—we need no statistics to tell us that . . . So with the conversion experience—that it should for even a short time show a human being what the high-water mark of his spiritual capacity is, this is what constitutes its importance—an importance which backsliding cannot diminish."

U-turners themselves are arguably in the best position to know if a turn has happened—if they have reached, in James's words, a spiritual "high-water mark." It might not be observable. Their external behavior need not change that much. As the Zen proverb goes, "Before enlightenment—eat rice, clean bowl. After enlightenment—eat rice, clean bowl." It *need* not.

But, almost invariably, it does.

Hence Max Weber's standard for measuring the validity of the U-turn experience: Observe what the U-turner actually does, out there in the world. Frequently, as the Harvard psychologist Howard Gardner pointed out recently, we may think we've changed our mind when we haven't. "If in fact you believe that your mind has been changed on some point, but you continue to behave exactly the way you did before, then you're basically fooling yourself." Conversely, "Often you behave differently and you realize your mind changed and you weren't really aware of it." (Somehow the message of all those *Wall Street Journal* editorials seeped in.) The proof of enlightenment, of conversion or real mind change, then, comes the moment you demonstrate it through your behavior. The moment you write a check to the other party, or visit your sworn enemy in the hospital, or lie down in front of your employer's bulldozer, or tell your racist father he's wrong. In all U-turns, there are actually two shifts, and this one is the second. The first is an internal shift—wherein, after much subconscious grinding of gears, the "truth" emerges. The second is the external shift: The newly "awakened" changes her life accordingly. Just as "a religious experience is understandable only through the context of its outcome in social action," as Max Weber put it, so too with secular turns: It is only actions that make it up onto the scoreboard.

Plucked from his exalted public perch, and jailed for indecency, Oscar Wilde wrote to his friends from Reading prison of the transformation that had taken place within him. He now saw the world "with changed eyes," Wilde said. "My reckless pursuit of mundane pleasure, my extravagance, my senseless ease, my love of fashion, my whole attitude toward life, all these were wrong." Wilde claimed that after his time in prison he actually *thought* differently. "Violin variations don't interest me." He no longer reflexively turned everything he was feeling into a witty epigram. He found that, suddenly, he was thinking more frequently about the "feelings and happiness of others."

We have to take on faith Wilde's testimony of a private sense of transformation. But after the event, there were clear differences in his *observable* life—not only in the way he conducted his art, but in the way he treated people. The "old" Wilde was prolific. After the epiphany, he wrote virtually nothing. The old Wilde was, though extravagant, not an especially generous man. The new Wilde, virtually penniless now, routinely shared with others whatever small income he received.

T. S. Eliot's late-in-life conversion to Christianity was a private shift. (Given that it was seen—coming as it was from the poet laureate of existential despair—as something of an intellectual betrayal, Eliot might have been wise to keep it under his hat.) But a poet's interior life *becomes* his exterior life. Up the flagpole it went in "Ash Wednesday," the first major poem he wrote after his conversion. There's no mistaking this Eliot for the secular poet who wrote *The Waste Land*. The subsequent publication of the magisterial *Four Quartets*—the Waste Land in full Christian bloom—silenced the atheist fans who were hoping the "Ash Wednesday" nonsense might just be a phase.

The Calculated Turn

There is a species of fish called the goby that swims in the reefs of Australia. It's an odd creature; it remains sexually immature, finning among the anemones until it has identified a potential mate, at which point it promptly turns into the opposite sex. This is the dig against many U-turners: They are goby fish. Their transformations are simply opportunistic—which would seem to render them "inauthentic," by definition.

The crux of all morality, Kant believed, is not what we do but our motive for doing it. A U-turn performed for the right reason, an end in itself, is evidence of what he called the "jewel within." The problem is, the jewel within can't be seen, and therefore can't be objectively evaluated: Only the actions that flow from it can. A further criterion to judge the "legitimacy" of a turn, then, is to ask, To what degree is the convert profiting from it?

If you buy the carpet-magnate Ray Anderson's conversion from resource-gobbler to child of Gaia as genuine, what about Robert Congel's? The developer aims to build a mega-mall near Syracuse, which if it unfolds as planned will be the largest manmade structure on the planet. The twist is that Congel, historically no friend of the environment (he's a big Bush supporter, and the twenty-five malls he has built have displaced acres and acres of arable land) wants to make Destiny USA a light sandalprint on upstate New York, a fossil-free zone "powered exclusively by renewable energy sources like solar and wind." This wasn't the original plan—Destiny was to be a conventional sprawling megaplex, designed solely to revive the sluggish local economy—but Congel called a halt to that kind of project, based on a vision that came to him almost overnight.

U-Turn

He was vacationing on the beaches of Normandy shortly after 9/11. "There I was looking at those pure white graves of tens of thousands of kids that died for freedom," Congel reflected to a *New York Times* reporter. "Today our kids are dying in a war for oil. Petroleum addiction is destroying our country, our economy and our environment."

Congel returned home and feverishly started rewriting the plans for the mega-mall, wiping fossil fuel out of the equation and establishing, in his mind, a new standard for green development.

The happy spin on this story: Never underestimate the power of one man's conscience. Do you accept that? If not, why not?

There are lots of reasons a developer would pull a radical, public about-face that aren't necessarily connected to conscience. The PR surrounding the human-interest story will surely attract plenty of corporate sponsors who want to be part of Destiny's nuclear glow of goodwill. Grand visions—the mall that saved America—feed big egos. And the new vision has the potential of saving Robert Congel a bundle in taxes, even if he doesn't meet his goals. On the other hand, expedience as a driving motive is all but impossible to prove. The standard might better be expressed not as "To what degree is the U-turner profiting from the u-turn?" but rather, "To what degree *does he appear* to be profiting from it?"—which is a much slipperier proposition, and rife with potentially unfair judgments of character.

Perhaps the most reliable strategy is to draw an inference from the late Harvard psychologist Gordon Allport's work on religious commitment. Allport distinguished between what he called "extrinsic" and "intrinsic" commitment. Extrinsic commitment is conditional: The person is simply trying to win social points or maybe just get in God's good graces. Not so the intrinsically devout soul, whose commitment is deep and private, an end in itself. The proof is to be found in the person. Look deep into his eyes, and keep looking. The intrinsically committed are at peace, Allport found. The extrinsically committed are not.

However byzantine a U-turner's private motivation, it has to come from within: On that most would agree. Few hold Patty Hearst responsible for her sudden U-turn toward fanaticism at the barrel of a gun—or believe that she had found, in her role within the Symbionese Liberation Army, her "essential self." But there are other U-turners in the same ballpark who were more subtly seduced, and history has not let them off the hook for their actions.

Katherine Ann Power, the Catholic school valedictorian–turned– America's most-wanted fugitive, elicited little sympathy after she turned herself in in 1993. (When her gang killed a beloved police officer in a botched bank robbery, public opinion fell heavily against her, even among many who sympathized with the causes of the radicalized students of the sixties.) But one professor who taught at Power's Berkeley alma mater at the time put her turn in perspective: She was in a crushing double bind. "Impossible moral burdens were put on students," he said. "They were told that legitimate sources of money for the [antiwar] movement had dried up. Students like Kathy Power, in their enormous desire to do good, took it as a personal mandate. She became enormously confused. The liberal system and legitimate action within that system were denounced, with no thought of where that could lead." Thus vulnerable, Power then met the apotheosis of that climate of discord and dissent, a charismatic thug who physically escorted her over the line into violent conflict.

If you examine the turns of the celebrity reinventors, from Courtney Love to Dennis Rodman—an earnest sweetheart who cried when he won the NBA's defensive player of the year award cum circus clown who head-butted referees and married himself—you tend to find a lot of other hands on the levers. In many cases, these celebrities are heavily pressured to remake themselves by agents, handlers, advisors, and industry gurus. Or simply used as puppets for someone else's political ends.

When rocker Tommy Lee, chastened and spending a few quiet, reflective months in prison (for spousal abuse), decides he is grateful for the time to "just chill and check in with Tommy"; and he then gets a life coach, puts out a book called *Tommyland*, and presents himself to the world as a good man just and true, suspicion is justified.

But should it diminish our surprise or admiration at his turn to learn that Virgil Butler, the slaughterhouse worker–turned–vegan, is a poster boy for People for the Ethical Treatment of Animals, and his story, prominently displayed on the PETA Web site, "turned more people vegetarian than anything we did last year," as the PETA executive who produced the spot told me?

The use of the conversion story as a political tool is time-honored, after all—and sometimes it's the converter himself who uses it. As a youth, Darrell Issa was arrested for stealing cars. As a man, he became a successful businessman selling car alarms; the ironic symmetry of that reversal was repeated again and again—"I've done just the opposite of being a car thief!"—as Issa announced his candidacy in 2003 for governor of California.

One of the more fascinatingly complicated stories in this vein—where other people's self-interest murks up the water of a person's turn of conscience—is that of Norma McCorvey, better known as "Jane Roe."

McCorvey, the lead plaintiff and titular star of *Roe v. Wade*, the January 1973 Supreme Court decision legalizing abortion for American women, is now a pro-life Catholic. "I am Norma McCorvey," she declared in a press conference at the National Memorial for the Unborn, in Chattanooga, Tennessee, on March 23, 1997, a quarter-century after the landmark case. "I am now a child of God, a new creature in Christ; I am forgiven and redeemed. Today, I publicly recant my involvement in the tragedy of abortion. I humbly ask forgiveness of the millions of women and unborn babies who have experienced the violence of abortion. In this place of healing, the National Memorial for the Unborn, I stand with those who honor the worth of every unborn child as created in the image of God. I will strive, in the name of Jesus, to end this holocaust."

McCorvey had been working as a marketing director at an abortion clinic in Dallas, trying to ignore the pro-life protesters gathered outside. But one of those protesters, the Reverend Philip Benham of the fundamentalist Operation Rescue, struck up a playful friendship with her, and she converted not long after. She was a potent communicator, and her public pronouncements thereafter served as powerful ammunition in the meme cannons of the pro-life movement. One anecdote, ofttold, has McCorvey forlornly surveying a deserted playground, observing that the swings are empty "because there's no children because they've all been aborted." The drama is in the contrast. You can imagine Jane Roe before and Jane Roe after staring uncomprehendingly at each other across a gulf of time and ideology, a line as keen as the blade of a knife.

But to hear McCorvey tell it, the conversion was neither swift nor clean. A little research clouds the narrative further.

McCorvey had a rough life. She was a former drug dealer, alcoholic, and domestic-abuse victim, and after the court decision, a still clearly adrift McCorvey "converted" to atheism, and even flirted with a satanic cult, she told CNN—before landing on the safer ground of Benham's fundamentalist church, where she was recently baptized. "Jesus Christ has reached through the abortion mill wall and touched the heart of Norma McCorvey," said Reverend Benham, who performed the baptism.

McCorvey comes off, in light of her backstory, as vulnerable, malleable, and plucky. Both sides, the pro-choice and pro-life movements, have at one time or another propped Jane Roe up in the shop window. And just as the devil can quote scripture for his own ends, each side can find usable pull-quotes in her on-the-record comments. "I am pro-life," she told a Dallas radio station. "I think I've always been pro-life, *I just didn't know it.*" More recently, she clarified to CNN and other news sources that she defends a woman's right to abortion in the first trimester.

"If anything, Norma McCorvey's statements reflect her own confusion about the manifold aspects of abortion and the psychological turmoil within her own life," one commentator recently said. "Jane Roe was a role on the stage of American history, which took courage and just plain guts; how much harassment and threatening did McCorvey endure?"

Perhaps just enough to stir up the anxiety, guilt, and angst that, at least for some, is relieved by transforming yourself into the opposite of what you once were.

U-turns coincident with "born again" experiences can be problematic that way: For to a charismatic church, there's no better marketing tool, no better testament to the power of God, than the case study of a sinner who saw the light, and is willing to tell the story. But again, it's an error of logic to suppose that the involvement of a third party's interest necessarily obviates the "authenticity" of the conversion—by Norma McCorvey or anyone else.

A true, conscience-driven U-turn is not grandiose. If it even has the whiff of impression-management about it, of image building, of publicity seeking, we are right to suspect it. So-called "spiritual materialists," folks who, as the science-fiction writer Spider Robinson once put it, "drag their muffler a bit," and announce the coming of their spiritual selves a bit too loudly, rightly meet raised eyebrows.

The Bible has some strong opinions on grandiosity ("Beware of practicing your piety before men in order to be seen by them—" Matthew 6:1.) Jesus seemed to care little about deed and a lot about intention. Other religious and philosophical traditions make similar valuations. The tenth-century philosopher Maimonides believed that the most spiritually evolved level of giving is the gift bestowed anonymously (that enables the recipient to become self-sufficient). So making a public show of your U-turn—whether it be almsgiving or conscientious objecting—would therefore seem to diminish its value, and its authenticity.

If the hero's laurels are bestowed posthumously, that's another story.

That's what Pat Tillman has going for him. Tillman—the Arizona Cardinals' star who, following the 9/11 attacks and at the peak of his career, quit football and joined the Marines, presumably to avenge those American deaths where he thought they were manufactured, in Afghanistan—made the decision that this was a better use of a young athlete's body than falling into zone coverage a few hours a week. When he quit, Tillman didn't make a big show of it, saying simply, "My country needs me more than this game does." He just left. Not once, between the time he cleaned out his locker in Phoenix and the time he was killed by friendly fire in Afghanistan, did he grant a media interview. This wasn't about self-aggrandizement; this was a private thing. Tillman's actions are not necessarily beyond reproach. But, for the most part, even fierce critics of the war admit that what he did took courage, and showed integrity. At the very least, he did the wrong thing for the right reasons. He acted on his convictions.

Judging the credibility of U-turns by applying certain criteria, looking for elements of the story that ought to be in place, is not a bad start. But a big piece of the puzzle still remains: The U-turner him- or herself. A jurist needs to assess the credibility of witnesses in order to figure out how much weight to give their testimony. So too with U-turners.

The Parole Board's Dilemma

We might, for example, be less likely to believe a new convert's assurance that he has found the "answer" (and his aggressive entreaties to us to follow the same path, so that we might find it, too), if he has a history of turns. Wedding guests tend to shop at Wal-Mart, not Cartier, when picking out a gift for a friend who has met "Mr. Right" for the third time. The assumption with such folks tends to be that this current position, no matter how strong the conviction with which it's held, is a rest stop en route to some other destination, probably back up the road.

The James Frey Problem

The folks who tell the most compelling and dramatic stories about what has happened to them tend to be extreme personalities. Many whistle-blowers fall into this category: Often, they are the kind of people who, were you a defense attorney, you might think long and hard before calling as a witness. Credibility issues frequently swirl around their lives in ways that cast the legitimacy of the moral U-turn into doubt.

I routinely encountered such people while researching this book. I had no doubt that their stories were true. But they are the kind of stories that would give magazine fact-checkers fits. They are full of unverifiable detail. Necessarily so, because they are reports from within subcultures—the Church of Scientology, CIA-funded shell companies, private slaughterhouse operations—that don't exactly invite open scrutiny.

One way to handle the problem is simply to tell their stories and then say of their veracity, as the editor of *Multinational Monitor* did in his review of John Perkins's *Confessions of an Economic Hit Man*, "You be the judge." (That's a little bit of a cop-out, in that most readers don't have the facts to be in a position to judge—that's why they're reading the book.) Perkins tells a breathtaking story of his life in the National Security Agency (Zelig-like, Perkins seems to be blending into the wallpaper at every major backroom diplomatic moment of the '70s, '80s, and '90s), capped by full-blown repentance for that life and the exploitation he was party to. When *Hit Man* appeared in bookstores and on reviewers' desks, you could almost hear editors shouting to their research departments,

"Get me background on this guy!" You could imagine them retrieving a Googleprint on Perkins, digging through backlists. And—alarm bells! The profile that emerges is of a New-Age environmentalist self-help writer who penned books, and led workshops, on Native American spirituality. They find he has written a book called *Psychonavigation: Techniques for Travel Beyond Time*—more shamanic delvings. They cannot reconcile the New-Age flake with the high-rolling imperial man of finance. He simply cannot, to their minds, be both. "In the wake of the controversy over James Frey," a *New York Times* reporter put it, "one feels obliged to ask: Is it all true?"

Frey is, of course, the author of *A Million Little Pieces*, a dramatic U-turn memoir—incorrigible drug addict comes clean through his own macho bootstrapping—that was riddled with factual holes. But if the public's cynicism about redemption narratives has increased, so too has its willingness to see an "essential truth" beneath murky surface details. As long as the yarn's compelling, is labeled true, and falls into the category of *should be* true, that's enough. Frey's book was a smash bestseller—and, more tellingly, so was the sequel, which emerged after the fraud had been exposed. John Perkins's book hit the *New York Times* best-seller list even without the benefit of a single review in the big mainstream media. (The movie rights have been purchased by Beacon Pictures, which hopes to turn it into a Harrison Ford vehicle.)

Virgil Butler, the slaughterhouse worker–turned–vegan, is not a well-educated man. He describes himself as a "hillbilly," and when he smiles you think of Stonehenge. He is a recovering alcoholic. There are enough problems in his personal life that a psychologist, called to testify against him in a libel case, might say his animal-rights "awakening" was simply a case of a lost man needing to bring meaning to his life. (From a fellow with no dreams living in a trailer, he now has a whole community of people who are inspired by him—a pretty successful solution to an existential problem.) The *Los Angeles Times* ran a story about Butler a few years ago. Some minor factual inaccuracies in his story prompted the paper to run a retraction, and no big media outlet has covered Virgil Butler since. Tyson's take on Virgil Butler is that he is a disgruntled worker who invented tales of slaughterhouse horror only after he lost his job. "Some of the things he says are outrageous," spokesman Ed Nicholson said.

The Parole Board's Dilemma

But his story is mostly true. Virtually everything Butler said about the chicken plant corroborates what other whistleblowers and undercover investigators have found. And if you measure the sincerity of a conversion by its durability, this one was sincere—for the born-again Virgil has not wavered from his new identity.

The problem that bedevils whistleblowers is that even if you're right, you're going to be discredited. If you're a hillbilly trying to expose a big organization, you'll lose the PR war. Especially if it's a corporate giant with the resources to manufacture campaigns to smear a whistle-blower's reputation. Or a doggedly defensive outfit like, say, the Church of Scientology.

That happened, to some extent, with Gerry Armstrong, the former L. Ron Hubbard biographer who turned apostate and critic of the church. When *60 Minutes* was preparing an investigative piece on Scientology, Armstrong sat down for lengthy interviews with Mike Wallace. In the end, the show didn't use him, choosing instead to quote Omar Garrison, the writer with whom Armstrong collaborated, a man with nice suits and a hypnotic British accent. The *60 Minutes* segment, critical of the church in the main, depended largely on personal accounts of ex-members. Scientologists are known to attack the credibility of those ex-members who speak out against it, so the interview subjects *60 Minutes* quoted had to be, to the satisfaction of the producers, beyond reproach. (In the end CBS went with Laura Sullivan, who was the personal PR agent to Hubbard, and Paulette Cooper, an articulate author who had written a critical book.) But other news outlets—from Britain's Channel 4 to CBC's *Fifth Estate* to ABC's *20/20*—*did* deem Gerry Armstrong credible enough to go on air with his story.

When people who are contrarians by nature tell you a transformation story, you can't help but suspect that their turn is, at least in part, just another brick in the wall of their self-image: In other words, it's more about them, their identity, than it is about the issue.

We trust the story if we trust the person, and we trust the person, if we like him, find him smart, think he's a little like us. We tend, writes Anthony Storr in *Feet of Clay*, "to diagnose mental abnormality in the socially incompetent and overlook it in the socially dominant." (We discredit the Virgil Butlers, that is, and cut too much slack for the Ted Turners.) Conversion experiences, as described by those who have them, so closely resemble mental illness that Storr asks why we don't dismiss all religious converts as mentally ill. In fact, we pick and choose: The same story is taken more or less seriously depending on the mouth it issues from.

It's worth remembering, then, as we confront U-turners who strike us as simply mad, that madness is at least partly a cultural construct. Someone deemed "mad" may simply be ahead of the curve with an idea that will be mainstream in twenty or thirty years but which almost no one yet hews to. (See chapter 10.) For now, he has "adopted a fiction that's not supported by society," as the guru Bhagwan Shree Rajneesh, who may have been mad but probably wasn't, once put it. (The sane person, by contrast, is one whose fiction *is* supported by society.) But even a credible diagnosis of mental illness doesn't obviate the possibility of true, positive change of character at the end of the ride.

There's a great line attributed to Henry James that turns up frequently in the literature of life changes: "Adventures happen to people who know how to tell it that way." Some of us are simply better yarn-spinners, and have more invested in the yarn. In Reading jail, Oscar Wilde turned his decline—from feted artist to public disgrace—into something more noble. He tried, as the University of Oregon psychologist William Todd Schultz says, "to impose on his fall the organizing structure of a conversion narrative," to "wring from his story of ruin not a disaster but a higher kind of triumph: a triumph of soul."

So is the lost-now-found U-turner, whose life story so moves us, *really* describing a life of redemption, or did he just choose to remember it that way? Probably a little of each. Self-consciousness about our own stories creates a weird kind of doubling. There is the life, as lived, and there is our reconstruction of it, as remembered and told. The one doesn't replace the other, but rather overlays it, creating something like a multiply exposed photograph. The story the U-turner tells, then, is the truth, but it's stylized. It's not the objective truth. But, then, objective truth doesn't really exist at all.

* * *

The Parole Board's Dilemma

The problem with anticipating criticism is that if you take every cavil and carp seriously you end up misrepresenting the relative strength of the two sides. It's true that we prefer inspiring stories of individual courage. History burnishes the moral narrative, boosts the element of conscience in human biography, and downplays the other elements—chance, coercion, fear—that made a person, or a whole culture, change its ways. But rare is the significant life change in which conscience isn't a factor.

In short, there are strong grounds to be skeptical *of the skeptics*—the ones who claim people don't change, or at least don't change abruptly (those, that is, who aren't outright faking a change out of self-interest). A skeptic, you might say, is just someone it hasn't happened to.

The essayist Nicholson Baker was deeply suspicious of the whole notion of the epiphanic U-turn, preferring to believe that changes of mind almost always happen incrementally, imperceptibly. And then he had one himself. "I was plodding along, writing my little books, and then suddenly this thing speared into my life and it just took me over," he told David Gates in *Newsweek*: "This thing" was the Bush presidency—or rather, Baker's surprisingly strong reaction to it. You could say the cognitive shift it prompted, the philosophical U-turn, was from aesthete to propagandist. Baker swung from detached micro-observations of daily life to full social and political engagement, at least for the time it took him, weeping as he punched the keys, to write the novel that gushed forth, called *Checkpoint*.

The high-minded have historically had an impossibly sharp eye for expedience. "The more glittering the deed, the more I subtract from its moral worth, because of the suspicion aroused in me that it was exposed more for glitter than goodness," wrote Michel de Montaigne. William Ian Miller drops that quote in his book *Faking It*, and you can practically see the law professor's eyes twinkling as he composes the killer rebuttal: "Because virtue looks good, it looks bad. What are the virtuous to do? Pretend to vice?"

Under a powerful enough microscope, *nobody* can escape the charge of hypocrite. The notion that all do-goodism is motivated by self-interest, an idea the British philosopher Simon Blackburn calls the Grand Unifying Theory of Pessimism, is more than cynical. It doesn't hold up as an argument. "It kidnaps the word 'self-interest' for whatever the person we're talking about happens to be concerned about. In other words, it's a cynical 'explanation' that, because it purports to apply to everything, actually explains nothing." In plenty of instances, people actually "*neglect* their own interest or sacrifice their own interest to other passions or concerns."

Sometimes we just do the right thing, Miller says flatly, "and don't worry that it may be good business to do so."

If you drew back, and back, until you were looking at the Earth from space, you'd see the vectors of people trying to do the right thing crossing. The planet would look as if, mortally wounded, it had been stitched up by a team of blind surgeons working against the clock.

For every Pat Tillman there is a Stephen Funk, for every John Walker Lindh a Mike Hood. For every high-profile joiner and abstainer, in other words, for every business titan and talk-show host and university professor who has had a wake-up call and made a turn, there are dozens of folks whom you've never heard of and never will who have done the same thing. Not heroes, necessarily. Just people struggling to find a way to be fully human in the world that seems to offer few examples.

THIRTEEN

The Earth As Seen from Space
Is America Ripe for a Mass U-Turn?

I wasn't born for an age like this;
Was Smith? Was Jones? Were you?

—George Orwell, "Why I Write"

In the closing weeks of 1994 there came to pass, in quick succession, a series of extraordinary events. Paul Stiles, a twenty-nine-year-old bond trader working in the International Emerging Markets division of Merrill Lynch, in the North Tower of the World Financial Center on Wall Street, interpreted these events first as a bizarre coincidence and then as an omen.

The first was the news that Orange County was bankrupt. The *entire county*: a financial fiasco that surpassed in magnitude even New York City's insolvency during the 1970s. Much of the blame circled around the investment bank that had underwritten a lot of the county's investments, which turned out to be far riskier than the city's administrators had been led to believe: one Merrill Lynch.

Stiles was new to the trading desk of Merrill, having just transferred from the bond-marketing department. The day after his first trade—he sold a Mexican bond, on the instructions of his boss—Mexico devalued its currency, igniting a "peso crisis" that caused trillions of dollars in capital to vanish in one day. The very next day, news filtered onto the trading floor that a former Merrill Lynch systems analyst had been arrested after blowing up a homemade firebomb on a New York City subway car. Three days *after that*, Stiles opened his *New York Times* to read a business piece, buried among the ads for cars and watches: "Among the world's countries, the income gap between rich and poor in Manhattan is surpassed only by a group of 70 households near a former leper colony in Hawaii."

It was now Christmastime, and there being few senior people on the bond desk to train him, Stiles decided, with his wife, Sarah, to get far away for a week. They landed on a remote peninsula in Costa Rica—stepping onto the actual soil of those very "emerging markets" Stiles was abstractly manipulating. They canoed into a river lodge and spent a solitary New Year's Eve there.

Stiles returned to Merrill to find that his job has been eliminated. (Simple belt-tightening, employees were told in a group meeting.) He found a temporary post in another division of the firm, but was already thinking about where to send his résumé: perhaps to a venerable foreign bank like Britain's Barings, steward of the queen's money. But no sooner had *that* plan begun forming in his mind than a startling piece of news broke: Barings was bankrupt. The sudden collapse was, preposterously, being blamed on a single "rogue trader," a twenty-eight-year-old man named Nick Leeson whom Stiles, somewhat to his surprise, found himself rooting for. A working-class guy who was, it occurred to Stiles, merely exercising the same self-interest the banks themselves did.

For Stiles, the individual data points began to coalesce into a kind of parable. What had alarmed him about the peso crisis, when it erupted, was how uncontrollable it became almost immediately. The Mexican economy was being tweaked by a handful of young guys like him, and, for at least a couple of weeks, no government on Earth had the power to stabilize it. The Nick Leeson scandal merely confirmed his growing impression of the global money markets as a kind of Ponzi scheme that claimed millions of victims who didn't even know they were in the game, and one so volatile that a crisis in confidence in a single East Asian country would soon jump borders and oceans and bring ruin to working people in Latin America and Russia. The game wasn't immoral, exactly—it was *a*moral, which somehow made it all the more chilling.

By early in the new year, Stiles's job was becoming an issue for him on a couple of levels. As an employee of the most powerful bank on Wall Street, he was, demonstrably, part of the problem. And it was the corrosiveness of that knowledge—more than the long hours and bad nutrition and lack of sunlight—that seemed to be aging him prematurely. His face was filling out, gray hair was sprouting at his temples. He suffered pounding headaches, for which his doctor prescribed Valium. Until now Paul Stiles had always been able to claim a kind of moral high ground—he wasn't a "slick" like some of the other traders who did high-volume damage—just a high school teacher's son with lofty ambitions and a firm goal (weren't you supposed to have firm goals?) to work on Wall Street for ten years, make a bundle, and get out. But now he was on a slippery slope down—he could feel it—and moving faster the better he got at his job.

The problem had gone unarticulated, but not unnoticed. A few months earlier he had been invited by a client on a fishing trip to New Mexico's San Juan River. The San Juan is an artificially bountiful river, dammed and stocked, and Stiles watched the fellows around him pulling record numbers of fish, oblivious to the humiliation, even embarrassment, that ought to come when you play a game rigged in your favor. Of that event, he wrote in his journal an almost Melvillean meditation:

"They were a uniform crowd, each trying to draw something from the water, yet mindless of why. Somewhere along the way their choices had been lost. They had set out to find nature and been led to this turbocharger. To prove without doubt that their choice had been the right one—to feel secure about what they were doing with their lives—there was everyone else here doing just what they were doing, wearing just what they were wearing, reaffirming how they were supposed to feel, what they were supposed to do. If all the trout fishermen are here, I must be here. Trout fishing is about catching big trout. If I catch a big trout, I am happy. From the loftiest heights of man, from his need for beauty, for nature, for a spiritual connection, they now stood naked in a stream, naked in their greed for the big fish."

Stiles's ascension—a road paved by stopovers in the navy, the National Security Agency, and the captaincy of an Internet business for travelers founded during the dot-com boom—was the very definition of the American dream. Yet his stay on the summit—Wall Street—was only a few months old and already "I felt my entire constitution—moral, physical, and emotional—under attack."

There is a poem by W. B. Yeats that is torn out and posted on the wall by people who have bottomed out completely, and, in that dark place, been forced to confront who they really are, and what they really believe. "Now that my ladder's gone / I must lie down where all the ladders start / in the foul rag-and-bone shop of the heart." Paul Stiles had to face it now, all of it, the sense of a poisoning of basic assumptions and loyalties he would later tell me felt like the breakup of a marriage. It was the "emotional upheaval of having climbed to the top and found out that it's actually the bottom."

His thoughts became almost Zoroastrian. Light and dark.

"Fundamentally, on Wall Street, I came face to face with the way things are," he says. "The material and nonmaterial sides of life are literally at war. Wall Street is the material side, and it's extinguishing the other side every day. And you either submit to that and be lost, or reject it and save yourself."

On March 3, 1995, Stiles went into work, late. He hung his coat on the seat back and settled in before the blinking touchscreen, which was alive with incoming calls from all over Latin America. He sat there staring at it. He had made a decision in bed the night before that his body was only now registering. He could not move. He got up and went to the men's room, looked at his face, washed it, and walked to the lunchroom. The *rhubarb rhubarb rhubarb* of the trading hall sounded like surf. He watched, through the gaps in the window screens, commuters moving soundlessly far below. Eventually, he reached for his keyboard and sent an e-mail to his banking friend in Tokyo: "Time is short."

"There's a point you reach when the system no longer makes sense, when your trust is withheld by habit, when your country shimmers like a mirage and the man you once were is a painful memory," Stiles would later write in a memoir about his tenure at Merrill, which ended abruptly a few days after that paralytic moment in front of his computer, when he was summoned into his boss's office and told that he was being let go outright. "It is then that you build your own little world. Finally, you focus on finding a quiet niche where you can enjoy your fleeting moment on this earth." For Stiles, that niche has been writing. Not long after leaving Wall Street, he began composing a book called *Is the American Dream Killing You?*, a dense three-hundred-page exegesis on the radioactive effects of consumer capitalism on the human psyche.

The Cultural Flashpoint

Was it something about that particular time and place, that convergence of events, that produced a sudden change in Paul Stiles, or was it something about Paul Stiles that made him an early detector of a coming tsunami? He himself duly noted the details of what seemed to be a historical moment, even as it was unfolding. You read the story of his personal metamorphosis as a metaphor for larger, social shifts. "The peso crisis," he would conclude, "signified a change in eras, the shift from a Cold War dominated by political-military affairs to a new world order run by the Market—a shift from White House to Wall Street." To be working at Wall Street's most powerful investment bank at this precise juncture in history was to happen to be standing in the Bernauer Strasse and have the Berlin Wall fall on you, or shelving books at the depository in Dealey Plaza. It was to be, unwittingly, at the epicenter of a perfect storm with deep moral implications. "Implicit in this historic change was a shift in values," he writes. "American democracy is the mother of both power and principle. But the Market cares only about profits."

As we've seen, the conditions that prepare the ground for U-turns are both internal and external: What's happening both within one's own developing psyche and outside of it conspire to produce the moment of clarity. And so, to native temperament and particular life circumstances (you're of a certain age and class, or you're circumstantially constrained from expressing your virtue and goodness), we add the third and final factor in the nexus of change: what's happening in the world.

To understand why individuals make U-turns, it's worth investigating in this way why whole cultures do—because the same dynamics often seem to be at work.

When the now-early-middle-aged women (like the writers Denise Ryan and Caitlyn Flanagan) try to figure out what happened to their moms who morphed from June Cleaver to hopped-up Betty Friedan and left the family in a lurch, they generally conclude that a receptive personality collided with the front edge of a strong cultural force. Denise's mom, Angeline Kyba wasn't responding to the women's movement when she threw down the mop and picked up a paintbrush—at least not consciously. She was just trying to be who she had to be. (In fact, the decision was so unusual that when Denise's parents separated, a special meeting was called at her school to explain to the other students what "separation" and "divorce" actually meant.) But the move reverberated down the leafy boulevards of her tony old Toronto neighborhood. Erstwhile squeaky-clean matriarchs were soon drinking and smoking joints, too. "The funny thing is, eventually *everyone on our street* got divorced," Angeline says. (More curious still: Almost all the moms went to art school.) "She was like Typhoid Mary," Denise says of her mom—the first enlistee in a war none of the June Cleavers realized they had been drafted into, but which all joined willingly once they understood what was at stake (and how bad it felt to be consigned to the side of the enemy). The about-face of the fifties mom was a surprisingly common occurrence, so much so that it seems like a great untold story of that era. In 2000, Denise wrote an exquisite story about her mom's wake-up call and its impact on the family in the online magazine Salon.com. The response was immediate and overwhelming. "Maybe a hundred readers wrote in to say, basically: 'That's *my* life.'"

The late sixties were a cultural flashpoint that turned obeisant kids into radicals. Katherine Ann Power defines the extreme, but plenty of others fell like rain along the continuum.

"I could cite you case after case of this," says Jerome Kagan, who has thought a lot about the mass moral shift of students in that period of 1969 to 1971, when college campuses politicized around the Kent State shootings and the Vietnam War. In fact, the examples he knows personally—like the unmarried graduate student who quit and moved to California's Topanga Canyon to write children's stories—have convinced Kagan that if you took a sample slice from that particular historical moment—people born between, say, 1950 and 1953—and compared them to a group born earlier and one born later, "you would see dramatic differences. That's the power of the historical moment."

The Earth As Seen from Space

Social movements are often backlashes against the perceived sins of the fathers in much the same way that U-turns are backlashes against the perceived sins of the life lived thus far. Both are corrective reactions to a system out of balance. And both are typically slow to materialize, because core cultural identities, like individuals' core identities—resist change. The former New York senator Daniel Patrick Moynihan once described a kind of insidious process that happens to societies in which civility is allowed to subtly, gradually degrade. He called it "defining deviance down." People learn to tolerate behavior they really shouldn't, behavior that is not in the culture's character, that is not in that sense *authentic*; they tolerate it because the changes in behavior happen so incrementally that no one even notices.

On the eve of the selection of the most recent pope, Richard McBrien, a historian and the author of *Lives of the Popes*, told CBS's Morley Safer that the biggest challenge facing the pontiff wasn't contraception or ordaining women—these are small things to sort out. "By far the biggest challenge will be to turn around a culture that puts the seat of happiness in consumption and creature comforts, and get it to redefine happiness as community service."

That's a task that sounds a bit like waiting for evolution to unfold. But, in fact, these kinds of big cultural changes can happen relatively suddenly, like paleomagnetic reversals, as unseen forces reach a kind of critical mass—and, for no obvious reason, the system turns turtle.

Michel Foucault called these sorts of moments *ruptures*, when they happen from time to time in the human sciences—psychiatry, medicine, linguistics, economics, and biology. Ruptures occur when the rules governing these disciplines suddenly fail to hold. Much better known as the proponent of a similar idea is Thomas Kuhn, whose contention, in *The Structure of Scientific Revolutions*, is that whole scientific communities—and, by extension, whole cultures—can get stuck. A culture gets stuck when we "have fallen so in love with our current ideas that we are blind to alternatives," says the psychiatrist Anthony Storr. Stuck cultures, like stuck tectonic plates, only come unstuck abruptly. The force comes from a kind of critical mass of disillusionment.

Value systems, like ideologies, and faiths, follow a sine-wave cycle. The merits of a particular way of living are exaggerated, setting up unrealistic expectations in the generation coming up. These expectations are inevitably shattered, the pendulum swings back, and the disillusioned pilgrims search for something like the opposite of the paradigm that has just betrayed them.

It was disillusionment with the corruption of the church that sparked the mass swing toward atheism during the Enlightenment—and then disillusionment with what atheism wrought that sparked a mass swing away from it as the extent of the murderous folly of Maoism became apparent. That's generally how it goes: The faithful stream into the room en masse until the floor collapses, then the faithless move in (and vice versa). Likewise, whenever a culture drifts too far to the right politically, when the market is allowed to become too unregulated, a kind of scramble response of the society's immune system kicks in as people try to protect their social relationships that have come under siege.

Change, in other words, is not efficiently brought about by force or even direct lobbying; it's better kindled by the creation of an oppositional force around which resistance can galvanize. A band of teetotalers singing the virtues of sobriety will have less impact than a wave of dangerous reprobate drunks.

Writing in the late-1960s, the psychologist Paul Watzlawick and his colleagues (now at the Mental Research Institute in Menlo Park, California) took Jung's theory of reversals and ran with it, making what must at the time have seemed like a ludicrous projection. "To cast a brief glance into the future, it is a fairly safe bet that the offspring of our contemporary hippie generation will want to become bank managers and will despise communes, leaving their well-meaning but bewildered parents with the nagging question: Where did we fail our children?"

The Restoration of the World

It's not just in religion and politics that backlash cycles occur with clockwork predictability. You can see it in literary trends—for new writers, the great writers of the past stand as father figures that have to be overthrown. "Overthrowing" Dad by doing the opposite of what he did is, arguably, the MO of all artists: It's how culture advances, and builds a tight little cultural elite, which eventually dictates the direction for the society as a whole—until the next generation overthrows *that*.

Not long ago, the *New York Times* science reporter Natalie Angier wrote a column about her own lapsed faith, and eventual ensconcement in atheism. The change was inevitable, she said, as her experience and the breadth of her knowledge grew. If breadth of knowledge and education are enough to produce major life-direction shifts, then, because those are conditions that can be overlaid on any life, *we're all capable of radical reversals*. And if *that's* true, whole societies are capable of radical reversals once they become sufficiently enlightened. Once, that is, they wake up.

Life-changing epiphanies, to the Buddhist way of thinking, are merely windshield-cleaners. They're not about suddenly seeing the world differently, but simply suddenly *seeing the world*—and in this respect they evoke the image of the businessman calling his office one morning: "I've been sick for the last twenty-five years and today I'm well, so I won't be coming in." Understood this way, *enlightenment*—"the sense of transcendence that changes us, that makes life worth living," as Karen Armstrong said recently—isn't really anything supernatural at all. It's a perfectly reasonable process.

"We accept it as completely normal that we can look at things we looked at as a child and understand them quite differently now," the social historian Walter Truett Anderson said, "but we seem to have a hard time with the idea that we may in the future be able to look at the things we look at right now and see *them* quite differently."

At the species level we are changing, and at a faster rate than ever before, and one of the dimensions on which we're changing is human nature itself. There's evidence that such traits as trust, aggressiveness, even intelligence, have evolved in response to environmental demands. (Whole cultures become congenitally trusting, for example, when it's in their collective interest to do so, and paranoid in turbulent times when self-protection is required.) Proof of the kind of fierce selective pressure that the last ten thousand years have produced is found in the human genome itself: Portions of it appear to have been reshaped during that time. It seems virtually certain that human nature has been tweaked as the genome has changed. We are becoming the people that environ-mental and social conditions are forcing us to become.

And what are those conditions?

The signal condition, perhaps, is that for the first time human beings are capable of doing themselves in—either with sudden intention or through the casual brutality of environmental degradation or through setting up the conditions for inevitable economic collapse. A species, to survive in such uncertain times, might adapt a kind of sixth sense, a kind of warning bell about our own behavior when it starts doing damage—at the individual or collective level. Maybe, just maybe, that's what people like Ray Anderson, Madeline Nelson, Michael Allen Fox, and Paul Stiles—in the perplexing extremes of their adaptations to life—are responding to.

If that's true, the development of such new radar isn't something we would expect to see right away. To predict mass enlightenment after, say, an event like 9/11, is to misunderstand the time scale of evolutionary change. (Therefore, this theory is what Stephen Jay Gould would call a "bad theory"—it's not provable or disprovable in our lifetimes.) But, if true, it would help explain the kinds of moral U-turns we're talking about. The tiny sampling of people it's happen-ing to, selected because of some complex commingling of individual personality traits and circumstance, are at the front end of a social movement marked by a shift from little-picture to big-picture think-ing. From an ethic of freedom to an ethic of responsibility, not just to those around us but for those coming up behind. Call them Seventh-Generation X.

Mario Beauregard, the University of Montreal neuroscientist, is convinced that the epiphanic shifts we see in certain individuals por-tend something much bigger—a "global evolution of consciousness" that will transcend differences between secular and religious as we think of those descriptors now. Since his work has been publicized, he told me, "I've received e-mails from all over the world of people reporting spontaneous awakenings, a fusion with the universe and so on, without being religious at all."

"I think he's right," the Apollo astronaut Ed Mitchell said when I men-tioned Beauregard's work. "My take on all of these types of experiences is that it's ground-state resonance with the zero-point energy field, which I consider the ground of our being."

I understood almost none of that. So Mitchell repackaged it.

What some of us are tuning in to, he suggested, might be distress signals from the planet itself. "As the system is threatened and needs to be innovative and creative in order to sustain itself, to survive, these kinds of experiences are going to appear in greater number."

And you won't have to be an Apollo astronaut to have one?

"No."

And so, even though I, living in a city, may feel completely detatched from the natural environment . . .

"Doesn't matter."

. . . I'm still linked to it.

"Yup."

And the signals that will come to me will come in the same sort of way, if I'm open to them, that they did to you.

"Yup."

I ran past Ed Mitchell my term *secular epiphany*.

"It's just a transcendent experience, a metanoia, being 'born again,' whatever you want to call it," he said. "It's really just a deep shift in your value system and your mind-set. I don't believe in extra dimensions— I'm speaking strictly metaphorically when I talk about the 'other side.' But once you've seen that, once you've felt what you felt, you can't go back. It's irreversible."

There is a familiar notion, particularly among followers of Eastern philosophies, that a collective awakening is the result of a growing number of individual awakenings. This is the proverbial "cool revolution," a *proactive* mass movement that kindles change subtly, gradually, and peacefully. No single charismatic leader drives the agenda. "When people have transformed their minds, they will naturally transform the society," says Robert Thurman. The dynamic is the opposite of the lonely crowd: Think of it as the collective individual.

"I have always said that no one heals alone—we heal through and for one another," writes the psychologist and psychoneuroimmunologist Joan Borysenko, who in her mind-body work often refers to her husband, who survived the concentration camps with the help of other survivors. "In Judaism this is referred to as *tikkun olan*, the healing or restoration of the world."

Following what was by most measures the most violent century in history, the dust has cleared to reveal the landscape. And the great surprise is that nobody seems to be around. At least, they're not in view front-and-center. The population has scattered and stand huddled up at the margins, at the polar extremes. In America, particularly, it's hard to find a dimension of political or social life that doesn't force or promote partisan thinking, and with it a kind of perpetual instability.

A two-party system means that a minute shift of wind or policy can upset the balance of a perfectly split electorate; if even a few outliers among the entrenched tribes change their mind, a whole vast region can toggle from Red to Blue or vice-versa. A culture of faithful versus faithless spins off all sorts of other touchy binaries, like the culture of life versus the culture of death (pro-life versus assisted suicide). The media, with its mutually annihilating messages coming in from right and left, is starting to seem like those hotel sinks that have a hot tap and cold tap and no plug: On average, the water is pleasantly lukewarm, but it's impossible to wash your hands. (And so the sink becomes useless). Consumer capitalism itself, a nest of oppositions (buyer/seller, producer/consumer) that depends on the continual trashing of the old for the new, is also dependent on fundamental judgment errors. Consistently overestimating how happy, say, a new plasma screen will make us is what keeps consumer capitalism humming along; it depends on the very disillusionment it produces, like a machine that burns its own gears.

A whole generation that believed the promise that they can "have it all" instead found themselves boomeranging between extremes (each pole—the "life" without the work, and the work without the life—quickly becomes unsustainable, but for different reasons). Brave attempts at balance have generally ended badly as the truth dawns that the economics of Western cultures just don't seem to allow it.

The most staggering polarization is surely the one remarked on most. America's wealthy and poor are metaphorical worlds apart: First World and Third World. Some have speculated that it's that fact—a gap between rich and poor in the United States that's three times as large as in any European country, and the rapidly inflating real estate bubble creating a new age of serfdom—that explains the strange, mass embrace by Americans of organized religion over the last thirty years, when much of the Western world is abandoning it.

"The way to feel virtuous in America today, to feel assurance that we're 'okay,' is through material wealth," Jerome Kagan told me. "The income gap leaves too many people feeling they have a damaged or compromised sense of their worth. So how do you reassure yourself that you're 'good'? By becoming religious. And it works. It works. I happen to know very well two brothers. One brother is very successful in the secular world; and the other isn't. And it bugged that second brother. And he suddenly turned religious. It was his way of saying, you see, actually *I* win, because I'm more moral."

But religion isn't the only way for those left behind in the materialism game—or, more to the point for the typical U-turner, disillusioned by it—to express their "goodness." A commitment to some social-welfare issue may work just as well.

The richest vein of U-turn stories that I found, by far, concerned converts to animal rights. There were animal-rights activists who used to be cattle ranchers and butchers and animal experimenters, and even a guy who was employed as Ronald McDonald who ditched the getup for militant veganism. The killing of animals for food and shoes, no longer strictly necessary, is something that most of us carry some residual guilt about. Eric Markus, an author who is now an animal-rights activist, captured the discord in a nutshell, and in a phrase that could stand in for the intellectual and moral struggles of a lot of the U-turners in this book: "The way my parents brought me up was fundamentally opposed to the way they taught me to eat. I had to get rid of one or the other." To become a vegetarian is a fairly gentle way to expose the hypocrisy of the family script, without actually being written out of the will. So long as they wear it lightly, new vegetarians, like all new converts to a more ostensibly "ethical" way of living, can feel the sense of piety and humility that comes with stepping down a rung on the ladder of human entitlement. That kind of settling of accounts approaches a religious feeling. In such a coming-clean, there is a kind of baptism into a new life, a genuine sense of becoming a nobler agent in the world, without a foot being set in church.

An Unstable Load Will Shift

The great irony of the information age, as social historians have pointed out, is that having access to the full spectrum of information hasn't made us more open-minded and bipartisan; it has just made it easier for us to find views that confirm our own biases. So we are driven daily even further to the extremes, into communities with little variance in their tastes and politics. A weird social phenomenon thus kicks whole cultures into its vortex: "group polarization." The more partisan we become, the more partisan we become. People unwittingly morph into warped versions of their true selves, rationalizing away all kinds of views and behaviors as they strain to stay with the tribe they joined way back when they were—and it was—something completely different. Until? Until?

The U-turners in this book are, you could say, people who fell out of balance, but in lots of different ways. The restorative snap back depended on what, in particular, they were thinking too much about, and what they were neglecting as a result. But what they have in common is that the gap between personal values (like being kind or raising a family or volunteering) and social values (like making money) just became too great, reaching the point where they didn't recognize themselves. The social self and the private selves became strangers to each other. And when that happens, something has got to give.

A system out of balance always corrects itself: The rule applies at the individual level as well as at the level of a whole culture. At a crucial, loaded moment, someone makes the needed gesture, gives the needed speech, strikes the needed chord. In Britain, a literate former slave publishes an arresting memoir, the first "inside story" of the slave trade, just as growing guilt and increasing threats of revolts from the slaves themselves have prepared the ground for the abolitionist movement. In India a bespectacled little man leads six dozen followers to the sea to peacefully protest a British law forbidding Indians to make their own salt, just as unrest reaches critical mass. (The march prompts mass civil disobedience in sympathy and marks the beginning of the end of British colonial rule in India.)

In the December of 1968, Apollo 8 astronaut Bill Anders snaps a photograph of the whole Earth suspended in blackness. The image appears on magazine covers just as the first stirrings of an extremely marginal environmental movement are being felt, and there is no one who doesn't understand in a new way how tiny and fragile the planet is, a little neighborhood, really, where the trash you pitch over the fence inevitably lands in someone else's yard. The effect of the image turns out to be exactly as predicted by a Cambridge University astrophysicist named Fred Hoyle twenty years earlier: "Once a photograph of the Earth, taken from outside, is available," Hoyle said, "we shall, in an emotional sense, acquire an additional dimension. Once the sheer isolation of the Earth has become plain to every man, whatever his nationality, or creed, a new idea as powerful as any in history will be let loose."

Not long ago the conservative commentator David Brooks, usually a pretty mirthful guy, weighed in from his perch on the *New York Times* op-ed page in an uncharacteristically grave and hushed tone. Hurricane Katrina had just turned the Gulf Coast into an open sewer. Brooks saw the event as a cultural inflection point. Not a tipping point—more than that: a "bursting point." How had America acquitted itself? The poor were abandoned and the rich got out, and nobody much cared before it was too late. In this decade, for the first time, the country glimpsed its Jungian shadow. The same character trait that showed itself as fashionable, clinical detachment in the cultural spheres showed itself here, larger and uglier, as detachment from the concerns of people not much like us. That shadow is creeping up, asserting itself. And so, Jung would say, a rebalancing is imminent. It is, the economist Karl Polanyi believed, a historical inevitability. A kind of spasm response of "spontaneous social reactions" always happens when the good of society as a whole is tamped down too long.

Brooks believes a big progressive resurgence may be at hand. Or perhaps a call for law and order as unrest reaches a critical mass. "All we can be sure of is that the political culture is about to undergo some big change." Historians have noted that the intervals between big social shifts have grown shorter and shorter. No one can quite agree on what

285

the next great shift will be, but the assumption that it will happen *in our lifetimes* is something many scientists have staked their life's labors on.

A certain type of psychologist is inclined to pose the kind of question we've already explored: Is there a type of person most likely to have a midlife reversal? But a mimetic theorist—one who studies how ideas spread—would take issue with that approach. It assumes that people themselves determine what beliefs they're going to have. Mimetic theory asks instead, What is it about certain ideas that leads them to collect many "hosts" for themselves? "The question," says the University of Toronto's Keith Stanovich, "is not *how do people acquire beliefs, but how do beliefs acquire people?*"

In other words, it's not about who's involved or what the catalyst is: If the conditions are right—politically, socially, culturally—ideas that capture the moment will spread. The pressure of events cannot, beyond a certain critical point, be contained. In a sermon shortly after the buses of Montgomery, Alabama, were desegregated, and the civil rights movement had begun, Martin Luther King made a memorable remark: Rosa Parks, he said, "had been tracked down by the zeitgeist." But if it hadn't been Rosa Parks, it would have been someone else. (Indeed, Rosa Parks was not the first black Montgomerian to challenge the bus laws and be arrested; it's just that she was deemed the most sympathetic figure, and so the nascent desegregation movement put her on display.) We think of Olaudah Equiano's book, but there were no doubt other literate slaves, whose stories were waiting to be told. We think about authors who launched their big idea—*The Other America* (Michael Harrington), *The Lonely Crowd* (David Riesman), *Silent Spring* (Rachel Carson) —just when the culture was ready for them, and kindled change. But it could just have easily been some other player, another "possible self" in the drama of that particular historical moment, who heard the cue and stepped on stage.

The specific catalyst itself is, then, if not quite immaterial, at least not the most important part of the equation—just as the catalytic event that sparks individual life reversals is so often trivial. It is simply an entry point, an event that, for whatever reason, causes the fog to clear on the big collective notion that had formed undercover. The new ideology that the U-turner embraces is simply *an irresistible truth whose time has come.*

The Earth As Seen from Space

Karen Armstrong views our own moment in history—with its staggeringly rapid expansion of knowledge and scientific advancement—as every bit as transformative a period in history as the one that hatched the great faiths 2,500 years ago. But there is one major difference. The pathbreaking today is exclusively intellectual. No great visionaries have emerged to shepherd the benighted masses to a new understanding of *how to be* in the world. Where once the world's sharpest minds spent as much time and energy on tackling spiritual problems as we do on curing cancer, today such pursuits are considered just so much screwing around on the margins—not the domain of the best and brightest, but the refuge of the ethereal, the eccentric, and the damaged. Thus, there is no one to remind people of the conclusion pretty much all the sages of the ancient world arrived at: There *is* a secret answer at the back of the book. The way to some measure of peace and happiness is not so mysterious. Consider the interests of others as equivalent to your own, and act accordingly. The notion is that, in the end, it's not what you acquire, or what you learn, or even what you believe: It's how you live your life that will save you.

Long after he fled Wall Street there came, for the former Merrill Lynch bond trader Paul Stiles, a final, decisive epiphany. As it happened, he was in the middle of writing his backlash book *Is the American Dream Killing You?* The chapter he was working on concerned urban sprawl.

"I was driving my kids to school," he recalls. "And I entered this environment near Annapolis, which is just the most garish sprawl: fast-food joints and lube joints and strip malls and traffic and blacktop and spaghetti wire everywhere, and I just started to feel physically ill, driving through it. Because I understood not just that it was ugly but the whole thing that had produced it. Why would you do this to a place you live? It's like throwing trash on the street. I'd reached a new level of sensitization to it.

"And this produced the straw that led to the decision to leave the country. I remember this so distinctly. We had stopped at a traffic light right near my son's school. And there were these two kids on the sidewalk, and they were maybe eleven or twelve years old. One of them had this half-crazy walk, and this wild hair and a black T-shirt. And he was wearing a hockey goalie's mask. And this is June. He was imitating a serial killer. I just sat there pondering all the people who had been involved in the long chain of events that had led to him wearing that on the street. Think this through. Someone selling the idea for these slasher films to Hollywood; people making them; someone handing out the knives on the set; someone splattering the blood. Marketing teams getting the word out and people going to watch them. And the movie posters. And then, of course, the parents of this kid, and the administrators of the school watching him walk down the hall with this thing on his face. And it seemed to symbolize—not just that it itself was a problem—but that so many people didn't seem to notice anymore."

A lot of thoughts coalesced in a few seconds.

"I'm forty-one," was the first. "Half of my life's over. Do I want to continue to live in the United States? The answer was an immediate no. It was a real gut-check: You ask your subconscious a question and you have to answer right away. No.

"I actually made a vow at that point. That no matter what happened—positive or negative—I was getting my kids out of this place. It's like one of those times in your life when you make that pledge to yourself—like, I'm never going to drink that much again—I made that vow, and carried it out. I went to the Spanish embassy, and I walked in, and said, I'm interested in leaving the country, and emigrating." The citizenship was, surprisingly, approved right away, and they were gone within a year. On the way out, Stiles sold both his cars to a guy who paid for them with cashier's checks. He moved the family of four to Tenerife, in the Canary Islands, where they found a little farmhouse with a view of the mountains and the sea, and the kids would learn Spanish, and every vestige of the tension-flush of trader's sunburn would leave his face, and he could forget about what he'd left behind.

Almost. Not long after arriving, he received a call from the bank about those cashier's checks from the guy back in the states who bought their cars.

They had bounced.

Notes

Introduction

2 **businesswoman and part-time model** "From the Beaches to the Forests," Claudia Stoicescu, *Corporate Knights* magazine (January 5, 2006).

3 **"I almost felt like an invisible person was grabbing my arm"** Hill, *The Legacy of Luna*, 12.

4 **"like the answer to a question I didn't even know I was asking."** Ibid., 24.

7 **coined the term *metanoia*** Abukuma Moriyuki, "A Weberian Sociology of Religious Experience," http://www.ne.jp/asahi/moriyuki/abukuma/moriyukis/intro/Religious_Experience.html (accessed June 2006).

7 **former chess grand master Paul Morphy** Paul Hoffman, "The Pandolfini Defense," *The New Yorker* (June 4, 2001).

One: The Burning Spear

11 **the Atlanta office of Ray Anderson** Author interviews. See also Anderson, *The Journey from There to Here.*

12 **whole lagoons of petroleum** Paul Hawken, Amory Lovins, and L. Hunter Lovins, *Natural Capitalism: Creating the Next Industrial Revolution* (Back Bay Books, 2000), 138.

13 **"In terms of combining social responsibility"** Charles Fishman, "Sustainable Growth: Interface Inc." *Fast Company* magazine (April 1998).

16 **fifties matriarch** "A Tale of Two Mothers," Salon.com, http://archive.salon.com/mwt/feature/2000/05/09/art_mom/index.html (accessed June 2006).

16 **"room of one's own"** Author interviews.

17 **"He will be wise but less cocksure"** Palmer, *Inner Knowing*, 5.

18 **Pat Tillman—before he picked up the phone** Tim Layden, "Not Standing Pat," *Sports Illustrated*, June 3, 2002; and Gary Smith, "Code of Honor," *Sports Illustrated*, May 3, 2004.

Notes

20   **documented some of the '99 disasters** Po Bronson, *The Nudist on the Late Shift: And Other True Tales of Silicon Valley*, Broadway Books, 2000.

20   **South-Asian tsunami** "Disaster Ignites Debate: Was God in the Tsunami?" Ron Rosenbaum, *New York Observer* (January 10, 2005).

20   **the archbishop of Canterbury** Richard N. Ostling, "Asia's Tsunami Crisis Revives Perennial Question: 'Where Was God'?" *Asbury Park Press* (January 23, 2005).

22   ***"Fuck them,"* he thought.** James Kennedy, *About Face*, 131.

23   **"I have been wading in a long river"** "Midwestern Primitive," *Time* magazine, (February 28, 1949); see also, "On the Virtues of Idleness," Mark Slouka, *Harper's* (November 2004).

24   **W. S. Merwin's narrator** "For the Anniversary of My Death," *The Lice*, Macmillan, 1967.

Two: The Time of Reckoning

29   **Five-Dollar Philanthropist** For more details on Tom Williams' ventures, see his website: www.givemeaning.com.

31   **the average reckoning point** Elliott Jacques, "Death and the Midlife Crisis," *International Journal of Psychoanalysis*, no. 46 (1965).

31   **Hardened violent criminals sometimes mysteriously reform** Jack Block and Norma Haan, then at the Berkeley Institute for Human Development, observed that "the decade from twenty-five to thirty-five is a guilty period." George Vaillant, *Adaptation to Life*, 332.

32   **A quirk of human neurochemistry** Leanne M. Williams et al., "The Mellow Years? Neural Basis of Improving Emotional Stability over Age," *Journal of Neuroscience* 26 (29), June 14, 2006.

32   **at the precise point of intersection . . . comes enlightenment** David Whyte, "Fionn and the Salmon of Knowledge," in Whyte, *The Heart Aroused*, 145.

32   **"I was taught that God was love"** "The Lost Tycoon," Ken Auletta, *The New Yorker* (April 23, 2001).

33   **the "social clock"** Bernice Neugarten, "Time, Age and the Life Cycle," *The Meanings of Age: Selected Papers*, in Dail Neugarten, ed. (University of Chicago Press, 1996), 25.

33   **the "subjective midpoint" in most lives is around age twenty** Robert Lemlich, in Ingram, *The Velocity of Honey*, 192.

33   **"Work hard—you don't have as much time as you think you do."** "Remembering Michael Kelly," *The New Republic* (April 4, 2003).

34   **"I have become everything I hate"** Whyte, *Crossing the Unknown Sea*, 155.

34   **"Our marriages fail"** "Fat, Forty and Fried," Nigel Marsh, *Guardian* (May 20, 2006).

Notes

37   **the ruthless Helen Kushnik** Author's conversation with Dennis Miller, 1992.

38   **"If you start giving the salute to something you aren't"** Leslie Kane, ed., *David Mamet in Conversation*, University of Michigan Press, 183.

38   **"Looking back on it,"** "Smedley Butler on Interventionism," 1933, www.fas.org/man/smedley.html (accessed June 2006).

39   **Dave Dellinger was raised** "Fresh Air," NPR (April 9, 1993).

40   **"the day my conscience came out of hiding"** "Buyers Naude," obituary, *The Economist* (September 16, 2004).

42   **"The book of our lives is open"** Robert Coles, "Two Tolstoy Stories," *Harvard Diaries*, 97.

Three: The Likely Candidate

43   **a bliss Ed Mitchell would liken to romantic love** Smith, *Moondust*, 59.

44   **NASA, predictably, has distanced itself from Mitchell** "I couldn't help noticing that, unlike books by the other moon-walkers, none of Ed Mitchell's writings were available in the bookshop at the Kennedy Space Center," Smith, *Moondust*, 40.

47   **"What Slayton wanted was impregnability."** Smith, *Moondust*, 328.

49   **Both "lacked the stomach to repress their moral emotions"** Janet Landman, "The Crime, Punishment, and Ethical Transformation of Two Radicals: or How Katherine Ann Power Improves on Dostoevsky," in McAdams, *Turns in the Road*, 35.

49   **When you delve into the past** See the example of Carl Jung in Storr, *Feet of Clay*, 85–94.

49   **a condition called *chrometophobia*** "Trivial Money Matters," FW The Art of Living, www.myfw.com/money/Article_100014.asp (accessed June 2006).

50   **"Did this polymorphous man have a firm center?"** "Gandhi's Truth," in Coles, *The Erik Erikson Reader*, 389.

50   ***Homo religiosus*** James E. Loder, *The Transforming Moment*, 140.

51   **which teams of psychologists and sociologists** Involved in the project are, among others, Jeffrey Victoroff and Jessica Stern of Harvard.

51   **We do not, as a culture, cut the "prodigal daughter" much slack.** *Sound and Spirit*, Public Radio International (March 28, 2004).

51   **"messianic morality"** Jordan Peterson, "Lost Boys," *Toronto Star* (June 11, 2006).

51   **"More prodigies, more idiots"** Steven Pinker, in debate with Elizabeth Spelke, "The Science of Gender and Science," Edge.org (May 16, 2005), www.edge.org/3rd_culture/debate05/debate05_index.html (accessed June 2006).

51   **why engineers . . . love Monty Python** Studio 360, Public Radio International (August 21, 2005).

51   **The comic novelist Mark Leyner** "Spilling the Beans," *O* magazine (June 2002).

Notes

52 **"What are the conditions for self-actualization"** Maslow, *The Farther Reaches of Human Nature*, 204.

53 **"The Case for a Simpler Life"** Laurance Rockefeller, *Reader's Digest* (February 1976).

53 **a plane, a sixty-five-foot speedboat** Laurence Rockefeller obituary, Michael T. Kaufman, *New York Times* (July 11, 2004).

53 **"cultural creatives"—a cohort 50 million strong** Ray and Anderson, *The Cultural Creatives*, 17.

53 **"The Palestinian bombers tend to be middle class"** There is an explanation for this, though. It's not that the poor are less inclined to radicalism, necessarily. "Individuals with low ability or little education are most likely to volunteer to join the terrorist organization," Ethan Bueno de Mesquita of Washington University in St. Louis concluded. But "the terrorist organization screens the volunteers," he noted, and only the best candidates make it through. Cited in "The Quality of Terror," *American Journal of Political Science* (July 2005).

54 **"They think, 'My life should be rich and rewarding . . .'"** Watzlawick et al., *Change*, 47.

54 **the natural shift to "postformal" thinking** McAdams, *The Stories We Live By*, 200.

55 **"The rest is nonunderstanding, or incomplete understanding"** Gurdjieff, paraphrased in Peter Ouspensky, *The Psychology of Man's Possible Evolution*, 102.

55 **"Living in Luna," she writes** Julia Hill, *The Legacy of Luna*, 187.

55 **Shirley swings wildly** McAdams, *The Stories We Live By*, 174. *Shirley Rock* is a pseudonym assigned by McAdams to his research subject.

56 **Without Elsinore** Lorissa MacFarquhar, "A Dry Soul Is Best," *The New Yorker*, October 25, 2004.

56 **Che Guevara was a rebel from the get-go** "The Real Che," Anthony Daniels, *The New Criterion* (October 2004). Che would come to identify himself as "Ese, el que fue"—"myself, the man I used to be"—as his daughter, the Havana physician Aleida Guevara, noted. Cited in "Riding My Father's Motorcycle," *New York Times* (October 9, 2004).

57 **the writer David Auerbach** Storr, *Feet of Clay*, 217.

57 **Christian who longed . . . to become "a savage"** Holland Cotter, "Gauguin's Paradise: Only Part Tahitian and All a Fantasy," *New York Times* (March 5, 2004).

57 **"we deal with the vicissitudes of human intention"** McAdams, *The Stories We Live By*, 29.

58 **The research psychologists Robert McCrae and Paul Costa, Jr.** McAdams, Ibid., 196. Some people, McCrae and Costa point out further, are also more inclined *to report* a midlife crisis. Certain people simply seem to crave novelty and variety (Gauguin and Whitman and William James are often included in this group), and this proclivity is part of a personality trait called "Openness." "Men and women who are open to experience," note McCrae and Costa, "are more likely to make midcareer shifts." McCrae and Costa, in "Openness to Experience," in R. Hogan and W. H. Jones, eds., *Perspectives in Psychology*, vol. 1., 146–172, (1985).

Notes

58 **"happy carrot"** *Tapestry*, CBC1 (September 26, 2004).

58 **Tristan Flora and her grandson** The story of mother and son inspired the Mario Vargas Llosa novel *The Way to Paradise*.

59 **University of Minnesota scientist named Thomas Bouchard** Robert Winston, "Why Do We Believe in God?" *Guardian* (October 13, 2005).

59 **an innate, unique "set point"** Psychologist Jonathan Haidt, quoted in "Pursuing Happiness," John Lanchester, *The New Yorker* (February 27, 2006).

59 **"Trying to be happier is like trying to be taller"** David Lykken, in John Lanchester, "Pursuing Happiness," *The New Yorker* (February 27, 2006).

60 **the "devil's advocate"** V. S. Ramachandran and Sandra Blakeslee, *Phantoms in the Brain*, 136; see also Lauren Slater, *Opening Skinner's Box*, 129.

60 **"a Kuhnian paradigm shift"** Ramachandran, Ibid.

60 **a gene called VMAT2** "The Brain Chemistry of the Buddha," Laura Sheahen, Beliefnet.com, http://www.beliefnet.com/story/154/story_15451_1.html (accessed June 2006).

61 **the spiritual intuitive** "Robert Wright interviews Huston Smith," MeaningofLife TV. http://meaningoflife.tv/video.php?speaker=smith&topic=complete (accessed June 2006).

61 **a *moral dimension* of our personalities may be innate** See James Wilson's *The Moral Sense*.

62 **Women's double-X chromosome** "In males, there's no hiding your X," the science writer Olivia Judson pointed out. In males, a genetic variant for extreme behavior such as, say, pulling a U-turn, would never be brought to heel. Judson, "Different but (Probably) Equal," *New York Times* (January 23, 2005).

62 **waiting to be dunked** Tom Wolfe, "Sorry, But Your Soul Just Died," *Hooking Up*, 78.

62 **"your soul just died"** Ibid., 78.

62 **Somewhere between a third and three-quarters** Steven Pinker, "Robert Wright interviews Steven Pinker," MeaningofLife TV, http://meaningoflife.tv/video.php?speaker=pinker&topic=complete (accessed June 2006).

Four: The Condemned Twin

67 **"The self I had killed in the first prison"** Sidney Rittenberg, *The Man Who Stayed Behind*, 408.

68 **the self as "a project"** *Internet Encyclopedia of Philosophy* www.iep.utm.edu/s/sartre-ex.htm.

71 **Glanville would write a gripping memoir** *The Goldberg Variations*.

72 **"happiness" studies** See Jon Gertner, "The Futile Pursuit of Happiness," *New York Times Magazine* (September 7, 2003).

73 **"Every psychiatrist has seen cases"** Anthony Storr, *Feet of Clay*, 93.

73 **For the psyche to regain equilibrium,** Jolande Jacobi, *The Psychology of C. G. Jung*, 53–60.

Notes

73 **"in the world of dogma"** Jung, "Psychology and Alchemy," *Collected Works of C. G. Jung*, vol. 12.

73 **"the blackness of the whiteness"** Ibid.

74 **It is the very connection of opposites,** Ibid. It's useful to think of Jung's opposing halves not as two faces of a coin but as the two pincers of a pair of pliers: Their usefulness, their very *meaning*, is in their opposition.

74 **"It seems radical, . . ."** In Matherne's review of *A Life of Jung* by Ronald Hayman, www.doyletics.com/arj/lifejung.html (accessed June 2006).

74 **midlife U-turns are relatively rare** Midlife crises, too, are rarer than we're sometimes led to believe. Twenty-six percent of Americans reported that they had a midlife crisis, according to one recent study. Elaine Wethington, "The Myth of the Middle-Age Crisis," *Motivation and Emotion*, vol. 24, no. 2 (October 2000.)

75 **Hendra's "drug of choice"** Sarah Hampson, "The Hampson Interview: Tony Hendra," *Globe and Mail* (June 19, 2005).

75 **"The power of paradox is that it proves"** Watzlawick et al., *Change*, 18.

76 **"Great believers and great doubters may *seem* like opposites"** Jennifer Hecht, *Doubt*, 364.

76 **Vidocq was a flamboyant and cunning French criminal** Philip John Stead, *Vidocq: A Biography*.

78 **a more superficial one** Timothy D. Wilson, *Strangers to Ourselves*, 65.

80 **the same core person** Other psychologists and philosophers have used different names for this "true identity." Karen Horney called it the "real self "; Kazamierz Dabrowski, the "higher self "; Schopenhauer the "true self," which "lies immeasurably above that which you usually take to be your self."

80 **It will reject that promotion** John Vaillant, *The Golden Spruce*, 189.

81 **"messianic fantasies"** Michael Kaufman, *Soros*, 16.

81 **"the white cliffs of Dover"** Jean Vanier on *Tapestry*, CBC Radio1 (January 1, 2006).

81 **So the legendary advertising man Stan Freberg** Terry O'Reilly, *O'Reilly on Advertising*, CBC Radio1 (June 29, 2005).

82 **The American-religion scholar Randall Balmer** Balmer, *Growing Pains*.

82 **"It's weak and delicate and subtle"** Maslow, *Toward a Psychology of Being*, 6.

82 **He called the fruition of potential idea *entelechy*** The writer Geoff Dyer expressed the idea of entelechy neatly: "Destiny, I think, is not what lies in store for you; it's what is already stored up inside you—and it's as patient as death." ("On the Roof," Granta no. 80.)

82 **The great film director Walter Murch** Michael Ondaatje, *The Conversations*, 9.

83 **It dawned on the singer-songwriter Paul Simon** Alec Wilkinson, "The Gift: Paul Simon's Search for the Next Song," *The New Yorker* (February 1, 2003).

83 **"most of our most important thinking"** Emilie Griffin, *Turning*, 32.

Notes

84 **Colin Duffy of Glen Ridge, New Jersey** Susan Orlean, "The American Man at Age Ten," *The Bullfighter Checks Her Makeup*, 1.

84 **"When Shirley Rock was ten years old"** Dan McAdams, *The Stories We Live By*, 174.

85 **the "five-factor model" of human personality** Steven Pinker, *The Blank Slate*, 375.

86 **he discovered that Sonny Liston** What George Foreman didn't know "was that Liston was illiterate. Poor Sonny was *drawing* his name." Richard Hoffer, "Born Again and Again," *Sports Illustrated*, December 2, 2003. See also George Foreman with Edwin Slake, "Man, Big George Is Back," *Sports Illustrated*, December 15, 1975.

86 **the search equation exactly backwards** Parker Palmer, *Let Your Life Speak*, 3.

88 **some other "possible self"** The term "possible self " was coined by Hazel Rose Markus, now a psychology professor at Stanford. Markus believes that vividly imagining *positive* possible selves helps us realize those selves. But *"feared* selves also have an important role to play in promoting change," she told *Psychology Today* (April 1988). Often, a feared self is suddenly made vivid and palpable where it wasn't before."

89 **the "Unitarian Darwinian"** As a youth, Hardy "refused to believe in chance, or luck, or coincidence, and regarded such explanations as completely unscientific." Geoffrey Leytham, "Alister Clavering Hardy and Spiritual Evolution." www.scimednet.org, http://www.scimednet.org/Leadarts/Leytham_Hardy.htm (accessed June 2006).

Five: The Revolutionary Evolution

96 **"It can be a moment of extreme drama"** *Tapestry*, CBC1 (December 11, 2005).

97 **C. S. Lewis's conversion** Lewis, *Surprised by Joy*, 235.

98 **like a pack of hounds** Ibid., 223.

98 **Jean Vanier, founder of the social services network** *Tapestry*, CBC1 (January 1, 2006).

100 **Evolution is discontinuous** Stephen Jay Gould, with Niles Eldridge, called it the theory of "punctuated equilibria."

100 **A character in a play cannot *phase in* to a scene** Dan McAdams, *The Stories We Live By*, 128.

102 **Anwar Shaikh, born in what is now Pakistan,** Ibn Warraq, ed., *Leaving Islam: Apostates Speak Out.*

104 **"a state of near-siege"** Peter Rhodes, "grim warning of a man under siege" *Express and Star* (September 8, 2004).

104 **the *crystallization of discontent*** Roy Baumeister, "Can Personality Change?" excerpted in William Miller, and Janet C. de Baca, *Quantum Change*, 282.

108 **"fatally overcommitted to what they are not"** Robert Coles, ed., *The Erik Erikson Reader*, 290.

Notes

108 **T. S. Eliot's image of the spiral staircase** Karen Armstrong, *The Spiral Staircase*. See also *Fresh Air*, NPR (March 18, 2005).

109 **"as if from a voice that had spoken before he had quite listened."** Coles, ed., *The Erik Erikson Reader*, 402.

109 **"on the feet of doves . . ."** Ibid., 412. That is, the moment of truth is suddenly there, "unannounced and pervasive in its stillness," as Erik Erikson put it. "But it comes only to him who has lived with facts and figures in such a way that he is always ready for a sudden synthesis and will not, from sheer surprise and fear, startle truth away."

109 **In 1927, Bluma Zeigarnik** Zeigarnik revealed her conclusions in a paper published in 1927 in *Psychologische Furschung* 9, no. 1, p. 85. Her theory has found its broadest application in the field of memory and information retention. Professional tutoring agencies advise students to take regular breaks, in the middle of uncompleted study sessions—the better to keep in mind what they have read.

110 *inert knowledge* The term has been popularized by psychologist John Bransford.

110 **the Harvard cognitive psychologist Howard Gardner** Gardner, *Changing Minds*, 24.

111 **"philosophical friends"** Jacob Needleman, "The Sacred Impulse," in Richard Carlson, *Handbook for the Soul*, 158.

111 **"our inner fire goes out"** Albert Schweitzer, Wikiquote. http://en.wikiquote .org/wiki/Albert_Schweitzer (accessed June 2006).

111 **Chana Ullman's comprehensive study of conversion experiences** Ullman, *The Transformed Self*.

111 *but as you have the potential to be* Needleman, "The Sacred Impulse," in Carlson *Handbook for the Soul*, 158.

111 **a Zazen monk named Joshu Sasaki Roshi** See James Adams, column, *Globe and Mail* (April 16, 2005), and Tim de Lisle, "Who Held a Gun to Leonard Cohen's Head?" *Guardian* (September 17, 2004).

112 **"If he'd been a professor of German in Heidelberg . . ."** Shelagh Rogers, *Sounds Like Canada*, CBC1 (February 6, 2006).

112 **"anxiety fades, naturally, on its own,"** Tim de Lisle, *Guardian* (September 17, 2004).

112 **"While we were talking, Ray Kurzweil approached . . ."** Bill Joy, "Why the Future Doesn't Need Us," *Wired* magazine (April 2000).

114 **"strength of weak ties"** Mark Granovetter, "The Strength of Weak Ties," *American Journal of Sociology*, 78 (1973). For a précis of Granovetter's theory, see Duncan Watts's *Six Degrees*, 19–39.

117 **"Emotional occasions are extremely potent . . ."** William James, *Varieties of Religious Experience*, 220.

118 **"had found [his] place in the world."** William Kunstler, *My Life As a Radical Lawyer*, 43.

Notes

118 **There are three kinds of drug addict** Harry Frankfurt, *The Importance of What We Care About*, 17–24. See also Doug Saunders, "Support Your Local Hypocrite," *Globe and Mail* (June 12, 2004).

119 **"destabilizing the first-order desire"** Keith Stanovich, *The Robot's Rebellion*, 71.

Six: The Crying Baby

120 **"A paid industry hack."** Tom Abate, *San Francisco Chronicle* (June 10, 2002).

120 **Reagan found it profoundly unjust** Gore Vidal, *Palimpsest*, 362. See also Edmund Morris, "The Unknowable," *The New Yorker* (June 28, 2004).

121 **"Ronald Reagan would never have been President"** Gore Vidal, *Palimpsest*, 362.

121 **Clancy had had one in the other direction** Bruce Grierson, "A Bad Trip Down Memory Lane," *New York Times Magazine* (July 27, 2003).

121 **John Adams and Thomas Jefferson** Howard Gardner, *Changing Minds*, 163.

122 **"If your baby cries at night, do you pick him up?"** George Lakoff, *Moral Politics*, Introduction.

123 **Generation after generation of the Left's best minds** "Ex-Conservatives and Other Silly Folk," Jonah Goldberg, *National Review Online* (January 24, 2001; accessed July 2006).

123 **True enough, there is no shortage of examples** "From Max Eastman to Eugene Genovese, Whittaker Chambers to Ronald Radosh, intellectuals migrate from left to right almost as if obeying a law of nature," writes Corey Rubin, in "The Ex-Cons: Right-Wing Thinkers Go Left!" *Lingua Franca* (February 2001). (Rubin, however, is setting the premise up to shoot it down.)

124 **"I had learned to judge it by the evil it had done."** David Horowitz, *Radical Son*, 361.

124 **The philosophies of secular liberals are all about uncertainty** There remains strong social programming for this definition of the "good liberal," as Stanley Fish (derisively) defined the type, weighing in after the Danish cartoon flap in 2006. ("On Faith in Letting it All Hang Out," *New York Times* [February 12, 2006].) "No matter how strongly felt or extreme are their private religious views, these views must be worn lightly in public, and especially not foisted on others."

125 **stronger Daddies than the ones heading up their side** "Nine-eleven changed me," Dennis Miller told his audience during the debut of his most recent late-night cable show, "and quite frankly I'm shocked it apparently didn't change everyone out there." In a time of reckoning, Miller wanted action. "I [asked] liberal America, well, what are you offering?" he told *Time* magazine, "and they said, well, we're not going to protect you and we want some more money." So he went right. (Rebecca Winters, "Ten Questions for Dennis Miller," *Time* [December 14, 2003].)

125 **the wake-up call came inside the Houston Astrodome** Michael Lind, *Up from Conservatism*, 67.

Notes

126 **"for the foreseeable future . . . the honorable name of conservatism"** Ibid., 70.

126 **Francis Fukuyama's moment** Louis Menand, "Breaking Away," *The New Yorker* (March 27, 2006).

127 **"a capitalist nightmare"** Corey Rubin, "The Ex-Cons," *Lingua Franca* (February 2001).

127 **And there are plenty more** Daniel Bell, Mickey Kaus, Glen Loury, and Arianna Huffington, to name a few.

128 **neo-conservatism the "new Marxism"** Shadia Drury, "Educating Stephen," *Globe and Mail* (June 26, 2004).

128 **"a communitarian concern for the economically disadvantaged . . ."** *The Connection*, NPR (October 26, 2001).

128 **"Self-interest itself . . ."** Martha Nussbaum, *Upheavals of Thought*, 321.

128 ***against* the natural grain of things** George Lakoff, *Moral Politics*. One group of researchers of a federally funded study even speculated that conservatism is a pathology that stems from "an underlying emotional conflict involving feelings of hostility directed at one's parents." See "Political Conservatism as Motivated Social Cognition," The American Psychological Association's *Psychological Bulletin* 129, no. 3 (2003): 339–375.

129 **"communal" archetype** Dan McAdams, *The Stories We Live By*, 71.

129 **The screenwriter David Milch** "The Misfit," Mark Singer, *The New Yorker* (February 14 and 21, 2005).

129 **men . . . become less libertarian and more communitarian** Carol Gilligan sums up the basic differences in male and female morality thus: Male morality is oriented toward justice, while female morality inclines toward responsibility.

130 **Men become . . . more like women** This appears to support a right-to-left migration, but there is a catch. Women, as they mature, flesh out the underdeveloped "justice" component of their morality—the morality of rights—the same theory holds. They become, in other words, more like men. About all you can conclude is that the maturity corrects imbalances. It drifts toward a recognition of the complementarity of opposites.

130 **If you knew your vote was the last hope** Jon D. Hanson and Adam Benforado, "The Drifters: Why the Supreme Court Makes Justices More Liberal," *Boston Review*, (Jan/Feb 2006).

130 **You can always build a case** Both liberals and conservatives claim their view best fulfills this criterion. Nonetheless, a prominent economist recently made a strong case, in terms of pure utilitarianism, for one direction over the others. If you were interested strictly in improving aggregate human happiness, which way would you vote? George Lowenstein, the Carnegie-Mellon economist who worked with Harvard psychologist Daniel Gilbert on his affective-forecasting work, was asked this very question. Would you vote as a liberal or a conservative? Well, "The data make it all too clear," Lowenstein said, "that boosting the

Notes

living standards of those already comfortable, such as through lower taxes, does little to improve their levels of well-being; whereas raising the living standards of the impoverished makes an enormous difference." Given that, Lowenstein said, "I don't see how anybody could study happiness and not find himself leaning left politically." Jon Gertner, "The Futile Pursuit of Happiness," *New York Times Magazine* (September 7, 2003).

Seven: The Change of Heart

134 **"a million 'nearly insignificant complaints'"** Nicholson Baker, "Changes of Mind," in *The Size of Thoughts*, 6.

135 **"My father had now seen a woman beaten ..."** Charles Baxter, *Believers*, 163.

135 **"Because my intellect hasn't caught up with my emotions yet."** Dan McAdams, *The Stories We Live By*, 206.

135 *resonance* Howard Gardner, *Changing Minds*, 57.

136 **One theory for why conservative American judges** Jon D. Hanson and Adam Benforado, "The Drifters: Why the Supreme Court Makes Judges More Liberal," *Boston Review*, (Jan/Feb 2006).

136 **"The promptings of one's own heart ..."** Howard Gardner, *Changing Minds*, 57.

136 **"gut knowledge"** The University of Virginia psychologist Jonathan Haidt argues that our moral responses are formed not by reason, but based on a primitive sense of revulsion and disgust. When something is morally wrong, we sense it, on the deepest gut level. Haidt calls this phenomenon "moral dumbfounding." Paul Bloom, "To Urgh is Human," *Guardian* (July 22, 2004).

136 **The Japanese refer to the region as *hara*** Helen Palmer, *Inner Knowing*, p. 24.

136 **convictional knowing** James E. Loder, *The Transforming Moment*, 93.

138 **"push and pull the mental apparatus around ..."** Roy Baumeister in Miller and Delaney, eds., *Judeo-Christian Perspectives on Psychology*, 62.

138 **"Like geological upheavals ..."** Nussbaum, *Upheavals of Thought*, from the Introduction.

139 **"law of primacy of feeling."** "What's your law?" Edge.org, tkhttp://www.edge.org/q2004/q04_print.html (accessed June 2006).

139 **Oliver Sacks recounts the story of a judge** Steven Wise, *Rattling the Cage*, 67.

139 **It's the activation of emotion** See Damasio, *Descartes' Error*, from the Introduction.

140 **"right into the heart of human nature."** V. S. Ramachandran, *Phantoms in the Brain*, 137.

140 **neuroeconomists have determined ...** John Cassidy, "Mind Games," *The New Yorker*, (September 18, 2006).

140 **Emotions concern themselves with human potential** Nussbaum, *Upheavals of Thought*, 58.

Notes

140 "'hold its breath' for a while" Coles, ed., *The Erik Erikson Reader*, 404.

140 "conversion of the intellect" and "conversion of the heart." Emilie Griffin, *Turning*, 50.

141 "the most beautiful place on Earth" Bill McKibben, "McCain's Lonely War on Global Warming," *OnEarth* magazine (online) (April 1, 2004; accessed July 2006).

141 McCain's "coming out" moment Ibid.

141 Ignatieff went to visit his grandfather's grave Michael Ignatieff, *Blood and Belonging*, 124.

142 The work was *L'Allegro, il Penseroso ed il Moderato* Studio 360, Public Radio International (August 14, 2002).

143 The James-Lange theory The notion that the body precedes the mind, that we come to understand what we feel and think by observing what we do, recalls the old joke about the two behaviorists who have just made love. "One says to the other, 'I know it was good for you, but was it good for me?'" Timothy D. Wilson, *Strangers to Ourselves*, 205.

144 *"that the body has already begun to solve."* Antonio R. Damasio, *The Feeling of What Happens*, 284.

144 "universal" emotions Antonio R. Damasio, *Descartes' Error*, 133.

144 called it *Jen* Coined by Confucius—and said to be the core element of all his teachings—the *Jen* has also been translated as "social virtue."

144 "Compassion is the natural response of the heart..." Sylvia Boorstein, *It's Easier Than You Think*, 134.

145 "We discover that we can be selfish together." Sam Harris, *The End of Faith*, 187.

145 "Why are kings without pity for their subjects?..." *The Connection*, NPR (October 26, 2001).

145 "Where there would be room for guilt..." Ibid.

145 "belief in a just world." Candace Clark, *Misery and Company*, 46.

146 "Misfortune is the great leveler" David Cayley, "Enlightened by Love: The Thought of Simone Weil." Audiocassette. Originally broadcast on *Ideas*, CBC1 (August 2002).

146 When Dellinger, in later life, *Fresh Air*, NPR (April 9, 1993).

147 Of Aristotle's three conditions Martha Nussbaum, *Upheavals of Thought*, 331–400.

147 our "moral circle" See "Natural-born Dualists: A Talk with Paul Bloom," Edge.org (May 13, 2004), http://www.edge.org/3rd_culture/bloom04/bloom04_index.html (accessed June 2006).

147 Amnesty International founder Peter Benenson Peter Archer, Benenson obituary, *Guardian* (February 28, 2005).

148 a hike one day David Kirby, "'Danger on Peaks': Ars Longa, Vita Longa," *New York Times Book Review* (November 21, 2004).

149 "as if the monks' brains..." Sharon Begley, "Science Journal," *Wall Street Journal* (November 5, 2004).

Notes

150 **"Our life is nothing."** Sidney Rittenberg, *The Man Who Stayed Behind*, 19.

151 **"a tall pine tree is oblivious . . ."** to borrow British philosopher Simon Blackburn's analogy.

151 **Rationalizations "consist in lies . . ."** Simon Blackburn, "Ethics and Morality," *The Connection*, NPR (June 28, 2000).

152 **with Peter Singer** You might think of Michael Fox's shift as one away from the ethics of rational abstraction and toward the ethics of care—a more feminine model of morality.

Eight: The Kandinsky Decision

154 **the "persistence" school** Paul Watzlawick et al., *Change*, 1.

155 **". . . it's underestimating the power of resistance"** *On Point*, NPR (February 12, 2004).

155 **psychologist Leon Festinger** Lauren Slater, *Opening Skinner's Box*, 114.

156 **"The vast majority of people . . ."** Ibid., 123.

156 **". . . he is incapable of self-correction."** Philip Gourevich, "Bushspeak," *The New Yorker* (September 13, 2004).

157 *contrition of the heart* William Ian Miller, *Faking It*, 84.

157 **there's evidence that we *all* got a good set of moral radar** See, among many sources for this assertion, James Wilson's *The Moral Sense*.

157 **"strong evaluations"** Keith Stanovich, *The Robot's Rebellion*, 73.

157 **"You can't get out of jail . . ."** R. D. Laing, *Did You Used to Be R. D. Laing?* A documentary film by Tom Shandel and Kirk Tougas.

157 **your "true nature"** Keith Stanovich, *The Robot's Rebellion*, 73.

158 **Oasis of False Promise** David Perkins, *The Eureka Effect*, 76. U-turns, in the first, perceptual phase, require what Perkins calls "breakthrough thinking," in the following way: To take the big dramatic step and take on a new life, you must first *see* that alternative path, and recognize it as a legitimate option.

158 **"the very nature of integrity"** Christopher Hitchens, *Why Orwell Matters*, 13.

158 **he ended up imprisoned . . . in Gorky** Howard Gardner, *Changing Minds*, 170.

158 **"Rosa Parks decisions"** Parker Palmer, *Let Your Life Speak*, 32.

159 **a "hallmark" of the fanatic** Eric Hoffer, *The True Believer*, 110. Hoffer also calls proselytizing "more a passionate search for something not yet found than a desire to bestow upon the world something we already have."

159 **"Remember your humanity and forget the rest."** Holcolm B. Noble, Joseph Rotblat obituary, *New York Times* (May 17, 2005).

160 **the First Things First Manifesto** *Adbusters* (Fall 1999/Spring 2000).

161 **The progression in commitment of Howard Lyman** "Ex-Cattleman's Warning Was No Bum Steer," Reilly Capps, *Washington Post* (January 5, 2005).

161 **Sam Harris made the argument** Natalie Angier, "Against Toleration," *New York Times Book Review* (September 5, 2004).

Notes

162 **what difficulty and risk lie on that path.** *Tapestry*, CBC1 (September 26, 2004).

162 **". . . but it's in all of us."** M. Scott Peck, from a lecture at the University of Victoria, British Columbia, attended by the author, 1988.

162 **John Gabriel Stedman, an eighteenth-century British seaman,** From John Gabriel Stedman's diary, *Narrative of a Five Years Expedition Against the Revolted Negroes of Surinam* (Johns Hopkins University Press, 1988). See also David Brion Davis's review of same in the *New York Review of Books* (March 30, 1989).

164 **If Isaac Newton hadn't been so committed** Anthony Storr, *Feet of Clay*, 180.

165 **as R. D. Laing put it, "if others view it as blue."** *Did You Used to Be R. D. Laing?*

165 **"distortion of perception."** "Is it Human Nature to Conform?" *Mind Changers*, BBC Radio 4, December 9, 2003.

165 **Stanley Milgram, whose work on obedience to authority** For an excellent summary of Milgram's work, see Ian Parker, "Obedience," *Granta* no. 71.

166 **Wilm Hosenfeld is a high-ranking Nazi officer** *The Diary of Wilm Hosenfeld*, excerpted in *The Pianist: The Extraordinary True Story of One Man's Survival in Warsaw*, afterword.

168 **in the words of Wolf Biermann** Afterword, *The Diary of Wilm Hosenfeld*, in *The Pianist*.

168 **Rabbi Sheila Peltz once visited Auschwitz** www1.bbiq.jp/quotations/peltz.htm (accessed July 2006).

169 **David Foster Wallace popularized the term *democratic spirit*** Wallace, "Tense Present: Democracy, English, and the Wars over Usage," *Harper's* (April 2001).

Nine: The Road to Damascus

170 **Lee Strobel was an award-winning** Strobel, *The Case for Christ*.

172 **"It is hard not to suspect . . ."** Elizabeth Fox-Genovese, *Crisis* magazine (June 1, 2002).

174 **a close correlate of electrical activity in the brain in real time** Real-time brain scans are quite marvelous, but the confidence they have given us that we now know how the mind works is misleading. We still have no real idea, for instance, how the regions of the brain speak to each other.

174 **different regions of their brains came alive** Mario Beauregard and Vincent Paquette, "Neural Correlates of the Mystical Experiences of Carmelite Nuns," *Neuroscience Letters* (in press).

174 **Andrew Newberg . . . ushered Tibetan monks** Andrew Newberg et al., "A measurement of regional cerebral blood flow during the complex cognitive task of meditation: a preliminary SPECT study," *Psychiatry Research*, Neuroimaging section, 101 (2001), 113–122.

174 **the neuroscientist Richard Davidson and his team** Jonathan Knight, "Religion and Science: Buddhism on the Brain," *Nature* 432, 670 (December 9, 2004).

Notes

174 **Marc Jung-Beeman and his colleague Edward Bowden** E. M. Bowden and M. Jung-Beeman, "Aha! Insight experience correlates with solution activation in the right hemisphere, *Psychonomic Bulletin and Review* 10 (2003), 730–37.

175 **James Austin . . . thinks the insight researchers are starting to get warm** Are the researchers who are studying the eureka phenomenon via word tests actually mapping the moment of kensho satori? Austin allows that some elements of the two experiences seem similar, including the tension that prevails before a solution pops to mind. But his conclusion is no, not quite. "This is not yet research into the kinds of spontaniously generated major shifts that resolve massive existential crises relating to the self," he writes in *Zen-Brain Reflections* (273). In short, solving a word puzzle won't change your life.

177 **And is that same circuitry activated** It's safe to say that the moment of true, life-changing insight has not yet been mapped by neuroscience, for a simple reason. If this is indeed a once-in-a-lifetime event, there's only one way to capture it: Research subjects would be ushered into the lab at age six and wheeled out at age eighty, a method that's unlikely to pass muster with the ethics boards.

178 **"to God, who is our home."** William Wordsworth, *Ode: Intimations of Immortality from Recollections of Early Childhood*, cited in Emilie Griffin, *Turning*, 20.

178 **"You cannot imagine the relief . . ."** Deirdre McCloskey, *Crossing*, 89.

179 **following this new path will invest my life with meaning.** William Barclay, *Turning to God*, 31.

179 **secular descriptions just aren't up to the job.** We often reach for religious metaphors because religious stories are at the root of so many of our culture's myths. From very early on, we're taught myths sometimes as if they're secular, and sometimes as if they're religious. And what tends to happen in the telling of stories is that the footnotes fall out. The sources of the various component myths—classical, Judeo-Christian, or more contemporarily literary—are lost. The U-turn myths are powerful because they're universal, the Kool-Aid we're all drinking, mixed from the same water.

179 **the case with John Perkins** Perkins, *Confessions of an Economic Hit Man*. Also, Amy Goodman's radio interview with Perkins on *Democracy Now* (November 9, 2004, archived at democracynow.org).

180 **"Now it's your turn"** John Perkins, *Confessions of an Economic Hit Man*, 224.

181 **The protagonist in Og Mandino's slim novel** Mandino, *The Greatest Salesman in the World*. It was, incidentally, picking up Mandino's book that changed the life of Matthew McConaughey. The actor was enrolled at the U of Texas at the time, studying psychology and philosophy, aiming for law school. He was studying for exams, and on a break he found Mandino's book, thumbed through it, and read right to the end. The next day he switched to film studies. (Sarah Hampson, "The Hampson Interview: Matthew McConaughey," the *Globe and Mail* [April 2, 2005].)

Notes

181 **"an inner spiritual change in the hearts of men"** Anthony Storr, *Feet of Clay*, 142.

181 **the Greek *epistrephein*** William Barclay, *Turning to God*, 20.

181 **the army lawyer James Kennedy** Kennedy, *About Face*, 148.

182 **"If only this were funny."** "Blinded by the Right," Dennis Cass, Slate.com (February 6, 2004). For a clever satire of the comic's rightward swing see, "The Miller's Crossing," by Rick Chandler, on the Black Table (May 29, 2003), www.blacktable.com/chandler030529.html (accessed June 2006).

182 ***Guardian* writer Zoe Williams** Williams, "Tee-totalitarianism" *Guardian* (June 3, 2003).

182 **"propagating" what you've learned** Solomon ben Judah ibn Gabirol (1020–1057). The other steps are "silence," "listening," "remembering," and "practicing." The epiphany itself, Gabirol believed, comes in the middle, after the "silence" and the "listening."

182 **"The Christian is called upon"** William Barclay, *Turning to God*, 31.

183 **But spreading the word is only one of many duties.** Ibid., 28.

183 **In Deepa Mehta's film *Water*** "Follow your religion" was the explicit instruction the Hindu faithful lived by in 1930s India. To tens of millions of widows, that command—to follow the letter of some two thousand-year-old sacred texts—meant resigning themselves to a cursed life of isolation and self-denial. But by the end of the decade another message was rising in opposition, from the mouth of Mahatma Gandhi: "Follow your conscience."

183 **An active conscience conveys a sense** C. Steven Evans, "The Relational Self," in Miller and Delaney, eds., *Judeo-Christian Perspectives in Psychology*, 87.

184 **In 1976, after William Powell** *The Anarchist Cookbook*, Customer Reviews, Amazon .com.

186 **"It has nothing to do with any religion whatsoever."** Torcuil Crichton, "I Had a Vision of Jesus," the British *Sunday Herald* (January 22, 2006).

186 **Kevin Rowland, founder of the British band** Various sources, including Stuart Jeffries, "Decade of Decadence," *Guardian* (January 17, 2002).

187 **Ricky Williams, the prized young running back** "The Runaway," Chris Jones, *Esquire* (December 2004). Williams had failed a drug test and faced suspension by the league. After leaving the NFL, he attempted a comeback in the Canadian Football League, which does not honor the NFL drug-suspension rules.

188 **"The Haunting of the Lingards,"** Jincy Willett, *Jenny and the Jaws of Life*.

189 **When Jeffrey Wigand, the chemist** From a public lecture in Vancouver attended by the author.

190 ***"The soul has to be prepared"*** Seyyed Hossein Nasr, *Tapestry*, CBC1 (December 11, 2005).

191 **Helen Palmer had a series of premonitions** Palmer, *Inner Knowing*, Foreword.

191 **Like Jung's famously stuck patient** C. G. Jung, *Synchronicity*, 22–31.

192 **He shelved his plans** It was Erwin Stresemann, Germany's most renowned ornithologist, who validated Mayr's sighting of the pochards, and ultimately

convinced Mayr to switch tracks. He lured Mayr to Berlin to work for him, classifying bird specimens at the Natural History Museum there, and persuaded him to pursue an ornithology doctorate under him.

192 **Philip Benham did for "Jane Roe"** Conrad Goeringer, "'Jane Roe' Baptised, Converts to Christianity," Theistwatch, skepticfiles.org, http://www.skepticfiles .org/american/15aug95.htm (accessed June 2006).

192 **"implicate order"** This was not the first time that the conversation with a U-turner swung around to quantum mechanics. I wondered why it kept happening. Was it because it's a fashionable subject—or is it because when something extreme happens to us, we look for extreme explanations? Quantum physics is the one place where science and fabulism coexist unapologetically, where secular explanations sound like spiritual ones, where intuitive reality is suspended and paradox rules and everything is connected. It is a Lewis Carroll world where to reverse course in midlife sounds like a perfectly normal thing to do.

193 *A Prayer for Owen Meany* Eugene Peterson's *Subversive Spirituality*, 7.

194 **The brain is a "belief engine"** Michael Shermer, *How We Believe*, 32–43.

194 **It is akin to a biological drive** We *need*, at almost a cellular level, "to find answers to the big questions, or explanations to the big mysteries." Andrew Newberg, *Why God Won't Go Away*, 58.

194 **The anthropologist Bronislaw Malinowski** Michael Shermer, *How We Believe*, 41.

194 **Conversions tend to happen within two years** "The two-year period preceding the conversion was for the majority of converts dominated by despair, doubts in their own self-worth, fears of rejection, unsuccessful attempts to handle rage, an emptiness, and an estrangement from others." Chana Ullman, *The Transformed Self*, 19.

195 **"The corrective," Loder writes, "is the intentional turn inward . . ."** James E. Loder, *The Transforming Moment*, 173.

195 **Jung insisted he never met a client** Jung first expressed this point in his paper "Psychotherapy or the Clergy?" Michael Argyle, *Psychology and Religion*, 519.

195 **He brings immediate relief**. If you think of the "function" of religious faith in evolutionary terms—social cohesion, the imposition of a value system—then any community-building behavior can substitute for it. In evolutionary terms, in other words, a secular, moral shift fulfills the same needs as religious conversion.

195 **"I am willing to do anything—*anything*"** M. Scott Peck, *Further Along the Road Less Traveled*, 122.

195 **"Self-questioning isn't something we do naturally . . ."** Po Bronson, *The Fanny Kiefer Show*, Studio 4 (January 19, 2004).

197 **"The commonest of men . . ."** Arthur Miller's essay *Tragedy and the Common Man*. See also Rick Salutin on Miller in the *Globe and Mail* (February 18, 2005).

197 **He was frankly psychotic.** Danish psychiatrist Dr. Paul J. Reiter described pretty much all of Luther's twenties and much of his thirties as "one long *krankheit-sphase*, a drawn-out state of nervous disease." Erikson, "Young Man Luther," in Coles, *The Erik Erikson Reader*, 27.

197 **"Is Conan Doyle Mad?"** *Sunday Express*, www.csicop.org/si/2002-3/polidoro.html

197 **a diagnosis of Borderline Personality Disorder** Benedict Carey, "Who's Mentally Ill . . . ? Deciding Is Often All in the Mind," *New York Times* (June 12, 2005).

198 **"Insanity is a perfectly rational adjustment . . ."** R. D. Laing, *Didn't You Used to Be R. D. Laing?*

198 **"double bind"** Gregory Bateson's original research involved children who received mixed messages from their mothers.

198 **The psychiatrist Robert Coles once wrote to Anna Freud** "The Spiritual Life of Children, Part Two," in Coles, *Harvard Diary*, 138.

199 **who coined the term *spiritual emergency*** Stanislav Grof, "Examples of Psychoreligious Problems," *The Journal of Nervous and Mental Disorders* (1992). That the field is being defined by a New Age pioneer—Grof is the founder of Transpersonal Psychology, Division 36 of the American Psychological Association—shows how distinctly contemporary it is.

Ten: The Good Hypocrite

201 **he openly opposed the war** Craig Lambert, "Literary Warrior," *Harvard Magazine* (May/June 2005).

201 **"If you're consistent . . ."** Ibid.

202 **"You've got to keep making decisions"** *Touching the Void*, directed by Kevin MacDonald, 2004.

202 **"the person you previously were . . ."** Bradford Keeney, "The Luckiest Man Alive?" *Utne Reader* (June 24, 2003). See also "Tripping Yourself," in Keeney, *Everyday Soul*, 45.

203 **"McEnroe might be a bit of a dilettante"** Robert Lloyd, "Television Review," *Los Angeles Times* (July 10, 2004).

203 **he threw beer cans out the window of a truck.** ". . . as he drove at high speed through the desert he assailed others for despoiling." See Ecology Hall of Fame, at Ecotopia.org, http://www.ecotopia.org/ehof/abbey/ (accessed June 2006).

203 **"It becomes more and more tiresome"** *Sounds Like Canada*, CBC1 (February 6, 2006).

203 **"Those who are frankly self-serving . . ."** Stanovich, *The Robot's Rebellion*, 58.

204 **"It is wrong for a man to say . . ."** Michael Shermer, *Why We Believe*, 7.

205 **but we cannot infer causality.** But as the psychoanalyst Adam Phillips noted recently: Psychoanalysis "turns up historically at the point at which traditional

societies begin to break down and consumer capitalism begins to take hold." Adam Phillips, "A Mind Is a Terrible Thing to Measure," *New York Times* (February 26, 2006).

205 **It makes no sense** As loggers hollered up at Julia Hill to let the tree go—she was just delaying the inevitable—she shot back, Why not just kill your grandparents? Letting them live, you're just delaying the inevitable! Hill, *The Legacy of Luna*, 68.

206 **"not in otherness but in oppositeness."** "The Phony Authenticity of American Psycho Lindh," Ron Rosenbaum, *New York Observer* (December 24, 2001).

206 **"Doing graphic design that's anti-consumerist . . ."** The letter-writer was riffing on the old Vietnam-era oxymoron, "Fighting for peace is like fucking for chastity."

207 **There are some fairly strong arguments** Indeed, certain kinds of U-turns are hard to defend. The cognitive scientist Keith Stanovich makes the distinction between what might be called smart turns and dumb turns. Any kind of U-turn involving the coming to, or changing of, faith is in some sense maladaptive, for faith is, by Darwinian lights, a "junk meme"—a powerful replicator that exists to serve itself, its own propagation, and does not serve us. Stanovich believes we actually have a duty not to let ourselves be taken in by such junk memes. Both religious conversions and deconversions (from belief in God to certainty that there is no god) are "dumb" turns in the sense that they are irrational. (The falsity or truth of a belief system can't be disproved, so they fail the basic test of the scientific method.) The only rational journey, and therefore the only "smart" turn involving faith, is the *loss* of faith: in which a believer becomes an agnostic, and admits: *There is just no way to know.*

207 **"nothing to lose by saying . . ."** Lauren Slater, *Opening Skinner's Box*, 124.

207 **"you're getting farther from your true self . . ."** C. S. Lewis, *Mere Christianity*, 86.

208 **"The serious thing for each person to recognize . . ."** Abraham Maslow, *Toward a Psychology of Being*, 7. On the other hand, Maslow believed, "if we do something honest or fine or good, it registers to our credit." Chand Singh Yadav, "As You Sow, So Shall You Reap," the *Tribune* (July 13, 2002).

208 **a midlife hiccup** George Vaillant, private correspondence.

209 **". . . the disease called sleeping sickness?"** Albert Schweitzer, *The Spiritual Life*, Foreword.

209 **"It is tragic . . ."** Ibid.

209 *evasion of one's destiny* Abraham Maslow, *The Farther Reaches of Human Nature*, 34.

209 **Aristotle's notion** The major religions each have a term for the apparently human flaw that holds people back from reaching their potential, noted Huston Smith. "Christianity calls it original sin; Judaism, "missing the mark." Islam says we are "forgetful of our true nature." Buddhism reminds us we're unenlightened. And they all agree on what the flaw is: putting our own needs ahead of others." ("Robert Wright interviews Huston Smith, MeaningofLife TV.)

Notes

210 "**If you don't do it . . .**" http://meaningoflife.tv/video.php?speaker-smith& topic-complete. *Sound & Spirit*, Public Radio International (October 5, 2003).

210 "**to build modern buildings that had the feel of ancient ruins.**" *My Architect: A Son's Journey*, directed by Nathaniel Kahn, 2003.

210 "**It always frightens me to think . . .**" "Lies My Father Told Me," Simon Houpt, the *Globe and Mail* (February 19, 2004).

211 "**Whenever and wherever man abandons . . .**" Coles, ed., *The Erik Erikson Reader*, 159.

211 *Only by finding and acting* See Charles Foran, "Burning Man: How to Change Your Life and End Global Suffering," *The Walrus* (April 11, 2005).

211 **George Vaillant evoked the image of a twisted old seaside tree** Vaillant, *Adaptation to Life*, 360.

212 **We want to feel moral and virtuous** "Morality is, in fact, the defining trait of the human species." Jerome Kagan, *Three Seductive Ideas*, 155.

212 "**At first I felt like Lord Bountiful . . .**" William Kunstler, *My Life As a Radical Lawyer*, from the Foreword.

212 **reason ripens into real moral conviction** The paradoxical thing about emotion is that it both triggers epiphanies and delays them. This is why you find the most dramatic U-turn stories in what Howard Gardner calls the "charged domains" of politics, scholarship, and religion: These are the realms steeped in human values. "They are the parts of life that mean the most to people." You could say that the natural progress of the U-turner is from self-interest to sympathy to commitment. From what the philosopher Harry Frankfurt called a "first-order desire," where there's a personal payoff, to a values-driven "second-order desire," where there isn't, necessarily.

213 **the night the "dam broke"** Deirdre M. McCloskey, *Crossing*, 49.

213 "*it is knowing yourself, instead of knowing about yourself*" Ibid., 51.

214 "**The Costs and Benefits of Womanhood**" Ibid., 51–53.

216 "**You were not of course invited . . .**" Ibid., 226.

216 **How far does duty extend?** Ibid., 227.

216 **Twenty years ago, Chuck Collins** Ian Parker, "The Gift," *The New Yorker* (August 2, 2005).

219 **the obligation to show "by clear and constant signs"** Alexander Nehamas, *Nietzsche: Life as Literature*, 172.

219 "**. . . you have some moral obligation to be telling people**" Keith Stanovich, author interview.

220 "**Evolution makes you the kind of person others can trust**" "Robert Wright interviews Steven Pinker," MeaningofLife TV, http://meaningoflife.tv/video.php ?speaker=pinker&topic=complete (accessed June 2006).

221 "**an awful lot of shooting.**" From Seymour Hersh's speech at the Stephen Wise Free Synagogue, archived at *Democracy Now* (January 26, 2005), http://www. democracynow.org/article.pl?sid=05/01/26/1450204 (accessed June 2006).

Notes

Eleven: The Thought Experiment

224 **Eastern spiritual traditions are rich** In Hindu mythology there is a transcendent place outside of time and space—what we might call enlightenment—represented by the Sanskrit word *moksha*. But it won't come to you. There are a few paths in: love, work, or meditation.

225 **the *I Ching*** From Ritsima and Karcher, *The I Ching*

225 **"confusion technique"** Paul Watzlawick et al., *Change*, 101.

226 **The cryptic nature of these stories** Ibid., 101.

227 **"moral, poetic, erotic and almost spiritual refusal"** Sadie Plant, *The Most Radical Gesture*, 8.

228 **"Sometimes I request people never to tell anything true"** "Tripping Yourself," Bradford Keeney, *Everyday Soul*, 64.

228 **Where your intellect and your intuition converge** Emilie Griffin, *Turning*, 47.

228 **The philosopher Mark Kingwell** From a public lecture at Vancouver Public Library.

230 **"To examine the logical consistency of [our] beliefs . . ."** Alexander Nehemas, *The Art of Living*, 42.

230 **vintage Bugatti roadster** "The Singer Solution to World Poverty," *New York Times Magazine* (September 5, 1999).

231 ***Theory of Justice*** Martha Nussbaum, *Upheavals of Thought*, 343.

231 **"To make an experiment of oneself"** Gandhi, in this vein, called his autobiography *Experiments in Truth*.

236 **the artist John Freyer** "Did it change my life?" Freyer asks rhetorically about his experiment. "Well, I'm still in Iowa City. I'm sitting in a studio that's full of stuff acquired at the same places I used to acquire stuff at. I still hold on to things; I'm just not accumulating at the same rate that I used to. The irony is that the goal of this project was to leave. But today I live in the place I was trying to escape from, with a woman I met through the project [she bought his kitchen table] and we have a child." The answer, in other words, is yes.

238 **"I used to feel that I had to be good"** Ian Parker, "The Gift," *The New Yorker* (August 3, 2005).

239 **"What if someone needed [my last kidney]"** "An Organ Donor's Generosity Raises the Question of How Much Is Too Much," *New York Times* (August 17, 2003).

239 **"I think in terms of maximum human utility"** To Paula Zahn, CNN (August 18, 2003).

239 **"What I aspire to is a kind of ethical ecstasy"** Ian Parker, "The Gift," op. cit.

240 **"Having redefined his life"** Ibid.

240 **Kevin Kelly made of his life** "Shoulda Been Dead," *This American Life*, NPR (January 17, 1997).

Notes

242 **And so, with tiny pirates and angels** On the eve of his imagined death, watching trick-or-treaters in goblin costumes come to the front door, Kelly composed this haiku: "Like odd Buddhist monks / unconcerned with ugliness / begging for tidbits."

243 **Camus's notion of the "apprenticeship in death"** William Todd Schultz, "The Riddle That Doesn't Exist: Ludwig Wittgenstein's Transmogrification of Death," *Psychoanaloytic Review* 86, no. 2 (1988).

244 **his own outsized fear of death** Ibid.

Twelve: The Parole Board's Dilemma

245 **"If you see the Buddha on the road, kill him."** Mortals couldn't even perceive a true agent of the divine—so the fellow you think is the Buddha is an imposter, a manifestation of your own *wish* for enlightenment. And he's doing you no good. See Sharlet and Manseau, *Killing the Buddha*, 1.

245 **the savage Joe Queenan** *My Goodness*.

247 **"But then I found that his life didn't really fit..."** Adam Hochschild, "Bury the Chains," *On Point*, NPR (January 10, 2005).

249 **"the way things never were but always are"** The political writer Jane Kramer hatched a theory that we should be suspicious of a U-turner's redemption narrative to the degree that that person wields power. "People at the center of power always present you with a well-crafted public self," she told the anthologist Robert Boynton. "They are propagandists for themselves." The margins of society produce more honesty, in her experience. Boynton, *The New New Journalism*, 189.

249 **"I love ascents—who doesn't love ascents?"** *Poetry Daily* interview with Robert Bly (April 6–7, 1997). Archived at poems.com, www.poems.com/blyinter.htm (accessed June 2006).

250 **"It has long been known that the surest route to journalistic stardom..."** Eric Felten, "Mr. Lind's Clever Little Joke," *Washington Times* (August 7, 1996).

250 **"The consummate creature of our times"** Norah Vincent, "Tit for Tat, David Brock is a Turncoat's Tale," *Los Angeles Times* (June 5, 2001).

250 **"Maybe it's me..."** "It Takes One to Know One," CBS *60 Minutes* (May 22, 2005).

251 **"would have put James Bond to shame."** "Kevin Poulsen" *Cybercrime* (October 2004), www.thinkquest.org/04oct/00460/poulsen.html (accessed June 2006).

251 **"conspired to steal classified military orders..."** Ibid.

253 **"The young soldier who enlists..."** Anthony Swofford to Dave Weich, conversation archived at www.powells.com/authors/swofford.html.

253 **"That's not the easiest way out of the military"** *The Tavis Smiley Show*, NPR (March 18, 2004).

Notes

253 **"crystallized since you joined . . ."** Bill Galvin, *The Tavis Smiley show*, NPR (March 18, 2004).

254 **Regret is amoral; remorse, moral.** Although, as the Michigan law professor and author William Ian Miller notes, there's an element of remorse that is selfish, too. We may not be feeling bad for the one we wronged, but for ourselves—because now "we're "going to get it from God." Miller, *Faking It*, 64.

255 **"The Christian message provoked different reactions . . ."** William Barclay, *Turning to God*, 47.

255 **"quantum change"** William Miller, and Janet de Baca, *Quantum Change*, 4.

256 **why the producers of reality shows shoot so much footage** Psychologist Gene Ondrusek, who helped choose the first round of contestants on the original *Survivor*. *The Infinite Mind*, NPR (July 1, 2004).

256 **"Drugs make you make bad fashion decisions."** "Courtney Love's Anti-Drug Campaign," *E Online* (October 31, 1997).

256 **"I used to be a rock-'n'-roll cliché."** *E Online* (October 31, 1997).

257 **"may represent the one true hallmark . . ."** Dan McAdams et al., *Turns in the Road*, 84.

257 **"What is truly important in a conversion . . ."** William James, *Varieties of Religious Experience*, 209.

257 **"If in fact you believe that your mind has been changed . . ."** *The Connection*, NPR (April 6, 2004).

258 **"a religious experience is understandable . . ."** Max Weber, *The Sociology of Religion*, 10.

258 **"Violin variations don't interest me."** William Todd Schultz, "De Profundis," in Dan McAdams et al., *Turns in the Road*, 67.

259 **evidence of what he called the "jewel within."** Kant quoted in Simon Blackburn, *Being Good*, 115.

260 **"There I was looking at those pure white graves . . ."** Amanda Griscom Little, "The Mall That Would Save America," *New York Times* (July 3, 2005).

260 **"extrinsic" and "intrinsic" commitment** See Gordon Allport, and J. Michael Ross, "Personal Religious Orientation and Prejudice," *Journal of Personality and Social Psychology*, no. 5 (1967).

261 **"Impossible moral burdens were put on students"** Lucinda Franks, *The New Yorker* (June 13, 1994). See also Janet Landman, "The Crime, Punishment and Ethical Transformation of Two Radicals, or How Katherine Power Improves on Dostoevsky," Schultz, *Turns in the Road*, 35.

261 **"just chill and check in with Tommy"** Alex Kuczynski, "Can Tommy Lee Change His Spots?" *New York Times* (October 24, 2004).

262 **"I've done just the opposite of being a car thief!"** The entrepreneurial Darrell Issa, the San Diego congressman leading the effort to recall Governor Gray Davis, "was prosecuted in 1980 for allegedly faking the theft of his Mercedes and selling the vehicle to a car dealer." Associated Press, June 26, 2003.

262 **"I am now a child of God . . ."** *The Human Life Review*, (Summer 1999).

Notes

262 **"because there's no children because they've all been aborted."** Laurie Goodstein, "Jane Roe Renounces Abortion Movement," *Washington Post* (August 11, 1995).

263 **"Jesus Christ has reached through the abortion mill . . ."** Conrad Goeringer, "'Jane Roe' Baptised, Converts to Christianity," skepticfiles.org, http://www.skeptic files.org/american/15aug95.htm (accessed June 2006).

263 **"I think I've always been pro-life . . . "** Ibid.

263 **"If anything, Norma McCorvey's statements . . ."** Ibid.

266 **"In the wake of the controversy over James Frey . . ."** Landon Thomas, Jr., *New York Times* (February 19, 2006).

266 **The movie rights have been purchased by Beacon Pictures . . .** Ibid.

266 **"Some of the things he says are outrageous"** Tyson spokesman Ed Nicholson on Virgil Butler, "A Killing-Floor Chronicle," Stephanie Simon, *Los Angeles Times* (December 8, 2003).

267 **"to diagnose mental abnormality . . ."** Anthony Storr, *Feet of Clay*, 170.

268 **"adopted a fiction that's not supported by society"** Ibid., 199.

268 **"to impose on his fall . . ."** William Todd Schultz, "De Profundis," in Dan McAdams et al., *Turns in the Road*, 67.

269 **changes of mind almost always happen incrementally** Nicholson Baker, *The Size of Thoughts*, 3.

269 **"I was plodding along . . ."** Baker, who wrote the first draft of the book during the siege of Fallujah, conceded that he was so consumed with rage he could think of almost nothing else. David Gates, "Target: The President," *Newsweek* (August 9, 2004).

270 **In plenty of instances, people actually *"neglect* their own interest . . ."** Simon Blackburn, *Being Good*, 27.

270 **Sometimes we just do the right thing** William Ian Miller, *Faking It*, 29.

Thirteen: The Earth As Seen from Space

273 **"They were a uniform crowd . . ."** Paul Stiles, *Riding the Bull*, 235.

274 **the "emotional upheaval of having climbed to the top . . ."** Conversation with the author.

274 **"The material and nonmaterial sides of life . . ."** Ibid.

274 **"There's a point you reach when the system no longer makes sense . . ."** Paul Stiles, *Riding the Bull*, 322.

275 **"American democracy is the mother of both power and principle."** Ibid.

276 **Denise wrote an exquisite story about her mom's wake-up call** "A Tale of Two Mothers," Salon.com, www.salon.com/mwt/feature/2000/05/09/art_mom/index .html (accessed June 2006)

277 **"defining deviance down."** Nathan Glazer, "Master Builder: Pat Moynihan's Legacy," *The New Republic* (April 14, 2003).

Notes

277 **"By far the biggest challenge . . ."** "Il Papa," CBS *60 Minutes* (April 3, 2005).

277 **like paleomagnetic reversals** This may be the closest-fitting metaphor for U-turns—individual or cultural. Paleomagnetic reversals work like this: Every quarter-million years or so, on average, unpredictably and in the relative blink of an eye, Earth's magnetic fields flip-flop: Suddenly north is south, and south is north. It happens because convection currents are continually nosing out of the Earth's core and into the planet's magnetic field, weakening it in those spots. Things are quietly destabilizing. If those weak spots grow to a certain critical size, they disturb the twin dynamos—the electromagnetic generator—at the Earth's core and trigger the polarity flip. So even though the flip-flop appears to have come in the blink of an eye out of nowhere, it's in fact an event the perfect conditions for which were a few hundred thousand years in the making.

278 **Likewise, whenever a culture drifts** See Karl Polanyi, *The Great Transformation.*

278 **it's better kindled by the creation** See Saunders, "This Year, Save a Blessing for the Unbelievers," *Globe and Mail* (December 24, 2004).

278 **"Where did we fail our children?"** Paul Watzlawick et al., *Change,* 21.

278 **father figures that have to be overthrown** Harold Bloom, *The Anxiety of Influence,* 54.

279 **New York Times science reporter Natalie Angier** *New York Times* (September 5, 2004).

279 **"the sense of transcendence that changes us"** Karen Armstrong, *Fresh Air,* NPR (March 18, 2005).

279 **"We accept it as completely normal . . ."** Walter Truett Anderson, "The Next Enlightenment," *Tapestry,* CBC1 (July 31, 2005).

279 **At the species level we are changing** Nicholas Wade, "The Twists and Turns of History, and of DNA," *New York Times* (March 12, 2006).

281 **"cool revolution"** Robert Thurman, *Inner Revolution,* 95.

282 **" . . . tikkun olan, the healing or restoration of the world."** Joan Borysenko, *Handbook for the Soul,* 46.

283 **"I had to get rid of one or the other."** Eric Markus is an author and podcaster. See his Web site, EricMarkus.com.

284 **The more partisan we become, the more partisan we become.** David Brooks, "Circling the Wagons," *New York Times* (June 5, 2004), and "Age of Political Segregation," *New York Times* (June 29, 2004).

284 **In Britain, a literate former slave** Olaudah Equiano.

285 **"a new idea as powerful as any in history will be let loose"** Fred Hoyle, as it happened, had made a profound spiritual U-turn of his own. It was Hoyle who pioneered a lot of our knowledge about the quantum mechanics of the nuclear furnaces of the stars. The work forced him to peer deeply into the origins of the universe. And as he crunched the algorithms, and the sheer unlikelihood of human life became apparent—at the molecular level, at a billion bifurcation moments, the universe "made the right choice" every time to support

313

Notes

eventual life—Hoyle threw up his hands and converted to Christianity.) See "Robert Wright interviews John Polkinghorne," MeaningofLife TV. http://meaningoflife.tv/video.php?speaker=polkinghorne&topic=complete (accessed June 2006).

285 **the conservative commentator David Brooks** "The Bursting Point," *New York Times* (September 4, 2005).

286 **". . . *how do beliefs acquire people?*"** Keith Stanovich, *The Robot's Rebellion*, 123.

287 **The pathbreaking today** Karen Armstrong, *Talk of the Nation*, NPR (March 28, 2006).

287 **It's how you live your life that will save you** See Michael Valpy "Rigidity, Be Gone," *Globe and Mail* (April 3, 2006).

Selected Bibliography

Abagnale, Frank Jr. *The Art of the Steal*. Broadway Books, 2001.

Adler, Mortimer. *Six Great Ideas: Truth, Goodness, Beauty, Liberty, Equality, Justice*. Macmillan, 1981.

———. *A Second Look in the Rear-View Mirror: Further Autobiographical Reflections of a Philosopher at Large*. Macmillan, 1993.

Allport, Gordon Willard. *The Individual and His Religion: A Psychological Interpretation*. Macmillan, 1950.

Anderson, Ray. *The Journey from There to Here: The Eco-Odyssey of a CEO*. Peregrinzilla Press, 1995.

Argyle, Michael. *Psychology and Religion: An Introduction*. Routledge, 2000.

Aristotle, *De Anima*, Hugh Lawson-Tancred, trans. Penguin Classics, 1987.

Armstrong, Karen. *The Spiral Staircase: My Climb Out of Darkness*. Anchor (reprint ed.), 2005.

———. *The Great Transformation: The Beginning of Our Religious Traditions*. Knopf, 2006.

Austin, James H. *Zen and the Brain: Toward an Understanding of Meditation and Consciousness*. MIT Press, 1999.

———. *Zen-Brain Reflections*. MIT Press, 2006.

Baker, Nicholson. *The Size of Thoughts: Essays and Other Lumber*. Vintage Contemporaries, 1997.

Balmer, Randall. *Growing Pains*. Brazos Press, 2001.

Barclay, William. *Turning to God: A Study of Conversion in the Book of Acts and Today*. Epworth Press, 1963.

Baxter, Charles. *Believers: A Novella and Stories*. Vintage, 1998.

Beja, Morris. *Epiphany in the Modern Novel*. University of Washington Press, 1971.

Selected Bibliography

Bell, Daniel. *The Radical Right*. Transaction Publishers, 2001.

Berman, Philip, ed. *The Search for Meaning: Americans Talk About What They Believe, and More*. Ballantine, 1990.

Bertolucci, Bernardo. *Bernardo Bertolucci: Interviews*. Edited by Fabien Gerard, T. Jefferson Kline, and Bruce Sklarew. University Press of Mississippi, 2000.

Besen, Wayne R. *Anything But Straight: Unmasking the Scandals and Lies Behind the Ex-Gay Myth*. Harrington Park Press, 2003.

Blackburn, Simon. *Being Good: A Short Introduction to Ethics*. Oxford University Press, 2003.

Bloom, Harold. *The Anxiety of Influence: A Theory of Poetry*. Oxford University Press, 1997.

Boa, Fraser. *The Way of Myth: Talking with Joseph Campbell*. Shambhala, 1989.

Boorstein, Sylvia. *Happiness Is Free: And It's Easier Than You Think*. Sedona Press, 2002.

Boyd, Andrew. *Life's Little Deconstruction Book: Self-Help for the Post-Hip*. W.W. Norton, 1998.

Boynton, Robert S. *The New New Journalism: Conversations With America's Best Nonfiction Writers on Their Craft*. Vintage, 2005.

Bridges, William. *The Way of Transition*. Perseus Publishing, 2001.

Brock, David. *Blinded by the Right: The Conscience of an Ex-Conservative*. Crown, 2002.

Bronson, Po. *The Nudist on the Late Shift: And Other True Tales of Silicon Valley*. Broadway Books, 2000.

———. *What Should I Do with My Life?: The True Story of People Who Answered the Ultimate Question*. Random House, 2002.

Brusset, Frederic and Mary Ann. *Spiritual Literacy: Reading the Sacred in Everyday Life*. Scribner's, 1996.

Butler, Smedley D. *War Is a Racket*. Feral House, 2003.

Campbell, Joseph, ed. *The Portable Jung*. Penguin, 1971.

Carlson, Richard, and Benjamin Shield, eds. *Handbook for the Soul*. Back Bay Books, 1996.

Chambers, Whittaker. *Witness*. Random House, 1952.

Clark, Candace. *Misery and Company: Sympathy in Everyday Life*. University of Chicago Press, 1998.

Coles, Robert, ed. *The Erik Erikson Reader*. W.W. Norton, 2000.

Coles, Robert. *Harvard Diary: Reflections on the Sacred and the Secular*. Crossroads, 1988.

Dabrowski, Kazamierz. *Change Through Positive Disintegration*. Gryf Publications, 1970.

Selected Bibliography

Damasio, Antonio R. *The Feeling of What Happens: Body and Emotion in the Making of Consciousness*. Harcourt, 1999.

———. *Looking for Spinoza*. Harcourt, 2003.

———. *Descartes' Error: Emotion, Reason and the Human Brain*. Penguin, 2005.

Dellinger, David. *From Yale to Jail: The Life Story of a Moral Dissenter*. Pantheon, 1993.

DeVries, Peter. *The Mackerel Plaza*. Penguin, 1986.

Dostoevsky, Fyodor. *The Double: Two Versions*, translated by Evelyn Harden. Ardis, 1985.

Eggers, Dave, ed. *The Best American Nonrequired Reading*. Houghton Mifflin, 2004.

Eliot, T. S. *Collected Poems, 1909–1962*. Harcourt, Brace & World, 1963.

Elkington, John. *Cannibals with Forks: The Triple Bottom Line of 21st Century Business*. New Society Publishers, 1998.

Equiano, Olaudah. *The Interesting Narrative of the Life of Olaudah Equino, or Gustavus Vassa, the African, Written by Himself*. Lakeside Press, 2004.

Feldman, Robert S., ed. *Development Across the Life Span*. Prentice Hall, 2002.

Fowler, James W. *Stages of Faith: The Psychology of Human Development and the Quest for Meaning*. Harper & Row, 1981.

Frankfurt, G. Harry. *The Importance of What We Care About: Philosophical Essays*. Cambridge University Press, 1988.

Freyer, John. *All My Life for Sale*. Bloomsbury USA, 2002.

Gallagher, Winifred. *Spiritual Genius: The Mastery of Life's Meaning*. Random House, 2001.

Gardner, Howard. *Changing Minds: The Art and Science of Changing Our Own and Other People's Minds*. Harvard Business School Press, 2004.

Gilligan, Carol. *In a Different Voice: Psychological Theory and Women's Development*. Harvard University Press, 1993.

Glanville, Mark. *The Goldberg Variations: From Football Hooligan to Opera Singer*. HarperCollins UK (Flamingo), 2004.

Green, Donald, Bradley Palmquist, and Eric Schickler. *Partisan Hearts and Minds*. Yale University Press, 2004.

Griffin, Emilie. *Turning: Reflections on the Experience of Conversion*. Doubleday, 1980.

Haidt, Jonathan. *The Happiness Hypothesis*. Basic Books, 2005.

Hamer, Dean. *The God Gene: How Faith is Hardwired Into Our Genes*. Doubleday, 2004.

Harris, Sam. *The End of Faith: Religion, Terror and the Future of Reason*. W.W. Norton, 2004.

Hassan, Steve. *Combatting Cult Mind Control*. Park Street Press, 1988.

Selected Bibliography

Hecht, Jennifer: *Doubt: The Great Doubters and Their Legacy*, HarperSanFrancisco (reprint ed.), 2004.

Hendra, Tony. *Father Joe: The Man Who Saved My Soul*. Random House Trade Paperbacks, 2005.

Hill, Julia Butterfly. *The Legacy of Luna: The Story of a Tree, a Woman, and the Struggle to Save the Redwoods*. HarperSanFrancisco, 2001.

Hitchens, Christopher. *Why Orwell Matters*. Basic Books, 2002.

Hochschild, Adam. *Bury the Chains: Prophets and Rebels in the Fight to Free an Empire's Slaves*. Houghton Mifflin, 2005.

Hoffer, Eric. *The True Believer: Thoughts on the Nature of Mass Movements*. HarperCollins Perennial, 1989.

Hornby, Nick. *How to Be Good*. Riverhead Books, 2001.

Horowitz, David. *Radical Son: A Generational Odyssey*. Free Press, 1998.

Hosenfeld, Wilm. The Diaries of Wilm Hosenfeld, excerpted in *The Pianist: The Extraordinary Story of One Man's Survival in Warsaw, 1939–45*. V. Gollancz, 1999.

Huxley, Aldous. *The Doors of Perception and Heaven and Hell*. Harper Perennial Modern Classics, 2004.

Ignatieff, Michael. *Blood and Belonging: Journeys Into the New Nationalism*. Farrar, Straus & Giroux, 1995.

Ingram, Jay. *The Velocity of Honey: And More Science of Everyday Life*. Thunder's Mouth Press, 2005.

Jacobi, Jolande, *The Psychology of C. G. Jung*. Yale University Press, 1973.

James, William. *The Varieties of Religious Experience*. Modern Library, 1999 (originally published 1902).

Jamison, Kay Redfield. *Exuberance: The Passion For Life*. Alfred A. Knopf, 2004.

Jung, Carl Gustav. *The Collected Works of C. G. Jung*. Edited by Herbert Read, Michael Fordham, Gerhard Adler. Pantheon Books, 1953–1983.

———. *Memories, Dreams, Reflections*. Collins, 1967.

———. *Synchronicity: An Acausal Connecting Principle*. Princeton University Press, 1973.

Kagan, Jerome: *Three Seductive Ideas*. Harvard University Press, 1998.

Kane, Pat. *The Play Ethic: A Manifesto for a Different Way of Living*. Macmillan, 2004.

Karcher, Stephen. *The I Ching: First Complete Translation with Concordance*. Vega, 2002.

Kaufman, Michael. *Soros: The Life and Times of a Messianic Billionaire*. Alfred A. Knopf, 2002.

Selected Bibliography

Keeney, Bradford. *Everyday Soul: Awakening the Spirit in Daily Life*. Riverhead Books, 1996.

Kennedy, James E. *About Face: A Gay Officer's Account of How He Stopped Prosecuting Gays in the Army and Started Fighting for Their Rights*. Carol Publishing Corporation, 1995.

Kimmelman, Michael. *The Accidental Masterpiece: On the Art of Life and Vice Versa*. Penguin, 2005.

Korten, David. *When Corporations Rule the World*. Kumarian Press/Berrett/Koehler Publishers, 1995.

Kübler-Ross, Elisabeth. *Living with Death and Dying*. Macmillan, 1981.

———. *On Death and Dying*. Scribner's, 1997.

Kuhn, Thomas S. *The Structure of Scientific Revolutions*. University of Chicago Press, 1970.

Kunstler, William. *My Life As a Radical Lawyer*. Carol Publishing, 1994.

Laing, R. D. *The Divided Self: An Existential Study in Sanity and Madness*. Penguin (reprint ed.), 1965.

Lakoff, George. *Moral Politics: How Liberals and Conservatives Think*. University of Chicago Press, 2002.

Lamott, Anne. *Traveling Mercies: Some Thoughts on Faith*. Pantheon Books, 1999.

Landman, Janet. *Regret: The Persistence of the Possible*. Oxford University Press, 1993.

Lasn, Kalle. *Culture Jam: The Uncooling of America*. Eagle Brook, 1999.

Levinson, Daniel J. *The Seasons of a Man's Life*. Alfred A. Knopf, 1978.

Lewis, C. S. *Mere Christianity*. HarperSanFrancisco, 2001.

———. *Surprised by Joy: The Shape of My Early Life*. Harvest Books, 1966.

Lind, Michael. *Up from Conservatism: Why the Right is Wrong for America*. Free Press, 1997.

Loder, James E. *The Transforming Moment*. Helmers and Howard, 1989.

Lourie, Richard. *Sakharov: A Biography*. Brandeis University Press, 2002.

McAdams, Dan. *The Stories We Live By: Personal Myths and the Making of the Self*. Guilford Press, 1993.

McAdams, Dan, ed. (with Ruthellen Josselson and Amia Lieblich). *Turns in the Road: Narrative Studies of Lives in Transition*. American Psychological Association, 2001.

Mack, John. *Abduction: Human Encounters With Aliens*. Scribner's, 1994.

McCloskey, Deirdre M. *Crossing: A Memoir*. University of Chicago Press, 1999.

Mamet, David. *David Mamet in Conversation*. Edited by Leslie Kane. University of Michigan Press, 2004.

319

Selected Bibliography

Mandino, Og. *The Greatest Salesman in the World*. F. Fell, 1976.

Manseau, Peter, and Jeff Sharlet. *Killing the Buddha: A Heretic's Bible*. Free Press, 2004.

Maslow, Abraham. *The Farther Reaches of Human Nature*. Penguin USA (reprint ed.), 1993.

———. *Toward a Psychology of Being*, 3rd ed. Wiley, 1998.

Miller, William, and Janet C. de Baca. *Quantum Change: When Epiphanies and Sudden Insights Transform Ordinary Lives*. Guilford Press, 2001.

Miller, William Ian. *Faking It*. Cambridge University Press, 2003.

Miller, William R., and Harold D. Delaney, eds. *Judeo-Christian Perspectives on Psychology: Human Nature, Motivation and Change*. American Psychological Association, 2004.

Morris, Jan, *Conundrum*. Harcourt Brace Jovanovich, 1974.

Muggeridge, Malcolm. *Jesus Rediscovered*. Doubleday, 1969.

Murray, Henry. *Endeavors in Psychology: Selections From the Personology of Henry A. Murray*. Edited by Edwin Schneidman. Harper & Row, 1981.

Nehamas, Alexander. *Nietzsche: Life as Literature*. Harvard University Press, 2003.

———. *The Art of Living: Socratic Reflections from Plato to Foucault*. University of California Press, 2000.

Neibuhr, Rheinhold. *The Essential Rheinhold Niebuhr: Selected Essays and Addresses*. Edited by Robert McAfee Brown. Yale University Press, 1986.

Neugarten, Bernice. *The Meanings of Age: Selected Papers*. Edited by Dail Neugarten. University of Chicago Press, 1996.

Newberg, Andrew. *Why God Won't Go Away: Brain Science and the Biology of Belief*. Ballantine, 2001.

Nussbaum, Martha. *Upheavals of Thought: The Intelligence of Emotions*. Cambridge University Press, 2003.

Ondaatje, Michael. *The Conversations: Walter Murch and the Art of Editing Film*. Vintage Canada edition, 2002.

Orlean, Susan. *The Bullfighter Checks Her Makeup: My Encounters with Extraordinary People*. Random House, 2002.

Ouspensky, Peter. *The Psychology of Man's Possible Evolution*. Alfred A. Knopf, 1954.

Pagels, Elaine. *Beyond Belief: The Secret Gospel of Thomas*. Random House, 2003.

Palmer, Helen, ed. *Inner Knowing: Consciousness, Insight, Creativity and Intuition*. J. P. Tarcher/Putnam, 1998.

Palmer, Parker. *Let Your Life Speak: Listening for the Voice of Vocation*. Jossey-Bass, 1999.

Peck, M. Scott. *The Road Less Traveled*. Touchstone (reprint ed.), 1998.

———. *Further Along the Road Less Traveled*. Simon & Schuster, 1993.

Selected Bibliography

Perkins, David. *The Eureka Effect: The Art and Logic of Breakthrough Thinking*. W.W. Norton, 2001.

Perkins, John. *Confessions of an Economic Hit Man*. Berrett-Koehler, 2004.

Peterson, Eugene. *Take and Read*. Eerdmans Publishing Co., 1996.

————. *Subversive Spirituality*. Eerdmans Publishing Company, 1997.

Pinchbeck, Daniel. *Breaking Open the Head: A Psychedelic Journey into the Heart of Contemporary Shamanism*. Broadway Books, 2002.

Pinker, Steven. *The Blank Slate: The Modern Denial of Human Nature*. Penguin, 2003.

Plant, Sadie. *The Most Radical Gesture: The Situationist Internationale in a Postmodern Age*. Routledge, 1992.

Polanyi, Karl. *The Great Transformation*. Beacon Press, 2001.

Queenan, Joe. *My Goodness: A Cynic's Short-lived Search for Sainthood*. Hyperion, 2001.

Ramachandran, V. S. *Phantoms in the Brain*, Harper Perennial, 1999.

Rawls, John. *A Theory of Justice*. Harvard University Press, 1971.

Ray, Paul H., and Sherry Ruth Anderson. *The Cultural Creatives: How 50 Million People are Changing the World*. Three Rivers Press, 2001.

Rittenberg, Sidney, with Amanda Bennett. *The Man Who Stayed Behind*. Duke University Press, 2001.

Robbins, Tom. *Fierce Invalids Home from Hot Climates*. Wheeler Publishing, 2000.

Rosen, Sidney, ed. *My Voice Will Go with You: The Teaching Tales of Milton H. Erickson, M.D.* W. W. Norton, 1982.

Rosenbaum, Ron. *Explaining Hitler: The Search for the Origins of His Evil*. Harper Perennial, 1999.

Runyan, William McKinley. *Life Histories and Psychobiography*. Oxford University Press, 1984.

Salamon, Julia. *Rambam's Ladder: A Meditation on Generosity and Why It Is Necessary to Give*. Workman Publishing, 2003.

Schweitzer, Albert. *The Spiritual Life: Selected Writings of Albert Schweitzer*. Ecco Companions, 1996.

Seligman, Martin. *Authentic Happiness*. Free Press (reprint ed.), 2004.

Sharlet, Jeff, and Peter Manseau. *Killing the Buddha: A Heretic's Bible*. Free Press, 2004.

Shermer, Michael. *Why People Believe Weird Things: Pseudoscience, Superstition and Other Confusions of Our Time*. W. H. Freeman, 1997.

————. *How We Believe: Science, Skepticism, and the Search for God*. Owl Books, 2003.

————. *The Science of Good and Evil: Why People Cheat, Gossip, Care, Share, and Follow the Golden Rule*. Times Books, 2004.

Selected Bibliography

Shore, Bill. *The Light of Conscience: How a Simple Act Can Change Your Life*. Random House, 2005.

Singh, Jaspreet. *Seventeen Tomatoes: Tales from Kashmir*. Vehicule Press, 2004.

Slater, Lauren. *Opening Skinner's Box: Great Psychological Experiments of the Twentieth Century*. W. W. Norton, 2004.

Smith, Andrew. *Moondust: In Search of the Men Who Fell to Earth*. Harper Perennial, 2006.

Smith, Huston. *Why Religion Matters: The Fate of the Human Spirit in an Age of Disbelief*. HarperSanFrancisco, 2001.

Stanovich, Keith. *The Robot's Rebellion: Finding Meaning in the Age of Darwin*. University of Chicago Press, 2005.

Stead, Philip John. *Vidocq: A Biography*. Staples Press, 1954.

Stedman, John, *Stedman's Suriname: Life in an Eighteenth-Century Slave Society*. Johns Hopkins University Press, 1992

Stiles, Paul. *Riding the Bull: My Year in the Madness at Merrill Lynch*. Random House, 1998.

———. *Is the American Dream Killing You? How "the Market" Rules Our Lives*. Collins, 2005.

Storr, Anthony. *Feet of Clay: Saints, Sinners and Madmen: A Study of Gurus*. Free Press, 1996.

Strawson, Galen. *The Self?* Blackwell Publishers, 2005.

Strobel, Lee. *The Case for Christ*. Willow Creek, 1998.

Swimme, Brian. *The Universe Is a Green Dragon: A Cosmic Creation Story*. Bear & Company, 1984.

Talen, Bill. *What Should I Do If Reverend Billy Is in My Store?* New Press, 2005.

Thurman, Robert. *Inner Revolution*. Riverhead, 1998.

Ullman, Chana. *The Transformed Self: The Psychology of Religious Conversion (Emotions, Personality and Psychotherapy)*. Plenum Press, 1989.

Vaillant, George. *Adaptation to Life*. Harvard University Press, 1995.

———. *The Golden Spruce*. Knopf Canada, 2005.

Vaughan, Diane. *Uncoupling: Turning Points in Intimate Relationships*. Vintage, 1990.

Vidal, Gore. *Palimpsest: A Memoir*. Random House, 1995.

Wallace, David Foster. *Consider the Lobster: And Other Essays*. Little, Brown, 2005.

Warraq, Ibn. *Leaving Islam: Apostates Speak Out*. Prometheus Books, 2003.

Watts, Duncan J. *Six Degrees: The Science of a Connected Age*. W.W. Norton, 2003.

Selected Bibliography

Watzlawick, Paul, with John Weakland and Richard Fisch. *Change: Principles of Problem Formation and Problem Resolution.* W.W. Norton, 1974.

Weber, Max. *The Sociology of Religion.* Beacon Press (reprint ed.), 1993.

Wechsler, Lawrence. *Vermeer in Bosnia: A Reader.* Pantheon Books, 2004.

Whyte, David. *The Heart Aroused: Poetry and the Preservation of the Soul in Corporate America.* Currency Doubleday, 1996.

————. *Crossing the Unknown Sea: Work as a Pilgrimage of Identity.* Riverhead Trade, 2002.

Willett, Jincy. *Jenny and the Jaws of Life: Short Stories.* St. Martin's Press, 1987.

Wilson, Bill. *Alcoholics Anonymous: The Story of How Many Thousands of Men and Women Have Recovered from Alcoholism.* Alcoholics Anonymous World Services, 1955.

Wilson, James Q. *The Moral Sense.* Free Press, 1993.

Wilson, Timothy D. *Strangers to Ourselves: Discovering the Adaptive Unconscious.* Belknap Press of Harvard University Press, 2002.

Wise, Steven. *Rattling the Cage: Toward Legal Rights for Animals.* Perseus Publishing, 2001.

Wolfe, Tom. *Hooking Up.* Picador, 2001.

Acknowledgments

For their help at various stages of the manuscript, from tire-kicking to polishing, I wish to thank Benjamin Adams, Dominic Ali, Gillian Blake, Dennis Brown, Diana Drew, Drew Jackson, Sam Stoloff, Greg Villepique, and Jennifer Williams.

And I especially want to thank the folks who told me their stories.

Index

327

Index

Index

Index

Index

Index

Index

Index

Index

Index

Index

Poyner, Rick, 161
pragmatism, 168
Prayer for Owen Meany, A (Irving), 193
Precautionary Principle, 204–5
premonitions, 191
pride, 163–64
primacy of feeling, law of, 139
proselytizing, 159, 182–83, 188–89
psychic adaptation, theory of, 72–73
psychotic break, 7
Pugwash Manifesto, 159–60
purity, 49

Quakerism, 87–88
quantum change, 255
Quartz, Steve, 139
Queenan, Joe, 245–46
Queen's Quarterly, 152

Radosh, Ronald, 123
Rajneesh, Bhagwan Shree, 268
Ramachandran, V. S., 59–60,
    139–40, 176
rationalizations, 151
Rawls, John, 128, 231
Razor's Edge, The (Maugham), 58
Reagan, Ronald, 120–21, 123, 127
receptivity, 46–48, 190, 192,
    223–24, 226–27, 275, 286
Red Cross, 20
redemption myths, 49
redemption script, 88
reinvention, 9
relativity effect, 33
religious conversions, 2, 5–6, 170–72
    authenticity of, 255–59
    born-again, 84–85, 181, 188, 263,
    281

consistency among, 195
contrition of the heart, 157
emotion as catalyst in, 136,
    137–44
inner freedom in, 152
instructions given to, 190–91
of the intellect vs. the heart, 140
leap of faith in, 204–5, 207
moderates vs. extremists in, 161
mystical states in, 177–78
pathology similar to, 198–99, 268
and proselytizing, 159, 182–83,
    188–89
public backlash against, 185,
    188–89
receptivity to, 190, 192
revolutionary, 117
spiral staircase as metaphor for,
    108
unio mystica in, 173–74
religious fundamentalism, 59
resistance, power of, 155–56
resonance, 135–36, 178
resources, 165
restlessness, 59
"Reverend Billy," 91–94
reversals, theory of, 278
revolutionary, mind-set of, 197
revolutionary change, 96–98, 117
Riesman, David, 286
risk aversion, 140
risk-taking, 59
Rittenberg, Sidney, 64–67, 90, 104,
    150–51, 163–64, 229
Rittenberg, Yulin, 64
Robertson, Pat, 126
Robinson, John, 225
Robinson, Spider, 264

Index

Index

Index

A Note on the Author

Bruce Grierson has been nominated for eight Canadian national magazine awards, and is the coauthor of *Culture Jam*. He lives in Vancouver with his wife and daughter.